MANAGING INTEGRATED HEALTH SYSTEMS

JOHN M. (JAY) SHIVER, MHA, FAAMA, LFACHE

Department of Health Administration and Policy
George Mason University
Fairfax, VA

JOHN CANTIELLO, PhD

Assistant Professor
Department of Health Administration and Policy
George Mason University
Fairfax, VA

JONES & BARTLETT
LEARNING

World Headquarters
Jones & Bartlett Learning
5 Wall Street
Burlington, MA 01803
978-443-5000
info@jblearning.com
www.jblearning.com

Jones & Bartlett Learning books and products are available through most bookstores and online booksellers. To contact Jones & Bartlett Learning directly, call 800-832-0034, fax 978-443-8000, or visit our website, www.jblearning.com.

Substantial discounts on bulk quantities of Jones & Bartlett Learning publications are available to corporations, professional associations, and other qualified organizations. For details and specific discount information, contact the special sales department at Jones & Bartlett Learning via the above contact information or send an email to specialsales@jblearning.com.

08039-1

Production Credits

VP, Executive Publisher: David D. Cella
Publisher: Michael Brown
Associate Editor: Lindsey Mawhiney
Associate Editor: Nicholas Alakel
Production Manager: Tracey McCrea
Senior Marketing Manager: Sophie Fleck Teague
Manufacturing and Inventory Control Supervisor: Amy Bacus

Composition: Cenveo® Publisher Services
Cover Design: Kristin E. Parker
Rights & Media Research Coordinator: Amy Rathburn
Media Development Editor: Shannon Sheehan
Cover Image: © Serp/Shutterstock
Printing and Binding: Edwards Brothers Malloy
Cover Printing: Edwards Brothers Malloy

Library of Congress Cataloging-in-Publication Data
Managing integrated health systems / [edited by] John M. Shiver, John Cantiello.
     p. ; cm.
  Includes bibliographical references and index.
  ISBN 978-1-284-04449-2 (pbk.)
  I. Shiver, John M., editor.   II. Cantiello, John, editor.
  [DNLM: 1. Community Medicine—economics—United States.   2. Delivery of Health Care, Integrated—organization & administration—United States. W 84 AA1]
  RA971.3
  362.1068—dc23
                                    2015014284

6048
Printed in the United States of America
19 18 17 16 15   10 9 8 7 6 5 4 3 2 1

Dedication

Jay

This effort is dedicated to my wife, Debbie, who gave me the inspiration and latitude, and to my parents, Art and Lucy, who gave me the focus and discipline. And, of course, to the wonderful students who taught me so much.

John

This book is dedicated to my parents, Gail and Jonathon. Thank you for your encouragement, support, and inspiration.

Contents

About the Authors

John M. (Jay) Shiver, MHA, LFACHE, FAAMA
Department of Health Administration and Policy
College of Health and Human Services
George Mason University

Jay has over 40 years of experience in healthcare management as a health system executive, physician practice manager, consultant and academic. He has extensive experience successfully leading change, creating new and innovative business models, developing and implementing strategic visions, and aligning incentives. He is an expert in ambulatory care delivery. He is the author of numerous books and articles and speaks nationally.

Education

BS, The Citadel, Charleston, SC
MHA, Medical College of Virginia/Virginia Commonwealth University, Richmond, VA

John Cantiello, PhD
Assistant Professor
Department of Health Administration and Policy
College of Health and Human Services
George Mason University

John teaches and advises students in the health administration undergraduate program at George Mason University. His research interests include health insurance coverage, access to and coordination of health services, and underserved populations.

His experience in the healthcare field includes working in medical facilities and hospitals in an administrative capacity, working for the Orange County Health Department as an operations management consultant, working for the Florida Center for Nursing as a research assistant, and serving as a health agency site evaluator with the Florida Department of Health in a joint effort to reduce racial and ethnic health disparities.

Education

PhD, Public Affairs, University of Central Florida, 2008
MS, Health Services Administration, University of Central Florida, 2004
BS, Health Services Administration, University of Central Florida, 2002

Contributors

James O. Cleverley, MHA
Principal
Cleverley and Associates
Columbus, OH

William O. Cleverley, PhD
President
Cleverley and Associates
Professor Emeritus
The Ohio State University
Columbus, OH

Jonathan De Shazo, PhD
Assistant Professor
MHA Program Director
Virginia Commonwealth University
Richmond, VA

Keith William Diener, PhD
Assistant Professor of Business
   Law and Ethics
Richard Stockton College
Galloway, NJ

**Salvador J. Esparza, RN, FACHE,
   DHA**
Assistant Professor
California State University
Northridge, CA

Andrew Heyman, MD, MHSA
Director of Graduate Education
Program in Integrative Medicine
The George Washington
   University
Washington, DC

Thomas R. Hoffman, JD, CAE
Associate General Counsel
American College of Radiology,
   Legal Department
Reston, VA

**Renee Brent Hotchkiss, MSHSA,
   PhD**
Associate Professor and Program
   Director
Rollins College
Winter Park, FL

Douglas E. Hough, PhD
Associate Director, MHA
   Program
Johns Hopkins School of Public
   Health
Baltimore, MD

P.J. Maddox, EdD, RN
Professor and Chair
Department of Health
   Administration and Policy
George Mason University
Fairfax, VA

Douglas McCarthy, MBA
Senior Research Director
The Commonwealth
   Fund
New York, NY

Carrie Rich, MHA
President
Global Good Fund
Washington, DC

David Schott, MSPH, CPH
Research Assistant
Georgia Southern University
Statesville, GA

Knox Singleton, MHA
President
Inova Health System
Fairfax, VA

Paula H. Song, PhD
Assistant Professor
Division of Health Services
  Management and
  Policy
College of Public Health
The Ohio State
  University
Columbus, OH

Sandra K. Warner, MBA, PHR
Assistant Vice President
Human Resources
Adventist Health
Roseville, CA

James Yang, MD, MPH
Medical Director and Internist
Integrative and Functional
  Medicine
George Washington University
Washington, DC

James S. Zoller, PhD
Professor
College of Health Professions
Medical University of South
  Carolina
Charleston, SC

Acknowledgments

We would like to acknowledge the invaluable assistance and teamwork of Sheryl Rivett. Sheryl conducted, and documented, the luminary interviews that accompany this text. Her effort throughout this endeavor is very much appreciated. We wish her the very best. She is a gifted writer.

We also want to thank Dr. PJ Maddox, Chair, Department of Health Administration and Policy of George Mason University for her ongoing support.

Interviewees

David Bernd, MS, FACHE
Chief Executive Officer
Sentara Healthcare
Norfolk, VA

Don Berwick, MD, MPH
Clinical Professor of Pediatrics
    and Health Care Policy
Harvard Medical School
Cambridge, MA
President and CEO
Institute for Healthcare
    Improvement
Cambridge, MA

Teri Fontenot, FACHE
Chief Executive Officer
Woman's Hospital
Baton Rouge, LA

Jeff Goldsmith, PhD
President
Health Futures, Inc.

Charlottesville, VA
Associate Professor
University of Virginia
Charlottesville, VA

Sister Carol Keehan, DC, RN, MS
President and Chief Executive
    Officer
Catholic Health Association
Washington, DC

Alex Nason, MBA, MHA
Vice President
Clinical Care Services
Specialists on Call
Reston, VA

Rich Umbdenstock, MS, FACHE
President and Chief Executive
    Office
American Hospital Association
Washington, DC

Introduction

It can be hard to comprehend in concrete terms how quickly medical advances have been made in healthcare delivery. Consider this story: A middle-aged son accompanies his elderly mother to an ophthalmology appointment. After listening to the ophthalmologist explain that his mother needs cataract surgery, the son turns to his mother to explain in clearer terms what will be happening: "Mom, the doc is saying you need cataract surgery. That means you need to be in the hospital the night before the procedure for tests. You can't eat anything the night before. The next morning...."

Twenty years later, the same son is no longer middle aged. After a recent visit to his own ophthalmologist, he tells his wife, "I'm headed to the doctor's office for cataract surgery. Should be home in time for tonight's game!"

The evolution of the healthcare industry in recent years has brought profound and rapid changes to the industry itself and the requisite professional skills, knowledge, and expertise necessary to manage this very complex business. This text provides those engaged in and studying health care the understanding and knowledge required to succeed in this dynamic industry.

The primary intent of this text is to provide accessible, practical, and applied knowledge and guidance to the every day management and operations of these multifaceted organizations. To this end the authors selected to contribute their expertise to this work have been chosen on the basis of their real-world skills. Authors have experience in the field and in academia. Of particular note and of unique pertinence to this text, you'll find insightful, revealing interviews with highly recognized, innovative, and successful experts from the field who offer practical expertise and wisdom on pertinent topics. Their keen knowledge of these evolving systems and their critical impact on the effectiveness and efficiency of the U.S healthcare system overall, is invaluable.

WHY A NEW APPROACH?

Prior to World War II, the healthcare industry was a cottage industry consisting of a limited range of professionals with relatively little formal education.

In the decades following the war, health care in the United States transitioned from physicians practicing out of home offices to a mega-industry representing a significant portion of the country's gross domestic product (GDP) (**Figure P–1**). Today, the ever-increasing cost of health care has become an issue of national importance; it is talked about at the family dinner table, argued about in the boardrooms of *Fortune* 500 companies, and debated in the chambers of Congress. Health care is no longer a small business with only personal importance, but rather a national concern that impacts everyone.

Readers may note that the traditional term "healthcare delivery system" is less prominent in this text than the term "health system." Health care is now transforming into an industry that is held accountable and compensated not just for restoring the health of individual patients, but for managing the ongoing health of society as well—that is, the overall health of the population and the management of the resources consumed to maintain community health. Managers in this industry are no longer just healthcare delivery system managers; rather, they have evolved into managers who are accountable for the health of the people they serve. Caring for the ill and the injured is no longer sufficient. The successful healthcare system of the future will positively impact the health of an entire community.

Why does this matter? Until recently, the focus and incentives were on fixing problems and curing illness. Looking forward, for future healthcare managers, the focus and incentives will be more on the improvement of population health, so that there is less injury and illness and a reduced need for medical care. This utopian ideal will not be realized quickly or easily. In the interim, changing incentives will focus on improvements in the quality

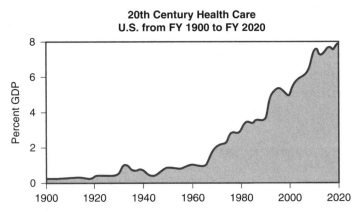

Figure P–1 20th Century Health Care U.S. from FY 1900 to FY 2020
Courtesy of www.usgovernmentspending.com.

of the delivery of care, society, and the marketplace, motivating healthcare industry participants to reduce costs and redundancy in their systems.

The accomplishment of successful integration and management of the overall health of a defined population will require an understanding of how to manage the efforts of exceptionally complex organizations that have inherently conflicting internal incentives. Examples of the conflicting but ultimately necessary components of the system that must be juggled can be found in the effort to maximize a balance between quality, service, efficiency, and cost. It is our hope that readers will better understand and appreciate these dynamic interests and will take away the skills that prepare them to ensure the best health possible for a population, while simultaneously managing available resources in a responsible manner.

Resistance to change is always the challenge to management in any industry, yet the ability to overcome and manage change is the hallmark of a successful leader. Comprehending the enormity of the ongoing changes in health care requires a contextual framework to illustrate four important components of this evolution: the rapidity of change, the fiscal scope of the changes, the place for changes in public policy, and the overall social impact.

LEGISLATIVE HISTORY

It has only been since World War II that an industry built around healthcare delivery truly took hold on a national scale. Prior to this era, health care was decidedly local and of limited capability. Outside major metropolitan areas, hospitals were rare. Physicians practiced alone and mostly from home offices; many traveled to their patients' homes. Nursing care was rudimentary and typically provided by family members and neighbors. The average life expectancy was approximately 69.5years (**Figure P–2**) and healthcare expenditures accounted for less than 2% of the GDP.

In 1946, Congress passed the Hill-Burton Act, which provided federal assistance for building and expanding hospitals across the United States. In just the first six months after its launch, the program approved grants for 347 new hospitals, and in the end provided for the spending of $3.7 billion in new construction and facility modernization new hospitals across the country (Clark, 1980).

This rapid expansion of hospital beds shifted the focus of health care away from the traditional solo-practice physician and care delivered by community members to a more institution-centric delivery model. Supply of healthcare services increased exponentially, with the increased access being quickly followed by a comparable rise in utilization. In a few short years, Americans began to consider world-class treatment and accessibility as "de

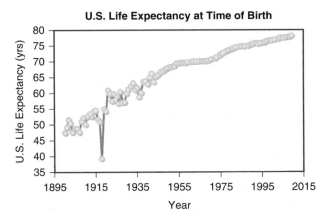

Figure P–2 U.S. Life Expectancy at Time of Birth

Data from Arias E. United States life tables, 2006. National vital statistics reports; vol 58 no 21. Hyattsville, MD: National Center for Health Statistics. 2010.

rigueur" and the days of dying early from common communicable diseases began to fade from the collective memory. During this same period, health-care insurance became a significant benefit provided by employers. Prior to World War II, health insurance had been a relatively insignificant benefit. During the war years, however, employers began offering health insurance as a way to recruit workers despite federally imposed wage restrictions; by the end of the war, health insurance had become an expected employee benefit. The poor and the elderly, who were not part of the workforce, still bore the cost of care without access to affordable health insurance.

Providing financial access to healthcare services for the poor and elderly was a key initiative of President John Kennedy's administration in the early 1960s. It was not until after Kennedy's assassination that his successor, Lyndon Johnson, signed into law the first truly significant fiscal expansion to healthcare coverage. In 1965, healthcare coverage expanded under the Medicare and Medicaid programs. Following the passage of Medicare and Medicaid it took until 1970 for healthcare expenditures to reach 2% of the U.S. GDP (U.S. Government Spending, n.d.) (**Figure P–3**).

In the following years, healthcare costs continued to increase, although Medicare and Medicaid costs did not rise as high as the private-sector spending. Readers can refer to **Figure P–4** and the following website for detailed statistics regarding healthcare growth in the United States: http://www.cms.gov/Research-Statistics-Data-and-Systems/Statistics-Trends-and-Reports/NationalHealthExpendData/Downloads/tables.pdf.

The health industry wasted little time in expanding to serve the newly insured elderly and poor. Within just a decade of the implementation of

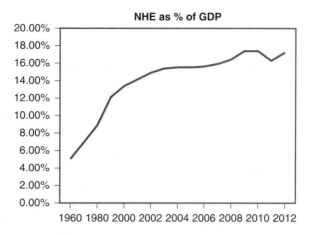

Figure P–3 NHE as % of GDP

Data from Martin AB, Lassman D, Washington B, Catlin A, and the National Health Expenditure Accounts Team. Growth In US Health Spending Remained Slow In 2010; Health Share Of Gross Domestic Product Was Unchanged From 2009. Health Affairs, vol 31, no 1. (2012):208–219.

Medicaid and Medicare, the growing costs and expansion of healthcare services became a major topic of legislative concern. Two especially notable pieces of legislation were passed during the first half of the 1970s in an

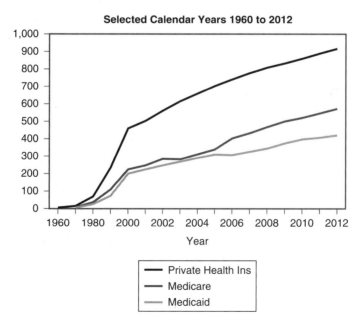

Figure P–4 NHE by Source Selected Calendar Years 1960 to 2012

Data from CMS, Office of the Acturary, NHSG.

effort to constrain the continually increasing costs: the Health Maintenance Organization Act of 1973 and the Health Planning and Resources Development Act of 1974. The former was designed to introduce greater competition and cost controls into the then fee-for-service reimbursement methodology. The latter placed restrictions on capital expenditures for new services. Other significant legislative efforts have since been implemented as further attempts to gain control of escalating medical inflation, such as the Prospective Payment Act and the Health Insurance Portability and Accountability Act. Nevertheless, these laws have had only a limited impact in slowing medical inflation.

In early 2010, President Barack Obama signed into law the Patient Protection and Affordable Care Act (ACA). This bill represents the federal government's most ambitious effort to create structural changes in the financing and delivery of health care. The ACA continues to be implemented, but its impact has already been felt throughout the United States. Nowhere are the effects of the law felt more acutely than within the healthcare delivery system. Every component of the current U.S. healthcare system is directly impacted by the ACA, which also directly impacts every citizen, every healthcare provider, every insurer, and the basic structure of our entire national health system. The only element of the health system not explicitly addressed by this law is the information technology arena—though that area was covered in the HITECH Act signed into law in March 2009. Readers will be provided with an in-depth examination of both of these laws and their impact in this text.

MARKET PRESSURES

Legislated change is not the only challenge for emerging health systems; the overall healthcare market has also evolved and its impact on the healthcare industry cannot be underestimated.

From a financial perspective, healthcare costs currently represent about 18% of the U.S. GDP and have increased steadily for the past 60 years with modest decrease in growth over the past few years. For private employers, 55% of which offer health insurance to employees (Kaiser Family Foundation, 2014), medical inflation is exemplified by the increased costs to purchase health insurance plans for their employees. This important employee benefit has increased by 26% over the past five years (Kaiser Family Foundation, 2014).

As a reaction to the rising costs of health insurance, employers have increased pressure on providers and legislators. The burden of the growing costs is ultimately borne by employees. Employers are transferring the increased costs to their employees through means such as cost shifting, increased deductibles, and copayments. Health insurance benefit costs are shifting to employees or have been eliminated or reduced as an employment benefit. Increasingly, many employers are offering only defined contribution plans in which employers contribute a predetermined amount of money toward the purchase of health insurance, not unlike the trend to eliminate defined benefit retirement plans in lieu of programs such as the 401(k) defined contribution plans.

The shifting of risk and costs to employees for health insurance protection has had a profound impact on individuals and their families. Purchasers of healthcare services today bear more of the first dollar expense, and consequently consumers are becoming increasingly aware of and sensitive to the cost of services. This new consumer awareness has placed growing pressure on providers to justify costs and deliver results—a new dynamic for providers who have historically determined which services to deliver without having had to explain those choices to the consumer.

CHALLENGES

Managers working within the health industry must meet the challenge of dealing with the multifaceted impact of new laws and a complex changing private insurance market. The knowledge, skills, and abilities required to be a successful leader in the evolving healthcare systems include those related to healthcare services delivery, population health, health information technology, and sophisticated financial management. Many of these knowledge arenas may be familiar to the traditional healthcare system manager, but much is new. For example, many individuals who work in the delivery system are not versed in the health insurance business model or familiar with the scope and depth of population health management. Moreover, healthcare information technology—traditionally a discipline unto itself—must now be managed as an integral component of any current health system.

The new healthcare enterprise is growing into a broad, diverse, and multidisciplinary industry. Today's healthcare leader is required to understand and meld essentially conflicting agendas of intrinsically unbalanced organizations. Not unlike the modern fighter aircraft, the new healthcare organization has built into its very structure a certain degree of dynamic instability; without the active engagement of computers, new fighter aircrafts are unable to fly. Today's health system executives must navigate business enterprises encompassing often conflicting interests—a balancing act that requires sophisticated management skills, leadership, vision, and an understanding of the appropriate application technology to manage successfully.

The dynamic tensions among the various components of the new health-care system require a level of knowledge and skills heretofore not experienced in the profession. Balancing these conflicting interests requires managers to have an intimate understanding of all the diverse components, while also creating a culture that allows the various pieces to maximize their performance for the overall benefit of the organization and the population served. This text provides the reader with an understanding of the many—often moving—components of the healthcare system and a foundation of knowledge required to overcome the system challenges. The reader will explore facets of healthcare finance, delivery, knowledge integration, community and population health, and change management. In each arena, the focus is on the future needs of the emerging business model.

We open with an overview of the concept of integrated health systems and the history of their evolution. The role of such existential factors as public policy, finance, technology, globalization, and both quality and safety requirements are discussed in the context of leadership and change management. With a baseline understanding of the future state of health care, the authors provide an applied and theoretical framework for creating a culture characterized by responsible leadership. Through these chapters and interviews with luminary leaders in the field, the reader will discover that today is truly an exciting time to study health administration.

Included in this study are the existential forces of the market, politics, and economics, all of which are shaping the current changes in the industry. As previously mentioned, the historically consistent trend of rising healthcare costs has put significant financial pressure on all purchasers, including employers and government. These pressures have been felt throughout the economy, but in particular they are being experienced by individual beneficiaries through increased out-of-pocket expenses and cost shifting. These trends have created changes in consumer behavior as well as in the care delivery systems.

One of the most visible changes is the appearance of retail medicine outlets in pharmacies and "big box" stores across the United States. With consumers bearing more of the cost of health care directly, new, innovative, lower-cost, and more-convenient delivery systems have appeared in communities. Retail healthcare delivery systems such as urgent care kiosks staffed by nurse practitioners, telemedicine practices, and others have become commonplace. Tied closely to the changes in the delivery of allopathic medicine are the growing interest in and influence of complementary and integrative medicine, as well as other services. These new and creative ways of bringing lower costs and convenience to the market are forcing the health system to rethink its current business model, which is quickly becoming outmoded and unsustainable.

One of the more unique aspects of health care is reflected in the many ways in which people do not respond in accordance with classical economic theory. The traditional economist would posit that people make choices regarding health care in much the same way that they would make a consumer appliance purchase. However, a growing number of studies have demonstrated that healthcare decisions do not follow the traditional economic decision-making theory. This deviation from much of the classic economic model has puzzled health system managers for decades. This text offers insights into why the health system does not always act in the ways predicted by the classic economic models and suggests how healthcare managers might better invest capital resources so as to achieve the greatest value and benefit for the population served. The discussion will also consider how this economic irrationality might be applied to structure healthcare services in ways that more closely match the needs and behavior of consumers.

As previously mentioned, the Patient Protection and Affordable Care Act (Public Law 111-148), signed into law by President Obama on March 23, 2010, is perhaps the most visible and widely known legislative force impacting modern health care in the United States. The role of government policy and law in the health affairs of the citizenry has increased immensely over the past few decades. The Patient Protection and Affordable Care Act is simply the most recent example of this trend, though perhaps the most impactful. Legislative acts can be game changing for those who are concerned each day with delivering care and maintaining health at a local level. Unless the health industry takes a proactive role in the legislative process, it will find itself overrun by more politically active players such as the pharmaceutical industry, employers, and payers. The role of healthcare system leaders in the political process has always been a sensitive one and must be handled with care. Historically, hospital executives and physicians have not played significant roles in the political process. At this point in time, however, the stakes are too high to ignore: Health system leaders can no longer simply abdicate responsibility for the legislative process. For the sake of their communities, they must be active participants in the process. In this text, readers will learn how the legislative process works and how healthcare leaders can serve as advocates and sources of expertise in the political process. The authors show how health leaders can create real impact and provide knowledge to other members of the government.

Central to the federal government's model of healthcare reform, as outlined by the ACA, is an understanding of the need for payment reform. The accountable care organization (ACO) is a payment reform model that is described in some detail within the ACA, though considerable discretion is allowed regarding the actual governance, organization, and operation of these organizations. This text examines a number of ACOs and reviews their performance. The effectiveness of the various ACO models is examined relative to the impact of the incentives—in particular, the impact on reducing costs of healthcare delivery and improving outcomes and satisfaction of both the consumer and the provider.

Integral to the reform of health care and healthcare financing is the concept of population health, which recognizes that a healthy population consumes fewer resources. Attaining this lofty goal is easier said than done, as society has scant experience in creating a healthy population. Health care and medicine in the United States have traditionally centered on curing the sick and repairing the injured. Indeed, the health insurance industry is built around paying for such services. This text explores in some detail, strategies for achieving the goal of improving the overall health of the population. Readers will examine state-of-the-art techniques for addressing population health.

The potential of large-scale data analytics, machine learning, and artificial intelligence for transforming health care is enormous, beyond current comprehension. Prior to passage of the HITECH Act of 2009, health industry participants had very limited access to large statistically significant data sets for creating new knowledge and examining best practices across entire populations. That is, providers were essentially small businesses with only limited local information. Until recently, each component of the healthcare delivery system kept only the records it needed to operate its individual business; these records were maintained within the enterprise, and information was shared only when providers were required to do so. Consequently, every encounter, every test, every therapeutic procedure, and every surgery engendered a new, discrete written record, which was maintained and available only at the physical site where the service occurred. Within the past decade, however, healthcare providers have started to move away from handwritten notes and toward adoption of fully integrated open architecture data platforms that are available anywhere, anytime. Health systems are now in the midst of a transition from paper-based, unconnected data sets to a fully integrated nationwide information system. Today's information technology revolution is having a major impact on the delivery of care and everything else in the healthcare industry: It is not only creating better care and service, but also engendering changes in the organization and structure of healthcare delivery systems.

It is impossible to envision all of the opportunities for improving health that might be realized through the use of the data now being assembled and analyzed. Contained within these data is information that will allow us to improve the health of generations to come. The data will be used to create the evidential basis for making important changes in health care and in the way in which it is provided. New data mining and machine learning technologies will be used to ascertain new knowledge to guide even more research. The health insurance industry has traditionally maintained significantly larger data sets than the providers of care, but this information has been proprietary and, within the larger scheme of things, relatively small and skewed by the individual business models of the insurance industry organizations. Federal data sets, while large, have focused on tracking government-insured populations—an approach that also skewed the information tracked. Recent advances in the science of machine learning and data mining will become increasingly important as larger and more valid data sets created by integration across the healthcare industry become available. Past experience from other industries tells us that these larger data sets have the potential to generate information that is unimagined today. The reader will be asked to imagine how this massive set of data, accessible anywhere and capable of being mined for new information, can help improve health and the quality of health care.

Telemetry and its various iterations now allow health services to be obtained in heretofore inaccessible environments and places. The ability to access healthcare expertise virtually anywhere, including below the surface of the globe and in outer space, is allowing for medical care to be provided to millions of previously unreachable populations. Even robotic technology has moved into the healthcare realm. Robots are found both in clinical settings and in more mundane logistical services. Today it is possible to perform surgery by combining the technology of robotics and telemetry. Physicians can use surgical robotics to perform surgery while they are located thousands of miles away from their patients; they can consult with patients at small regional hospitals via telemetry and robots. Moreover, supplies, medicine, meals, and laundry are routinely delivered throughout health facilities by robots. The military is currently testing robots for use in combat to retrieve wounded soldiers. Such technology continues to be developed and will one day expand the capabilities of—or replace—people who have traditionally performed certain roles.

CONCLUSION

It was George Santayana who famously said, "Those who do not learn from the past are condemned to repeat it." The history of health care in the United States is marked by many efforts to create change. Some have succeeded; some have failed. Progress forward should always be the objective.

The exciting thing about modern health care is that every day we are moving forward at an unusually fast pace.

There is no way to accurately predict how much progress we can achieve, but we *can* be certain that this field of endeavor will provide everyone who participates in it the opportunity to contribute to its improvement. The future of healthcare management has never been brighter. As individuals, we live healthier, longer lives than those who came before us. As leaders in the health industry, we have the opportunity—rather, the obligation—to create a positive legacy for the generations who follow us.

John M. (Jay) Shiver, MHA, FAAMA, FACHE

REFERENCES

Clark, L. J., Field, M. J., Koontz, T. L., & Koontz, V. L. (1980). The impact of Hill-Burton: An analysis of hospital and physician distribution in the United States, 1950-1970. *Med Care, 18*, 532–550.

Kaiser Family Foundation. (2014). 2014 Employer Health Benefits Survey. http://kff.org/report-section/ehbs-2014-abstract/

U.S. Government Spending. (n.d.). US Health Care Spending History from 1900. http://www.usgovernmentspending.com/healthcare_spending

Chapter 1

Integrated Healthcare Delivery Models in an Era of Reform

—Douglas McCarthy

LEARNING OBJECTIVES

- Understand the historical background against which healthcare systems are evolving.
- Analyze the impact of culture on organizational development.
- Analyze and critique the requirements for a successful integrated health system.
- Explain and analyze the characteristics of some of the best integrated systems.

INTRODUCTION

Healthcare delivery in the United States is shifting from a fragmented "cottage industry" of solo and small physician practices paid on a fee-for-service basis to more organized forms in which physicians join with other providers in efforts to improve the quality and efficiency of care. In the midst of this historic change—which is being driven by both market forces and public policy—it is useful to reexamine where the United States has come from in terms of healthcare delivery models and where the current pathways are leading. This chapter describes how models of integrated healthcare delivery have provided inspiration and ideas for recent policy reforms, and traces the evolution of such models into new and emerging ways of integrating care.

A Brief History

Early in the twentieth century, experts began taking note of the benefits of large **multispecialty group practices (MSGP)** that employ primary and specialty care physicians who share common governance, infrastructure, and finances, and refer patients to one another for services offered within the group (Falk, Rorem, & King, 1933). At the Mayo Clinic, for example, all patients are assigned a coordinating physician to ensure that they have an appropriate care plan, that all ancillary services and consultations are scheduled in a timely fashion, and that patients receive clear communication throughout and at the conclusion of an episode of care. Such multispecialty groups sometimes became the nucleus of **integrated delivery systems (IDS)** that included hospitals and an array of other services such as home health and skilled nursing care.

In a major innovation, some multispecialty groups began accepting a fixed payment for a defined set of services in lieu of separate fees for services (Enthoven & Tollen, 2004). The example of these prepaid group practices inspired the U.S. federal government to support the development of **health maintenance organizations (HMOs)** in the 1970s as a means of controlling costs by integrating the financing and delivery of care. To reduce the effort required to start HMOs, looser models sought to achieve integration among networks of independent physicians, albeit with mixed results. After a period of rapid growth, HMOs lost momentum in the 1990s as consumers reacted against the restrictions they placed on choice. (Many HMOs have since gained membership by enrolling elderly beneficiaries in the Medicare Advantage program.)

Meanwhile, physicians in many markets began forming single-specialty group practices, which may create efficiencies and ensure bargaining clout in price negotiations with insurers, but lack the natural opportunities for care coordination inherent in multispecialty practice (Liebhaber & Grossman, 2007). Although integrated delivery systems and large multispecialty groups gained a footing in California, the upper Midwest, and some other urban and rural areas of the country, they generally have remained the exception in U.S. health care.

Charting a New Path

Recently, there has been renewed interest in learning how the experience of integrated delivery systems can help address the shortcomings of uncoordinated fee-for-service medicine that lead to undesirable patient experiences, suboptimal outcomes, and unnecessarily high costs (Schoen, How, Weinbaum, Craig, & Davis, 2006). The Commonwealth Fund's Commission on a High Performance Health System (2007) called for the nation to "embark on the organization and delivery of health care services to end the fragmentation, waste, and complexity that currently exist. Physicians and other care providers should be rewarded, through financial and non-financial incentives, to band together into traditional or virtual organizations that can provide the support needed to physicians and other providers to practice 21st century medicine." Similar recommendations were issued by the Institute of Medicine (2001) and the Medicare Payment Advisory Commission (2009).

In the four years since the enactment of the Patient Protection and Affordable Care Act (ACA), this vision has taken concrete form. Provisions in the law allow the Medicare program to test new payment models to foster coordination of care through bundled services and the formation of **accountable care organizations (ACOs)**. Several states are redesigning their Medicaid programs in pursuit of accountable care (Silow-Carroll et al., 2013), while commercial insurers are partnering with health care providers in new arrangements that seek to reward value rather than volume of services (Van Citters et al., 2013).

To illustrate the potential of integrated care delivery, the Commonwealth Fund has sponsored a series of case studies of organizations located across the United States (**Figure 1–1**) that have been recognized for innovation

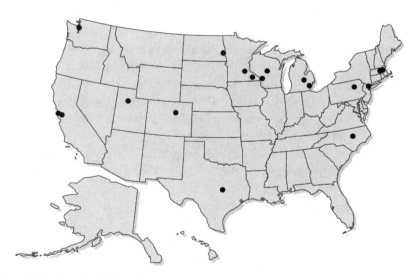

Figure 1–1 Case Study Locations

Reproduced from Shih, A., Davis, K., Schoenbaum, S., Gauthier, A., Nuzum, R., & McCarthy, D. 2008. *Organizing the U.S. Health Care Delivery System for High Performance*. New York, NY: The Commonwealth Fund.

and performance (McCarthy & Mueller, 2009b; McCarthy, Klein, & Cohen, 2014).* In this chapter, the term *integrated healthcare delivery* means that "care providers have established relationships and mechanisms for communicating and working together to coordinate patient care across health conditions, services, and care settings over time" (Institute of Medicine, 2001). It may also mean the use of payment mechanisms for sharing financial risk that foster accountability for outcomes over the continuum of care.

The following sections describe how these organizations exemplify the ideal attributes of healthcare delivery identified by the Commission (Shih et al., 2008; **Exhibit 1–1**) and synthesize key lessons from their experiences to guide other healthcare leaders in the accountable care era.

Exhibit 1–1 Six Attributes of an Ideal Health Care Delivery System

- *Easy access to appropriate care.* Patients have convenient access to care and information that is appropriate to their needs at all hours, there are multiple points of entry to the system, and providers are culturally competent and responsive to patients' needs.
- *Information continuity and integration.* Patients' clinically relevant information is available to all providers at the point of care and to patients through electronic health record (EHR) systems and related information technologies.
- *Care coordination and transitions.* Patient care is coordinated among multiple providers, and transitions across care settings are actively managed.
- *Peer review and teamwork for high-value care.* Providers and care teams both within and across settings have accountability to each other, review each other's work, and collaborate to reliably deliver high-quality, high-value care.
- *Continuous innovation.* The system is continuously innovating and learning so as to improve the quality, value, and patients' experiences of healthcare delivery.
- *System accountability.* There is clear accountability for the total care of patients.

Information from Shih, A., Davis, K., Schoenbaum, S., Gauthier, A., Nuzum, R., & McCarthy, D. 2008. *Organizing the U.S. Health Care Delivery System for High Performance.* New York, NY: The Commonwealth Fund.

---

*Information for the case studies was gathered from interviews with organization leaders, internal material provided by the sites, and external sources.

IDEAL ATTRIBUTES OF INTEGRATED HEALTHCARE DELIVERY

Easy Access to Appropriate Care

Co-locating multispecialty services in a single facility can promote convenient access to care. Many of the study sites have reengineered their work processes to reduce waiting times for appointments by offering same- or next-day access to primary care and after-hours alternatives (e.g., nurse call lines and urgent care centers) to emergency department (ED) care. Some also offer group visits that provide peer support for making lifestyle changes and adhering to self-care routines. Several of Kaiser Permanente's large medical centers offer culture-specific patient care modules allowing patients to communicate in their native language with a bilingual care team oriented to their cultural norms, which can be critical to providing effective treatment.

Prepaid care has encouraged some study organizations to offer virtual telephonic and Web-enabled visits and secure electronic messaging as convenient alternatives to face-to-face encounters for patients with non-urgent needs, and as an efficient means for care teams to reach out to patients in need of follow-up (Pearl, 2014; Reid et al., 2013). HealthPartners—an integrated delivery system in Minnesota—reported that its online clinic garnered high customer satisfaction while saving the health plan an average of $88 for simple care episodes compared with face-to-face visits (Courneya , Palattao, & Gallagher, 2013). Several study sites use telehealth technologies for home monitoring of patients with chronic conditions or to provide remote consultations and diagnosis for patients in rural areas.

Information Continuity and Integration

Integrated delivery systems have been leaders in implementing health information technology (IT) and electronic health record (EHR) systems that facilitate coordination of care, promote the delivery of evidence-based care with decision support tools, and make laboratory and imaging tests results available when needed. Some have created Web portals that allow authorized community physicians to view the records of their patients or to make electronic referrals into the system. Several are creating or collaborating with other stakeholders to develop networks for electronic information exchange.

Many of the study sites have developed capabilities to identify patients who could benefit from more intensive care management, and several have systems to alert physicians or care managers to follow up with patients who use hospital services or transition from the hospital. Some evidence suggests that the use of an EHR in an integrated practice environment can improve chronic care management and reduce hospital use (Weber, Bloom, Pierdon, & Wood, 2008). Although EHRs require more of physicians' time than paper records, they create efficiencies for the care team or organization as a whole (e.g., by reducing the time to process prescription refill requests) while improving patient care.

EHRs also figure in efforts to improve access to appropriate care. For example, advice nurses at the Marshfield Clinic use the EHR to view a patient's treatment plan when speaking to the patient on the telephone and add a record of the call to the EHR for the patient's primary care physician to review and follow up as needed. Some integrated delivery systems operate walk-in convenience clinics, located in retail stores, that are linked to the system's EHR to help preserve continuity of care. Moreover, Web portals linked to the EHR can promote engagement in their care.

Study sites had made substantial investments in health information technology (IT) prior to the advent of financial incentives offered by the federal government for providers to adopt EHRs. Intermountain Healthcare's leaders observed that the organization did not realize the full value of its investment until the EHR became a key enabler of a broader clinical improvement strategy (described later in this chapter). Healthcare organizations will need to identify similar intrinsic motivations, as new technologies will require ongoing investments to support them after the federal financial incentive program ends. While some new ACOs are finding it challenging to uniformly spread EHRs among independent physicians and to integrate IT systems across organizational boundaries, their leaders observed that sharing even rudimentary data across ACO partners (e.g., a daily hospital patient census) can offer actionable insights to improve care coordination.

Care Coordination and Transitions

Integrated delivery systems can provide a supportive environment for developing primary care "medical homes," which aim to make patient care more accessible, continuous, comprehensive, patient centered, and coordinated. They often adopt a population-management approach that stratifies patients according to their health risks and leverages physician time by enhancing the roles of other care team members to support patients in need of preventive care, disease or medication management, transitional care, and self-care education. Several sites have developed navigation programs for patients with cancer or other intensive treatment needs. Many facilitate effective "hand-overs" from hospitals to post-acute and community care settings.

In recognition of the role that psychosocial and behavioral factors play in improving health and treatment adherence, care teams may include social workers and psychologists as well as nurses, pharmacists, and case managers to address patients' needs in a holistic manner. Care teams may be embedded in clinical sites with sufficiently large patient volumes, or they may work virtually from central locations when clinical sites are small or geographically dispersed. Referring patients to centralized care management programs, such as anticoagulation management for high-risk patients, appears to work well when those patients account for only a small number of any one physician's practice, or when such services benefit from linkage to specialty care.

Peer Review and Teamwork for High-Value Care

The study sites typically convene interdisciplinary teams of clinical experts to develop and spread evidence-based guidelines and standard care processes, often by embedding them in the EHR. A robust measurement infrastructure enables routine monitoring and feedback of provider and group performance, sometimes in an identifiable or "unblinded" manner to strengthen peer accountability within the group or unit. Physicians also serve as "clinical champions" to identify and promote the adoption of best practices. They are typically involved in decision making both through formal leadership roles, often in partnerships or "dyads" with administrative leaders, and through involvement in committees that complement vertical management structures.

At its best, multispecialty group practice fosters a cohesive group culture that helps to minimize and resolve "turf battles" between disciplines and departments as physicians work together and with other staff to achieve common goals. In the words of one observer, "Everyone is in the same boat, pulling together." Working as part of a self-governing physician group appears to involve a trade-off in which physicians sacrifice some of their individual autonomy for the benefits of group practice, such as the expertise and resources to jointly determine best practice protocols. Groups that are accountable for both financial and clinical outcomes under capitated payment find that it protects their clinical freedom from outside micromanagement.

Continuous Innovation and Organizational Learning

Integrated delivery systems take advantage of their scale and infrastructure to improve healthcare quality and value. They bring together experts from across medical and administrative disciplines to lead continuous improvement efforts. Many are enthusiastic about the potential of equipping frontline staff with "lean" techniques (borrowed from the manufacturing industry) so that they can design process improvements, minimize waste, and determine measures by which their performance will be evaluated. They have discovered that clinicians are more amenable to the idea of standardizing their work processes when they can see that it avoids "wasted" time and frees them to spend more time on clinically oriented tasks with or for their patients. Denver Health, an integrated public safety-net system, used such techniques to conduct nearly 100 rapid-cycle improvement projects to redesign strategic "value streams," thereby realizing almost $50 million in reduced costs or increased revenue over five years.

System Accountability

Typically, no single physician or entity takes responsibility for the total care of patients in unorganized fee-for-service care. Some study sites address this gap by assigning an accountable physician or a medical home for a patient. The cases documented examples where the delivery system as a whole assumed accountability for patients or members—most notably when a patient is covered by a health plan owned by an integrated delivery system. Other sites have found it is more economical to provide care management programs for all patients in need of such services, regardless of their insurance, with the cost covered by pay-for-performance or shared savings programs that reward improvements in care. Others have filled in gaps by focusing efforts on patients not eligible for programs available to those enrolled in managed healthcare plans.

Supporting a culture of accountability, the study organizations reported engaging in rigorous performance measurement—not only to promote peer accountability, but also to demonstrate the results of their efforts to purchasers, patients, and other stakeholders. Accountability is further reinforced by public performance reporting in competitive urban marketplaces such as California, where purchasers have structured the market to reward plans that deliver higher value. One leader noted that external transparency fosters honesty, awareness, and commitment to improvement throughout the organization's workforce.

CASE EXAMPLES OF INTEGRATED HEALTHCARE DELIVERY

The case study sites represent diverse types of organizations that range from fully integrated delivery systems that provide the full scope of healthcare services and insurance coverage to looser networks of physicians. The structure of an integrated delivery system may be envisioned as the framework on which its attributes or functional capabilities can be built, which in turn influences its performance and outcomes.

Kaiser Permanente

Kaiser Permanente (KP) has grown from industrial worksite healthcare programs in the 1930s to become the largest not-for-profit integrated delivery system and group-model HMO in the United States, serving more than 9.1 million members in eight regions. KP comprises three interdependent entities that exist in a "partnership of equals" through exclusive contracts built on common vision, joint decision making, and aligned incentives.

- Kaiser Foundation Health Plan contracts with purchasers (individuals, employers, and government programs) to finance healthcare services for its members.
- Kaiser Foundation Hospitals (and its subsidiaries) arranges inpatient, extended, and home health care for Kaiser Health Plan members in owned and contracted facilities.
- Permanente Medical Groups are locally governed professional corporations or partnerships of physicians that work in Kaiser facilities and accept a fixed payment from Kaiser Health Plan to provide medical care exclusively for Kaiser members.

Working in cooperation with health plan and facility managers, KP physicians take responsibility for clinical care, quality improvement, resource management, and the design and operation of the care delivery system in each region. Permanente physicians are salaried and have the opportunity to earn bonuses based on group and individual performance.

KP's three-tiered population-health management model builds on a robust shared EHR system and a strong primary care orientation as the most efficient way to interact with most patients most of the time, while recognizing that some patients who have—or who are at risk for developing—chronic diseases need additional support and specialty care to achieve good outcomes. Patients are stratified into three levels of care:

1. Primary care with self-care support, for those 65% to 80% of patients whose conditions are generally responsive to lifestyle changes and medications
2. Assistive care management, for those 20% to 30% of patients whose diseases are not under control at level 1
3. Intensive case management and specialty care, for those 1% to 5% of patients with advanced disease and complex comorbidities or frailty

Focusing on the entire spectrum of prevention for cardiac care management has contributed to multiple improvements in the northern California region, such as a 25% decline in the adult smoking rate, increased use of therapies to control risk factors for cardiovascular disease, a near-doubling in blood pressure control among patients with hypertension, and reductions in hospitalization rates for cardiovascular conditions and in heart disease deaths.

Kaiser Permanente has long enjoyed a price advantage in the California market due to its integrated financial and clinical model, through which it reaps the benefits (and can reinvest the savings) from efforts to reduce the use of hospitals and other expensive services. Its competitors (such as Hill Physicians Medical Group) learned to achieve similar gains, in part by emulating KP's strategies. Financial losses in the late 1990s and the advent of public performance reporting, reinforced by unblinded internal performance feedback within the medical group, energized the organization to demonstrate the potential of its model by making a stronger push for innovation and quality (McCarthy & Mueller, 2009a).

Hill Physicians Medical Group

Hill Physicians Medical Group (HPMG), founded in 1984 and northern California's largest independent practice association (IPA), contracts with health plans to provide care to more than 300,000 patients enrolled in commercial HMOs, Medicare Advantage plans, and California's Medicaid Program. HPMG contracts, in turn, with 3,800 independent providers, including some 900 primary care physicians and 38 hospitals. A subset of physician-shareholders elect a governing board, which contracts with a management services organization for day-to-day operations. HPMG receives a fixed payment from health plans and reimburses physicians on a fee-for-service basis plus bonuses (funded in part by participation in purchasers' pay-for-performance programs) for meeting performance goals for service utilization, clinical quality, and use of EHRs. HPMG engages physicians in its programs by ensuring that its members represent a sizable proportion of a physician's patient panel.

To avoid losing a very large customer base in the Sacramento market—the California Public Employees' Retirement System (CalPERS)—HPMG joined with Dignity Health (a multihospital system) and Blue Shield of California to create a commercial ACO for the Sacramento market in January 2010. The shared goal was to bring Blue Shield's premiums for CalPERS members below Kaiser Permanente's premiums. Because CalPERS structured its benefit offerings so that its beneficiaries are cost-conscious when choosing among competing health plans, the ACO partners were united by a common threat of losing health plan members—and therefore patients—to KP's HMO. To achieve the overall premium savings target, the partners set spending budgets by type of service and agreed to share any savings that exceeded the target as well as the financial risk if they exceeded their budgets.

Working together, the ACO partners decreased hospital admissions and readmissions, emergency department visits, and spending in the venture's first three years, resulting in $59 million in savings or $480 per CalPERS member per year. The ACO's leaders credit their success to developing a mutual understanding of one another's strengths and challenges, which they say was a prerequisite for improving care coordination, increasing patient education, and reducing duplication of services and unwarranted variations in care. In effect, market competition was structured so that the ACO partners realized mutual benefit by acting together like a virtually integrated delivery system (Cohen, Klein, & McCarthy, 2014).

Marshfield Clinic

The Marshfield Clinic is a large, nonprofit multispecialty group practice that employs more than 700 physicians who practice in 41 clinic sites in central Wisconsin. The Clinic is building on its successful participation in Medicare's Physician Group Practice Demonstration—a precursor to Medicare's Shared Savings Program—to enhance and extend care management programs to benefit all patients, not just those attributed to its Medicare ACO. The Clinic's sophisticated, internally developed EHR system and enterprise data warehouse enable the identification of gaps and best practices in care and internal transparency in performance reporting, which has galvanized physician support for quality improvement efforts.

The ACO is part of the Marshfield Clinic's continuing investment in developing advanced primary care coordination and disease-specific care management capabilities, which have yielded reductions in hospitalization and readmission rates. Its track record of savings for Medicare ($118 million over the five-year Physician Group Practice Demonstration) offers evidence that success with accountable care is possible with a strong institutional mission and a shared commitment to performance improvement among physicians in group practice. Because the Clinic is the sole sponsor of its ACO, it did not share savings with independent community hospitals, nor did it face any threat of lost revenue due to reductions in inpatient stays (Klein, McCarthy, & Cohen, 2014).

Group Health Cooperative

Group Health Cooperative (GHC), one of the United States' first member-governed, staff-model HMOs, has evolved into a mixed-model health plan serving 600,000 members in Washington state and northern Idaho. More than half of its members receive care from an integrated multispecialty group practice employing more than 1,000 physicians in the Puget Sound and Spokane areas. Other members receive care from contracted community providers.

In recent years, as GHC faced stronger competition in the marketplace, it began to see unintended consequences of a "production-oriented" approach to primary care in the integrated medical group: swollen patient panels, increasing specialty-care referrals, rising costs of hospital and emergency care, and signs of burnout in its workforce. In response to these challenges, in 2007 GHC began to design and test a medical home model at a primary care clinic in a Seattle suburb (**Exhibit 1–2**). Although many elements of the medical home were already in place at GHC, the pilot strengthened them so as to promote proactive care planning and patient engagement, using the EHR to identify and address patient care needs, expanding and enhancing the roles of the care team to reduce panel size, planning work during daily team huddles, and using phone calls and secure electronic messaging as alternatives to face-to-face visits when appropriate.

The medical home pilot site demonstrated improvements in patient experience and clinical quality, reduced provider burnout, and fewer ED and urgent care visits and hospitalizations (Reid et al., 2010). The model was subsequently extended to all 25 GHC clinic sites, leading to small declines in primary care office visits corresponding to a large increase in electronic messages

---

Exhibit 1–2 Core Principles of a Medical Home at Group Health Cooperative

1. The relationship between the personal care physician and the patient is the core of all that we do. The entire delivery system and the organization will align to promote and sustain this relationship.

2. The personal care physician will be a leader of the clinical team, responsible for coordination and integration of services, and together with patients will create collaborative-care plans.

3. Continuous healing relationships will be proactive and will encompass all aspects of health and illness. Patients will be actively informed about their care and will be encouraged to participate in all its aspects.

4. Access will be centered on patients' needs, will be available by various modes 24/7, and will maximize the use of technology.

5. Our clinical and business systems are aligned to achieve the most efficient, satisfying, and effective patient experiences.

Reproduced from McCarthy, D., Mueller, K., & Tillmann, I. 2009. *Group Health Cooperative: Reinventing Primary Care by Connecting Patients with a Medical Home*. New York, NY: The Commonwealth Fund.

and telephone encounters. Emergency department visits declined 18.5% by the second year after accounting for preexisting trends in network practices (Reid et al., 2013). GHC's leaders say these improvements are renewing the organization's culture and making it a more attractive place to work.

Intermountain Healthcare

Intermountain Healthcare, a large multihospital system serving communities throughout Utah and Idaho, created an integrated medical group from scratch in a span of a few years. By recruiting community physicians with a "collaborative bent" and emphasizing core values and a common work ethic, the medical group self-selected compatible members and became a stable unit with a shared culture. Focusing on quality and service, rather than on productivity alone, allowed physicians to develop an internally motivated pride for achieving excellence both clinically and financially (McCarthy & Mueller, 2009b).

Intermountain applied the improvement principles espoused by W. Edwards Deming to develop a clinical integration strategy that seeks to reduce costs by improving quality (James & Savitz, 2011). The program rests on four pillars: (1) identifying key clinical processes to focus effort, (2) designing management information systems for integrated clinical and financial management, (3) developing an integrated clinical and operations management structure, and (4) using incentives that support improvement. Care process models support physicians with evidence-based protocols, decision-support tools, and patient educational materials. The model is used by multidisciplinary teams to design improved processes, such as the following:

- Consistent application of a protocol for elective induction of labor, which reduced inappropriate early induction, deliveries by cesarean section, admissions to the neonatal intensive care unit, and the time women spent in labor, altogether saving $50 million
- An evidence-based mental health integration program in primary care clinics, which led to improved detection of depression, lower treatment costs, increased productivity, and greater satisfaction among patients and staff (Reiss-Brennan, Briot, Savitz, Cannon, & Staheli, 2010)

Geisinger Health System

Geisinger Health System, founded in 1915, is a physician-led, not-for-profit integrated delivery system serving rural northeastern and central Pennsylvania. The multispecialty Geisinger Medical Group employs more than 1000 physicians who practice at 78 clinic sites and in several Geisinger-owned and non-Geisinger hospitals in the region. Many Geisinger patients are enrolled in the Geisinger Health Plan, a top-performing HMO that covers 450,000 members in several states. The health plan also contracts with a large number of independent healthcare providers and community hospitals in the region.

Geisinger has defined an "innovation architecture" to systematically improve the quality, satisfaction, and efficiency of care processes (Paulus, Davis, & Steele, 2008). It involves convening teams to identify the best care model, setting targets for care model redesign, developing a clinical business case for the redesign, applying improvement approaches, and culling promising innovations for expansion. Such efforts typically begin among patients insured by the Geisinger Health Plan, where clinical and financial interests are fully aligned (McCarthy, Mueller, Wrenn, 2009).

ProvenCare is a portfolio of evidence-based quality and efficiency programs addressing acute and chronic conditions. Clinical workgroups redesign care processes to reliably deliver a coordinated bundle of evidence-based (or consensus-based) best practices that are "hardwired" in the EHR through templates, order sets, and reminders. For patients covered by the Geisinger Health Plan who are having certain surgical procedures, Geisinger charges the health plan a bundled payment that covers preoperative care, surgery, and 90 days of follow-up treatment at a Geisinger facility (in effect, a "warranty" against complications). The bundle, which is priced at a discount to create an incentive for efficiency, has led to improved clinical and financial outcomes for patients undergoing heart bypass surgery (Casale et al., 2007).

The same approach has been applied to other services. For example, in perinatal care, it led to a 32% decline in cesarean deliveries (Berry et al., 2011). The design of a primary care medical home model of care called ProvenHealth Navigator improved the quality of care, reduced hospital admissions (by 18%) and readmissions (by 36%), and lowered overall costs (by 4% to 7%) for Geisinger Health Plan's elderly Medicare Advantage members (Gilfillan et al., 2010; Maeng et al., 2012).

Genesys PHO

The Genesys PHO is a **physician–hospital organization (PHO)** that negotiates risk-based managed care contracts and participates in pay-for-performance programs with health plans on behalf of the nonprofit Genesys Regional Medical Center (GRMC) and a network of 160 community-based primary care physicians who serve 250,000 patients in a five-county service area around Flint, Michigan. PHO physicians refer their patients to GRMC for most inpatient care and to a closed panel of 400 specialists with privileges at GRMC who have agreed to follow the PHO's protocols for care coordination and utilization management. Half of the primary care physicians participating in the PHO are shareholder-members of the Genesys Integrated Group Practice (GIGP), a virtual group of small private physician practices. GIGP also owns and operates several diagnostic centers and after-hours clinics.

The Genesys PHO involves its primary care physicians in determining appropriate guidelines for clinical care and specialty referral and supports them in becoming primary care medical homes. Insurers have delegated authority for medical management under a capitated payment structure. This clinical and operational autonomy, together with a respectful relationship with the hospital that treats the physicians as true partners, appears to have given the Genesys PHO an endurance that was often lacking in other failed efforts to establish PHOs elsewhere in the United States.

The PHO partnered with the hospital and the specialty panel to participate in Medicare's Pioneer ACO program, in hopes that it would provide financial support to intensify care management for fee-for-service patients and increase risk-taking capacity as the partners prepare for a future in which value-based purchasing becomes the norm. Primary care physicians, specialists, and the hospital shared upside and downside risk in the Pioneer ACO program, limited to 10% of a benchmark in the first two years of the program.

Although Medicare requires that beneficiaries managed by an ACO maintain their freedom of choice of provider, the PHO's primary care physicians encouraged their ACO-covered patients to see their office as a medical home for routine care needs, such as monitoring chronic conditions and providing follow-up testing when a patient is stable after a heart attack. The PHO has also hired health navigators to reach out to patients at risk of incurring high costs to help improve transitions in care and connect them to needed services. Despite the fact that the ACO achieved quality targets and reduced Medicare costs during the first two years of the Pioneer program, the ACO lost money from Medicare because it did not outperform a national risk-sharing benchmark, which does not account for regional variations in spending (Beck, 2014). The PHO dropped out of the Pioneer program but subsequently joined the Medicare Shared Savings Program, which offers the opportunity to earn savings without risk of losses.

LESSONS LEARNED

Leaders of these organizations appeared to motivate the achievement of higher performance by fostering a mission-oriented culture that appeals to common values, such as patient welfare, professional pride, and shared responsibility for quality and outcomes. Leaders balance a focus on values with management discipline by setting clear and ambitious goals, communicating with and enlisting physicians and the workforce in carrying out a strategic vision, and marshalling resources to support implementation of agreed-upon strategies.

In general, greater integration makes it possible for a system to better understand and design programs to meet the needs of a population so as to improve the quality and efficiency of care. Case study organizations are taking multiple paths to integrating care, bringing together providers and services across disciplines and settings to focus on particular conditions or care episodes (e.g., diabetes, cancer, cardiac surgery). They also may apply this strategy across time and types of care, such as using every patient contact as an opportunity to schedule needed preventive care. Experience from these and other case studies (Robinson, 2013) suggests that combining cross-service integration with service-line specialization strategies may be effective in optimizing both care coordination and efficiency goals.

Determining which delivery system components to own or contract for depends on objectives, resources, and the local market environment, among other factors (Robinson & Casalino, 1996). Kaiser Permanente has found that owning hospitals and co-locating services in its California-based medical centers promotes tighter care coordination and efficiency. Likewise, critical-access hospitals, such as those profiled in the North Dakota case study, often serve as "one-stop shops" for integrating inpatient and outpatient care for rural communities. In contrast, Group Health Cooperative found that excess hospital bed capacity in the Seattle market made it more efficient to contract and coordinate with independent hospitals for inpatient care, which has freed up GHC to focus its expertise on ambulatory care delivery.

Simply owning the pieces of a system is not enough, however. The experience of organizations such as Henry Ford Health System suggests that integrated delivery systems, however configured, must actively pursue the opportunities for integration inherent in their model if they are to achieve the desired internal alignment and coordination between parts of the system. This entails realizing efficiencies ranging from eliminating redundant layers of administration to cross-marketing and in-sourcing services to avoid "leakage" of revenues outside the system—in short, taking advantage of an organization's core strengths.

Aligned Incentives

Alignment occurs at the organizational level by integrating care and coverage and/or by setting budgets centrally, so that services can be organized in ways that make the most sense operationally and clinically. For example, some integrated systems subsidize primary care services from other operations, having recognized that effective primary care delivery contributes to a more efficient system overall. Integrated delivery systems that include health plans, and ACOs that partner with commercial insurers, have stronger financial incentives to provide care coordination and care transition services that reduce overall costs because of fewer ED visits or hospitalizations. In other cases, provider organizations are collaborating with payers and purchasers to participate in value-based incentive programs and create payment reforms that help fund care management activities, a process facilitated by a prepared infrastructure. Nevertheless, integrated systems can lose money by doing the right thing when incentives are not aligned with payers.

The relationship between organization and system-level payment methods is depicted in **Figure 1–2**. The figure shows that, as the delivery system becomes more organized, more bundled payment methods and robust pay-for-performance programs are not only more feasible, but also more desirable. Bundled payment methods reward care coordination and efficiency, which more organized delivery systems should be able to achieve. In addition, with greater organization, it should be possible to increase the percentage of total reimbursement subject to pay-for-performance programs, and to focus these programs on clinical outcomes measures. Not only would this create incentives for high performance, but it would also counterbalance the risk that bundled payments would lead providers to deliver too few services. By contrast, it is not feasible to implement these payment methods at the small provider level (Shih et al., 2008).

At the physician level, the compensation method is aligned with the organization's objectives, values, and market environment. Some entities, such as the Mayo Clinic, believe that salaried physicians are motivated intrinsically

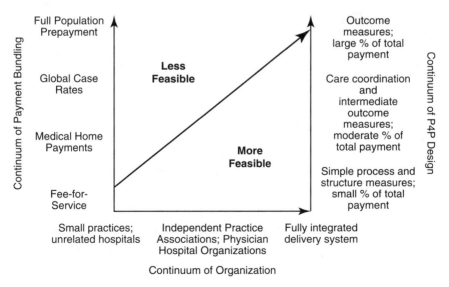

Figure 1–2 Organization and Payment Methods

Reproduced from The Commonwealth Fund (2009). *The Path to a High Performance U.S. Health System: A 2020 Vision and the Policies to Pave the Way*. Washington, D.C.: The Commonwealth Fund.

by professional and organizational culture to do their best for patients. Other organizations see a positive role for extrinsic rewards, including financial incentives, which may include productivity-based pay or bonuses for meeting quality and service goals. Physician payment incentives must be designed carefully, as they may have both intended and unintended consequences on behavior and satisfaction (Greene, Hibbard, & Overton, 2014).

Market Adaptation and Policy Evolution

Following an evolution in the market that has demanded choice of provider, several integrated systems with health plans "opened" their networks to contract with community physicians and accept payers other than their own health plan, thereby shifting their orientation away from an exclusive reliance on prepaid practice. These organizations have adapted to the market by developing performance information and incentives to help overcome the limitations of fee-for-service payment. Several of these "hybrid" organizations report an advantage from being able to influence other providers in the community who practice in their facilities or who contract with their health plans, and of creating a spirit of "competitive excellence" within their organization as they seek the loyalty of patients who have a choice of providers.

Because the Medicare Shared Savings Program is built on existing fee-for-service incentives, it was not seen as a logical progression by study organizations with health plans that participate in the Medicare Advantage program. The Medicare ACOs profiled were challenged in engaging with beneficiaries because the program's patient attribution model is based on care-seeking behaviors that are liable to change, resulting in turnover in the target population. Because Medicare beneficiaries are not formally "enrolled" in an ACO and cannot be offered incentives to change their behavior, Medicare ACOs must rely on patients to voluntarily comply with recommendations. That said, the sites have recognized the value of engaging patients in care management to identify personal goals for lifestyle change or treatment, and educating them about their treatment options, though all felt they could do more in this regard.

THE VALUE OF INTEGRATED DELIVERY

Commonly reported results of the initiatives and programs documented in the case studies included improved clinical quality of care and control of chronic diseases, increased patient satisfaction, shorter waiting times, and reduced hospitalizations, emergency visits, and prescription drug expenses (McCarthy & Mueller, 2009b). Organizational culture and what one leader calls "pride of purpose" appear to be key factors propelling excellent organizations to sustain such efforts over time. Although some institutions such as the Mayo Clinic have been developing their culture over decades, in other cases leaders describe how managers can engage the workforce to inculcate the behaviors and attitudes that shape a culture aimed toward higher performance, especially as it relates to keeping patients safe from harm (McCarthy & Blumenthal, 2006).

A review of the health services literature found that "more organized systems generally perform better than less organized systems on measures of clinical quality, show promise for reducing health care costs, and have a mixed record in terms of patients' experiences" (Shih et al., 2008). Similarly, in comparison to external benchmarking data, the study organizations generally performed better on clinical quality than on patient satisfaction metrics, although several have made strides in improving the patient experience. Not all the sites did equally well across all dimensions of performance, however. While their models of care delivery work well most of the time, the case studies documented some instances when they failed to live up to their promise. Moreover, not all physicians working in integrated systems perceive that they achieve their potential for integration and care coordination (Strandberg-Larsen et al., 2010). Nevertheless, their overall experience and achievements suggest that a greater degree of integration, if well executed, can be beneficial to improving the value of U.S. health care.

REALIZING THE POTENTIAL OF INTEGRATED DELIVERY

The cases studies illustrate that there are many ways of achieving more integrated delivery of health care. In seeking to develop or foster integrated delivery systems, managers and policymakers should adopt a flexible approach that takes into account not only what is most effective, but also what is most feasible in a local context and environment. While doing so, they should focus on building a guiding vision, integrative capabilities, and supportive organizational culture as much as the structural components of an organization.

More physicians are moving to employment relationships with hospitals (O'Malley, Bond, & Berenson, 2011)—a trend that might be harnessed to realize the fuller advantages of an employed group practice model (Minott et al., 2010). According to leaders, physicians are increasingly attracted to organized care settings and can be motivated to participate in and lead ACOs if they see that new arrangements offer a way to provide better care, sustain patients' loyalty, and maintain control over their own destiny. In other circumstances, physicians, hospitals, and other providers may find that it makes sense to develop alternative ways to organize and integrate care through independent private practices, though they may or may not enjoy all the levers for integration available to employed physician groups. However, the benefits of integrated care delivery may be mitigated if market consolidation results in higher prices and costs (Cutler, 2014).

The prospects for stimulating greater organization and integration of care in the United States depend in large part on continuing support for and refinement of payment policies that support delivery system reforms in the public and private sectors. For example, proposed federal legislation to revamp Medicare physician payment would create incentives for physicians to participate in value-based payment arrangements. Experts have proposed a tiered pathway for ACO evolution and qualification that would reward performance based on the degree of financial risk assumed by the ACO (McClellan, McKethan, Lewis, Roski, & Fisher, 2010; Shortell, Casalino, & Fisher, 2010). Additional changes to the regulatory, professional, and educational environments may be needed to support the infrastructure for higher performance (Shih et al., 2008).

Delivery system reforms to stimulate greater organization of care generally enjoy the support of both consumers and health system leaders (How, Shih, Lau, &, Schoen, 2008; Stremikis, Guterman, & Davis, 2009). Health system leaders see that impending demographic shifts and fiscal constraints are creating an urgent need to creatively bring these approaches to scale (Dentzer, 2010). Patients also may play a role in bringing about change as they demand greater responsiveness and convenience from the care system, such as the ability to communicate electronically with their care team, and as they make use of performance information to choose their care providers. The public availability of such comparative data—especially data focusing on system-level outcomes—can enable purchasers and policymakers to calibrate better policies and motivate providers to respond for the sake of professional pride and reputation.

ACKNOWLEDGMENT

The author is indebted to current and former colleagues and grantees of The Commonwealth Fund and staff at the Institute for Healthcare Improvement who gave advice and contributed to research from which this chapter is adapted in part. The views presented here are those of the author and not necessarily those of The Commonwealth Fund or its directors, officers, or staff.

CHAPTER SUMMARY

The experience of integrated healthcare delivery systems across the United States demonstrates how higher performance can be attained through convenient access to appropriate care, information continuity and integration, care coordination, team-oriented care delivery, and continuous innovation and improvement. Realizing these attributes requires the cultivation of values-based leadership and aligned incentives (both at the organizational and provider levels) supported by accountability for and transparency of results. Adapting and spreading these approaches more widely would help assure that more Americans can benefit from receiving care that is designed and delivered to assure optimal patient experiences and outcomes at a sustainable cost.

KEY TERMS AND CONCEPTS

Accountable care organization (ACO): A group of physicians, and possibly other healthcare providers such as hospitals, who come together voluntarily to accept collective accountability for the quality and cost of care delivered to their patients.

Health maintenance organization (HMO): A group that organizes the financing and delivery of a range of healthcare benefits for members enrolled in a health plan.

Independent practice association (IPA): An organized group of independent providers who contract with one or more health plans for the purpose of providing healthcare services to a defined population.

Integrated delivery system (IDS): A group of healthcare organizations that collectively provide an array of health-related services in a coordinated fashion to those using the system.

Multispecialty group practice (MSGP): A group that employs primary and specialty care physicians who share common governance, infrastructure, and finances; refer patients for services offered within the group; and are typically affiliated with a particular hospital or hospitals.

Physician–hospital organization (PHO): A partnership between a hospital and all or some of its affiliated physicians for the purpose of contracting with one or more health plans to provide health care services to a defined population.

Questions to Consider

1. Describe how health care experienced by you, or someone you know, might have differed had it been delivered in accordance with the six attributes of an ideal health system.

2. Do the case examples describe what you consider to be an ideal way for patients to receive care? Why or why not?

3. How could a physician group or hospital apply the lessons offered by the case examples to create an integrated system of care?

4. Is there anything the healthcare industry could learn from the consumer electronics industry about how to use information technology to improve operations or services?

5. In which ways can leaders shape the culture of an organization to improve performance?

6. Which behavior is each of the following methods of paying for health care likely to reward: (a) salary; (b) a fee for each service or unit of work; (c) a bundled payment for an episode of care; (d) fixed payment for all care needed in a given time period?

REFERENCES

Beck, M. (2014, September 25). A Medicare program loses more health-care providers. *The Wall Street Journal*.

Berry, S. A., Laam, L. A., Wary, A. A., Mateer, H. O., Cassagnol, H. P., McKinley, K. E., & Nolan, R. A. (2011). ProvenCare perinatal: A model for delivering evidence/guideline-based care for perinatal populations. *Joint Commission Journal on Quality and Patient Safety, 37,* 229–239.

Casale, A. S., Paulus, R. A., Selna, M. J., Doll, M. C., Bothe, A. E. Jr., McKinley, K. E., …, Steele, G. D. Jr. (2007). A provider-driven pay-for-performance program for acute episodic cardiac surgical care. *Annals of Surgery, 246,* 270–280.

Cohen, A., Klein, S., & McCarthy, D. (2014). *Hill Physicians Medical Group: A market-driven approach to accountable care for commercially insured patients.* New York, NY: The Commonwealth Fund.

Commonwealth Fund Commission on a High Performance Health System. (2007). *A high performance health system for the United States: An ambitious agenda for the next president.* New York, NY: The Commonwealth Fund.

Courneya, P. T., Palattao, K. J., & Gallagher, J. M. (2013). HealthPartners' online clinic for simple conditions delivers savings of $88 per episode and high patient approval. *Health Affairs, 32,* 385–392.

Cutler, D. M. (2014). Who benefits from health system change? *Journal of the American Medical Association, 312,* 1639– 1641.

Dentzer, S. (2010). Geisinger chief Glenn Steele: Seizing health reform's potential to build a superior system. *Health Affairs, 29,* 1200–1207.

Enthoven, A. C., & Tollen, L. A. (2004). *Toward a 21st century health system: The contributions and promise of prepaid group practice.* San Francisco, CA: Jossey-Bass.

Falk, I. S., Rorem, C. R., & Ring, M. D. (1933). *The costs of medical care: A summary of investigations on the economic aspects of the prevention and care of illness.* Chicago, IL: University of Chicago Press.

Gilfillan, R. J., Tomcavage, J., Rosenthal, M. B., Davis, D. E., Graham, J., Roy, J. A., …, Steele, G. D. Jr. (2010). Value and the medical home: Effects of transformed primary care. *American Journal of Managed Care, 16,* 607–614.

Greene, J., Hibbard, J. H., & Overton, V. (2014). A case study of a team-based, quality-focused compensation model for primary care providers. *Medical Care Research & Review, 71,* 207–223.

How, S. K. H., Shih, A., Lau, J., & Schoen, C. (2008). *Public views on U.S. health system organization: A call for new directions.* New York, NY: The Commonwealth Fund.

Institute of Medicine. (2001). *Crossing the quality chasm: A new health system for the 21st century.* Washington, DC: National Academy Press.

James, B. C., & Savitz, L. A. (2011). How Intermountain trimmed health care costs through robust quality improvement efforts. *Health Affairs, 30,* 1185–1191.

Klein, S., McCarthy, D., & Cohen, A. (2014). *Marshfield Clinic: Demonstrating the potential of accountable care.* New York, NY: The Commonwealth Fund.

Larson, B. K., Van Citters, A. D., Kreindler, S. A., Carluzzo, K. L., Gbemudu, J. N., Wu, F. M., ... Fisher, E.S. (2012). Insights from transformations under way at four Brookings-Dartmouth accountable care organization pilot sites. *Health Affairs,* 31(11), 2395–2406.

Liebhaber, A., & Grossman, J. M. (2007). Physicians moving to mid-sized, single-specialty practices. *Center for Studying Health System Change Tracking Report, 18,* 1–5.

Maeng, D. D., Graham, J., Graf, T. R., Liberman, J. N., Dermes, N. B., Tomcavage, J., ..., Steele, G. D. Jr. (2012). Reducing long-term cost by transforming primary care: Evidence from Geisinger's medical home model. *American Journal of Managed Care, 18,* 149–155.

McCarthy, D., & Blumenthal, D. (2006). Stories from the sharp end: Case studies in safety improvement. *Milbank Quarterly, 84,* 165–200.

McCarthy, D., & Mueller, K. (2009a). *Kaiser Permanente: Bridging the quality divide with integrated practice, group accountability, and health information technology.* New York, NY: The Commonwealth Fund.

McCarthy, D., & Mueller, K. (2009b). *Organizing for higher performance: Case studies of organized delivery systems. Series overview, findings, and methods.* New York, NY: The Commonwealth Fund.

McCarthy, D., Mueller, K., & Wrenn, J. (2009). *Geisinger Health System: Achieving the potential of system integration through innovation, leadership, measurement, and incentives.* New York, NY: The Commonwealth Fund.

McCarthy, D., Mueller, K., & Tillmann, I. (2009). *Group Health Cooperative: Reinventing primary care by connecting patients with a medical home.* New York, NY: The Commonwealth Fund.

McCarthy, D., Klein, S., & Cohen, A. (2014). *The road to accountable care: Building systems for population health management.* New York, NY: The Commonwealth Fund.

McClellan, M., McKethan, A. N., Lewis, J. L., Roski, J., & Fisher, E. S. (2010). A national strategy to put accountable care into practice. *Health Affairs, 29,* 982–990.

Medicare Payment Advisory Commission. (2009). Accountable care organizations. In *Report to the Congress: Improving incentives in the Medicare program.* Washington, DC: Author.

Minott, J., Helms, D., Luft, H., Guterman, S., & Weil, H. (2010). *The group employed model as a foundation for health delivery reform.* New York, NY: The Commonwealth Fund.

O'Malley, A. S., Bond, A. M., & Berenson, R. A. (2011). Rising hospital employment of physicians: Better quality, higher costs? *Center for Studying Health System Change Issue Brief, 136,* 1–4.

Paulus, R. A., Davis, K., & Steele, G. D. (2008). Continuous innovation in health care: Implications of the Geisinger experience. *Health Affairs, 27,* 1235–1245.

Pearl, R. (2014). Kaiser Permanente Northern California: Current experiences with Internet, mobile, and video technologies. *Health Affairs, 33,* 251–257.

Reid, R. J., Coleman, K., Johnson, E. A., Fishman, P. A., Hsu, C., Soman, M. P., . . ., Larson, E. B. (2010). The Group Health medical home at year two: Cost savings, higher patient satisfaction, and less burnout for providers. *Health Affairs, 29,* 835–843.

Reid, R. J., Johnson, E. A., Hsu, C., Ehrlich, K., Coleman, K., Trescott, C., Erikson, M., . . ., Fishman, P. A. (2013). Spreading a medical home redesign: Effects on emergency department use and hospital admissions. *Annals of Family Medicine, 11,* S19–S26.

Reiss-Brennan, B., Briot, P. C., Savitz, L. A., Cannon, W., & Staheli, R. (2010). Cost and quality impact of Intermountain's mental health integration program. *Journal of Healthcare Management, 55,* 97–113.

Robinson, J. C. (2013). Case studies of orthopedic surgery in California: The virtues of care coordination versus specialization. *Health Affairs, 32,* 921–928.

Robinson, J. C., & Casalino, L. P. (1996). Vertical integration and organizational networks in health care. *Health Affairs, 15,* 7–22.

Schoen, C., How, S. K. H., Weinbaum, I., Craig, J. E. Jr., & Davis, K. (2006). *Public views on shaping the future of the U.S. health system.* New York, NY: The Commonwealth Fund.

Shih, A., Davis, K., Schoenbaum, S., Gauthier, A., Nazum, R., & McCarthy, D. (2008). *Organizing the U.S. health care delivery system for high performance.* New York, NY: The Commonwealth Fund.

Shortell, S. M., Casalino, L. P., & Fisher, E. (2010). *Advancing national health reform: Implementing accountable care organizations.* Policy Brief. Berkeley: University of California, Berkeley, School of Law, Berkeley Center on Health, Economic & Family Security.

Silow-Carroll, S., & Edwards, J. N. (2013). *Early adopters of the accountable care model: A field report on improvements in health care delivery.* New York, NY: The Commonwealth Fund.

Strandberg-Larsen, M., Schiotz, M. L., Silver, J. D., Frolich, A. Andersen, J. S., Graetz, I., . . ., Hsu, J. (2010). Is the Kaiser Permanente model superior in terms of clinical integration? A comparative study of Kaiser Permanente, Northern California and the Danish healthcare system. *BMC Health Services Research, 8,* 91.

Stremikis, K., Guterman, S., & Davis, K. (2009). *Health care opinion leaders' views on slowing the growth of health care costs.* New York, NY: The Commonwealth Fund.

The Commonwealth Fund Commissio on a High Performance Health System. (2009). The path to a high performance U.S. health system: A 2020 vision and the policies to pave the way. New York, NY: The Commonwealth Fund.

Weber, V., Bloom, F., Pierdon, S., & Wood, C. (2008). Employing the electronic health record to improve diabetes care: A multifaceted intervention in an integrated delivery system. *Journal of General Internal Medicine, 23,* 379–382.

Chapter 2

Information Systems

—Jonathan P. DeShazo, PhD

LEARNING OBJECTIVES

- Understand the electronic health record (EHR) as indispensable to high quality, coordinated, and efficient care
- Understand that many types of information systems (IS) are needed to manage an integrated health system
- Appreciate how information systems are tightly integrated with the business and clinical functions of the health system
- Be aware of the leadership, personnel roles, and services commonly found in the IS function
- Be very familiar with how Information and data are key to management and clinical decision making
- Appreciate the role and relationship of analytics systems and their business and clinical functions
- Recognize how technology changes due to environmental forces such as policies and emerging payment models impact health care

INTRODUCTION

The **electronic health record (EHR)** is indispensable to provide high-quality, coordinated, efficient care and is mandated through federal policy. However, many more types of **information systems (IS)** are needed for an integrated health system to support its mission and remain competitive in the market. These information systems are tightly integrated with the business and clinical functions of the health system and are managed and supported by skilled professionals within the IS function of the organization.

This chapter discusses the EHR in detail as well as other significant clinical and administrative information technology (IT) found in integrated health systems. The leadership, personnel roles, and services commonly found in the IS function are explored as well. Information and data are key to management and clinical decision making; thus the role and relationship of analytics systems and their business and clinical functions are examined as important developments in healthcare IT. Finally, technology changes due to environmental forces such as policies and emerging payment models are discussed.

KEY INFORMATION SYSTEMS

Information system is a broad term used to describe both the technology (e.g., hardware and software) and the way that individuals use a system to perform their roles within the organization. Data also play an important role in information systems, making up the information component that is transferred between systems of computers and human users. For example, an EHR system consists of hardware (e.g., computers), software (e.g., the EHR application or program), and data (e.g., orders, lab results). The EHR system also consists of templates (structured guides) that are tightly integrated with clinical pathways (the step-by-step process that providers follow when giving care). Therefore, when thinking about the EHR, one must think about the technology as well as the way it is used.

The justification for understanding information systems as they pertain to managing integrated delivery systems is simple: Most, if not all aspects of a health system have been transformed by information systems. Indeed, first the revenue cycle, then operations, and now clinical delivery have not just been automated but truly transformed through the value-added capabilities of these systems. Therefore, a competitive advantage may be gained by managing the information technology function to its full capacity, and integrating this new information across all decision makers within the organization. In this section, we discuss important health information technology (HIT) systems used by clinical staff as well as healthcare administrators.

Electronic Health Record

All of a patient's medical information is documented within his or her health record. It is important to appreciate the breadth and depth of the information contained within the health record to better understand the challenges of keeping these data electronically and repurposing them later (**Figure 2–1**). Medical providers use the health record to document the health state of the patient as well as the care they provide. Providers also use it to communicate to one another. The health record is used as the source of billing codes, establishing what will be charged on the medical bill. In most cases, the health record is also a legal record of the patient's status, the provider's decision making, and exactly which procedures were performed. These very different usages are very important to consider when repurposing health records for research and analysis (**Table 2–1**).

Ideally, the health record has the following characteristics:

- *Longitudinal*, spanning medical encounters over the years
- *Comprehensive*, including all of the various types of health information (e.g., labs, procedures, images) in one place
- *Complete*, containing all of the encounters available regardless of hospital, setting, and geographic location

Currently, this ideal is rarely, if ever, achieved.

Figure 2–1 Screenshot of Practice Fusion EHR
Courtesy of Practice Fusion, Inc.

Table 2–1 Typical EHR functions and data elements

EHR Functions	EHR Data
Health information and data management[*]	Patient demographics
	Vitals
Structured templates	Allergies
Result management[*]	Diagnosis and problems
Order management[*]	Progress/nursing notes
ePrescribing	Physician notes
Order sets	History and physical examination
Formularies	Care setting
Decision support[*]	Medication
Alerting	Procedures
Additional information	Laboratory order and results
Electronic communication and connectivity[*]	Microbiology
	Radiology images
Health information exchange (HIE)	Consent and advance directives
Remote radiology	Patient-reported outcomes
Provider messaging	Chief complaint
Telehealth	
Patient support[*]	
Patient education	
Administrative processes and reporting[*]	
Reporting and population health[*]	
Disease registries	

[*] Denotes key functions as reported by Institute of Medicine (2003).

Many EHR products are designed to support general medicine practices and/or a large number of specialty services. However, some EHR software may be unique and tailored to a specific medical specialty. For example, ophthalmology practices may require special charting and drawing capabilities as well as the ability to communicate to special equipment. Moreover, EHRs are frequently designed to meet the needs of specific segments, such as ambulatory or acute care. To see other examples of EHR products and market segments, visit www.klasresearch.com, which is a rating service (think *Consumer Reports*) for EHRs and other health information technology.

The diversity of EHR needs across clinical settings represents a challenge to the integrated delivery system. Only the most expensive EHR vendors support large systems that incorporate high-quality inpatient and outpatient capabilities in the same product. Frequently, an integrated delivery system will support different EHR products across the enterprise due to cost requirements, the various needs of providers, or legacy situations. This proliferation of products (and standards) places an additional burden on system and user integration plans and maintenance across systems.

Patient health records have existed since the beginnings of medical practice. However, the transition from handwritten records to computerized records remains one of the great challenges of our era. There is strong evidence that EHRs are a requirement (but not sufficient themselves) to improve health outcomes. Such records can foster better clinical outcomes through improved documentation, error checking, and other decision support (Kern, Barrón, Dhopeshwarkar, Edwards, & Kaushal, 2013; Wu et al., 2006). Productivity and financial improvements may also be possible (Poissant, Pereira, Tambly, & Kawasumi, 2005).

Despite the relatively rapid computerization of other industries, EHR adoption has been slow (**Figure 2–2**). The slow pace of adoption of EHRs by hospitals and providers has been attributed to financial misalignment (Johnston et al., 2003), immature technology, and workflow interference (Ash & Bates, 2005). Conversely, improvements in these areas as well as new policies to incentivize EHR adoption are increasing adoption.

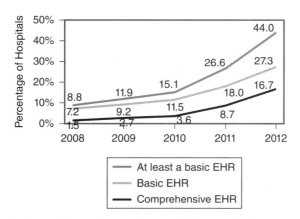

Figure 2-2 Adoption of Electronic Health Records by Hospitals, 2008–2012

© 2013. Robert Wood Johnson Foundation and Harvard School of Public Health, Mathematica Policy Research. "Health Information Technology in the United States: Better Information Systems for Better Care, 2013." Robert Wood Johnson Foundation. 2013. Used with permission from the Robert Wood Johnson Foundation. Data from DesRoches CM, Charles D, Furukawa M, et al. "Progress on Electronic Health Record Adoption Among U.S. Hospitals." *Health Affairs (Millwood)*. 2013;32(8). [Published July 9, 2013, ahead of print], archived and available at www.healthaffairs.org.

Consumer-Oriented Technologies and mHealth

This is the decade of **mobile health applications (mHealth)** and other consumer-oriented health technologies. Whereas the EHR may revolutionize medical practice, mHealth holds the potential to bridge the "last mile" of health care and connect clinical information systems to consumers in their homes and other nonclinical environments.

Patient portals and **personal health records (PHRs)** are consumer-oriented technologies that help individuals and caregivers manage healthcare information. Patient portals and PHRs can have similar capabilities, but PHRs are consumer controlled and independent of the provider organizations (**Figure 2–3**), whereas portals are the "online apps" available to patients of an integrated delivery system. Patients can log into the portal and perform a variety of value-added tasks. Common capabilities include the following:

- Schedule appointments
- View test results
- Patient–clinician messaging
- View current medications
- Problem lists
- View/update allergies
- Immunizations
- Prescription renewals/refill requests

Figure 2–3 Screenshot of Personal Health Record
Used with permission from Microsoft.

- Online billing services
- eVisits
- Save/export EMR data
- Education material
- Satisfaction surveys

For integrated delivery networks, patient portals are becoming instrumental communication channels through which to connect with patient and their caregivers across care settings and at home. For example, use of the online medication refill function in patient portals has been shown to improve patient medication adherence and key lab markers in diabetic patients (Sarkar et al., 2013). In addition, a growing body of evidence indicates that patient portals can improve use of preventive services, missed visits and care transitions, chronic disease management, and other aspects important to integrated care delivery systems. However, more research is needed, particularly on portal use among older and socioeconomically disadvantaged patients (Goldzweig et al., 2013).

The use of remote sensors and mobile devices is also growing in health care. Mobile devices (e.g., mobile phones and tablets) have the potential to reach large numbers of individuals in geographically dispersed places through a convenient and low-cost delivery mechanism. Mobile-based technologies have been used in chronic disease management, sexual health, general well-being, weight loss, tobacco cessation, and many other programs (Fiordelli, Diviani, & Schulz, 2013). Text messaging has been used to reduce missed visits, ensure medication compliance, and even make quicker diagnoses (Car, Gurol-Urganci, de Jongh, Vodopivec-Jamsek, & Atun, 2012; Krishna, Boren, & Balas, 2009).

The significant interest in mHealth is partly due to payment models and recent legislation that require healthcare provider organizations to be accountable for the health of their patients. In this environment, information technologies that support smoother transitions between care settings, improve communication between the patient and the provider outside of the traditional care setting, and go where the patient goes are growing in popularity.

Other Clinical Information Systems

An integrated delivery system typically includes a large number of clinical information systems in addition to the EHR. Many of these systems are tightly integrated with the EHR. The three ancillary systems that are the foundations of the EHR are the pharmacy, radiology, and laboratory systems. To fully capitalize on their promise, these ancillary systems should be integrated (or even centralized) across an integrated delivery system. Many providers choose ancillary systems offered by their existing EHR vendor to avoid the need for potentially complex and costly interfaces.

Although integrated delivery systems can have very diverse facility makeup (e.g., imaging centers, multiple outpatient clinics), it is typically beneficial for core information systems to be less geographically distributed. Ideally, the ancillary systems, like the EHR, should be centralized within and available across all care settings.

A number of lists identifying and defining clinical systems have been published by industry as well as researchers. The Health Information Management System Society's (HIMSS) EMR adoption model, known as EMRAM, is often used to describe the clinical information systems in an organization (**Figure 2–4**). The EMRAM is a score-based ranking from stage 0 (no clinical information technology) to stage 7 (the most capable information technology). It is cumulative, in that an organization must have all of the capabilities in Stage 1 before it should adopt Stage 2 capabilities. EMRAM contains information systems (e.g., data warehousing, pharmacy system) as well as capabilities that may be found within other clinical information systems (e.g., clinical decision support system, clinical documentation).

EMR Adoption Model[SM]

Stage	Cumulative Capabilities
Stage 7	Complete EMR; CCD transactions to share data; Data warehousing; Data continuity with ED and ambulatory
Stage 6	Physician documentation (structured templates), full CDSS (variance & compliance), full R-PACS
Stage 5	Closed loop medication administration
Stage 4	CPOE, CDSS (clinical protocols)
Stage 3	Nursing/clinical documentation (flow sheets), CDSS (error checking), PACS available outside Radiology
Stage 2	CDR, Controlled Medical Vacabulary, CDS, may have Document Imaging, HIE capable
Stage 1	Ancillaries – lab, rad, pharmacy - all installed
Stage 0	All three ancillaries not installed

Figure 2–4 EMR Adoption ModelSM
© 2011 HIMSS Analytics

The following is a breakdown of the most important elements in the EMRAM:[1]

- *Laboratory:* An application that streamlines the process management of the laboratory for basic clinical services such as hematology and chemistry.
- *Radiology:* An automated Radiology Information System that manages the operations and services of the radiology department. The functionality includes scheduling, patient and image tracking, and rapid retrieval of diagnostic reports.
- *Pharmacy:* An application that provides complete support for the pharmacy department from an operational, clinical, and management perspective, helping to optimize patient safety, streamline workflow, and reduce operational costs. It also allows the pharmacist to enter and fill physician orders and, as a by-product, performs all of the related functions of patient charging, general ledger updating, resupply scheduling, and inventory reduction/statistics maintenance.
- *Clinical data repository (CDR):* A central database in which to store and report on clinical data from various applications.
- *Health information exchange (HIE):* Provides the capability to access clinical data from external clinical information systems. Can be peer-to-peer or centralized through a health information exchange organization.
- *Clinical decision support system (CDSS):* An application that uses rules and guidelines based on clinical data to generate alerts and treatment suggestions. CDSS is key, but not necessarily sufficient, to encourage provider behavior changes.
- *Computerized provider order entry (CPOE):* The capability for providers to enter orders (e.g., medications, labs), typically using a structured format, into the computer system. It is frequently coupled with CDSS to provider drug-error alerts.
- *Closed loop medication administration:* The capability for a system to record and reconcile a prescription order with dispensary and administration details.

Administrative Information Systems

As with clinical systems, a great number and variety of information systems are available that support the administrative, operational, and strategic functions of the healthcare organization. In fact, administrative systems can generate a significant return on investment. A review of 57 articles on all types of health IT found that most of the positive financial effects of health information technology stem from administrative benefits. These benefits include savings on administrative goods, personnel, and pharmaceutical choice, and well as revenue gains from improved billing (Low et al., 2013).

Of the various types of administrative systems, billing systems have the longest history and most profound impact on healthcare organizations. A computerized billing system electronically documents information describing services provided and submits a claim to an insurance provider. Health system billing systems typically accommodate complex service and fee schedules, as well as other capabilities such as research billing and patient registration. Because billing systems play such a critical role in revenue generation, they are frequently the first IT system adopted; because of their primacy, they may then become a driver of analytic systems.

Enterprise resource planning (ERP) systems are becoming an indispensable management tool to integrated health systems. ERPs combine human capital and supply chain management with other available data to help organizations streamline equipment, supplies, personnel, and end-to-end fiscal control.

IS FUNCTION AND INTEGRATED HEALTH SYSTEMS

The information systems function within a health system is made up of people, technologies, and processes working together to support the mission and business goals of the organization. In health care, the IS function must support the operational needs of almost every type of end user, including healthcare providers, administrators and clerical workers, facilities and plant workers, scientific staff, and even patients. This diversity creates a challenging array of diverse information technology for the IS function to support.

To satisfy these diverse end-user requirements, health system IS functions must support systems such as the following:

- Clinical information systems
- Research information systems
- Business intelligence and performance/quality improvement systems
- Clerical and administrative systems
- Operations and financial systems
- Networking, interfaces, and telephony systems
- Billing systems

These systems perform a variety of service functions:

- System and software management
- Server/hardware management
- User provisioning and helpdesk support
- Health information management
- Backups and business continuity planning

Following business convention, the IS function of a health system is led by the **chief information officer (CIO)**. The CIO is the administrator responsible for IS technology, services, and personnel in a health system. A CIO's responsibility may include a single hospital, a large integrated delivery system, or an organization with a larger footprint. National- or regional-level CIOs may be supported by local CIOs at a smaller local level. For example, a large integrated delivery system may have a corporate level CIO, as well as CIOs for specific hospitals and ambulatory. CIOs typically report to the chief executive officer, but they may also report to other "C"-suite officers or directly to the board of directors (**Figure 2–5**).

In health care, the IS function is also led by the unique roles of **chief medical informatics officer (CMIO)** and **chief nursing informatics officer (CNIO)**. These two roles represent a structural coupling of clinical expertise with IS function experience. CMIOs are medically trained individuals responsible for the physician needs of clinical systems. Likewise, CNIOs are nurses responsible for the nursing needs of clinical systems. CMIOs and CNIOs will also likely lead a cadre of **physician and nurse informaticists**—providers who have frequently received training in clinical information systems and function as superusers and champions of clinical systems. The CMIO and CNIO may report to the CIO, and/or to the chief medical officer or chief nursing officer, respectively.

The **chief technology officer (CTO)** reports to the CIO and is responsible for enterprise-level strategy and issues related to information systems technology. The CTO should have a good command of current and emerging technologies and understand how they can be best applied operationally or used to further the organizational mission.

The **chief security officer (CSO)** is responsible for the development and enforcement of policies and technologies for information security as well as

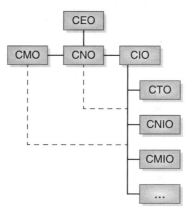

Figure 2–5 Organization chart of IS leadership

business continuity and disaster recovery planning. This is quickly becoming a complex and critical role as health care grows more dependent on information technology. Sometimes the CSO may also be responsible for compliance with the Health Insurance Portability and Accountability Act (HIPAA) and other privacy policies.

The **chief data officer**, who is also sometimes known as the chief health information officer, is an emerging role in health care. At one time a CIO may have had the appropriate level of knowledge regarding health data, but the recent explosive growth of data in health care is forcing organizations to develop leaders who specialize in data-centered roles (Versel, 2014). Data are now considered to be among a health system's most valuable assets, and how data are used will be the source of significant competitive advantage in the future (Aiken & Gorman, 2013).

Aside from senior leadership and reporting structure, how the IS function is organized within (or throughout) the integrated health system matters. Currently, most integrated delivery systems are moving toward a **centralized IS configuration** rather than a **decentralized** one. In a centralized IS configuration, most if not all, of the IS personnel work in a central headquarters or regional-based support center, rather than at each of the facilities. While a centralized approach has many benefits, including economies of scale, human resources/training, oversight/control, and ease of delivering a consistent service or product, it does have some drawbacks. For example, in a decentralized model, the IS personnel can develop closer relationships with their customers and have better insight into the end users' needs. Also, end users appreciate the proximity of IS support.

IS organizations can also be function based (e.g., where the emergency department has its own IS team), application based (e.g., where the billing system and EHR have their own teams), or organization process based (e.g., where all clinical systems fall under one team, and all revenue cycle systems fall under another team). Each of these configurations has unique advantages and disadvantages and performs differently depending on whether information systems are centralized or decentralized. An integrated health system will likely be a matrix organization including several of these arrangements. For example, in a semi-centralized arrangement, all IS teams may be process based except the clinical systems, which are subdivided by application-based teams.

IS process improvement is critical within integrated delivery systems. As organizations experience rapid changes (particularly within IS), there is a need to know which functions are currently operating well and which are outdated or even unnecessary. Process improvement frameworks are a structured method of assessing the performance of IS and making process improvement recommendations. A large number of process improvement

Table 2–2 Examples of Process Improvement Frameworks

	Website	IT Relevance	Healthcare Relevance	Level of Detail	Weaknesses	Strengths
IT infrastructure Library (ITIL)	www.itil.org	Yes	No	Detailed	Highly dependent on interpretation	Service and operations oriented
Six Sigma	www.isixsigma.com	No	No	Abstract	Difficult to apply in uncertain processes	Data driven, takes costs into account
Lean	www.Lean.org	No	No	Detailed	Just-in-time processes work best in stable systems	Oriented toward production-cycle improvement
CMMI	www.sei.cmu.edu/cmmi/?	Yes	No	Detailed	Does not address operations	Geared towered software development
Institute of Healthcare Improvement	www.ihi.org	No	Yes	Detailed	Slow, incremental progress	Good for addressing specific problems
Malcolm Baldrige	www.nist.gov/baldrige/?	No	Yes	Abstract	Holistic approach	Holistic approach

frameworks are available to adopt and follow, and an organization can certainly create its own from scratch or based on existing frameworks. The critical point is that the framework be consistently applied, measure important outcomes, and directly or indirectly lead to improvements. **Table 2–2** provides four examples of commonly used frameworks: IT infrastructure Library (ITIL), Six Sigma, Lean, and the Capability Maturity Model.

ANALYTICS AND BUSINESS INTELLIGENCE

The future of health care is data driven, and advanced analysis and business intelligence will be at the heart of it. **Business intelligence (BI) and analytics** is a collection of methods to extract and analyze data for better decision making. It can be applied for various purposes at almost any level from clinician, to department administrator, to corporate strategist. In health care, the move toward analytics is driven by need as well as the emerging sources of data produced by rapid EHR adoption.

Typically an integrated health system will employ BI to address the following areas:

- *Research and translational improvements:* A movement toward personalized medicine, genomic medicine, and comparative effectiveness analytics is driving business intelligence in this area.
- *Value-based care:* New reimbursement models are forcing integrated delivery systems to consider cost and value, as well as the effectiveness of their clinical processes. This new approach requires the clinical outcome data to be merged with operations and cost data.
- *Clinical and operational improvements:* Business intelligence may help improve clinical processes and operational processes, and identify opportunities for growth and savings that may lower costs.

The IS function of an organization plays a critical role in the success of BI systems. In addition to hosting and supporting the BI computer systems themselves, the IS function is largely responsible for the quality of the data represented. It is crucial for the primary information systems to capture clean, well-defined data. To ensure this demand is met, the computer systems capturing the data that flow into the BI systems may use front- and back-end data integrity checks, as well as routine end-user training. Coupled with data definitions lineage and good security, this effort will improve the data quality. The IS function (or preferably a chief information officer) then performs the following key functions to support business intelligence:

- *Data governance:* Governance focuses on managing data and data concepts from initial capture through aggregation and/or transformation to use. Types of data used in data governance include controlled terminologies and reference data.
- *Data integration:* This process includes the mapping of source data to target data, as well as a plan to load data from one system to another. Frequently, it includes data cleansing and quality control steps.
- *Data storage:* Data must be stored in a manner appropriate to the level of access and use needed. Data availability and disaster recovery are also considerations at this stage.

In 2009, the Health Information Technology for Economic and Clinical Health (HITECH) Act was enacted as part of the American Recovery and Reinvestment Act. This policy authorized the U.S. Department of Health and Human Services to spend $25 billion on healthcare IT adoption and research. The policy comprised an economic stimulus package as well as an EHR adoption incentive program. The HITECH Act expanded the Office of the National Controller for Health Care IT and created two new national committees: the HIT Policy Committee and the HIT Standards Committee. Several provisions of the act funded regional and state programs to encourage HIT adoption by providers as well as adoption- and effectiveness-oriented EHR research. However, the most impactful aspects of the law are the Meaningful Use program and the EHR adoption incentive program.

In the three-stage Meaningful Use program, hospitals and eligible providers are incentivized to adopt certified EHRs and to use these records in their practices. The complexity and capability of the systems used increase from one stage to the next. At the end of the five-year program, if hospitals and eligible providers are not "meaningful use compliant," incentives are replaced by penalties.

Due in large part to the drivers of the HITECH Act and Meaningful Use, more than half of all providers in the United States are currently using EHRs and another 25% are actively on their way to using EHRs in their practice. Time will reveal if meaningful use has been achieved and positive outcomes delivered by the policy.

Under another impactful policy, codified in the Patient Protection and Affordable Care Act, providers can take on more risk for their patients and be rewarded for achieving cost savings for their patient populations. Accountable care organizations, therefore, profit most when they demonstrate they are practicing evidence-based medicine and encouraging patient engagement, thereby avoiding unnecessary hospitalizations and healthcare costs.

Accountable care is a set of policies and processes, but IT can greatly impact the model used to implement it. The Certification Commission for Healthcare Information Technology (CCHITO recommends the following processes be closely supported by HIT: care coordination, cohort management, clinician engagement, financial management, reporting, and knowledge management.

CHAPTER SUMMARY

The Electronic Health Record, or EHR, is indispensable in providing high quality, coordinated, efficient care and is mandated through federal policy. However, there are many more types of information systems that are needed for an Integrated Health System to support its mission and remain competitive in the market. These information systems are tightly integrated with the business and clinical function of the Health System and are managed and supported by skilled professionals within the IS function of the organization.

This chapter discussed the EHR in detail as well as other significant clinical and administrative information technology found in integrated health systems. The leadership, personnel roles, and services commonly found in the IS function were reviewed then explored. Information and data are key to management and clinical decision-making and the business and clinical functions were discussed. Finally, technology changes due to environmental forces such as policies and emerging payment models were discussed.

KEY TERMS AND CONCEPTS

Business intelligence and analytics: A collection of methods to extract and analyze data for better decision making.

Centralized configuration: An information systems configuration in which most, if not all, of the IS personnel work in a central headquarters or regional-based support center, rather than at each of the facilities.

Chief data officer: Also known as the chief health information officer; an emerging data-centered role in health care.

Chief information officer (CIO): The administrator responsible for information systems technology, services, and personnel in a health system.

Chief medical informatics officer (CMIO): A medically trained individual who is responsible for the physician needs of clinical systems.

Chief nursing informatics officer (CNIO): A nurse who is responsible for the nursing needs of clinical systems.

Chief security officer (CSO): The administrator responsible for the development and enforcement of policies and technologies for information security as well as business continuity and disaster recovery planning.

Chief technology officer (CTO): The administrator responsible for enterprise-level strategy and issues related to information systems technology.

Decentralized configuration: An information systems configuration in which at least some of the IS personnel work at each of the facilities, rather than in a central headquarters or regional-based support center.

Electronic health record (EHR): A record that stores all of a patient's medical information. Medical providers use the health record to document the health state of the patient as well as the care they provide.

Enterprise resource planning (ERP) system: A system that combines human capital and supply chain management with other available data to help organizations streamline equipment, supplies, personnel, and end-to-end fiscal control.

Information system: A broad term describing both the technology (e.g., hardware and software) and the way that individuals use a system to perform their roles within the organization.

Mobile health applications (mHealth): Applications that connect clinical information systems to consumers in their homes and other nonclinical environments.

Patient portal: An "online app" available to patients of an integrated delivery system.

Personal health record (PHR): A consumer-controlled record of an individual's medical information that is independent of the provider organization.

Physician and nurse informaticist: A provider who may have received training in clinical information systems and functions as a superuser and champion of clinical systems.

Questions to Consider

1. How is the IS function organized? What are the leadership roles in IS function? Which services are provided by IS function?

2. What are the primary functions of the EHR? How is an EHR within an IDS different?

3. What are the consumer-oriented systems in an IDS?

4. What are the primary administrative systems in the IDS and which functions do they provide?

5. What is the role of IT in defining and measuring quality?

6. How does IT support analytics and business intelligence?

7. What role does IT play in supporting population-based care and value-based payment models?

REFERENCES

Aiken, P., & Gorman, M. (2013). *The case for the chef data officer*. Waltham, MA: Elsevier.

Ash, J. S., & Bates, D. W. (2005). Factors and forces affecting EHR system adoption: Report of a 2004 ACMI discussion. *Journal of the American Medical Informatics Association, 12*, 8–12.

Car, J., Gurol-Urganci, I., de Jongh, T., Vodopivec-Jamsek, V., & Atun, R. (2012). Mobile phone messaging reminders for attendance at healthcare appointments. *Cochrane Database of Systematic Reviews*, Issue 7. Art. No.: CD007458.

Fiordelli, M., Diviani, N., & Schulz, P. (2013). Mapping mHealth research: A decade of evolution. *Journal of Medical Internet Research, 15*, e95.

Goldzweig, C. L., Orshansky, G., Paige, N. M., Towfigh, A. A., Haggstrom, D. A., & Miake-Lye, I. (2013). Electronic patient portals: Evidence on health outcomes, satisfaction, efficiency, and attitudes: A systematic review. *Annals of Internal Medicine, 159*, 677–687.

Institute of Medicine. (2003). Key capabilities of an electronic health record system. *Electronic Health Record Functional Model: Letter Report*. Washington, DC: Institute of Medicine National Academies Press.

Johnston, J., Pan, E., Walker, J., Bates, D. W., & Middleton, B. (2003). The value of computerized provider order entry in ambulatory settings. Partners Healthcare System, Inc. *Clinical Informatics and Research Development.* Retrieved from http://www.partners.org/cird/pdfs/CITL_ACPOE_Full.pdf

Kern, L., Barrón, Y., Dhopeshwarkar, R. V., Edwards, A., & Kaushal, R. (2013). Electronic health records and ambulatory quality of care. *Journal of General Internal Medicine, 28,* 496–503.

Krishna, S., Boren, S. A., & Balas, E. A. (2009). Healthcare via cell phones: A systematic review. *Telemedicine and e-Health, 15,* 231–240.

Low, A. F., Phillips, A. B., Ancker, J. S., Patel, A. R., Kern, L. M., & Kaushal, R. (2013). Financial effects of health information technology: A systematic review. *American Journal of Managed Care, 19,* SP369–SP376.

Poissant, L., Pereira, J., Tamblyn, R., & Kawasumi, Y. (2005). The impact of electronic health records on time efficiency of physicians and nurses: A systematic review. *Journal of the American Medical Informatics Association, 12,* 505–516.

Sarkar, U., Lyles, C. R., Parker, M. M., Allen, J., Nguyen, R., & Moffet, H. H. (2013). Use of the refill function through an online patient portal is associated with improved adherence to statins in an integrated health system. *Medical Care, 52,* 194–201.

Versel, N. (2014). The evolution of health IT continues. *US News and World Report.* Retrieved from http://health.usnews.com/health-news/hospital-of-tomorrow/articles/2014/02/06/the-evolution-of-health-it-continues

Wu, S., Chaudhry, B., Wang, J., Maglione, M., Mojica, W., & Roth, E. (2006). Systematic review: Impact of health information technology on quality, efficiency, and costs of medical care. *Annals of Internal Medicine, 144,* 742–752.

Chapter 3

Managing Access to the Healthcare System

—John Cantiello, PhD

LEARNING OBJECTIVES

- Define access and its dimensions.
- Differentiate between the availability and provision of healthcare services.
- Identify the impact the Affordable Care Act has had on access.
- Distinguish between different models of care and explain how they are evolving.
- Explain how technology can facilitate access to healthcare services.
- Identify ways that healthcare managers can facilitate access.

INTRODUCTION

In the United States, a shortage of healthcare providers and limited access to care have resulted in a system that is geographically centered on providers. The changing requirements for population health management and pressures for greater convenience and services, however, are moving care deeper into the community and closer to the consumer. Ambulatory surgery now dominates surgical volumes. Today, most hospitals receive their largest amounts of revenue from ambulatory care services. Moreover, advances in technology have turned healthcare services into predominantly community-based services.

The implementation of the **Affordable Care Act (ACA)** has meant significant changes to the way many Americans access health services. A growing demand for easily accessible health care has prompted the development of new technology, and the ACA has changed the role of healthcare managers within healthcare organizations. The successful healthcare manager will be able to identify and implement collaborative strategies that focus on access to and coordination of healthcare services. Concepts, models, and different types of technologies that can facilitate access are discussed in this chapter.

DEFINING ACCESS AND ITS DIMENSIONS

The term **access** has been defined and examined differently throughout existing literature. The Institute of Medicine (2001) defines access as the "timely use of personal health services to achieve the best possible outcome" (Millman, 1993, p. 8). Rogers and Sheaff (2000) define optimal access as "providing the right service at the right time in the right place" (p. 866). Penchansky and Thomas (1981) explain that access to healthcare services depends on variables such as health insurance coverage, affordability of services, location of services, and the acceptability of services. Most definitions include the availability of healthcare services as well as the provision or delivery of actual healthcare services, the provision or delivery of the appropriate healthcare services, and some mechanism (i.e., health insurance) that facilitates access.

Donabedian (1973) categorized accessibility into socio-organizational and geographic accessibility. Socio-organizational characteristics include things that facilitate or hinder the efforts of an individual to acquire healthcare services (e.g., gender of the medical provider, cost of care). Geographic accessibility refers to the physical distance traveled to receive care. In other words, people in need may have access to healthcare services yet still have difficulty utilizing those services Aday & Andersen, (1981). Donabedian observed that "the proof of access is use of service, not simply the presence of a facility" (p. 111). The conceptualization of access has become increasingly complicated over time, and it is helpful to think of access as multidimensional.

Andersen and Newman (1973) have conceived and tested healthcare utilization pathways over the past several decades. Andersen's behavioral model of health services use is well known and commonly used as a framework for studying healthcare service utilization. The first version of the behavioral model of health services use, created in the 1960s by Andersen, examined three categories of healthcare access determinants: *predisposing characteristics, enabling characteristics*, and *need-based characteristics*. Predisposing characteristics represented the tendency for an individual to utilize healthcare services. Andersen and Newman argued that such predisposing characteristics dictate whether a person actually uses healthcare services. These characteristics include demographics, social status, and whether an individual believes health services are useful (p. 14). Andersen and Newman defined enabling characteristics as those that enable an individual to utilize healthcare services. Enabling characteristics include family and community resources. Family resources include socioeconomic status and geographic location; community resources include the presence of healthcare facilities within the community (p. 15). Finally, illness level or need-based characteristics encompass a person's perceived need for healthcare services. Andersen and Newman argue that an individual must perceive the existence of illness for the use of health services to take place. Such characteristics include symptoms and a general report of one's health (p. 16).

In the 1970s, Andersen's model was revised to include more variables. The newer version included the healthcare system as an overarching variable. The healthcare system includes health policy issues, resources, and organizations. Instead of focusing on the three characteristics in the previous model, the newer model included five concepts of healthcare access: *health policy, characteristics of the health delivery system, characteristics of the population-at-risk, utilization of health services*, and *consumer satisfaction* (Aday & Andersen, 1981). In the newer model, which was more detailed, primary determinants of access included population characteristics, the external environment, and the healthcare system (Racher & Vollman, 2002). Interestingly, the updated model included recognition that consumer satisfaction affects healthcare utilization. The perceived significance of consumer satisfaction has continued to increase in recent years.

In 1995, the behavioral model of health services use went through a third and final major revision. It was streamlined to include the categories of *primary determinants, health behaviors*, and *health outcomes*. Andersen (1995) categorized primary determinants as the main reason why people make certain health behavior decisions. He included demographics, the healthcare system, and the external environment as primary determinants (p. 7). The use of health services and maintaining a healthy lifestyle made up the second category, health behaviors (p. 7). The third category, health outcomes, was defined as one's perceived health status and patient satisfaction (p. 7). Andersen argued that the updated model shows "the multiple influences on health services' use and, subsequently, on health status" (p. 7).

The expansion of the behavioral model of health services use and its later restructuring illustrate that new conceptualizations of access become necessary as the healthcare system changes. When the model was first created, Aday and Andersen (1981) argued that the characteristics included in the model, while useful in identifying care pathways, were not enough to account for actual entry into the market. Aday and others have pointed out that one must consider the potential consumer's willingness to seek care to fully understand access (Mechanic, 1972). This willingness depends on one's attitude and the amount of information one has regarding healthcare services.

Penchansky and Thomas (1981) defined access as the ability to get care or the ease of getting care. These authors also explained that access to healthcare services should capture the relationship between supply and demand in five dimensions. Others have also argued that having access to healthcare services requires the availability of an adequate supply of health services (Gulliford et al., 2002). Again, it is helpful to think of access as a concept composed of multiple elements rather than only potential accessibility.

Penchansky and Thomas (1981) outlined five factors or dimensions that they believed affected supply and demand and influenced utilization of health services: *availability, accessibility, accommodation, affordability*, and *acceptability*. Availability refers to the quantity of healthcare services available. Accessibility is the relationship between the physical location of the supply of healthcare services and the physical location of the consumer. Accommodation refers to how easily the consumer can access care (e.g., hours of operation). Affordability refers to the resources that one has available to purchase care. Finally, acceptability relates to the social or cultural concerns of obtaining care (e.g., attitudes related to religion or gender).

Clearly, access is not a one-dimensional concept. Instead, it is helpful to think of access in terms of Aday and Andersen's (1981) streamlined model (primary determinants, health behaviors, and health outcomes) layered with Penchansky and Thomas's (1981) five dimensions (availability, accessibility, accommodation, affordability, and acceptability). In a broad sense, access refers to availability of medical care as well as the ease of obtaining it. Both availability and receipt of care should be considered.

COST AND ACCESS

The rising costs of medical services and insurance premiums are making health care unaffordable for and inaccessible to many Americans. Costs have been increasing for the past few decades for a variety of reasons, such as the introduction of new expensive technologies, a growing elderly population, new legislation and state mandates, and increases in malpractice insurance premiums for doctors (Rodriquez, 2003). A recent U.S. Census Bureau report produced by Smith and Medalia (2014) indicated that 42 million

Americans were uninsured in 2013. While this number is smaller than what had been previously reported, it is still large and concerning.

The existing literature indicates that the uninsured are a diverse segment of the population. This group comprises people of different ages, ethnic backgrounds, socioeconomic statuses, and health statuses. The uninsured population is largely made up of people who have been without health insurance for a relatively short amount of time. A smaller portion consists of people who are consistently uninsured, and an even smaller portion consists of people who do not have any type of health insurance for the long term (Joint Economic Committee, 2004). Many researchers have outlined the factors that contribute to the large uninsured population and explored how the uninsured affect the United States as a whole. The consequences of such a large uninsured population are immense and affect all of society through cost shifting, increased insurance premiums, and higher taxes. The nationwide impact of the uninsured was the major reason for the Obama administration's urgency in passing health insurance reform in 2010.

The United States is usually admired worldwide for its advanced science, technology, and medical research, and as a result many Americans benefit from being citizens of the country (American College of Physicians, 2000). Unfortunately, the benefits of American medicine are available only to those who can obtain healthcare services. For many Americans, a series of barriers prevent them from obtaining healthcare services.

In the United States, the most common barrier to receiving healthcare services is an inability to pay (Agency for Healthcare Research and Quality [AHRQ], 1997). The Henry J. Kaiser Family Foundation (2006) reports that the high cost of health insurance is the number one reason that people of any age are uninsured. "Uninsured Americans (38%) reported that they had delayed treatment for a serious illness during the past year" (Blendon, Brodie, Benson, Altman, & Buhr, 2006, p. 627). Because many of the uninsured do not have a regular source of care, they tend to wait longer to see a physician. They also lack regular access to preventive services. These two factors can result in a late-stage diagnosis of disease, leading to an even bigger health cost burden for the insured (Cairns & Viswanath, 2006). It is a known fact that the uninsured's access to care is less than the access afforded to the insured.

ACCESS AFTER THE AFFORDABLE CARE ACT

Health insurance reform, not health reform, was realized in the form of the ACA. The ACA brought broad sweeping changes to the U.S. healthcare delivery system. It guarantees access to healthcare services for more Americans and creates incentives for medical practitioners to focus on better coordination and higher quality services (Kocher, Emanuel, & DeParle, 2010).

The ACA and its changes are impacting multiple populations within the United States. The law expands health insurance to millions of individuals. Its changes target coverage expansion, equality, workforce growth, healthcare information, public health, overall wellness, and quality improvement (Somers & Mahadevan, 2010). By expanding coverage to nearly 16 million people, different healthcare service options have become available to many individuals.

The ACA proposes to improve access to health insurance in four main ways (Somers & Mahadevan, 2010). First, the individual mandate requires that all individuals have qualifying or acceptable coverage. Second, the employer mandate dictates that all employers with 50 or more employees must provide insurance coverage. Third, the regional and state health insurance exchanges allow individuals and small businesses to purchase coverage with varying benefits and costs and choose from subsidized plans. Fourth, the expansion of Medicaid eligibility extends Medicaid coverage to individuals living at up to 133% of the federal poverty level. Through increased awareness of service availability, individuals can increase their understanding of health care and adapt their behaviors accordingly.

The ACA took a major step toward reducing the uninsured population in the United States. As Kenney et al. (2012) explain, the act provides for coverage through Medicaid for people who have incomes below 138% of the federal poverty level and includes subsidies to those people who have incomes between 138% and 400% of the federal poverty level. Additionally, it prevents children with preexisting conditions from being rejected for coverage by health insurance providers, gives consumers more options for physician choices, allows for more preventive services, and extends coverage for young adults (Department of Health and Human Services [HHS], 2012). The Congressional Budget Office projects that the Affordable Care Act will increase the number of people with health insurance by 32 million (Kenney et al., 2012). However, one must keep in mind that insurance coverage does not necessarily guarantee access. Again, it is helpful to remember that actual access, in this case, requires the receipt of care.

Having health insurance is an extremely important tool for preventing illness (Shaffer, 2013). Under the Affordable Care Act, many preventive services are available for no cost or only a small fee. The importance of this factor should not be underemphasized. Having access to physicians for regular checkups and screenings can help prevent health complications down the road. If potential health problems are found early, their identification at an early stage can not only prevent costly medical bills and unexpected emergency room visits, but also save the patient from pain, suffering, and possible death. Access to primary care is critical in maintaining overall good health, and people who are covered by health insurance are more likely to access healthcare services such as primary care (HHS, 2012; Li, Dick, Fiscella, Conwell, & Friedman, 2011; Starfield & Shi, 2004).

Kocher, Emanuel, and DeParle (2010) summarized how the Affordable Care Act is likely to affect the healthcare delivery system in the future. Their predictions are helpful when trying to forecast how access to care will change in the coming years. They include a greater focus on the patient experience, changes in healthcare provider teams, accountable care organizations becoming more prominent, a focus on preventive care, and patients engaging in shared decision making related to delivery of services.

Kocher et al. (2010) suggest that bundled payments and incentive programs will make **accountable care organizations (ACOs)** and patient-centered medical homes more popular. The reorganization of physician reimbursement will have an impact on the way patients access physicians or **healthcare teams**. Related to the patient-centered medical home concept, the authors also argue that physicians will focus on proactively managing preventive care (p. 537). Others have also explained that education on disease prevention and the benefits of insurance will improve access to care (Hirasuna, 2007). This is an important concept in the new healthcare delivery system. Kocher et al. also forecast that patients will be engaging in more shared decision-making discussions with their physicians, another principle of the patient-centered medical home model.

As mentioned by Kocher et al. (2010), ACOs have the potential to impact the ease with which patients access the healthcare system. Gold (2011) describes an ACO as "a network of doctors and hospitals that shares responsibility for providing care to patients" (para. 4). ACOs existed before the Affordable Care Act was passed. They were first introduced into the lexicon in 2006 as a way to describe partnerships between hospitals and physicians to coordinate and deliver efficient care (Fisher, Staiger, Bynum, & Gottlieb, 2007). An ACO arrangement makes the provider of care and the patient jointly accountable for the well-being and health of the patient, which in turn provides incentives for providers to avoid unnecessary testing and procedures. Proponents of ACOs argue that these organizations not only allow physicians to provide better quality and slow spending growth, but also allow for patients to play a greater role in how they access the system (McClellan, McKethan, Lewis, Roski, & Fisher, 2010).

MODELS OF CARE AND HOW THEY ARE EVOLVING

Hospitals

Hospitals have traditionally been the foundation of the United States healthcare system and were at one point growing relatively quickly (Niles, 2010). In the 1970s, there were approximately 7123 hospitals nationwide, a significant increase since 1960 ("The Nation's Hospitals," 1971). This period of time also saw the growth of community hospitals that offered more complex procedures ("The Nation's Hospitals," 1971). In the 1980s, for-profit hospitals were becoming more common to the detriment of smaller nonprofit hospitals. In fact, more than 600 community hospitals closed during this time frame (Prince & Ramanan, 1994). Simultaneously, both for-profit and nonprofit hospitals began forming health systems. In the 2000s, many hospitals—especially public hospitals that served as safety nets—closed at an increasing rate (Wall, 2012).

Although hospitals still play an important role in the U.S. healthcare system, the method of their delivery of services changed over time. At the same time that health systems were growing, outpatient and other types of ambulatory care facilities became more common. Health insurance companies and the federal government's desire to control exploding healthcare costs both substantially contributed to this shift (Barr & Breindel, 1999). To adapt to the new cost-consciousness, more and more hospitals and health systems have integrated various types of outpatient services into their health systems (Niles, 2010). As Barr and Breindel (1999) explained, ambulatory care services include "diagnostic and therapeutic procedures and treatments provided to the patient in a setting that does not require an extended overnight stay in a hospital" (p. 431). While ambulatory care does not include a lengthy time in the hospital, this category of care can include hospital-based and non-hospital-based services.

Urgent Care Centers

Urgent care centers have become a popular type of walk-in clinic over the past several decades. While they are not the foundation of the U.S. healthcare system, they do play an important role in it. Urgent care centers emerged as early as 1970, then reached their peak in the mid-1980s. These types of clinics usually provide unscheduled acute but nonemergent care (McNeeley, 2012). Urgent care clinics usually provide extended primary care services during weekdays, evenings, and weekends on a walk-in basis (Yee, Lechner, & Boukus, 2013).

Access problems have helped pave the way for urgent care clinics to become more popular. As of 2012, there were approximately 9000 urgent care clinics spread across the United States (McNeeley, 2012). The shortage of primary care providers has left a gap in the provision of care, causing patients to move toward urgent care. Many healthcare providers and their related health systems are optimistic about the potential of these types of clinics to continue to improve access and reduce emergency department visits (Yee et al., 2013).

Patient-Centered Medical Homes

While having a primary care physician is not a new idea, the concept of patient-centered medical homes (PCMHs) is relatively new. The National Committee for Quality Assurance (NCQA; 2014) defines a PCMH as a model of care delivery where the emphasis is on **care coordination** and communication among the patient, primary care providers, and specialists. Collaboration and ongoing relationships are established to achieve and understand all medical needs, whether those needs are primary, secondary, acute, chronic, or preventive care, while actively engaging and educating the patient throughout the duration of his or her care. These concepts help to illustrate the idea of **patient-centered care**.

In 2007, the "Joint Principles of the Patient-Centered Medical Home" were articulated by the Patient-Centered Primary Care Collaborative (PCPCC), an umbrella organization involving four professional medical organizations representing primary care specialties. These principles include (1) the assignment of a personal physician, (2) a whole-person orientation, (3) coordination and integration of care, (4) the use of information technology and patient input to maintain and enhance quality and safety, (5) enhanced access to care, and (6) a payment schedule that appropriately recognizes the added value provided to patients who are members of a PCMH (PCPCC, 2007).

PCMHs are also intended to support the communication and coordination of care between primary care physicians and specialists (PCPCC, 2007). Recently, the NCQA operationalized these principles by identifying six "must-pass elements" for achieving NCQA recognition at any level access to care during office hours, the use of data for population management, care management, support of self-care processes, tracking of referrals and follow-up care, and the implementation of continuous quality improvement (NCQA, 2011).

The ACA provides physicians with incentives to change the way that they provide care. Overall, physicians and other medical professionals are seeking methods of coordinating their care efforts, resulting in patients getting the preventive care that they require. The medical home model provides a framework for physicians to coordinate care while providing patient-focused care. These are two very important developments following the implementation of the ACA.

Convenient Care Clinics

While they may appear similar to urgent care clinics, convenient care clinics (CCCs) are a more recent development. The CCC model provides an accessible, affordable entry point into the healthcare system. In this model, healthcare providers diagnose and treat common health problems, thereby reducing unnecessary visits to emergency departments and urgent care clinics (Lin, 2008). CCCs are primarily staffed by nurse practitioners or physician assistants, and there are an estimated 200 CCCs throughout the United States today. The clinics are often located in drug stores, food stores, and other retail settings with pharmacies, to enable patient accessibility. As Lin (2008) points out, these types of clinics usually make prices available before services are performed. This type of upfront pricing may be attractive to those who do not have health insurance.

Ownership of CCCs varies, with some being privately held and others being run by health systems or nonprofit organizations (Lin, 2008). In an era where coordination is being encouraged and incentivized, some argue that convenient care clinics pose a threat to quality. Both an ongoing relationship between the provider and the patient and provider access to patient medical records are essential to coordination (Hansen-Turton, Bailey, Torres, & Ritter, 2010). The existence of convenient care clinics is in direct conflict with this idea. In this type of setting, there is no ongoing provider–patient relationship, and providers usually do not have access to electronic health records. However, health systems may still see value in this easy-access model and decide to incorporate CCCs into their delivery service model. It will be up to healthcare leaders and decision makers to integrate these clinics into their systems or prepare to compete with them.

Federally Qualified Health Centers and Community Health Centers

The high cost of health insurance premiums has led many patients to seek care in community health clinics due to their lower costs (Stanley, Cantor, & Guarnaccia, 2008). Certain community health clinics qualify as federally qualified health centers (FQHCs). FQHCs receive grants under Section 330 of the Public Health Service Act (Health Resources and Services Administration (HRSA), n.d.). They also qualify for enhanced Medicare and Medicaid reimbursements. This healthcare safety net is intended to fill gaps in access to crucial health services for the uninsured and under-insured populations (Stanley et al., 2008). Previous studies have shown that, in general, community health centers help reduce the cost of ambulatory care–sensitive inpatient admissions, lower health disparities, lower medical costs, and are frequently associated with high quality and efficient care (Richard et al., 2012).

Many FQHCs have increased the number of services they provide and their responsibilities relative to patients in recent years (Hurley, Felland, & Lauer, 2007). Some of these organizations and health systems are forming associations with philanthropic organizations, safety net hospitals, and nonprofit hospitals to increase the amount of funding received for their services (Hurley et al., 2007).

Nurse-Managed Health Centers

One notable new model is the nurse-managed health center (NMHC). Similar to PCMHs, NMHCs focus on wellness promotion and disease prevention. The NMHC model of care emphasizes wellness promotion, disease prevention, and management of chronic disease. NMHCs can be either freestanding businesses or affiliated with universities or healthcare organizations (Institute for Nursing Centers Survey, 2008). Most of the care provided in NMHCs is provided by advanced practice nurses working in partnership with other healthcare workers (Pohl et al. 2010).

NMHCs have the potential to be successful after health insurance reform because they focus on preventive care and provide comprehensive care at a lower cost than other care providers. Thygeson, Van Vorst, Maciosek, and Solberg (2008) claimed that nurse-led models of care offer a significantly lower cost ($50–$55 per episode) than other models of care, such as the ones mentioned earlier in this chapter. Although the services provided in NMHCs vary and span the care continuum, they are usually divided into primary care practices or wellness clinics. The majority of clinics are wellness clinics (Institute for Nursing Centers Survey, 2008). In addition to offering low-cost options to consumers, the clinics have been cost-effective from a business standpoint, resulting in lower rates of hospitalization compared to other safety net options (Hansen-Turton et al., 2010).

TECHNOLOGICAL FACILITATION OF ACCESS

Technology has already had a huge impact on health care and will continue to do so as new technologies are developed and made available. Today, consumers have more information with which to make healthcare decisions because of the widespread availability of information technology. Healthcare providers, in turn, have more opportunities to utilize technology in care delivery, such as robotic surgery, e-prescribing, and clinical decision support systems that assist them with making diagnoses. The electronic health record (EHR) is an overarching tool that will continue to influence the way healthcare services are provided. The implementation of the EHR, which enables providers to share information about a patient's health history, will also provide the consumer with the opportunity to receive more cost-effective and efficient health care. EHRs allow for care coordination between patients, primary care providers, specialists, and other members of the healthcare team. However, EHRs alone will not facilitate total access; other types of technologies can also coexist with EHRs.

Telemedicine

Telemedicine utilizes computer technology to transmit data, voice, video, and a combination of the three with live video feeds. Telemedicine is emerging as a viable method of treating patients. A 2004 study found that patients receiving mental health services through two-way video conferencing had similar outcomes to those receiving traditional care with respect to the measurement of depression (Ruskin et al., 2004). Privacy can be maintained and perhaps even enhanced through the use of this technology. Treatment can be augmented with sensors that are worn to alert caregivers to changes in a patient's temperature, blood pressure, or biochemistry (Schopp, Demiris, & Glueckhauf, 2006).

In recent years, the use of video conferencing has become much more common, not only in the United States but around the world (Baer, Elford, & Cukor, 1997). While some providers have concerns about the provision of physical health services (e.g., diagnosis of physical ailments) via telemedicine, using telemedicine to diagnose and treat mental health issues is becoming more routine. Indeed, psychiatry appears to be an ideal specialty for the application of telemedicine because information is generally obtained using audiovisual communication (Baer et al., 1997).

In addition to the possibility of telemedicine becoming more routine, many argue that telemedicine is more cost-effective. While the initial purchase of this type of technology can be expensive, an increased patient volume can offset costs and help facilities implementing this technology realize positive financial returns (Ruskin et al., 2004).

The Health Resources and Services Administration (HRSA) has worked to increase the use of telemedicine in healthcare through the Office for the Advancement of Telehealth (OAT). OAT provides millions of dollars in competitive grants as an incentive for clinics to adopt telemedicine technology (Macrae, 2011). The very existence of OAT and the mention of telemedicine in the ACA illustrate the promise of this technology.

Mobile Health and Smartphone Apps

With the increased usage of smartphones and smartphone applications (apps) in the United States, it is no surprise the healthcare industry has introduction of mobile health options. "Mobile health" (mHealth) can be defined broadly as mobile technologies related to computing, medical sensors, and patient–provider communication (Istepanian, Jovanov, & Zhang, 2004). The difference between conventional telemedicine and mobile health is that mobile health involves portable devices. This type of technology provides yet another way for healthcare providers to evaluate and treat patients.

Although there are obstacles to mHealth implementation, portable devices are already being used in the U.S. healthcare delivery system. As of 2009, two-thirds of all physicians used some type of mobile technology in their practice of medicine, and more than 1500 healthcare-related apps were offered in Apple's App Store for the iPhone, iPad, and other devices (Sarasohn-Kahn, 2010). Healthcare apps can assist healthcare professionals with obtaining access to patient electronic medical records, reference systems, and decision support systems. They also provide a way for providers to interact with patients on a long-distance basis (Hamou et al., 2010). Patients can use these apps to communicate with their care provider (through video conferencing, text service, or basic voice communication) and to monitor and track their own health maintenance activities.

One downside to the growing use of smartphone apps is that the structure for service reimbursement is not yet in place (Noblin, Cortelyou-Ward, & Cantiello, 2012). While smartphone popularity does seem to be growing, not everyone has access to or can afford a smartphone—another constraint on the use of mHealth.

Health Kiosks

A health kiosk is a public access touchscreen or desktop/laptop interface (Jones, 2009). Integrated health kiosks are usually available in walk-in clinics, outpatient areas, community settings, pharmacies, and occupational settings. According to Glabman (2009), the use of health kiosks is a disruptive innovation that may have strong effects on the way healthcare services are delivered in the United States. One of the largest experimental health kiosk projects has been the Michigan Interactive Health Kiosk project, where more than 100 kiosks were placed in a community setting (Jones, 2009). Kiosks can facilitate "taking medical histories, health promotion, self-assessment, consumer feedback, patient registration, patient access to records, and remote consultations" (Jones, 2009, p. 1818).

Jones (2009) pointed out that many projects failed to achieve their goal of being used in routine practice, leading some to question the usefulness of health kiosks. However, some providers have been very successful in placing health kiosks in remote area pharmacies (Glabman, 2009). These kiosks have special attachments such as high-definition digital otoscopes, digital stethoscopes, and digital dermascopes. Such attachments allow a physician to obtain results that would normally be obtained from an in-person examination. In this setting, a technician or pharmacist collects a copayment and takes the medical history of the patient. Insurance companies have been willing to participate in this type of integrative model. Ensuring that services go beyond those offered over the Internet and that a technician is physically present to assist and collect payment are essential to ensuring the success of health kiosks.

The literature reveals that telemedicine—and other mobile health technologies, at least to some extent—can be successful in evaluating and treating certain physical and mental ailments. Health kiosks have also shown promise, but have yet to demonstrate long-term success. The type of technology used to implement telemedicine techniques and the infrastructure needed to support such technology do exist, but adoption of these technologies has not been rapid. To ensure their success, healthcare organizations and systems must be willing to operate in an open system that uses relevant telemedicine and mobile health technologies to their full extent, rather than just as adjuncts. The key for healthcare leaders is to focus on relevant technology that will move their organizations forward. As Collins (2001) has argued, technology should be an accelerator of momentum, not the creator of it. Healthcare organizations should build their delivery systems to support technology and integrate relevant services into their systems where appropriate.

HOW MANAGERS CAN FACILITATE ACCESS

The healthcare industry has entered a period of significant change, and as a result healthcare managers need to be prepared for numerous challenges on different fronts. These challenges relate to changes in reimbursement rates, EHR implementation, new models of care, and an increasing number of insured patients with access to the healthcare system (Fields, 2010, para. 1). Healthcare managers will need to determine which factors drive healthcare utilization. This is where the comprehensive definition of "access" becomes important. It will not be enough for healthcare managers to ensure access; they will also have to proactively ensure utilization.

Identifying who is likely to use specific services and when those services will be used will help organizations ensure the availability of appropriate healthcare services. Maintaining such a strategic outlook will also help managers identify new customers, spot consumer concerns, and ultimately increase customer satisfaction. This will require mass data collection techniques and research. Healthcare leaders should be employing evidence-based health services management. Kovner and Rundall (2006) asserted that both the application of clinical medicine and organizational behavior should be evidence based; this viewpoint should not be taken lightly by healthcare managers when studying consumer access behavior.

As noted previously, many hospitals have experienced financial problems in the past few decades. As a result of the increased competition with ambulatory and outpatient services (which are often more cost-effective, efficient, and consumer-friendly) and reduced reimbursement from Medicare and Medicaid, many hospitals have developed strategies to bolster their financial stability. In response to cost-containment measures, hospitals are forming huge hospital systems and building large physician workforces. To compete with the Affordable Care Act's mandated state healthcare exchanges, health insurance companies are also developing relationships with hospitals, creating joint marketing plans, and sharing patient data (Mathes, 2011). Again, the decision-making process behind such collaboration should include evidence from the field whenever possible.

While the list of models of care noted previously is not comprehensive, these models do provide examples of ways that outside parties can compete with established healthcare service providers in a given community. Healthcare managers need to be familiar with all of these possibilities. At the same time, healthcare managers may have opportunities to integrate these types of models into their own delivery systems. Indeed, many health systems have already embraced outpatient services as part of their patient care (Ambulatory Surgery Center Association, 2013). Regardless, healthcare managers should remember that in today's environment, coordination is of the utmost importance. The key to success is a fully integrated healthcare delivery system that focuses on care coordination and communication between healthcare providers (specialists and generalists), as well as other members of the healthcare team. Waste and the repetition of medical tests should be eliminated whenever possible. While healthcare managers do not provide direct patient care, they are involved with the provision of healthcare services and can implement efficient and high-quality models of care for patients. The role of healthcare leaders will hinge on their awareness of and openness to options for maximizing efficiency (reducing costs) while achieving the same or better outcomes.

CHAPTER SUMMARY

Competition in the private sector has led to innovative solutions that focus on disease management, evidence-based medicine, investments in technology, and **healthcare information technology**. Continued focus on new and innovative ideas is needed for healthcare leaders to ensure access. To address the challenges that are occurring as a result of massive changes in the healthcare industry, members of the healthcare team should utilize informed and innovative thinking, distinctive technological tools, coordinated care pathways, and teamwork.

Healthcare organizations should look into redesigning their current processes and reorganizing the services they offer. Healthcare systems should work to bring health services closer to the consumer. To successfully redesign health services, deal with change, and manage access under a changed healthcare system, solutions need to be implemented gradually and at different levels. However, all parts of the solution should be interrelated and focused on achieving the same goal. Ultimately, this goal should center on patients remaining healthy and having access to a healthcare system that is cost-effective and efficient. If these goals are met, healthcare leaders will greatly improve healthcare access.

The passage of the Affordable Care Act has created an environment that favors **integration** across the **continuum of care**. In the past, only major systems or healthcare plans were able to afford the necessary investments in information technology and management skills required for full integration. As healthcare providers reorganize themselves in different ways (e.g., patient-centered medical home practices, accountable care organizations), they are investing in information technology and proven business models (Kocher et al., 2010). Over time these tools are becoming more affordable, and the experimental analysis of health models is allowing for smaller healthcare entities to realize true integration. A focus on access to and coordination of healthcare services is essential to ensuring the provision of the right healthcare service at the right time for the right population.

The aforementioned ideas, models, and types of technologies will be helpful to healthcare leaders looking to adapt to a changing healthcare delivery system. However, these leaders should also pay special attention to the overall direction in which these models are moving the healthcare industry. Specific models should not box in healthcare leaders. Instead, leaders should develop the capacity to think ahead and be free to introduce new ideas within their organizations.

Key Terms and Concepts

Access: The availability of healthcare services as well as the provision or delivery of actual healthcare services, the provision or delivery of the appropriate healthcare services, and some mechanism (i.e., health insurance) that facilitates access.

Accountable care organization (ACO): A group of physicians, and possibly other healthcare providers such as hospitals, who come together voluntarily to accept collective accountability for the quality and cost of care delivered to their patients.

Affordable Care Act: Formally, the Patient Protection and Affordable Care Act; federal legislation passed in 2010 that guarantees access to healthcare services for more Americans and creates incentives for medical practitioners to focus on better coordination and higher quality services.

Care coordination: Cooperation among physicians and other medical professionals to ensure patients get the care that they require.

Continuum of care: The full range of healthcare services options.

Healthcare information technology: Information systems and technologies that support the delivery of healthcare services; these information systems are tightly integrated with the business and clinical functions of the health system and are managed and supported by skilled professionals within the IS function of the organization.

Healthcare teams: Groups of healthcare providers who coordinate their efforts to ensure patient-centered care.

Integration: In health care, a system in which "care providers have established relationships and mechanisms for communicating and working together to coordinate patient care across health conditions, services, and care settings over time" (Institute of Medicine, 2001).

Patient-centered care: The establishment of collaboration and ongoing relationships to achieve and understand all medical needs, whether those needs are primary, secondary, acute, chronic, or preventive care, while actively engaging and educating the patient throughout the duration of his or her care.

Questions to Consider

1. Differentiate between the availability and provision of healthcare services.

2. How do high insurance premiums make access to healthcare services difficult?

3. Summarize the main ways that the implementation of the Affordable Care Act will affect access to healthcare services in the United States.

4. Which models of care do you see being the most successful after the implementation of the Affordable Care Act?

5. Summarize how technology can facilitate access to healthcare services.

6. What can healthcare managers do to facilitate access to healthcare services?

REFERENCES

Aday, L. A., & Andersen, R. M. (1981). Equity to access to medical care: A conceptual and empirical overview. *Medical Care, 19*(suppl), 4–27.

Agency for Healthcare Research and Quality (AHRQ). (1997). Millions face barriers to obtaining medical care. Retrieved from http://archive.ahrq.gov/news/press/barriers.htm

Ambulatory Surgery Center Association. (2013). Ambulatory surgery centers: A positive trend in health care. Retrieved from http://www.ascassociation.org/Resources/ViewDocument/?DocumentKey=7d8441a1-82dd-47b9-b626-8563dc31930c

American College of Physicians. (2000). No health insurance? It's enough to make you sick: Scientific research linking the lack of health coverage to poor health. Retrieved from http://www.acponline.org/acp_policy/policies/no_health_insurance_scientific_research_linking_lack_of_health_coverage_to_poor_health_1999.pdf

Andersen, R. M. (1995). Revisiting the behavioral model and access to medical care: Does it matter? *Journal of Health and Social Behavior, 36*, 1–10.

Andersen, R., & Newman, J. F. (1973). Societal and individual determinants of medical care utilization in the United States. *Milbank Memorial Fund Quarterly: Health and Society, 51*, 95–124.

Baer, L., Elford, R., & Cukor, P. (1997). Telepsychiatry at forty: What have we learned. *Harvard Review of Psychiatry, 5*, 7–17.

Barr, K. W., & Breindel, C. L. (1999). Ambulatory care. In L. F. Wolper (Ed.), *Health care administration: Planning, implementing, and managing organized delivery systems* (3rd ed., pp. 507–546). Sudbury, MA: Jones and Bartlett.

Blendon, R. J., Brodie, M., Benson, J. M., Altman, D. E., & Buhr, T. (2006). Americans' views of health care costs, access, and quality. *Milbank Quarterly, 84*, 623–657. doi: 10.1111/j.1468-0009.2006.00463.x

Cairns, C. P., & Viswanath, K. (2006). Communication and colorectal screening among the uninsured: Data from the Health Information National Trends Survey (United States). *Cancer Causes Control, 17*, 1115–1125.

Collins, J. C. (2001). *Good to great: Why some companies make the leap—and others don't*. New York, NY: HarperBusiness.

Department of Health and Human Services (HHS). (2012). Justification of estimates for appropriations committees. Retrieved from http://www.cms.gov/About-CMS /Agency-Information/PerformanceBudget/downloads/CMSFY12CJ.pdf

Donabedian, A. (1973). *Aspects of medical care administration: Specifying requirements for health care*. Cambridge, MA: Harvard University Press.

Fields, R. (2010, September 14). 5 ways hospitals will change over the next 10 years. *Becker's Hospital Review*. Retrieved from http://www.beckershospitalreview.com /hospital-management-administration/5-ways-hospitals-will-change-over-the-next-10-years.html

Fisher, E. S., Staiger, D. O., Bynum, J. P. W., & Gottlieb, D. J. (2007). Creating Accountable Care Organizations: The Extended Hospital Medical Staff. *Health Affairs, 26*, 44–57.

Glabman, M. (2009, January). Disruptive innovations that will change your life in health care. *Managed Care Magazine*. Retrieved from http://www.managedcaremag.com /archives/0901/0901.disruptive.html

Gold, J. (2011). Accountable care organizations, explained. Retrieved from http://www .npr.org/2011/04/01/132937232/accountable-care-organizations-explained

Gulliford, M., Figueroa-Munoz, J., Morgan, M., Hughes, D., Gibson, B., Beech, R., & Hudson, M. (2002). What does "access to health care" mean? *Journal of Health Services Research & Policy, 7*, 186–188.

Hamou, A., Guy, S., Lewden, B., Bilyea, A., Gwadry-Sridhar, F., & Bauer, M. (2010). Data collection with iPhone Web apps efficiently collecting patient data using mobile devices. *Proceedings of the 12th IEEE International Conference on e-Health Networking Applications and Services, Lyon*, 235–239. doi: 10.1109/HEALTH.2010.5556565

Hansen-Turton, T., Bailey, D. N., Torres, N., & Ritter, A. (2010). Nurse-managed health centers: Key to a healthy future. *American Journal of Nursing, 110*, 23–26.

Health Resources and Services Administration. (n.d.). Telehealth. Retrieved from http://www.hrsa.gov/ruralhealth/about/telehealth/

Henry J. Kaiser Family Foundation. (2006). Employee health benefits: 2007 annual survey. Retrieved from http://www.kff.org/insurance/7672/index.cfm

Hirasuna, D. (2007). Universal health coverage: An economist's perspective. Retrieved from http://www.house.leg.state.mn.us/hrd/pubs/univhlth.pdf

Hurley, R. E., Felland, L. E., & Lauer, J. (2007, December). Community health centers tackle rising demands and expectations. Retrieved from http://www.hschange .com/CONTENT/958/

Institute for Nursing Centers Survey. (2008). Retrieved from http://nursingcenters.org /PDFs/INC%20Highlight%20Report%2010_6_08.pdf

Institute of Medicine. (2001, March). Crossing the quality chasm: A new health system for the 21st century. Retrieved from https://www.iom.edu/~/media/Files /Report%20Files/2001/Crossing-the-Quality-Chasm/Quality%20Chasm%20 2001%20%20report%20brief.pdf

Istepanian, R. S. H., Jovanov, E., & Zhang, Y. T. (2004). Introduction to the special section on m-health: Beyond seamless mobility and global wireless health-care connectivity. *Information Technology in Biomedicine, 8*, 405–414.

Joint Economic Committee. (2004). *The complex challenge of the uninsured.* Washington, DC: U.S. Government Printing Office.

Jones, R. (2009). The role of health kiosks in 2009: Literature and informant review. *International Journal of Environmental Research and Public Health, 6,* 1818–1855. doi: 10.3390/ijerph6061818

Kenney, G. M., Zuckerman, S., Dubay, L., Huntress, M., Lynch, V., Haley, J., & Anderson, N. (2012, August). Opting in to the Medicaid expansion under the ACA: Who are the uninsured adults who could gain health insurance coverage? Retrieved from http://www.urban.org/uploadedpdf/412630-opting-in-medicaid.pdf

Kocher, R., Emanuel, E. J., & DeParle, N. M. (2010). The Affordable Care Act and the future of clinical medicine: The opportunities and challenges. *Annals of Internal Medicine, 153,* 536–539. doi: 10.7326/0003-4819-153-8-201010190-00274

Kovner, A. R., & Rundall, T. G. (2006). Evidence-based management reconsidered. *Frontiers of Health Services Management, 22,* 3–22.

Li, C., Dick, A. W., Fiscella, K., Conwell, Y., & Friedman, B. (2011). Effect of usual source of care on depression among Medicare beneficiaries: An application of a simultaneous-equations model. *Health Services Research, 46,* 1059–1081.

Lin, D. Q. (2008). Convenient care clinics: Opposition, opportunity, and the path to health system integration. *Frontiers of Health Services Management, 24,* 3–11.

Macrae, J. (2011). Process for becoming eligible for Medicare reimbursement under the FQHC benefit. Retrieved from http://bphc.hrsa.gov/policiesregulations/policies/pal201104.html

Mathes, S. (2011). Implementing a caring model. *Creative Nursing, 17,* 36–42.

McClellan, M., McKethan, A. N., Lewis, J. L., Roski, J., & Fisher, E. S. (2010). A national strategy to put accountable care into practice. *Health Affairs, 29,* 982–990. doi: 10.1377/hlthaff.2010.0194

McNeeley, S. (2012). Urgent care centers: An overview. *American Journal of Clinical Medicine, 9,* 80–81.

Mechanic, D. (1972). *Public expectations and health care.* New York, NY: Free Press.

Millman, M. (Ed.). (1993). Institute of Medicine (U.S.), Committee on Monitoring Access to Personal Health Care Services. *Access to health care in America.* Washington, DC: National Academy Press.

National Committee for Quality Assurance (NCQA). (2011). NCQA's patient center medical home (PCMH) 2011. Retrieved from http://www.ncqa.org/portals/0/programs/recognition/PCMH_2011_Overview_5.2.pdf

National Committee for Quality Assurance (NCQA). (2014). Patient-centered medical home recognition. Retrieved from http://www.ncqa.org/Programs/Recognition/Practices/PatientCenteredMedicalHomePCMH.aspx

Niles, N. J. (2010). *Basics of the U.S. health care system.* Burlington, MA: Jones & Bartlett Learning.

Noblin, A., Cortelyou-Ward, K., & Cantiello, J. (2012). Utilizing telemedicine techniques to confront rural mental health care challenges: The progression towards a technological health ecosystem. *Journal of Health & Medical Informatics, 7,* 1–5. doi: 10.4172/2157-7420.S7-001

Patient-Centered Primary Care Collaborative (PCPCC). (2007, February). Joint principles of the patient-centered medical home. Retrieved from http://www .aafp.org/dam/AAFP/documents/practice_management/pcmh/initiatives /PCMHJoint.pdf

Penchansky, R., & Thomas, J. W. (1981). The concept of access: Definition and relationship to consumer satisfaction. *Medical Care, 19*, 127–140.

Pohl, J. M., Tanner, C., Batkauskas, V. H., Gans, D. N., Nagelkerk, J., & Flandt, K. (2010). Toward a national nurse-managed health center data set: Findings and lessons learned over 3 years. *Nursing Outlook, 58*, 97–103. doi:10.1016/j. outlook.2009.10.003

Prince, T. R., & Ramanan, R. (1994). Operating performance and financial constraints of Catholic community hospitals. *Health Care Management Review, 19*, 38–48.

Racher, F. E., & Vollman, A. R. (2002). Exploring the dimensions of access to health services: Implications for nursing research and practice. *Research and Theory for Nursing Practice: An International Journal, 16*, 77–90. doi: 10.1891/088971802780956651

Richard, P., Ku, L., Dor, A., Tan, E., Shin, P., & Rosenbaum, S. (2012). Cost savings associated with the use of community health centers. *Journal of Ambulatory Care Management, 35*, 50–59. doi: 10.1097/JAC.0b013e31823d27b6

Rodriquez, M. (2003). Young, happy—and uninsured. Retrieved from http://www .mvhealth.com/local/03-08-29-insured.htm

Rogers, A., & Sheaff, R. (2000). Formal and informal systems of primary healthcare in an integrated system: Evidence from the United Kingdom. *Healthcare Papers, 1*, 47–58.

Ruskin, P. E., Silver-Aylaian, M., Kling, M. A., Reed, S. A., Bradham, D. D., Hebel, J. R., & Hauser, P. (2004). Treatment outcomes in depression: Comparison of remote treatment through telepsychiatry to in-person treatment. *American Journal of Psychiatry, 161*, 1471–1476.

Sarasohn-Kahn, J. (2010, April). How smartphones are changing health care for consumers and providers. Retrieved from http://www.chcf.org/publications /2010/04/how-smartphones-are-changing-health-care-for-consumers-and-providers

Schopp, L. H., Demiris, G., & Glueckauf, R. L. (2006). Rural backwaters or front-runners? Rural telehealth in the vanguard of psychology practice. *Professional Psychology: Research and Practice, 37*, 165–173.

Shaffer, E. R. (2013). The Affordable Care Act: The value of systemic disruption. *American Journal of Public Health, 103*, 969–972.

Smith, J. C., & Medalia, C. (2014). *Health Insurance Coverage in the United States: 2013*. U.S. Census Bureau, Current Population Reports, P60-250. Washington, DC: U.S. Government Printing Office. Retrieved from http://www.census.gov/content /dam/Census/library/publications/2014/demo/p60-250.pdf

Somers, S. A., & Mahadevan, R. (2010). Health literacy implications of the Affordable Care Act. Retrieved from http://www.iom.edu/~/media/Files/Activity%20Files /PublicHealth/HealthLiteracy/Commissioned-Papers/Health%20Literacy%20 Implications%20of%20Health%20Care%20Reform.pdf

Stanley, A., Cantor, J. C., & Guarnaccia, P. (2008). Holes in the safety net: A case study of access to prescription drugs and specialty care. *Journal of Urban Health: Bulletin of the New York Academy of Medicine, 85,* 555–571.

Starfield, B., & Shi, L. (2004). The medical home, access to care, and insurance: A review of evidence. *Pediatrics, 113,* 1493–1498.

The nation's hospitals: A statistical profile. (1971). *Hospitals, 44,* 463–468.

Thygeson, M., Van Vorst, K. A., Maciosek, M. V., & Solberg, L. (2008). Use and costs of care in retail clinics versus traditional care sites. *Health Affairs, 27,* 1283–1292. doi: 10.1377/hlthaff.27.5.1283

Wall, B. M. (2012). Hospitals: From charitable guesthouses to scientific centers. Retrieved from http://www.nursing.upenn.edu/nhhc/Essays/History_of_Hospitals_edited10_02.pdf

Yee, T., Lechner, A. E., & Boukus, E. R. (2013, July). The surge in urgent care centers: Emergency department alternative or costly convenience? Retrieved from http://www.hschange.com/CONTENT/1366/1366.pdf

Behavioral Economics and the Challenges of Managing an Integrated Healthcare System

—Douglas E. Hough, PhD

LEARNING OBJECTIVES

- Understand the concepts of behavioral economics.
- Analyze issues in health care through the lens of behavioral economics.
- Create strategies for managing clinicians based on the principles of behavioral economics.
- Create strategies for influencing the behavior of the population served by an integrated healthcare system, based on the principles of behavioral economics.

INTRODUCTION

The behavior of patients and healthcare providers has fascinated economists for decades. To what extent can patients really be consumers, especially in those instances when their "demand" is for acute care? Even in the cases of decisions that do not need to be made immediately, do patients ever have sufficient information to act as effective consumers? To what extent do physicians act like profit-maximizing firms? Do physicians act like effective agents on behalf of their patients, or do they create demand by ordering more services than patients really need?

Mainstream, neoclassical economists have struggled to explain patient and provider behavior in health care. Neither patients nor physicians seem to follow the standard economic models. Patients do not appear to be making "rational" decisions: They lack information (and do not appear to demand information the way they do for other goods and services); they do not seem to have pre-set preferences regarding treatment (except that "more care is better care"), and their decisions are often swayed by the opinions of others and by how options are presented to them. For their part, physicians do not act like true profit-maximizers—or like demand manipulators. They seem to make clinical and business decisions based on habit and rules of thumb. It appears as if the assumptions of neoclassical economics just do not fit the behavior of those in health care.

The scenario in health care involves imperfect people making imperfect decisions. Patients often insist on receiving a prescription for a drug or an order for a lab or imaging test when they visit a physician. Physicians often accede to these patient demands, even though they know that the prescriptions or tests are—at best—placebos. For example, Barnett and Linder (2014) found that physicians prescribed antibiotics for 60% of the patient visits related to sore throat, even though antibiotics are appropriate in only 10% of such cases. In another study, the researchers found that physicians prescribed antibiotics for 73% of the bronchitis cases that were presented (although only 5% of bronchitis cases are bacterial in origin). The irony is that despite this bias for action, only 75% of patients actually get their prescriptions filled, and 25% of those who do fill their prescriptions fail to adhere to the medication instructions (DiMatteo, 2004; Fischer et al., 2010).

For their part, physicians exhibit similar kinds of irrationality. Almost all physicians are dedicated to serving their patients and would never do anything to jeopardize the health of their patients. Yet, more than 160 years after Ignaz Semmelweis discovered the connection between physician hand washing and the transmission of disease, physicians adhere to good hand washing practices only half of the time (World Health Organization, 2009).

Neoclassical economists have a difficult time in explaining this seemingly irrational behavior. Traditional economics has assumed that people may not be perfect, but—at least, most of the time—they act "as if" they are making decisions perfectly. If they do make mistakes, they make random mistakes. An emerging field of economics, known as behavioral economics, offers a much different approach, by accepting the imperfections and biases of human decision making. Behavioral economics is only beginning to be applied to health care, but its approach has considerable potential to better explain and predict what is happening in this arena.

In this chapter, we present the core concepts of behavioral economics and contrast them with those of neoclassical economics. We discuss the policy levers that behavioral economics presents for influencing behavior. We than apply behavioral economics concepts to health care, specifically to explain the operations of integrated delivery systems and to suggest ways that the behavior of patients and providers can be improved to advance their own interests and achieve the goals of integrated delivery systems. Finally, we consider some "what if" scenarios and questions to ponder to build on the concepts presented here.

CORE CONCEPTS IN BEHAVIORAL ECONOMICS

Differences Between Neoclassical and Behavioral Economics

Before we consider the specific aspects of behavioral economics, we should note the differences between this field and standard, neoclassical economics. Every theory of economics rests on several critical assumptions about how a market is structured and how buyers and sellers behave in this market. Here is where neoclassical economics and behavioral economics first diverge. Let us consider five basic assumptions in these fields.

The first assumption is irrationality. Neoclassical economics assumes that everyone is rational. That is, buyers and sellers, individuals and organizations, always act in their own best interests. (Otherwise, they will not make decisions that promote their well-being, as measured by happiness/satisfaction for consumers and profits for sellers, and neoclassical economics then would be unable to explain or predict human behavior.) Behavioral economics, in contrast, acknowledges that not everyone is rational, at least not all the time. As a result, buyers and sellers do not always act in their own best interests.

The second assumption deals with preferences. Neoclassical economics assumes that all participants in the market know their preferences. In fact, consumers have a "utility function," which maps out their preferences and the trade-offs that they would be willing to make among different goods and services. Behavioral economics assumes that people do not have a utility function, but rather learn their preferences through experience, via trial and error. In addition, they make decisions based on their current situation (which acts like a reference point), not from some overarching utility function.

Third, neoclassical economics assumes that all participants in the market have full information—about the products in the market, their features and drawbacks, and the prices being offered and asked. Understandably, if consumers are not aware of the alternatives that are available to them, it will be difficult for them to make the right decisions. Similarly, sellers need to know about the preferences of consumers and the range of products being offered by competitors if they are to offer the right product at the right price. Behavioral economics assumes that information is incomplete and asymmetric. Sometimes the buyer does not have enough information, such as when she is buying a used car from its owner. Sometimes it is the seller who lacks information, such as an insurance company writing a life insurance policy for an individual; the buyer knows his behavior, health history, and other risk factors, but the insurer does not.

A fourth, somewhat less intuitive assumption of neoclassical economics is that consumer preferences and decisions are path independent. That is, consumers' preferences and decisions do not depend on how they arrive at those preferences or decisions. Conversely, behavioral economists assert that preferences are, indeed, path dependent. Economic decisions are often influenced by factors independent of the individual: Consumers buy differently if they are shown a more expensive house before a less expensive house, a fully equipped car before a stripped-down model, a 52-inch LCD television before a more modest one.

Finally, even neoclassical economists admit that consumers and producers sometimes make mistakes. Nevertheless, these economists assume that the mistakes are random. Thus, if people miss the mark in making decisions that improve their situation, sometimes they will be above the mark, and sometimes they will be below it—and we have no way to predict which mistakes they will make. Behavioral economists, however, contend that deviations from rational choice are systematic and predictable. It is perhaps this aspect of behavioral economics that ultimately sets it apart conceptually from neoclassical economics and provides the focal point for testing the relative effectiveness of the two approaches for understanding human behavior.

Another difference between behavioral and neoclassical economics involves the process by which people make decisions. Daniel Kahneman, winner of the Nobel Prize in Economics in 2002 for his work on behavioral economics, posits two distinct approaches to decision making: System 1 and System 2. Some psychologists have called System 1 "experiential" or "intuitive" and System 2 "analytic" or "reflective," but Kahneman uses the neutral terms to indicate that both approaches have value (and drawbacks). **System 1 thinking** is fast, effortless, and automatic, and often is used when the decision maker is skilled and experienced in the task at hand. In fact, she might be so skilled and experienced that she cannot explain how she made the decision. **System 2 thinking**, in contrast, is relatively slow, effortful, controlled, and deductive. The decision maker can explain—sometimes in great detail—how he made the decision (Kahneman & Frederick, 2002).

Neoclassical economics assumes (at least implicitly) that people use System 2 thinking in making economic decisions. They take their time, weigh alternatives, and factor in costs. They may not be experts and they may make mistakes, but they can explain—and justify—their decisions. Behavioral economics, for its part, recognizes that people use both System 1 and System 2 thinking when they make decisions, economic related or otherwise. As we shall see, this orientation allows behavioral economics to explain certain behaviors in health care more accurately than does neoclassical economics.

Core Concepts

With this background, we turn to a series of concepts that are fundamental in behavioral economics. Although the field is only three decades old and still in the process of solidifying the theory (and even the terminology), certain concepts have been tested and found to be robust. Those robust concepts that will be discussed here include the following:

- Loss aversion
- The endowment effect
- Framing
- The power of the default (also known as opt-in versus opt-out)
- Hyperbolic discounting

Loss Aversion

Behavioral economics begins with the observation that people hate losses; in fact, evidence suggests that they hate losses almost twice as much as they like gains. This behavior, which Kahneman and Tversky (1979) termed "loss aversion," contradicts the contention of neoclassical economics that people maximize the expected utility of gains and losses.

The exact form of this behavior is shown in **Figure 4–1**. The figure on the left-hand side indicates that behavioral economics assumes that people do not start with a fully formed utility function; rather, they start from their current position, the status quo. They view changes as either gains to, or losses from, that reference point. Kahneman and Tversky (1979) posit that people tend to be risk averse in gains, but risk loving in losses (hence, the tendency of gamblers to "double down" when they are losing). In addition, the figure shows that a gain of x generates a much lower value than a loss of x generates a loss of value—hence, loss aversion is present.

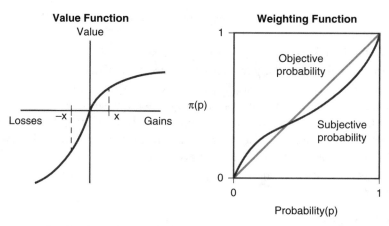

Figure 4-1 The Simple Analytics of Behavioral Economics

The figure on the right-hand side shows another aspect of loss aversion: People do not simply apply objective probabilities when they evaluate risks. Rather, they tend to overweight small probabilities and underweight large probabilities. In fact, a number of studies (e.g., Kunreuther, Novemsky, & Kahneman, 2001) have shown that people do not meaningfully distinguish among a one in 10,000 chance, a one in 100,000 chance, and a one in 1 million chance. If that is the case, then the expected utility theory of neoclassical economics breaks down.

The Endowment Effect

One way in which loss aversion manifests itself is in a concept known as the "**endowment effect**," which states that people tend to value something—a thing, a product, an idea—more highly once they have it. Behavioral economists have found the endowment effect in a wide variety of situations. The experiment that first demonstrated this effect in economics was conducted by Jack Knetsch (1989) with three classes of students. In the first class, students were given a coffee mug, and told that it was in compensation for their completing a short questionnaire. When they handed in the questionnaire, they were given the option to trade their mug for a bar of Swiss chocolate. (The mug and the chocolate had about the same retail value.) In the second class, students were given the bar of Swiss chocolate and then asked to complete the same short questionnaire. When they were finished, they were given the option to trade their chocolate bar for a coffee mug. Finally, students in the third class were given a choice between the mug and the chocolate bar before they completed the questionnaire. Neoclassical economists would predict that roughly the same percentage of students in each class would select the coffee mug. After all, people know whether they like coffee mugs or chocolate bars, and the different sequence and timing should make no material difference. That is not what happened, however. Although 56% of those in the third class chose a coffee mug, 89% of those in the first class chose to keep their coffee mug, and only 10% of those in the second class chose to trade their chocolate bar for the mug.

What happened? Knetsch concluded that possession of the coffee mug or the chocolate bar changed the students' perception of the value of the product. Perhaps they felt that they "earned" what they were given, or perhaps they perceived that having to make a decision between the two was too taxing. Or perhaps they felt that surrendering what they had just been given represented a loss—one that was greater than the expected gain from getting the other object. That is, they may have experienced loss aversion.

Framing

Given that people view gains and losses differently, it is not surprising that they view alternatives in different ways depending on whether the alternatives are presented as gains or losses. Tversky and Kahneman (1986) termed this phenomenon *framing*. According to these authors, "Framing is controlled by the manner in which the choice problem is presented as well as by norms, habits, and expectancies of the decision maker" (p. S257). As noted earlier, neoclassical economists contend that rational individuals will see through the framing and focus on the objective facts of the situation. Unfortunately for them, a number of studies (as well as centuries of product marketing) have demonstrated otherwise.

A classical study of framing in health care was conducted by Barbara McNeil and her colleagues (McNeil, Pauker, Sox, & Tversky, 1982). Three distinct groups of people—238 men with chronic medical problems, 424 radiologists, and 491 MBA students from Stanford Business School—were asked to consider that they had just been told that they had lung cancer, which was treatable by either surgery or radiation therapy. Half of each group were given the following statistics: Of 100 people having surgery, 90 live through the postoperative period, 68 are alive at the end of the first year, and 34 are alive at the end of 5 years. Of 100 people having radiation therapy, all live through the therapy period, 77 are alive at the end of the first year, and 22 are alive at the end of 5 years. The other half were told the following: Of 100 people having surgery, 10 die during surgery or the postoperative period, 32 die by the end of the first year, and 66 die by the end of 5 years. Of 100 people having radiation therapy, none die during the therapy period, 23 die by the end of the first year, and 78 die by the end of 5 years. A careful reader will note that the information in both presentations is identical, except that the first was presented in a survival frame and the second in a mortality frame. Despite the expectations of neoclassical economics that individuals ought to be able to make the same decision regardless of the presentation frame, 18% preferred radiation therapy in the survival frame and 44% preferred that treatment in the mortality frame. Perhaps equally surprising, the framing effect occurred with the same magnitude for all three groups—physicians, patients, and students—despite their significant differences in age, income, education, and experience with illness.

Power of the Default

Many situations have an unavoidable initial position; we have to start somewhere. We use English measurements or the metric system. Features on new cars are either standard or optional. The candy can be placed in the middle of the supermarket or at the checkout lane. What behavioral economists have discovered is that where you start makes a difference: The initial, or default, position has a powerful effect on behavior.

A famous study illustrates this point. Eric Johnson and Daniel Goldstein (2003) examined the rate at which adults in European countries register to be potential organ donors. In four of the countries—Denmark, the Netherlands, the United Kingdom, and Germany—between 4% and 27% of adults are registered organ donors. In the other seven countries—Austria, Belgium, France, Hungary, Poland, Portugal, and Sweden—the organ donation rate ranges from 86% to 99%. Although there are some cultural and historical differences among these countries, there is seemingly nothing that could explain these extraordinary differences. Johnson and Goldstein note that the first four countries use an "opt-in" or "explicit consent" approach, in which adults who want to be organ donors must sign up. The other countries have an "opt-out" or "presumed consent" system, in which adults are automatically enrolled as organ donors, but can opt out of the program if they wish. Neoclassical economists would argue that such differences would persist only if people were not informed of the initial assignment or told how to change their status, or if it were expensive (in time or money) to make a change. It turns out that none of these explanations addresses the seemingly anomalous behavior. It is fairly easy to change from the default position in these countries.

What does explain this dramatic difference in behavior? Several factors come into play. First, the default can act as an implicit recommendation or endorsement by the government or society: "Everyone else is registered as an organ donor. I haven't thought about it much, but I guess it must be a good idea." A second factor may be just inertia. People in Belgium or Portugal may want to opt out, but never quite get around to doing so. Third, the default could be an example of the endowment effect—that is, the default position becomes the endowment, and people will change from the default only if the alternative is demonstrably better. Finally, Richard Thaler and Cass Sunstein, in their book *Nudge* (2008), argue that defaults are a way by which the potentially ill-formed preferences of people can be given a push—a "nudge"— to what presumably they would have chosen themselves had they thought about it.

Hyperbolic Discounting

People prefer the present to the future; that is, they discount the future relative to the present. Hence, people demand a premium (i.e., an interest rate) to give up money today for money in the future. Economists have typically assumed that people have an exponential discount rate, which has two attractive properties: The discount rate is constant over time, and value declines proportionally over time. An exponential discount rate means that if an individual prefers $100 today to $200 two years from now, she would also prefer $100 eight years from now to $200 ten years from now. As it turns out, this behavior often does not happen; as has been demonstrated (Ainslie & Haslam, 1992), this individual is more likely to prefer the $200 ten years from now to the $100 in eight years. Her preferences are "time inconsistent" and follow what is called a hyperbolic discount function. People who exhibit hyperbolic discounting have a higher discount rate and prefer the present much more than the short-term future, but have a lower discount rate and are relatively indifferent between years in the long-term future. This becomes a problem because people will make decisions about the long-term future that they will regret once that future becomes the present, such as saving for their children's college, retirement, or nursing home care.

Policy Levers in Behavioral Economics

Neoclassical economics provides decision makers with essentially one instrument to influence behavior: price. It is price that drives much of economics, in large part because of the contention that individuals and organizations seek to balance the marginal benefits and the marginal costs of any action. As we have seen, people—and even organizations—can be driven by factors that are outside this rational calculus. Because it acknowledges and understands these factors, behavioral economics gives decision makers at governmental and organizational levels some additional levers to influence behavior. At the same time, it recognizes that human beings sometimes work in mysterious ways and cannot be expected to respond in lock-step fashion to all interventions. (As physicist and Nobel laureate Murray Gell-Mann once said, "Think how hard physics would be if particles could think.")

In some sense, an entire spectrum of approaches can be taken to influence behavior. The first such approach is information or education. It supposes that individuals intend to "do the right thing" but lack sufficient information to do so, in terms of either motivation or method. The second approach is persuasion: In addition to information, the individual needs to be convinced to do the right thing.

The third approach, which has been widely adopted in manufacturing, air travel, and, more recently, health care, is guidelines or checklists. Guidelines can represent the consensus or "best practice" methods used by experienced practitioners in the area. Checklists require practitioners to engage System 2 thinking on procedures that they perform routinely and, therefore, usually rely on System 1 thinking. The checklist is expected to ensure that the practitioner (e.g., airline pilot) addresses all salient and material issues involved in a procedure (e.g., pre-flight safety checks) for which errors may have disastrous results.

Penalties and rewards, the fourth potential approach, is the favorite of most neoclassical economists. People can be paid for performance, and they can be fined for lack of performance. By manipulating the size of the incentive, the policymakers can change the individuals' calculations of marginal benefits and marginal costs and, in turn, their decisions.

Behavioral economics provides several additional policy levers. The first is **commitment devices**—voluntary programs in which people in a rational state of mind use System 2 thinking to prepare for future situations in which they know that they will be less likely to behave rationally and fail to achieve an important goal. The model for commitment devices is "Christmas Clubs," which were popular in the first half of the twentieth century. With these programs, people would deposit money on a regular basis in a low- (or no-) interest-bearing savings account and would not be able to withdraw their money until December, when they could use it to buy Christmas presents. Those who used Christmas Clubs said that the programs gave them the discipline they needed to save. A contemporary version of the Christmas Club is stickK.com, in which people interested in achieving a goal develop a commitment contract on the site, which specifies the goals (e.g., weight loss, regular exercise), the stakes for not achieving the goals (e.g., money, reputation, and the recipient of the stakes), a designated referee, and a support group. The commitment device creates accountability both to oneself and to others.

A second policy lever from behavioral economics is defaults. As discussed earlier, defaults are based on the premise that a starting point must be selected. Given the power of many defaults, Thaler and Sunstein (2008) assert that policymakers have an important role in creating what they call "choice architecture." **Choice architecture** dictates, among other things, the form of the default, the extent to which the default reflects what the individuals would have chosen without the default, the degree of transparency of the default (so that the individuals can perceive that a default choice has been made for them), and the ease with which individuals can opt out of the default. As may be obvious, a beneficent nudge can turn into a dictatorial shove if the nudger believes that the nudgee is not sufficiently responsive to the nudge.

A variation on defaults is the forced choice. Instead of being presented with an opt-in or opt-out structure, the individual could be forced to make a choice, thereby revealing his or her true preference. For example, the Department of Motor Vehicles could require a motorist to choose whether to be an organ donor (that is, an explicit choice) before receiving a license renewal. This approach has the advantage of eliciting an individual's preferences directly rather than inferring or interfering with those preferences. Two downsides of this approach are that an individual may not be ready to make such a choice at that moment, and the person may make a hasty choice just to accomplish the original goal (i.e., obtain a driver's license).

Beyond these levers from behavioral economics, two others need to be mentioned. One is mandates, which remove choice but often leave a loophole (if enforcement is lax). In some sense, a mandate is a default without the opportunity to change the default. It is useful if the consequences of voluntary action are not sufficient. For example, parents might be mandated to have their children vaccinated, so as to ensure that communicable diseases do not spread throughout a community.

The other lever is coercion or compulsion. This approach—although extreme—could be appropriate (even in a democratic society) if the consequences of noncompliance threatened the society's very existence. An example would be a quarantine for those persons having an extremely infectious disease.

Within all these policy levers (especially those utilizing the concepts of behavioral economics) exist a multitude of details and variations that need to be considered. Although a comprehensive discussion of these factors is beyond the scope of this chapter, it is worthwhile to mention some of the basic details.

- Will the intervention employ **social norms** (i.e., "This is what we do here") or economic norms (i.e., "We will you give you this reward if you change your behavior")?
- If economic norms are used, will they be financial or nonfinancial (e.g., gift cards, tangible gifts, time)?
- Are the interventions intended to last for a short period or a long time?

- Do the behavior modifications require one-time, short-term or persistent, long-term changes?
- What is the possibility that the interventions (what Edward Deci [1971] calls "extrinsic motivation) crowd out and supplant people's intrinsic motivations to change their behavior?

APPLICATION OF BEHAVIORAL ECONOMICS TO INTEGRATED DELIVERY SYSTEMS

Organizations are beginning to use the insights from behavioral economics to improve their performance, and that of their employees and customers. (In fact, for decades marketers have exploited what is now known as behavioral economics to entice potential customers.) Examples include the following cases:

- Using defaults to improve employees' contributions to retirement plans (Madrian & Shea, 2001)
- Using incentives to encourage employee participation in wellness programs (Mattke et al., 2013)
- Setting monthly and per-use prices to encourage customers to select the more expensive monthly plans (DellaVigna & Malmendier, 2006)

Behavioral economics has only recently been used by healthcare organizations to improve employee, patient, and organization behavior. In this section, we review how the field has been applied and consider its potential.

Managing Healthcare Organizations and People

Today, healthcare organizations in the United States are undergoing significant stress. The theory of the business of hospitals, physicians, and health systems is becoming obsolete, and healthcare leaders know that they need to realign—if not reinvent—their organizations. Yet, they also know that many stakeholders in their organizations will resist any meaningful change. The causes for this resistance have been identified elsewhere, but the concepts of behavioral economics may yield some useful perspectives, and perhaps more importantly some new levers of change. Consider loss aversion and the endowment effect. Those in hospitals—employees, physicians, trustees, and even patients—are comfortable with the current structure and payment system (even if they bewail its inefficiencies and inequities). People will resist having their "endowment" taken away, especially if system leaders cannot guarantee that the new environment will be better.

How, then, to convince these naturally reluctant participants to change? Here are some potential solutions from behavioral economics.

- *Use the "none die" framing.* Make the case that staying the course will inevitably lead to a worse situation, including failure of the organization. Although hospitals have proved remarkably adept at surviving the many changes they have faced during the past three decades, leaders need to persuade employees, physicians, and trustees that this time really is different.
- *Create opportunities for early wins under the new paradigm.* As we saw earlier in this chapter, many people use hyperbolic discounting in their decision making. If all they see from change is financial and psychic costs for the time being, with prospects of benefits and better days delayed until the distant future, they will succumb to the "slough of despond" and lose productivity. To address this issue, leaders need to create shorter milestones for success and create tangible rewards for reaching those intermediate targets.
- *Give upfront contingent bonuses for reaching targets.* An intriguing study in a suburb of Chicago found that teachers responded most when they were given bonuses at the beginning of the school year, which they would have to give back if their students did not achieve targeted test scores (Fryer, Levitt, List, & Sadof, 2012). Such incentives in a healthcare organization might accomplish two things: demonstrate senior leadership's confidence in the workforce and take advantage of the endowment effect to induce reluctant employees to adopt the new paradigm.

Managing Physicians: A Special Case?

Obviously, physicians are a key element in creating and maintaining an integrated healthcare system. From an economic structure standpoint, the relationship between physicians and hospitals (or health systems) in the United States has been a peculiar one. For the most part, physicians have been neither employees nor owners of hospitals, yet they direct a large part of the allocation of resources in hospitals. This relationship has been changing rapidly, though, as hospitals and systems have been acquiring physician practices and employing physicians. Many healthcare organizations are finding it challenging to manage physicians profitably. Perhaps the concepts of behavioral economics can provide some helpful insights.

To see how this relationship might evolve, we should start with the basics. It has been known since the work of Ignaz Semmelweis in the 1840s that physician hand washing greatly reduces the transmission of disease to patients.

Yet, as mentioned earlier in this chapter, more than 160 years later physicians wash their hands, on average, less than half of the time that they should (World Health Organization, 2009). Why would physicians ignore a century and a half of history and evidence, given that they care about their patients and do not wish to do them harm? Clinicians themselves cite lack of time, irritation or dryness of hand washing agents, priority of patient needs, and even forgetfulness as reasons why they do not always wash their hands when they should. The core answer, however, may be something more fundamental. Think about the earlier discussion about System 1 and System 2. Physicians learn their craft using System 2, but over time they practice medicine largely using System 1. They use heuristics or rules of thumb in many patient encounters, and these heuristics serve them well. (For example, they need only a few seconds to determine that a patient who presents with fever and stiff neck most likely has meningitis.) Thus, over time, based on their own experience and what they see their colleagues do, physicians develop their own heuristics about hand washing. They may convince themselves that they are following best practices, even when they are not. One study found physicians estimated that they were 71% adherent to hand washing guidelines, when the observed rate was only 9% (Handwashing Liaison Group, 1999). Physicians will continue to use their own heuristics until they are given compelling evidence that other approaches are better (in particular, better for their patients).

Another, perhaps more dire, example is central line–associated bloodstream infections (CLABSIs). It was not until 2007 that the magnitude of this problem was revealed, when a Centers for Disease Control and Prevention (CDC) study reported that 82,000 CLABSIs occurred in U.S. hospital ICUs, leading to 20,000 deaths (Klevens et al., 2007). Dr. Peter Pronovost and his team at Johns Hopkins University developed a simple, five-step checklist for clinicians to use when they placed central lines into patients. They successfully implemented the checklist in 103 hospitals in Michigan, reducing infection rates to near zero (Pronovost et al., 2006). Despite this success, Pronovost was unable to replicate the Michigan success in New Jersey and Maryland (the home of Johns Hopkins), and efforts to reduce CLABSIs have taken much longer to implement than anyone would have expected. Why would this be so?

In his book on the topic, Pronovost relates his struggle to convince his colleagues at Hopkins to adopt the checklist: "What was striking was that nobody debated the evidence, nobody challenged the items on the checklist, and nobody questioned whether we should do them. But everyone objected to the change in culture. The doctors saw it as a loss—a loss of power and respect" (Pronovost & Vohr, 2010, p. 49). What the physicians were experiencing was loss aversion, even when they understood the benefits of change. In addition, Pronovost and his team were asking physicians to replace their longstanding heuristics. In the abstract, the new heuristic makes sense, but when the physician is faced with inserting a central line, he or she is likely to revert to the System 1 thinking and the previous heuristic.

How, then, to engage physicians to do what they know is right? The tenets of behavioral economics would suggest a couple of approaches:

- *Teach physicians to engage both System 1 and System 2 in their clinical decision making.* This recommendation may be obvious, but it also might sound naïve. Time-pressed physicians are not likely to slow down. However, Dr. Pat Croskerry (2009), an expert in medical decision making, advocates teaching medical students and young physicians what he calls "a universal model of diagnostic reasoning." In this process a physician engages both System 1 and System 2 thinking. If a patient presents with symptoms that are familiar to a physician, she uses System 1; if the symptoms are not as familiar, then she uses System 2. The key, according to Croskerry, is that the physician must allow either system to override the other.

- *Make new research findings more salient to the individual clinician.* Practicing physicians do not have time to review and integrate every new medical finding. Researchers and research consortia (such as the Cochrane Collaboration) need to frame their findings in ways that clinicians can use, especially if the findings represent a change from current practice.

- *Frame practice changes in terms of improving patient care and reducing harm to patients.* Recent research (Grant & Hofmann, 2011) demonstrated that hand washing adherence increased by almost 50% when the messaging focused on the impact of hand washing on patients rather than on the physician's own health. Physicians are altruistic by nature, so reminding them of their better nature will be a more effective nudge than other appeals.

- *Try lots of approaches.* A systematic review of strategies to disseminate and implement clinical guidelines for physicians found interventions that depended on a single intervention—education, reminders, performance feedback, or financial incentives—had only short-term effects (Grol & Grimshaw, 2003). By comparison, multifaceted interventions were much more successful in changing physician practice patterns and improving patient outcomes.

Managing Patients and Populations

Hospitals, physician practices, and integrated delivery systems have always been concerned with the health of the patients who present for diagnosis and treatment. With healthcare reform, it is highly likely that these organizations will also need to concern themselves with the health of the entire population in their service area, regardless of whether community members are "patients." Given that people can make imperfect decisions about their health care, we should consider the potential for behavioral economics to be able to explain and influence this behavior.

As I discuss in my book on behavioral economics and health care (Hough, 2013), there are any number of ways in which people do not act entirely rationally when it comes to their healthcare decisions:

- They insist on getting a prescription, shot, test, or some other intervention when they come to a physician with an illness, even though such treatments are unnecessary, and some may even be counterproductive.
- Even when they receive what they are asking for, they do not adhere to their treatment regimens.
- They make different treatment choices when benefits and risks are presented in different ways.
- Their bad habits (e.g., overeating, smoking, alcoholism) are easy to form and hard to break, and their good habits (e.g., exercising, eating nutritious food) are hard to form and easy to break.

These are significant challenges when hospitals, physicians, and health systems are dealing with patients. They become even more complex when these organizations are expected to be responsible for the health of populations, many of which will not engage with healthcare providers as traditional patients. In a sense, integrated delivery systems will need to manage both health behaviors and expectations. Behavioral economics may be able to provide some guidance in how to accomplish these tasks. One note of caution, however: A variety of experiments have tried to "de-bias" people—that is, to cure them of their irrational tendencies; almost none of these interventions have worked, suggesting that this behavior is deeply engrained in human beings. As a result, interventions should be targeted to working around the biases and irrationalities, rather than trying to educate people to do the right thing.

Consider the challenge of managing the expectations of patients and populations. The current social norm in health care goes as follows: (1) People can neglect their health until their health is threatened; (2) once ill, people can expect access to any and all health services as their right, with only partial financial responsibility; and (3) once treated, people can return to their prior lifestyles. This social norm has created a dynamic that may have been financially sustainable for health providers who were paid on a fee-for-service basis. In a population- and outcomes-based world, however, that norm is no longer viable. The challenge to integrated health systems is try to change the norm, a difficult but not impossible task. In fact, the public health field has demonstrated that it is possible to change norms; witness the effective campaigns in favor of seat belts and safe sex and against drunk driving and smoking in public places. But it was not easy: These campaigns required long-term, sustained efforts with multiple approaches that demonstrated high-profile consequences to the behavior to be changed. To transform the well-entrenched norms of health care will require an equivalent commitment.

Perhaps somewhat easier is changing the actual health behaviors of individuals. Kevin Volpp and his colleagues have found success in incentivizing people to lose weight (Volpp, John, Troxel, Norton, Fassbender, & Lowewenstein, 2008), stop smoking (Volpp et al., 2009), and improve medication adherence (Volpp, Loewenstein, et al., 2008). Even this work, however, demonstrates the difficulty of designing interventions that require long-term behavior change (in Volpp et al.'s studies, behavior regressed once the incentives ended) and that can be scaled up from small studies. Nevertheless, it is a first step.

Another health behavior that might be amenable to interventions from behavioral economics is medication adherence. As mentioned earlier in this chapter, one-fourth of patients fail to adhere to instructions regarding their medications: They do not take their medications at the right time, they take a different dosage than prescribed, or they stop taking the drugs before they are supposed to. Of course, a variety of potential reasons for such nonadherence exist: cognitive impairment, lack of trust in the prescribing physician, the complexity of treatment, or the cost of the medication (Osterberg & Blaschke, 2005). That being said, a significant body of evidence supports behavioral economics hypotheses regarding nonadherence. Several studies note that adherence rates are higher among patients receiving acute care than for those receiving chronic care, and among patients undergoing short-term treatment than among those undergoing long-term treatment (Sackett & Snow, 1979), which reflect hyperbolic discounting. In addition, adherence is higher when refills are sent automatically and when the patient expects to see the physician shortly.

More generally, an integrated delivery system needs to find other mechanisms for influencing the health of the population of the community, especially when the residents are not patients per se. Possibilities include the following measures:

- *Raising the "affect" of health behaviors.* One reason that people do not always engage in healthy behaviors (or avoid unhealthy ones) is they are not aware of the consequences of their behavior. Objective statistics rarely are influential; more powerful are descriptions of people like them who followed the good or bad behaviors.

- *Publicizing new social norms to both providers and lay people.* In 2012, the ABIM Foundation created the "Choosing Wisely" campaign, in which specialty societies named five tests or procedures in their discipline that have been found to be of little or no value (but which physicians often order or patients often request). Publicizing these tests and procedures could change the attitude of clinicians and patients, or at least give clinicians an authority to invoke when patients demand them.
- *Creating defaults.* In addition to publicizing the Choosing Wisely items, integrated delivery systems could create a default by which these kinds of tests and procedures are not scheduled unless the ordering physician provides sufficient evidence of their need. As we have seen with defaults in general, the mere presence of the default will dissuade many clinicians from ordering them.
- *Developing commitment devices.* Combined with the power of social norms, healthcare systems could sponsor contests among communities to lose weight (think "The Biggest Loser"), control diabetes, and minimize prescription drug abuse. Community leaders could pledge to perform menial—but useful—tasks in other communities if their area fails to meet its health targets. In addition, successful communities could be given cash prizes as well as public amenities not otherwise available.

FINAL THOUGHTS

The ideas presented in this chapter should be considered just a starting point for the application of behavioral economics to integrated healthcare systems. Here are some scenarios in which the tools of this field might be useful in finding creative solutions:

- Scenario 1: The health system has succeeded in creating an accountable care organization, and has been able to secure contracts with Medicare and the two largest private payers to accept financial risk for the population in its service area. The service area has an overweight rate of 73% and an obesity rate of 41%. About half of those who are overweight or obese are frequent users of the system, but the other half rarely come to a hospital, clinic, or physician practice associated with the system.
- Scenario 2: Orthopedic surgeons in each hospital in the system have agreed to use the same implant for all their knee surgeries. Unfortunately, the chosen implant differs from hospital to hospital. The system could save significant costs by ordering a single implant

from one manufacturer, and all of the devices perform about the same clinically. The surgeons are private practitioners and could switch their affiliation to a number of other, non-system hospitals if they think that the system is treating them unfairly or interfering with their practice autonomy.

- Scenario 3: The health system has offered wellness programs for its employees for about a decade and has seen spotty success with their usage. Some programs (e.g., free or deeply subsidized gym memberships, yoga classes) are well subscribed, but mostly by people who are already healthy. The system once mandated that all employees complete a free health assessment, but got significant pushback from many employees (and from the SEIU local representing service workers). The system is facing rapidly increasing costs for its self-insured employee health plan.

CHAPTER SUMMARY

Behavioral economics is an emerging field that yields new insights into human behavior by relaxing the neoclassical economics assumption of perpetual rationality. It reveals that people often act irrationally, albeit in a predictable way. Although the field is very new, a number of its key concepts—loss aversion, the endowment effect, framing, the power of defaults, hyperbolic discounting—have been validated in multiple experiments and applications. Behavioral economists have only recently begun to apply their concepts and tools to health care. However, it is evident that the field can explain and predict the behavior of patients, physicians, and managers.

In this chapter, we considered how behavioral economics could be applied to integrated healthcare systems, both in the current fee-for-service environment and in the nascent population health-based world. We found some interesting applications, and we should expect more to emerge in the future. Nevertheless, it is important to realize that we are analyzing human behavior, and humans have a way of making decisions that cannot be completely predicted.

KEY TERMS AND CONCEPTS

Choice architecture: A framework created by decision makers that dictates the form of a default, the extent to which the default reflects what individuals would have chosen without the default, the degree of transparency of the default, and the ease with which individuals can opt out of the default.

Commitment devices: Voluntary programs in which people in a rational state of mind use System 2 thinking to prepare for future situations in which they know that they will be less likely to behave rationally and fail to achieve an important goal.

Endowment effect: The concept that people tend to value something—a thing, a product, an idea—more highly once they have it.

Framing: The concept that people view alternatives in different ways depending on whether the alternatives are presented as gains or losses.

Hyperbolic discounting: The concept according to which people have a higher discount rate and prefer the present much more than the short-term future, but have a lower discount rate and are relatively indifferent between years in the long-term future.

Loss aversion: The contention of behavioral economics that people act to avoid losses.

Power of the default (opt-in versus opt-out): The concept that the initial, or default, position has a powerful effect on behavior.

Social norms: Accepted and expected behaviors in a society (i.e., "This is what we do here").

System 1 thinking: Thinking that is fast, effortless, and automatic, and often is used when the decision maker is skilled and experienced in the task at hand.

System 2 thinking: Thinking that is relatively slow, effortful, controlled, and deductive.

Questions to Consider

1. What is the evidence that patients, physicians, and managers in the U.S. healthcare sector do not always act rationally?

2. What is the evidence that patients, physicians, and managers in your system do not always act rationally?

3. To what extent could your system establish defaults to improve the health behaviors of patients and physicians?

4. How can employee wellness programs be structured to attract those who need it and save the system money?

5. What would be required to encourage physicians in the system to adopt state-of-the-art medical practices, without antagonizing them?

6. How can the health system engage those people in the community who rarely come to the system's facilities yet need to improve their health?

REFERENCES

Ainslie, G., & Haslam, N. (1992). Hyperbolic discounting. In G. Loewenstein, & J. Elster (Eds.), *Choice over time* (pp. 57–92). New York, NY: Russell Sage Foundation.

Barnett, L. J., & Linder, J. A. (2014). Antibiotic prescribing to adults with sore throat in the United States, 1997–2010. *Journal of the American Association Internal Medicine, 174*, 138–140.

Croskerry, P. (2009). A universal model of diagnostic reasoning. *Academic Medicine, 84*, 1022–1028.

Deci, E. L. (1971). Effects of externally mediated rewards on intrinsic motivation. *Journal of Personality and Social Psychology, 18*, 105–115. doi: 10.1037/h0030644

DellaVigna, S., & Malmendier, U. (2006). Paying not to go to the gym. *American Economic Review, 96*, 694–719.

DiMatteo, M. R. (2004). Variations in patients' adherence to medical recommendations: A quantitative review of 50 years of research. *Medical Care, 42*, 200–209.

Fischer, M. A., Stedman, M. R., Lii, J., Vogeli, C., Shrank, W. H., Brookhart, M. A., & Weissman, J. S. (2010). Primary medication non-adherence: Analysis of 195,930 electronic prescriptions. *Journal of General Internal Medicine, 25*, 284–290. doi: 10.1007/s11606-010-1253-9

Fryer, R. G., Levitt, S. D., List, J., & Sadof, S. (2012). *Enhancing the efficacy of teacher incentives through loss aversion: A field experiment.* Cambridge, MA: National Bureau of Economic Research.

Grant, A. M., & Hofmann, D. A. (2011). It's not all about me. *Psychological Science, 22*, 1494–1499. doi: 10.1177/0956797611419172

Grol, R., & Grimshaw, J. (2003). From best evidence to best practice: Effective implementation of change in patients' care. *Lancet, 362*, 1225–1230.

Handwashing Liaison Group. (1999). Hand washing: A modest measure—with big effects. *BMJ, 318*, 316.

Hough, D. (2013). *Irrationality in health care: What behavioral economics reveals about what we do and why.* Stanford, CA: Stanford University Press.

Johnson, E. J., & Goldstein, D. (2003). Do defaults save lives? *Science, 302*, 1338–1339.

Kahneman, D., & Frederick, S. (2002). Representativeness revisited: Attribute substitution in intuitive judgment. In T. Gilovich, D. Griffin, & D. Kahneman (Eds.), *Heuristics and biases: The psychology of intuitive judgment* (pp. 49–81). New York, NY: Cambridge University Press.

Kahneman, D., & Tversky, A. (1979). Prospect theory: An analysis of decision under risk. *Econometrica, 47*, 263–292.

Klevens, R. M., Edwards, J. R., Richards, Jr., C. L., Horan, T. C., Gaynes, R. P., Pollock, D. A., & Cardo, D. M. (2007). Estimating health care–associated infections and deaths in U.S. hospitals, 2002. *Public Health Reports, 122*, 160–166.

Knetsch, J. L. (1989). The endowment effect and evidence of nonreversible indifference curves. *American Economic Review, 79*, 1277–1284.

Kunreuther, H., Novemsky, N., & Kahneman, D. (2001). Making low probabilities useful. *Journal of Risk and Uncertainty, 23,* 103–120.

Madrian, B. C., & Shea, D. F. (2001). The power of suggestion: Inertia in 401(k) participation and savings behavior. *Quarterly Journal of Economics, 116,* 1149–1187.

Mattke, S., Liu, H., Caloyeras, J., Huang, C. Y., Van Busum, K. R., Khodyakov, D., & Shier, V. (2013). *Workplace wellness programs study: Final report.* Santa Monica, CA: RAND Corporation.

McNeil, B., Pauker, S., Sox, H., & Tversky, A. (1982). On the elicitation of preferences for alternative therapies. *New England Journal of Medicine, 306,* 1259–1262.

Osterberg, L., & Blaschke, T. (2005). Adherence to medication. *New England Journal of Medicine, 353,* 487–497.

Pronovost, P., Needham, D., Berenholtz, S., Sinopoli, D., Chu, H., Cosgrove, S., . . . Goeschel, C. (2006). An intervention to decrease catheter-related bloodstream infections in the ICU. *New England Journal of Medicine, 355,* 2725–2732.

Pronovost, P. J., & Vohr, E. (2010). *Safe patients, smart hospitals: How one doctor's checklist can help us change health care from the inside out.* New York, NY: Hudson Street Press.

Sackett, D. L., & Snow, J. C. (1979). The magnitude of compliance and noncompliance. In R. B. Haynes, D. W. Taylor, & D. L. Sackett (Eds.), *Compliance in health care* (pp. 11–22). Baltimore, MD: Johns Hopkins University Press.

Thaler, R. H., & Sunstein, C. R. (2008). *Nudge: Improving decisions about health, wealth, and happiness.* New Haven, CT: Yale University Press.

Tversky, A., & Kahneman, D. (1986). Rational choice and the framing of decisions. *Journal of Business, 59,* S251–S278.

Volpp, K. G., John, L. K., Troxel, A. B., Norton, L., Fassbender, J., & Loewenstein, G. (2008). Financial incentive-based approaches for weight loss: A randomized trial. *Journal of the American Medical Association, 300,* 2631–2637.

Volpp, K. G., Loewenstein, G., Troxel, A., Doshi, J., Price, M., Laskin, M., & Kimmel, S. (2008). A test of financial incentives to improve warfarin adherence. *BMC Health Services Research, 8,* 272.

Volpp, K. G., Troxel, A. B., Pauly, M. V., Glick, H. A., Puig, A., Asch, D. A., . . . Audrain-McGovern, J. (2009). A randomized, controlled trial of financial incentives for smoking cessation. *New England Journal of Medicine, 360,* 699–709.

World Health Organization. (2009). *WHO guidelines on hand hygiene in health care.* Geneva, Switzerland: Author.

Chapter 5

Financial Information, Financial Environments, Financial Viability, and the Decision-Making Process

—James O. Cleverley, MHA, William O. Cleverley, PhD,
and Paula Song, PhD

LEARNING OBJECTIVES

- Understand the importance of financial information in healthcare organizations.
- Identify the uses of financial information.
- Explain the common ownership forms of healthcare organizations, along with their advantages and disadvantages.
- Define financial functions within an organization.
- Understand the revenue cycles for healthcare firms.
- Describe factors that influence the financial viability of a healthcare organization.
- Identify the financial environment of the largest segments of the healthcare industry.

INTRODUCTION

In 1946, a small band of hospital accountants formed the American Association of Hospital Accountants (AAHA). They were interested in sharing information about and experiences in their industry, which was beginning to show signs of growth. A small educational journal, first published in

1947, attempted to disseminate information of interest to their members. Ten years later, in 1956, the AAHA's membership had grown to more than 2,600 members. The real growth, however, was still to come, with the advent of Medicare financing in 1965.

With the dramatic growth of hospital revenues came an escalation in both the number and functions delegated to the hospital accountant. Hospital finance, it quickly became apparent, encompassed much more than just billing patients and paying invoices. Hospitals were becoming big businesses with complex and varied financial functions. They had to arrange funding of major capital programs, which could no longer be supported through charitable campaigns. Cost accounting and management control were important functions to the continued financial viability of their firms. With this expansion in their responsibilities, hospital accountants soon evolved into hospital financial managers, and so the AAHA changed its name in 1968 to the Hospital Financial Management Association (HFMA).

The hospital industry continued to boom through the late 1960s and 1970s. Third-party insurance became the norm for most of the U.S. population. Patients either received it through government-sponsored programs such as Medicare and Medicaid or obtained it as part of the fringe benefit program at their place of employment. Hospitals were clearly no longer quite as charitable as they once were. There was money, and plenty of it, to finance the growth required through increased demand and the new evolving medical technology. By 1980, HFMA was a large association with 19,000 members. Its primary offices were located in Chicago, but an important office was opened in Washington, DC, to provide critical input to both the executive and legislative branches of government. On many issues that affected either government payment or capital financing, HFMA became the credible voice that policymakers sought.

The industry adapted and evolved even more in the 1980s, as fiscal pressure hit the federal government. Hospital payments were increasing so fast that new systems were sought to curtail the growth rate. Prospective payment systems (i.e., diagnosis-related groupings that are fixed in advance) were introduced in 1983, and alternative payment systems were developed that provided incentives for treating patients in an ambulatory setting. Growth in the hospital industry was still rapid, but other sectors of health care began to experience colossal growth rates, such as ambulatory surgery centers. To an ever increasing extent, health care was being transferred to the outpatient setting. The hospital industry was also no longer the only large corporate player in health care. In recognition of this trend, HFMA changed its name in 1982 to the Healthcare Financial Management Association so as to reflect the more diverse elements of the industry and to better meet the needs of members in other sectors.

In 2010, HFMA had more than 35,000 members in a wide variety of healthcare organizations. The daily activities of its members still involve basic accounting issues—patient bills must still be created and collected, and payroll still needs to be met—but strategic decision making is much more critical in today's environment. It would be impossible to imagine any organization planning its future without financial projections and input. Many healthcare organizations may still be charitable from a taxation perspective, but they are too large to depend on charitable giving to finance their business future. Financial managers of healthcare firms are involved in a wide array of critical and complex decisions that will ultimately determine the destiny of their firms.

This chapter is intended to improve decision makers' understanding and use of financial information in the healthcare industry. It is not an advanced treatise in accounting or finance, but rather an elementary discussion of how financial information in general and healthcare industry financial information in particular are interpreted and used. It is written for individuals who are not experienced healthcare financial executives. Its goal is to make the language of healthcare finance readable and relevant for general decision makers in the healthcare industry. Three interdependent factors are driving the need for such skills:

- Rapid expansion and evolution of the healthcare industry
- Healthcare decision makers' general lack of business and financial background
- Financial and cost criteria's increasing importance in healthcare decisions

The healthcare industry's expansion is a trend visible even to individuals outside the healthcare system. The hospital industry, which represents the major component of the healthcare industry, consumes about 5% of the United States' gross domestic product; other types of healthcare systems, although smaller than the hospital industry, are expanding at even faster rates. **Table 5-1** lists the types of major healthcare institutions and indexes their relative size.

Table 5-1 Healthcare Expenditures 2003-2012

	2012* (Projected)	2007*	2003*	Annual Growth Rate, 2007-2012 (%)
Total health expenditures	2930.7	2241.2	1734.9	5.5
Percentage of gross domestic product (%)	18.0	16.2	15.8	
Health services and supplies	2746.1	2098.1	1621.1	5.5
Personal health care	2446.3	1878.3	1447.5	5.4
Hospital care	931.7	696.5	527.4	6.0
Physician and clinical	604.5	478.8	366.7	4.8
Dental services	115.8	95.2	76.9	4.0
Home health	85.7	59.0	38.0	7.6
Other professional and personal health	180.7	128.2	99.4	7.1
Prescription drugs	288.8	227.5	174.2	4.9
Other medical products	71.3	61.8	54.5	2.9
Nursing home care	167.8	131.3	110.5	5.0
Expenses for prepayment and administration	213.4	155.7	121.9	6.5
Government public health	86.4	64.1	57.3	6.1
Research and construction	184.5	143.1	111.8	5.2

*Values are in billions of U.S. dollars, except for "Percentage of gross domestic product."
Courtesy of Centers for Medicare and Medicaid Services, Office of the Actuary.

THE IMPORTANCE OF FINANCIAL INFORMATION IN HEALTHCARE ORGANIZATIONS

The rapid growth of healthcare facilities providing direct medical services has substantially increased the number of decision makers who need to be familiar with financial information. Effective **decision-making** in their jobs depends on accurate interpretation of financial information. Many healthcare decision makers involved directly in healthcare delivery—physicians, nurses, dietitians, pharmacists, radiation technologists, physical therapists, and inhalation therapists—are medically or scientifically trained but lack education and experience in business and finance. Their specialized education, in most cases, did not include such courses as accounting. However, advancement and promotion within healthcare organizations (HCOs) increasingly entails assumption of administrative duties, requiring almost instant, knowledgeable reading of financial information. Communication with the organization's financial executives is not always helpful in this regard. As a result, nonfinancial executives often end up ignoring financial information.

Governing boards, which are significant users of financial information, are expanding in size in many healthcare facilities, in some cases to accommodate demands for more consumer representation. This trend can be healthy for both the community and the facilities. However, many board members, even those with backgrounds in business, may be over-whelmed by financial reports and statements. Important distinctions exist between the financial reports and statements of business organizations, with which some board members are familiar, and those of healthcare facilities. Governing board members must recognize these differences if they are to carry out their governing missions satisfactorily.

The increasing importance of financial and cost criteria in healthcare decision making is the third factor creating a need for more knowledge of financial information. For many years, accountants and others involved with financial matters have been caricatured as individuals with narrow vision, incapable of seeing the forest for the trees. In many respects, this depiction may have been an accurate portrayal. However, few individuals in the healthcare industry today would deny the importance of financial concerns, especially cost. Payment pressures from payers, as described in the scenario at the beginning of the chapter, underscore the need for atten-tion to costs. Careful attention to these concerns requires *knowledgeable* consumption of financial information by a variety of decision makers. It is not an overstatement to say that inattention to financial criteria can lead to excessive costs and eventually to insolvency.

The effectiveness of financial management in any business is the product of many factors, such as environmental conditions, personnel capabilities, and information quality. A major portion of the total financial management task is the provision of accurate, timely, and relevant information. Much of this activity is carried out through the accounting process. An adequate understanding of the accounting process and the data generated by it is, therefore, critical to successful decision making.

Information and Decision Making

The major function of information in general and financial information in particular is to "oil the wheels" of the decision-making process. Decision making is essentially the selection of a course of action from a defined list of possible or feasible actions. In many cases, the actual course of action followed may be essentially no action; decision makers may decide to make no change from their present policies. It should be recognized, however, that both action and inaction represent policy decisions.

Figure 5-1 shows how information is related to the decision-making process and gives an example to illustrate the sequence. Generating information is the key to decision making. The quality and effectiveness of decision making depend on accurate, timely, and relevant information. The difference between data and information is more than semantic: Data become information only when they are useful and appropriate to the decision. Many financial data never become information because they are not viewed as relevant or are unavailable in an intelligible form.

For the illustrative purposes of the ambulatory surgery center (ASC) example in Figure 5-1, only two possible courses of action are assumed: to build or not to build an ASC. In most situations, a continuum of alternative courses of action may exist. For example, an ASC might vary by size or the facilities included in the unit. In this case, prior decision making seems to have reduced the feasible set of alternatives to a more manageable and limited number of analyses.

Once a course of action has been selected in the decision-making phase, it must be accomplished. Implementing a decision may be extremely complex. In the ASC example, carrying out the decision to build the unit would require enormous management effort to ensure the projected results are actually obtained.

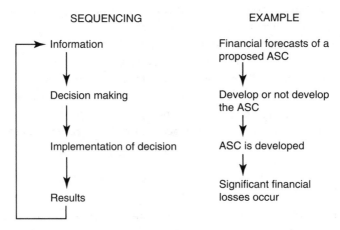

Figure 5-1 Information in the Decision Making Process

Periodic measurement of results in a feedback loop, as in Figure 5-1, is a method commonly used to make sure that decisions are actually implemented according to plan.

As previously stated, results that are forecast are not always guaranteed. Controllable factors, such as failure to adhere to prescribed plans, and uncontrollable circumstances, such as a change in reimbursement, may obstruct planned results.

Decision-making is usually surrounded by uncertainty. No anticipated result of a decision is guaranteed, because events may occur that have been analyzed but not anticipated. A results matrix concisely portrays the possible results of various courses of action, given the occurrence of possible events. **Table 5-2** provides a results matrix for the sample ASC; it shows that approximately 50% utilization will enable this unit to operate in the black and not drain resources from other areas. If forecasting shows that utilization of less than 50% is unlikely, decision makers may very well elect to build the facility.

A good information system should enable decision makers to choose those courses of action that have the highest expectation of favorable results. Based on the results matrix of Table 5-2, a good information system should specifically do the following:

- List possible courses of action
- List events that might affect the expected results
- Indicate the probability that those events will occur
- Estimate the results accurately, given an action–event combination (e.g., profit in Table 5-2)

Nevertheless, an information system alone does not evaluate the desirability of results. Decision makers must evaluate results in terms of their organizations' preferences or their own. For example, construction of an ASC might be expected to cause its owner to lose $200,000 per year, but it could provide a needed community service. Weighing these results and determining criteria

Table 5-2 Results Matrix for the ASC

Alternative Actions	Event		
	25% Utilization	50% Utilization	75% Utilization
Build unit	$400,000 loss	$10,000 profit	$200,000 profit
Do not build unit	0	0	0

are purely a decision maker's responsibility—not an easy task, but one that can be improved with accurate and relevant information.

THE USES OF FINANCIAL INFORMATION

As a subset of information in general, financial information is important in the decision-making process. In some areas of decision making, financial information is especially relevant. For our purposes, we identify five uses of financial information that may be important in decision making:

1. Evaluating the *financial condition* of an entity
2. Evaluating *stewardship* within an entity
3. Assessing the *efficiency* of operations
4. Assessing the *effectiveness* of operations
5. Determining the *compliance* of operation with directives

Financial Condition

Evaluation of an entity's financial condition is probably the most common use of financial information. Usually, an organization's financial condition is equated with its viability or capacity to continue pursuing its stated goals at a consistent level of activity. *Viability* is a far more restrictive term than *solvency*; some HCOs may be solvent but not viable. For example, a hospital may have its level of funds restricted so that it must reduce its scope of activity but still remain solvent. A reduction in payment rates by a major payer may be the vehicle for this change in viability.

Assessment of the financial condition of business enterprises is essential to the U.S. economy's smooth and efficient operation. Most business decisions in the economy are directly or indirectly based on perceptions of financial condition, including the decisions made by the largely nonprofit healthcare industry.

Although attention is usually directed at organizations as whole units, assessment of the financial condition of organizational divisions is equally important. In the ASC example, information on the future financial condition of the unit is valuable. If continued losses from this operation are projected, impairment of the financial condition of other divisions in the organization could be in the offing.

Assessment of financial condition also includes consideration of short-run versus long-run effects. The relevant time frame may change, depending on the decision under consideration. For example, suppliers typically are interested only in an organization's short-run financial condition because that is the period in which they must expect payment. By comparison, investment bankers, as long-term creditors, are interested in the organization's financial condition over a much longer time period.

Stewardship

Historically, evaluation of stewardship was the most important use of accounting and financial information systems. These systems were originally designed to prevent the loss of assets or resources through employees' malfeasance. This use remains very important. In fact, the relatively infrequent occurrence of employee fraud and embezzlement may in part reflect the deterrence effects of well-designed accounting systems.

Efficiency

Efficiency in healthcare operations is becoming an increasingly important objective for many decision makers. Efficiency is simply the ratio of outputs to inputs; it does not incorporate the quality of outputs (good or not good), but rather focuses on achieving the lowest possible cost of production. Adequate assessment of efficiency implies the availability of standards against which actual costs may be compared. In many HCOs, these standards may be formally introduced into the budgetary process. Thus, a given nursing unit may have an efficiency standard of 4.3 nursing hours per patient day of care delivered. This standard may then be used as a benchmark against which to evaluate the relative efficiency of the unit. If actual employment were 6.0 nursing hours per patient day, management would be likely to reassess staffing patterns.

Effectiveness

Assessment of the **effectiveness** of operations is concerned with the attainment of objectives through production of outputs, not the relationship of outputs to cost. Measuring effectiveness is much more difficult than measuring efficiency because most organizations' objectives or goals are typically not stated quantitatively. Because measurement of effectiveness is difficult, there is a tendency to place less emphasis on effectiveness and more on efficiency. This perspective may result in the delivery of unnecessary services at an efficient cost.

For example, development of outpatient surgical centers may reduce costs per surgical procedure, thereby creating an efficient means of delivery. However, the necessity of those surgical procedures may still be questionable.

Compliance

Financial information may be used to determine whether compliance with directives has taken place. The best example of an organization's internal directives is its **budget**, which comprises an agreement between two management levels regarding use of resources for a defined time period. External parties may also impose directives, many of them financial in nature, for the organization's adherence. For example, rate setting or regulatory agencies may set limits on rates determined within an organization. Financial reporting by the organization is required to ensure compliance.

THE USERS OF FINANCIAL INFORMATION

Table 5-3 presents a matrix of users and uses of financial information in the healthcare industry. It identifies areas or uses that may interest particular decision-making groups, but does not consider their relative importance.

Not every use of financial information is important in every decision. For example, in approving a HCO's rates, a governing board may be interested

Table 5-3 Users and Uses of Financial Information

	Users				
	Financial Condition	Stewardship	Uses Efficiency	Effectiveness	Compliance
External					
Healthcare coalitions	X		X	X	
Unions	X		X		
Rate-setting organizations	X		X	X	X
Creditors	X		X	X	
Third-party payers			X		X
Suppliers	X				
Public	X		X	X	
Internal					
Governing board	X	X	X	X	X
Top management	X	X	X	X	X
Departmental management			X		X

in only two uses of financial information: (1) evaluation of financial condition and (2) assessment of operational efficiency. Other uses may be irrelevant. The board wants to ensure that services are being provided efficiently and that the established rates are sufficient to guarantee a stable or improved financial condition. As Table 5-3 illustrates, most healthcare decision-making groups use financial information to assess financial condition and efficiency.

It is important to understand the management structure of businesses in general and HCOs in particular. **Figure 5-2** outlines the financial management structure of a typical hospital.

FINANCIAL FUNCTIONS WITHIN AN ORGANIZATION

Financial Executives International has categorized financial management functions as either controllership or treasurership. Although few HCOs have specifically identified treasurers and controllers at this time, the separation of duties is key to the understanding of financial management. Functions in the two categories designated by Financial Executives International are given here, along with an example of the type of activities conducted within each of these functions:

1. Controllership
   a. Planning for control: Establish budgetary systems
   b. Reporting and interpreting: Prepare financial statements
   c. Evaluating and consulting: Conduct cost analyses
   d. Administrating taxes: Calculating payroll taxes owed
   e. Reporting to government: Submit Medicare bills and cost reports
   f. Protecting assets: Develop internal control procedures
   g. Appraising economic health: Analyze financial statements

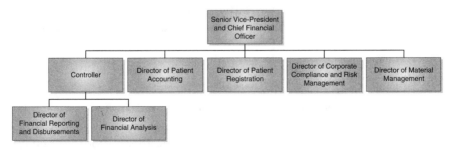

Figure 5-2 Financial Organization Chart of a Typical Hospital

2. Treasurership
    a. Providing capital: Arrange for bond issuance
    b. Maintaining investor relations: Assist in analysis of appropriate dividend payment policy (for-profit firms)
    c. Providing short-term financing: Arrange lines of credit
    d. Providing banking and custody: Manage overnight and short-term funds transfers
    e. Overseeing credits and collections: Establish billing, credit, and collection policies
    f. Choosing investments: Analyze capital investment projects
    g. Providing insurance: Managing funds related to self-insurance program

OWNERSHIP FORMS OF HEALTHCARE ORGANIZATIONS

More so than in most other industries, firms in the healthcare industry consist of a wide array of ownership and organizational structures. In health care, there are four main types of organizations (adapted from the American Institute of Certified Public Accountants Audit and Accounting Guide, *Health Care Organizations,* 2009):

- Not-for-profit, business-oriented organizations
- For-profit healthcare entities
    - Investor owned
    - Professional corporations/professional associations
    - Sole proprietorships
    - Limited partnerships
    - Limited liability partnerships/limited liability companies
- Governmental HCOs
- Nongovernmental, nonprofit HCOs

These four main types of firms differ in terms of ownership structure. Additionally, different HCOs require slightly different sets of financial statements.

Not-for-Profit, Business-Oriented Organizations

Not-for-profit HCOs are owned by the entire community rather than by investor-owners. Unlike its for-profit counterpart, the primary goal of a not-for-profit (also referred to as a nonprofit) organization is not to maximize profits, but rather to serve the community in which it operates through the healthcare services it provides. Not-for-profit HCOs must be run as a business, however, to ensure their long-term financial viability. With an annual budget of more than $10 billion, Ascension Healthcare is an example of one of the largest not-for-profit HCOs.

Not-for-profit organizations (described in Sec. 501(c)(3) of the Internal Revenue Code) usually are exempt from federal income taxes and property taxes. In return for this favorable tax treatment, not-for-profit organizations are expected to provide **community benefits**, which often come in the form of providing more uncompensated care (vis-à-vis for-profit firms), setting lower prices, or offering services that, from a financial perspective, might not be viable for for-profit firms. In addition to patient revenue in excess of expenses, not-for-profits can be funded by tax-exempt debt, grants, donations, and investments by other nonprofit firms.

The primary advantage of the not-for-profit form of organization is its tax advantage. It also typically enjoys a lower cost of equity capital compared with for-profit firms. The main disadvantage of this form of organization is that not-for-profit entities have more limited access to capital. Nonprofits cannot raise capital in the equity markets.

Although for-profit firms are becoming increasingly prevalent in many sectors of health care, nonprofits still dominate the hospital sector. Approximately 80% of U.S. hospitals are not-for-profit organizations. In the future, however, this sector may witness the growth of investor-owned organizations, mainly because they have easier access to the capital that will be necessary for adapting to the rapid changes in the healthcare system.

For-Profit Healthcare Entities

The main objective of most for-profit firms is to earn profits that are distributed to the investor-owners of the firms or reinvested in the firms for the long-term benefit of these owners. Managers in for-profit hospitals must strike a balance between their fiduciary responsibilities to the owners of the company and their other mission of providing acceptable-quality healthcare services to the community.

For-profit firms have a wide variety of organization and ownership structures. Such firms that buy and sell shares of their company stocks on the open market are referred to as **publicly traded companies**. A major advantage of being publicly traded is the ability to raise equity capital through the sale of company stocks. Publicly traded firms are subject to reporting requirements and regulation by the Securities and Exchange Commission. For-profit firms may also be privately held, meaning the shares of the company are held by relatively few investors and are not available to the general public. Privately held companies also have far fewer reporting requirements by the Securities and Exchange Commission.

Large for-profit firms are typically publicly traded. However, there are exceptions. For example, HCA, Inc., is a national for-profit healthcare services company headquartered in Nashville, Tennessee. Before 2005, HCA was the largest publicly traded hospital company. In 2005, it was purchased by a private equity firm and converted from a publicly traded to a **privately held company**. HCA, Inc., remains a privately held company and is still the largest for-profit hospital company, with 163 hospitals and related businesses in 20 states. In its fiscal year ending December 31, 2014, the company had a net income of $2.273 billion.

Both publicly traded and privately held for-profit firms are often referred to as "investor-owned" firms. **Investor-owned firms** are owned by risk-based equity investors who expect the managers of the corporation to maximize shareholder wealth. Most large for-profit firms use this legal form. Investor-owned firms have a relative advantage in terms of obtaining financing. In addition to debt, for-profit firms can raise funds through risk-based equity capital. They enjoy limited liability, but their earnings are taxed at both the corporate level and the shareholder level (so-called double taxation). In other words, the company pays corporate income tax, and the shareholder pays both tax on dividends paid by the company and gains made on the sale of the company's stock

A **professional corporation**, also called a professional association, is a corporate form for professionals who want to have the advantages of incorporation. A professional corporation does not, however, shield its owners from professional liability. Professional corporations and professional associations have been widely used by physicians and other healthcare professionals.

Sole proprietorships are unincorporated businesses owned by a single individual. They do not necessarily have to be small businesses. Solo practitioner physicians often are sole proprietors. This business form offers several advantages: It is easy and inexpensive to set up, there is no sharing of profits, the sole proprietor has total control, there are few government regulations and no special income taxes, and it is easy and inexpensive to dissolve. Its two main disadvantages are unlimited liability and limited access to capital.

Partnerships are unincorporated businesses with two or more owners. Group practices of physicians sometimes were set up with this form. A wide variety of partnership forms now exist. These businesses are easy to form, are subject to few government regulations, and are not subject to double taxation. On the down side, partnerships have unlimited liability, are difficult to dissolve, and create potential for conflict among the partners.

In a **limited partnership**, at least one general partner has unlimited liability for the partnership's debts and obligations. Limited partnerships offer limited liability to the limited partners along with tax flow-through treatment. The disadvantage to limited partnerships is that they require a general partner who remains fully liable for their debts and obligations.

A **limited liability company**, also called a limited liability partnership, is a business entity that combines the tax flow-through treatment characteristics of a partnership (i.e., no double taxation) with the liability protection of a corporation. In a limited liability company, the liability of the general partner is limited. Limited liability companies are flexible in the sense that they permit their owners to structure allocations of income and losses any way they desire, as long as the partnership tax allocation rules are followed.

Governmental Healthcare Organizations

Governmental HCOs are public corporations, typically owned by a state or local government. They are operated for the benefit of the communities they serve. A variation on this type of ownership is the **public benefit organization**. With a nonprofit public benefit corporation, the assets (and accumulated earnings) of the organization belong to the public or to the charitable beneficiaries the trust was organized to serve. In 1999, for example, Nassau County Medical Center (a 1,500-bed healthcare system on Long Island, New York) converted from county ownership to a public benefit corporation. The purpose of the conversion was to give Nassau County Medical Center greater autonomy in its governing board and decision making, so that it could compete more effectively with the area's large private hospitals and networks.

In some cases, governmental HCOs may have access to an additional revenue source through taxes—an option not available to other not-for-profit HCOs. Similar to other not-for-profits, government HCOs are not able to raise funds through equity investments and are exempt from income taxes and property taxes.

Governmental HCOs can face political pressures if their earnings become too great. Rather than reinvesting its surplus in productive assets, such a hospital might be pressured to return some of the surplus to the community, to reduce prices, or to initiate programs that are not financially advisable.

Nonprofit, Non–Business-Oriented Organizations

Non–business-oriented HCOs perform voluntary services in their communities; accordingly, they are often called **voluntary health and welfare organizations**. They are tax exempt and rely primarily on public donations for their funds. Examples include the American Red Cross and the American Cancer Society. Although these types of organizations provide invaluable services, the financial statements and financial management of these organizations are somewhat different from that of business-oriented firms.

REVENUE CYCLE FOR HEALTHCARE FIRMS

Almost any measure of size indicates that the U.S. healthcare industry is big business. Its size as a proportion of the U.S. gross domestic product has been steadily increasing for several decades, and it now accounts for approximately 16% of the gross domestic product, with more than $2 trillion in annual expenditures. Paralleling this growth, the pressures for cost control within the system have increased tremendously, especially at the federal and state levels for control of Medicare and Medicaid. Healthcare organizations not able to deal effectively with these pressures face an uncertain future. In short, as the expected demand for health services continues to increase during the next several decades as our population ages, successful HCOs must become increasingly cost efficient.

Healthcare firms are for the most part business-oriented organizations. Their ultimate financial survival depends on a consistent and recurring flow of funds from the services they provide to patients. Without an adequate stream of revenue, these firms would be forced to cease operations. In this regard, healthcare firms are similar to most business entities that sell products or services in the economy. **Figure 5–3** depicts the stages involved in the revenue cycle for a healthcare firm. The critical stages in the revenue cycle for healthcare firms are the provision and documentation of services to the patient, the generation of charges for those services, the preparation of a bill or claim, the submission of the bill or claim to the respective payer, and the collection of payment.

A simple review of the six stages of the revenue cycle in Figure 5–3 hides the significant degree of complexity involved in revenue generation for healthcare providers. No other industry in the U.S. economy experiences the same level of billing complexity that most healthcare firms face. Part of

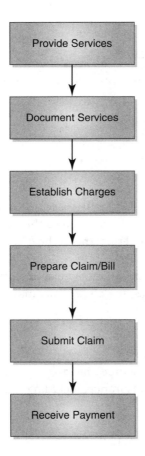

Figure 5–3 Revenue Cycle

this complexity is related to the nature and importance of the services provided. Regulation is also a factor that further complicates documentation and billing for health care.

FACTORS THAT INFLUENCE THE FINANCIAL VIABILITY OF A HEALTHCARE ORGANIZATION

Financial Viability

An HCO is a basic provider of health services but is also a business. The environment of an HCO viewed from a financial perspective is depicted in **Figure 5–4**.

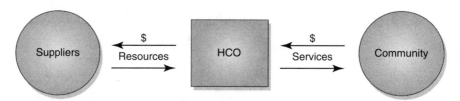

Figure 5–4 Financial Environment of Healthcare Organizations

Data from Centers for Medicare & Medicaid Services, Office of Financial and Actuarial Analysis, Division of National Cost Estimates.

In the long run, the HCO must receive dollar payments from the community in an amount at least equal to the dollar payments it makes to its suppliers. In very simple terms, this is the essence of financial viability.

The community in Figure 5–4 is the provider of funds to the HCO. The flow of funds is either directly or indirectly related to the delivery of services by the HCO. For our purposes, the community may be categorized as follows:

1. Patients
   a. Self-payer
   b. Third-party payer
      • Blue Cross and Blue Shield
      • Commercial insurance, including managed care
      • Medicaid
      • Medicare
      • Self-insured employer
      • Other

2. Nonpatients
   a. Grants
   b. Contributions
   c. Tax support
   d. Miscellaneous

In most HCOs, the greater proportion of funds is derived from patients who receive services directly. The largest percentage of these payments usually comes from third-party sources such as Blue Cross, Medicare, Medicaid, and managed care organizations. In addition, some nonpatient funds are derived from government sources in the form of grants for research purposes or direct payments to subsidized HCOs, such as county facilities. Some HCOs also receive significant sums of money from individuals, foundations, or corporations in the form of contributions. Although these sums may be small relative to the total amounts of money received from patient services, their importance in overall viability should not be understated. In many HCOs, these contributed dollars mean the difference between net income and loss.

The suppliers in Figure 5–4 provide the HCO with resources that are necessary in the delivery of quality health care. The major categories of suppliers are the following:

- Employees
- Equipment suppliers
- Service contractors
- Vendors of consumable supplies
- Lenders

Payments for employees usually represent the largest single category of expenditures. For example, in many hospitals, payments for employees represent about 60% of total expenditures. **Table 5–4** is an example of a statement of operations (similar to an income statement for a for-profit firm) that shows percentages of revenues and expenses for a hospital. Payments for physicians' services also represent important financial demands. In addition, lenders such as commercial banks or investment bankers supply dollars in the form of loans and receive from the HCO a promise to repay the loans with interest according to a defined repayment schedule. This financial requirement has grown steadily as HCOs have become more dependent on debt financing.

Sources of Operating Revenue

Table 5–5 provides a historical breakdown of the relative size of the U.S. healthcare industry and its individual industrial segments. The largest segment is the hospital industry, which absorbs about 31% of all healthcare expenditure dollars (in per capita terms). This percentage has been declining over the last few years and is expected to diminish further as other industry segments grow more quickly. The physician segment accounts for approximately 21% of total healthcare expenditures; this proportion has been steady in recent years but still represents a modest increase over the prior decade when expressed as a percentage of total healthcare expenditures. Prescription drugs represent the third largest healthcare segment, reflecting the rapid rise in prescription drug use. Whereas in the past nursing homes represented the third largest healthcare segment, prescription drugs have overtaken nursing homes. Prescription drugs now constitute about 10% of all per capita healthcare expenditures.

Another area experiencing significant growth has been the administration of private health insurance, which accounts for 7% of total U.S. health expenditures. The once-rapid increases in Medicare spending for skilled

Table 5–4 Statement of Operations for Memorial Hospital, Year Ended 20X7 (000s Omitted)

	20X7	%
Unrestricted revenues, gains, and other support		
Net patient service revenue	$85,502	85.84
Premium revenue	11,195	11.24
Other operating revenue	2913	2.92
Total operating revenue	$99,610	100.0
Expenses		
Salaries and benefits	40,258	40.41
Medical supplies and drugs	27,542	27.65
Professional fees	16,857	16.92
Insurance	5,568	5.59
Depreciation and amortization	3,952	3.97
Interest	1,456	1.46
Provision for bad debts	1,152	1.16
Other	523	0.53
Total expenses	$97,308	97.69
Operating income	2302	2.31
Investment income	1,846	1.86
Excess of revenues, gains, and other support over expenses	4,148	4.17
Net assets released from restrictions used for purchase of property and equipment	192	0.19
Increase in unrestricted net assets	$4340	4.36

Data from Centers for Medicare & Medicaid Services, Office of Financial and Actuarial Analysis, Division of National Cost Estimates.

nursing facilities (SNFs) have been tempered by the change to prospective payment. Annual growth rates in spending for nursing home care have been cut almost in half in recent years, as providers have reacted to the changes in reimbursement method. Demographic factors, however, will continue to put upward pressure on national nursing home expenditures. Many people believe that the nursing home segment will grow faster as the population ages.

Table 5–5 National Healthcare Expenditures

	2000	2008	2000–2008 Annual Growth	2019 Projected	2008–2019 Annual Growth
National health expenditures (millions of dollars)	1,855,389	2,338,746	6.0%	4,482,696	5.1%
Population (millions)	293.2	304.5	0.9%	334.8	0.7%
Per capita expenditures (millions of dollars)					
Hospital care	1,481	2,359	6.0%	4,105	5.2%
Physician and clinical services	1,026	1,629	6.0%	2,635	4.5%
Prescription drugs	429	769	7.6%	1,367	5.4%
Administration and net cost of private health insurance	291	524	7.6%	957	5.6%
Nursing home care	339	455	3.8%	735	4.5%
Investment: structures and equipment	225	374	6.6%	663	5.3%
Other personal health care	132	224	6.8%	551	8.6%
Dental services	220	332	5.3%	539	4.5%
Home health care	108	212	8.8%	459	7.3%
Government public health activity	153	228	5.1%	419	5.7%
Other professional care	139	216	5.7%	369	5.0%
Investment: research	91	143	5.9%	272	6.0%
Other nondurable medical products	106	128	2.4%	189	3.6%
Durable medical equipment	69	87	3.0%	129	3.6%
National health expenditures	4,808	7,681	6.0%	13,389	5.2%

Data from Centers for Medicare & Medicaid Services, Office of Financial and Actuarial Analysis, Division of National Cost Estimates.

Table 5–6 depicts the sources of operating funds for the four largest healthcare segments: hospitals, physicians, prescription drugs, and nursing homes. Dramatic differences in financing among these four segments can be readily seen.

The hospital industry derives more than 50% of its total funding from public sources, largely from Medicare and Medicaid. Of the two, Medicare is by far the larger, representing about 30% of all hospital revenue. This gives the federal government enormous control over U.S. hospitals and their financial positions. Few hospitals can choose to ignore the Medicare program because of its sheer size. Another 36% of total hospital funding comes from private insurance, largely from Blue Cross, commercial insurance carriers, managed care organizations, and self-insured employers. Direct payments by patients to hospitals represent approximately 3% of total revenue. The implication of this distribution for hospitals is the creation of an oligopsonistic marketplace. In other words, the buying power for hospital services is concentrated among relatively few third-party purchasers—namely, the federal government, the state government, Blue Cross, a few commercial insurance carriers, and some large self-insured employers.

Table 5–6 Sources of Health Services Funding: 2008 and Projected 2019

Source	Hospitals		Physicians		Prescription Drugs		Nursing Homes	
	2008	2019	2008	2019	2008	2019	2008	2019
Private payments (%)	43	38	65	65	63	53	38	33
Private health insurance	36	32	49	47	42	36	7	6
Out-of-pocket payments	3	3	10	11	21	17	27	24
Other private funds	4	3	6	7	0	0	4	4
Government payments (%)	57	62	35	35	37	47	62	67
Medicare	29	33	21	20	22	30	19	21
Medicaid	17	18	7	9	8	10	41	43
Other	10	11	7	6	7	8	3	3
Total payments (%)	100	100	100	100	100	100	100	100

Data from Centers for Medicare & Medicaid Services, Office of Financial and Actuarial Analysis, Division of National Cost Estimates.

The physician marketplace is somewhat different from the marketplace for hospital services. A much larger percentage of physician funding is derived from direct payments by patients (approximately 10%). Compared with hospital funding, a slightly larger percentage of physician funding results from private insurance sources, largely from Blue Cross and commercial insurance carriers. Physicians derive approximately 49% of their total funds from this source; the hospital segment derives 36% of total funds from this source. Public programs, although still significant, are the smallest source of physician funding, representing 35% of these funds. This situation results because more physician services, such as routine physical examinations and many deductible and copayment services, are excluded from Medicare payment.

Similar to the market for physicians, most payments for prescription drugs (42%) come from private insurance sources. The impact of Medicare coverage can be clearly seen in Table 5–6. By 2019, Medicare is expected to fund 30% of all prescription drug costs. Many state Medicaid plans (which are more than 50% federally funded) do provide prescription drug benefits. Medicaid represents more than 8% of prescription drug payments.

The nursing home segment receives almost no funding from private insurance sources. The major public program for nursing homes is Medicaid, not Medicare. However, the federal government pays more than 50% of all Medicaid expenditures. Medicare payments to nursing homes are largely restricted to skilled nursing care, whereas most Medicaid payments to nursing homes are for intermediate-level (custodial) care.

CHAPTER SUMMARY

The healthcare sector of the U.S. economy is growing rapidly both in size and complexity. Understanding the financial and economic implications of decision making has become one of the most critical areas encountered by healthcare decision makers. Successful decision making can lead to a viable operation capable of providing needed healthcare services. Unsuccessful decision making can and often does lead to financial failure. The role of financial information in the decision-making process cannot be overstated. It is incumbent on all healthcare decision makers to become accounting literate in today's financially changing healthcare environment. This literacy includes understanding the financial environment of the largest segments of the healthcare industry and the financial viability of an organization.

Before 1983, most hospitals were paid actual costs for delivering hospital services. With the introduction of Medicare's prospective payment system in 1983, hospitals now receive payments based on diagnosis-related groupings that are fixed in advance. Cost control and, therefore, cost accounting are critical in a fixed-price environment. The expansion of managed care has further restricted revenue and fostered greater interest in costing.

A nonprofit entity does not have the same opportunities for capital formation that an investor-owned organization does. Specifically, the nonprofit entity cannot sell new shares or ownership interests. Its sources of capital are limited to its accumulated funded reserves and to new debt. In some special situations, nonprofit organizations may receive contributions, but these amounts are usually not significant.

The hospital industry derives more than 50% of its total funding from public sources, largely from Medicare and Medicaid. Of the two, Medicare is by far the larger, representing about 30% of all hospital revenue. This gives the U.S. federal government enormous control over hospitals and their financial positions.

KEY TERMS AND CONCEPTS

Budget: An agreement between two management levels regarding use of resources for a defined time period.

Community benefit: Benefits provided by nonprofit organization in exchange for favorable tax treatment. It may take the form of providing more uncompensated care (vis-à-vis for-profit firms), setting lower prices, or offering services that, from a financial perspective, might not be viable for for-profit firms.

Decision making: The selection of a course of action from a defined list of possible or feasible actions.

Effectiveness: In regard to operations, the attainment of objectives through production of outputs.

Efficiency: The ratio of outputs to inputs.

Investor-owned firm: A firm owned by risk-based equity investors who expect the managers of the corporation to maximize shareholder wealth.

Limited liability company: Also called a limited liability partnership; a business entity that combines the tax flow-through treatment characteristics of a partnership with the liability protection of a corporation.

Limited partnership: An unincorporated business with two or more owners in which at least one general partner has unlimited liability for the partnership's debts and obligations.

Partnership: An unincorporated business with two or more owners.

Privately held company: A for-profit firm whose company stock is held by relatively few investors and is not available to the general public.

Professional corporation: Also called a professional association; a corporate form that is created by professionals who want the advantages of incorporation, but that does not shield them from professional liability.

Public benefit organization: A nonprofit company in which the assets (and accumulated earnings) of the organization belong to the public or to the charitable beneficiaries the trust was organized to serve.

Publicly traded company: A for-profit firm whose company stock is bought and sold on the open market.

Sole proprietorship: An unincorporated business owned by a single individual.

Voluntary health and welfare organization: A non–business-oriented healthcare organization that performs voluntary services in its community; it is tax exempt and relies primarily on public donations for its funds.

Questions to Consider

1. Only in recent years have hospitals begun to develop meaningful systems of cost accounting. Why did they not begin this development sooner?

2. Your hospital has been approached by a major employer in your market area to negotiate a preferred provider arrangement. The employer is seeking a 25% discount from your current charges. Describe a structure that you might use to summarize the financial implications of this decision. Describe the factors that are critical in this decision.

3. Which type of financial information should be routinely provided to board members?

4. Describe factors that influence the financial viability of a healthcare organization.

5. Describe the financial environment of the largest segments of the healthcare industry.

6. Discuss the major reimbursement methods that are used in health care.

Chapter 6

Legal Landscape: Challenges and Opportunities

—Thomas R. Hoffman, JD, CAE

LEARNING OBJECTIVES

- Identify legal issues that affect the management of healthcare organizations.
- Understand antitrust law.
- Describe why understanding the legal aspects of integration is so important when health organizations decide to go this route.
- Identify and explain the importance of laws related to patient health information and electronic health records.

INTRODUCTION

Health care represents one of the most critical—and highly regulated—fields in the United States. Public and private stakeholders continue to argue over the range of care that U.S. citizens and residents should obtain, and who should bear the costs of providing it. Vastly divergent approaches are proposed for both the delivery and financing of care. One leading trend, integration of health systems, occurs each week in numerous U.S. cities and towns. This integration is shaped by the multiple U.S. government agencies using the Patient Protection and Affordable Care Act (ACA) for policy and regulatory matters. For each solution that health managers find within the integrated approach, they must address additional challenges that the law presents.

This chapter addresses significant legal concepts that affect the management of integrated healthcare systems.[1] For example, executives who lead and manage systems must deal with the constantly shifting applications of federal **antitrust** laws and rules. Executives must recognize that antitrust laws protect competition, not competitors, when evaluating whether a health system may legally combine with one or more competing systems in the name of coordinated, effective health care. How will the 2011 Department of Justice (DOJ) and Federal Trade Commission (FTC) enforcement statements for accountable care organizations change the playing field for integrated systems? Can—and how can—a system use market data to improve community health, even if that may yield a competitive advantage? Will recent court decisions that prohibited large health systems from acquiring physician practices because they violated antitrust restrictions result in physicians becoming employees and, therefore, able to form unions? This chapter describes federal antitrust laws and analyzes what they mean for integration.

An additional key challenge for integrated health systems of the future will be to understand and comply with laws that govern the use and disclosure of patient health information. This chapter addresses mandates in the electronic health record (EHR) world, such as meaningful use regulations, which have drawn sharp criticism from professionals and vendors. Privacy and confidentiality issues remain fundamental. This chapter will review the recently amended HIPAA/HITECH regulations and forecast their impact on integrated systems.

ANTITRUST CONCERNS

Healthcare organizations and their executives should understand the roots of and the purpose of the law to be successful. Antitrust law illustrates the challenges and opportunities that arise between government and business. United States antitrust law originated in the late nineteenth century. In that era, "robber barons" or "trusts," such as Standard Oil and U.S. Steel, amassed extraordinary wealth and power, primarily by eliminating virtually all competition in their industries. As a consequence, the companies controlled both production and pricing without fear that anyone could underprice them. By the late 1880s, Congress grew to believe that these trusts, monopolies, and cartels harmed the public by restricting consumer choice and allowing artificially high prices (Shields & Hoffman, 2012).

---

[1] The author refers to "health systems" and "hospitals" interchangeably in this chapter.

Responding to these concerns, in 1890, Congress passed the Sherman Antitrust Act to prohibit business practices designed to restrain trade. The central language in Section 1 of the law states that:

> Every contract, combination in the form of trust or otherwise, or conspiracy, in restraint of trade or commerce among the several States, or with foreign nations, is declared to be illegal.[2]

Congress left enforcers and businesses, however, with a broad statute that lacked guidance.[3] What represents an illegal contract or combination? Did a dominant railroad or steel company violate the Sherman Act merely by its considerable size and healthy bottom line? Additionally, the vague law allowed management to exploit its ambiguity and crack down on labor unions because they were deemed to act outside of "commerce."

In 1914, Congress enacted the Clayton Act to ban certain practices left unguarded by the Sherman Act—namely, mergers and interlocking directorates (in which the same individual serves as a director on boards of competing companies) (Federal Trade Commission [FTC], n.d.). The Clayton Act also prohibits mergers and acquisitions "where the effect 'may be substantially to lessen competition, or tend to create a monopoly'" (FTC, n.d.).

A third critical antitrust statute, the Federal Trade Commission Act, bars "unfair methods of competition" and "unfair or deceptive acts or practices" (FTC, n.d.). This law gives the FTC jurisdiction over for-profit organizations, including for-profit health systems and physician group practices. The courts have affirmed that the FTC also has jurisdiction over nonprofit entities (Showalter, 2012). In recent cases, the regulatory agency has pushed back against several health systems' efforts to integrate their operations. The cases hold lessons for health systems executives and their teams around the United States.

For instance, the FTC has attempted to block numerous hospital mergers by asserting that the combined hospitals would have excessive market power. In the FTC's view, the antitrust "evils" that many mergers spawn would reduce access to health care and raise its costs. In making these judgments, the enforcement agency applied its traditional principles of the relevant product and geographic markets. However, one can question whether 100-year-old legal principles properly fit the evolving healthcare

---

[2]Title 15 United States Code, section 1, *et seq.*
[3]This process frustrates individuals and businesses such as health systems that have to live by the ambiguous laws enacted in Washington, D.C. Health executives must evaluate with qualified experts the "meat on the bones"—that is, the regulations and policy guidance that clarify the skeletal law.

arena or, instead, stifle innovation (Showalter, 2012, p. 406). Integration should succeed or fail based on how well (or not) people contribute to patient care, rather than whether organizations are slotted in a certain number on the Herfindahl-Hirschman index of supposed market concentration.

Fundamentally, these statutes—and all antitrust laws—safeguard the public as consumers, rather than the competitors who may be harmed by the prohibited practices (Shields & Hoffman, 2012, p. 28). Although the Department of Justice and the FTC share responsibility for civil antitrust enforcement, only the DOJ may bring criminal antitrust charges. Most states also have antitrust laws, and state attorneys general may enforce federal and state antitrust laws. Notably, individuals or organizations that claim harm by anticompetitive practices—including disgruntled physicians, other health professionals, and insurers may bring civil lawsuits as well (Shields & Hoffman, 2012). Criminal violations of the Sherman Act by individuals can result in fines up to $1 million and prison sentences as long as 10 years (FTC, n.d.). Corporate violators can face fines up to $100 million. Civil violations can result in payment of treble damages (three times the actual financial damages), plus attorneys' fees and costs. Class-action lawsuits can result in huge damage payments. The high financial stakes—and the incalculable effect on a health system's reputation from being the target of an antitrust investigation and/or lawsuit—should motivate healthcare organizations to value antitrust compliance. They must develop a focused compliance plan, acknowledge it at each corporate meeting, and refresh it regularly.

Antitrust considerations have given health executives pause in the era of the Affordable Care Act. A central question involves whether the integration wave will run aground because of antitrust law. Many organizations have sought out consolidation with their competing hospitals and medical practices as a means to reach "the next level" of cost-effective, quality patient care that is the core objective of the Affordable Care Act. However, health systems confront potential barriers in such mergers because the antitrust enforcers are closely monitoring integration in this industry (Statement of Edith Ramirez, 2013). Supporters of healthcare reform have touted one paradigm, the accountable care organization (ACO), as a promising vehicle for containing healthcare costs. An ACO constitutes a legal entity of a hospital system, physician practice (independent solo practice or completely integrated group), or other collection of healthcare providers that join forces to provide coordinated patient care (Centers for Medicare and Medicaid Services [CMS], n.d.). Government and private sector advocates maintain that patients will benefit from ACOs by obtaining the "right care at the right time" (CMS, n.d.).

Medicare, through the Patient Protection and Affordable Care Act of 2010, established a **"Shared Savings Program" (SSP)** that ACOs can join (Patient Protection and Affordable Care Act, 2010). The SSP authorizes an ACO to share in a portion of any savings it achieves by meeting particular quality performance standards (Federal Trade Commission & Department of Justice [FTC & DOJ], 2011). ACOs must commit to participate in the SSP for at least three years.

Which roadmap may a healthcare organization consult if it explores the ACO model? In 2011, the two antitrust enforcers, FTC and DOJ, issued a Statement of Antitrust Enforcement Policy on ACOs that sign onto the Medicare SSP. This Statement describes the agencies' legal and policy approach to evaluating potential collaborations.[4] According to this clarification of policy, ACOs may support providers who are attempting to "innovate in both the Medicare and commercial markets" and offer similar benefits to non-Medicare patients that the SSP would extend to Medicare beneficiaries (FTC & DOJ, 2011). Yet the regulators did not give ACOs a free pass, asserting that they might dampen competition and hurt consumers by promoting reduced quality of care and higher prices (FTC & DOJ, 2011).

For instance, the U.S. government will apply a "rule of reason" analysis to assess a health system that enters into a joint clinical care agreement with competing systems. This review balances an arrangement's potential pro-competitive, or legitimate, attributes against its potential anticompetitive, or illegal, aspects (FTC & DOJ, 2011, p. 67027). Multiprovider joint ventures that involve physicians or hospitals generally agree to share "substantial financial risk," as the FTC and DOJ define that term (FTC & DOJ, 2011). Consequently, they establish arrangements that seek clinical and operational efficiencies. When those efficiencies benefit patient care, the participating systems prosper financially and gain public confidence. When the efficiencies enhance competition, they pass muster in a legal sense. ACOs must qualify under the Affordable Care Act's eligibility criteria for the Centers for Medicare and Medicaid Services (CMS) to approve them. In particular, these organizations must establish a formal legal structure that enables them to receive payments from the government for shared savings and subsequently distribute those funds to providers within the ACO (FTC & DOJ, 2011). Additionally, ACOs must develop a leadership and management approach that focuses on clinical and administrative processes, reports on quality and cost measures, and coordinates care for Medicare

---

[4]Separate antitrust guidelines will apply to merger transactions, including those that may fit within the government's "safety zones" that protect collaborations among competitors.

beneficiaries (FTC & DOJ, 2011). Fortunately, the antitrust agencies concluded that the CMS eligibility requirements generally match well with their own analysis. Thus, an ACO that achieves cost and quality goals, among others, through a joint effort should pass the antitrust tests.

How does the U.S. government assess market conduct? The federal agencies exercise their antitrust due diligence by turning to contemporary health care's gold standard: data. FTC and DOJ scrutinize aggregate claims data from Medicare about allowable charges and fee-for-service payments to ACOs accepted into the SSP. Yet federal oversight of data poses a formidable challenge to health systems. Integrated—or integrating—health systems utilize data to assess patterns of care for sizable populations and their subsets (Geisinger Health System, 2013). Data analytics has become an essential attribute of modern health care. A national consortium of ACOs has observed that:

> The ACO requires accurate and timely data from CMS identifying their aligned beneficiaries and claims for their services. These data are valuable for evaluating subpopulations (i.e., patients with highly prevalent conditions or multiple chronic conditions), cost and utilization of services to identify areas of opportunity, and most importantly determining whether or not the ACO is achieving their financial goals (National Association of ACOs, 2014).

While data help a system fulfill its mission, they also contribute to the system's margin. For example, a health system might leverage population health data to gain a market edge that enforcers might then question. Suppose that a health system serves patients across two states with many underserved areas. This entity might consider merging or combining with a competitor to form an ACO and provide the needed primary care more efficiently. In such a situation, it would certainly want to learn more about its patients' needs. The competing system might have cultivated a rich database of payment rates for new therapies, enabling higher reimbursement. As the two potential partners conduct due diligence on each other's businesses, executives from both systems meet and agree to share their market information. Risky? Possibly. The FTC and DOJ assert in their Enforcement Policy Statement that exchanging "competitively sensitive information among competing participants could facilitate collusion and reduce competition" in offering services beyond the ACO (Statements of Antitrust Enforcement Policy, n.d.). In such a scenario, competition would suffer because patients might experience higher prices or lower quality or availability of healthcare services (Statements of Antitrust Enforcement Policy, n.d.).

To manage this kind of antitrust risk, current and prospective ACOs must develop measures that prevent these types of market "evils" (Statements of Antitrust Enforcement Policy, n.d.). For example, the governing boards of ACOs and other integrated healthcare systems should adopt and implement an antitrust code of conduct. This code should address how the organizations collect and distribute market data on industry pricing or sales. Most importantly, health systems must avoid taking collective action based on such data that might advance anticompetitive ends.

Recent cases illustrate that integrated health systems must balance innovation with prudence. In the past, U.S. courts have rejected numerous mergers and acquisitions between health systems and with physician practices on antitrust grounds. Although FTC and DOJ lost many challenges to hospital mergers in the 1990s (Showalter, 2012, p. 407), since 2007 they have successfully targeted attempts by multiple health systems to combine their operations (Berlin, n.d.[a]). One notable case in Idaho involved a major regional health system that sought to grow its market share by absorbing a major multispecialty group. St. Luke's Health System owns and operates seven Idaho hospitals and employs more than 500 physicians in Idaho and eastern Oregon. It acquired Saltzer Medical Group in 2012 (Shields & Hoffman, 2014). Saltzer represented the largest independent multispecialty medical practice in Idaho. In 2008, both organizations established an informal partnership that emphasized improving access to medical care, better coordinating that care, and "streamlining the health care delivery model" (Shields & Hoffman, 2014, p. 8).

St. Luke's also entered into a five-year professional services agreement (PSA) with the group. Significantly, the PSA contained an "exclusivity" provision that prohibited the Saltzer physicians from becoming employees of, or financially affiliating with, other health systems or hospitals (Shields & Hoffman, 2014, p. 10). Before the acquisition, Saltzer physicians had received a guaranteed salary with Relative Value Unit (RVU)-based compensation—plus compensation tied to risk or other quality-based incentives (Shields & Hoffman, 2014). Group leaders wanted a closer relationship to enable a shift to value-based compensation. They rejected a joint venture or looser affiliation. Additionally, the physicians sought to transition from fee-for-service payment and increase access to care for the sizable Medicare and Medicaid patient base in the local community (Shields & Hoffman, 2014, pp. 11–12).

St. Alphonsus Health System, a competing Idaho health system that employs more than 200 physicians, sued St. Luke's in federal and state courts. The FTC and Idaho attorney general filed a separate lawsuit against St. Luke's and Saltzer. All of the plaintiffs alleged that the combined

St. Luke's/Saltzer would create illegal anticompetitive effects in the relevant product and geographic markets. Specifically, they claimed that St. Luke's would unlawfully gain higher reimbursements from health plans, which would pass these increases on to their customers via higher premiums and out-of-pocket costs (Shields & Hoffman, 2014, p. 25).

The trial court praised St. Luke's intentions to enhance quality care, but it condemned the health system's methods, which caused the costs of such care to rise. Patients likely would have to pay higher billing rates at St. Luke's. Recognizing this risk, the court ruled that the acquisition violated the Clayton Act because its effect might be "substantially to lessen competition" (Shields & Hoffman, 2014, p. 41). St. Luke's moved to stay the court's judgment while appealing the ruling to a federal court of appeals (*Motion to Stay Judgment*, 2014). The health system claimed that there was no evidence that proved competition would be harmed by keeping the merger intact, pending the appeal. Rather, St. Luke's asserted, unwinding the merger would damage the physician group by causing its members to leave the group, thereby crippling the practice's ability to compete in the market (*Motion to Stay Judgment*, 2014).

The St. Luke's case matters in particular because it represents the FTC's first completely litigated action against a hospital-physician merger. The case may not be resolved for years. If it loses its appeal, St. Luke's would have to divest itself of the practice's physicians and assets. Antitrust experts indicate that the health system's predicament should instruct other merging entities to reevaluate their plans (Berlin, n.d.[b]). Do integrated systems want to spend their precious resources fighting agency and private plaintiff challenges? Would negotiating consent agreements with the government to avoid a crippling judicial loss represent a safer long-term move?

The high stakes of integration will pressure even more systems to combine forces in the future, because government and private incentives reinforce the old maxim, "That's where the money is." Such integration may take different forms. Some organizations may undertake a complete merger of their assets, as St. Luke's and the ProMedica systems have tried to accomplish, albeit unsuccessfully so far. Alternatively, organizations may form a clinically integrated provider network, like the two largest health systems in Michigan have established (New Mich. Network must tread, 2014).

Another key legal issue for executives to address involves the status of their health care professionals. Court or federal agency defeats of mergers and acquisitions may slow, but they will probably not halt the momentum toward greater physician employment. Many physicians, willingly or not, have become hospital employees after health systems acquired their independent practices. Their new status might drive physician-employees to consider banding together in a union, which federal labor law permits nonsupervisory individuals to do. However, physicians should pause before they "look for the union label." Will a sprawling health system have to bargain directly with a physician union? Or will unions force physicians to join a more generic group, akin to Service Employees International?

The boom in integration has drawn its critics. Some third-party payers maintain that health systems that integrate may tilt markets improperly (Kutscher, 2014). Executives should recognize that payers will oppose moves that they perceive as leading to higher prices and costs. Any health system transaction is associated with an antitrust risk that organizations will have to calculate and overcome.

PATIENT HEALTH INFORMATION

Electronic Health Records and Meaningful Use

Executives who lead integrated health systems also confront legal matters when their organizations use and disclose patient health information. Technological advances in health information management have created incredible opportunities for systems to personalize health records. This trend gained momentum when Congress enacted the **Health Information Technology for Economic and Clinical Health (HITECH) Act** in 2009. HITECH contains major financial incentives for health systems and other providers that incorporate EHRs. Many systems currently feature electronic health records that track every aspect of patient care encounters. EHRs facilitate a health professional's interaction with a patient and should save an organization both time and money. As of March 2014, CMS had provided funding of more than $12 billion in incentives for physicians and hospitals to adopt EHRs and to make "meaningful use" of their data, with another $30 billion in funding for this purpose from Medicare and Medicaid being allocated through 2019 (Flynn, 2014). Hospitals, physicians, and vendors, however, have complained that the burdensome EHR rules have frustrated their attempts to build health IT into their practices (AMA: Meaningful use, 2014). How can integrated systems take advantage of performance measures and navigate the government's EHR policy restrictions?

Initially, a health system must use "certified EHR technology" to become eligible for meaningful use incentive payments (Flynn, 2014, p. 1). The government defines "certified EHR technology" as a "qualified" EHR that is deemed as meeting standards that the Office of National Coordinator of Health IT (ONC) made applicable to the EHR system (either a portable electronic health record in a physician office or an inpatient health record in a hospital) (Flynn, 2014, pp. 1–2). Subsequently, a system must make "meaningful use" of the EHR platform to deliver patient care (Flynn, 2014, p. 2). The statute frames this concept as showing that "certified EHR technology is connected in a manner that provides ... for the electronic exchange of health information to improve the quality of health care, such as promoting care coordination" (Flynn, 2014). Such exchanges of information may occur between providers or between providers and patients (Flynn, 2014). Health systems and physicians have to demonstrate meaningful use by reporting performance measures. Specifically, a system or physician group must prove continuous meaningful use of EHR for 90 consecutive days in the first year of meaningful use (Flynn, 2014). Thereafter, it must establish continuous meaningful use in each subsequent year.

An integrated system that qualifies for meaningful use incentives needs to assemble outstanding IT teams and allow them to build a robust IT infrastructure that can use **protected health information (PHI)** creatively and responsibly. Just as important, executives must rely on in-house and outside experts to advise them on the shifting regulatory landscape. The U.S. Department of Health and Human Services' Office of Inspector General (OIG), CMS, and the ONC have each issued rulemakings for EHRs with which health systems must be familiar. In 2006, OIG led the way by publishing a regulation that offered a "safe harbor" for entities that provided interoperable EHR software or IT and training services (*Federal Register*, 2006). Under this regulation, health systems and hospitals were permitted to donate EHR items and services to physicians, including referring doctors, and escape liability under the federal anti-kickback law. To avoid this penalty, however, they must comply with the rule's criteria. For example, systems must provide EHRs that work across IT platforms and have received certification of interoperability by a certifying body of which ONC approves (*Federal Register*, 2013). CMS issued a similar rule that established an exception in its Stark self-referral law for donated EHR products and services. For its part, ONC has carved out its own regulatory niche with distinct standards: It certifies EHR vendors' technology that satisfies meaningful use requirements and non-meaningful use requirements (EHR's interoperability should be ONC's priority, 2014).

Physicians have not rushed to adopt EHRs en masse. In one study of primary care group practices, one-third of respondents that indicated they had an EHR noted that some of their physicians were not using it two years after initially adopting the system (Burns, Goldsmith, & Sen, 2013).

The high economic stakes in EHRs may also motivate questionable behavior. Some hospitals and referring physicians reportedly have pressured other physicians to adopt their EHR technology or else lose patient care business. Referring physicians, however, may wish to perform services at unaffiliated entities for quality of care or patient convenience reasons (American College of Radiology, 2013). Unfortunately, physicians such as radiologists cannot send imaging results to patient records outside their own system when their system's donated technology does not interface with another EHR platform. OIG has warned industry that hospitals and vendors must not donate technology as part of a plan to "lock in" data or patient referrals between donors and recipients; such a quid pro quo arrangement may violate the anti-kickback and Stark laws (Office of Inspector General, 2013). To avoid running afoul of these restrictions, health systems should confer with qualified healthcare counsel to assess and manage legal and business risk throughout a transaction, and they also need to participate in the rulemaking arena. CMS and ONC staffs have welcomed input on the industry perspective, especially the practical challenges in dealing with EHR systems.[5] Health systems have an opportunity to engage decision makers in key agencies and to play an important role in educating them.

Medical liability for EHR technology presents another legal hurdle for integrated systems. Reports of patient injuries, and even deaths, in which EHRs played a role have led to questions about the basic premise of more efficient, effective health care through utilization of technology. A 2011 study revealed that the Food and Drug Administration received 436 reports of serious adverse events related to health information technology, including electronic records (Robertson, 2013). Patients apparently suffered harm in 46 of those instances, in which four people reportedly died (Magrabi, Ong, Runciman, & Coiera, 2011). For example, a problem with a computerized physician order entry system led to an inadvertent medication overdose that caused one death. Another patient died after a health professional entered a portable X-ray image into a radiology archiving system under the wrong name, causing an incorrect diagnosis and consequent procedure that may have contributed to the patient's death (Magrabi et al., 2011). All technologies have inevitable, inherent glitches. However, systems that aim to coordinate their care processes via technology must account for how the data points in the system will affect the disease process.

EHR Risk Management

Health systems must continually evaluate their EHR platform, performing due diligence in researching and selecting a qualified, reliable vendor through

---

[5] http://www.imagingbiz.com/portals/radinformatics/q-acrs-michael-peters-portals-and-beyond-mu-1-2-and-3

very solid references. National associations offer policy briefs and guidelines that outline clinical and technological strategies.[6] Executives and their staffs should also negotiate indemnification clauses that, at a minimum, hold an EHR vendor liable for gross negligence and willful misconduct, including reportable adverse events that entail serious injury or death.

HIPAA (Amended HITECH Regulations): Impact on Integrated Systems

Antitrust enforcement and EHR challenges may keep many compliance officers awake at night. Health information privacy and confidentiality issues may make their hearts beat faster. Why? Because integrated health systems combine patient data from multiple components, such as hospitals, physician practices, and pharmacies. As health information flows more freely, system executives must ensure that their organizations safeguard it, both to comply with the law and to preserve trust in their clinical bona fides. How integrated health systems use and disclose patient health information will help determine their legal and business fates.

Which rights, for both patients and their health data, must systems honor? Under state law, hospitals and physicians have traditionally owned and maintained physical custody of patients' medical records (Showalter, 2012, p. 511). Now, however, patients have a formal right to get access to their records, under state law and the **Health Insurance Portability and Accountability Act of 1996 (HIPAA)** (U.S. Department of Health and Human Services, Office for Civil Rights, n.d.[a]). Thus, health systems and the professionals within them must allow patients to inspect and copy their medical records, request that errors be corrected, ask that the copies be sent to any new physician they specify, and permit authorized representatives to view the documents (Showalter, 2012, p. 511). Health systems may refuse to grant this access only if they or physicians determine that disclosing health information to a patient would impair his or her physical or mental health (Showalter, 2012, p. 511). Executives should consult their state law to verify what their organizations are required to do. One useful resource that summarizes state access laws is a 2009 report from RTI International, completed on behalf of the

---

[6] See, for example, American Hospital Association's guide to hospital contracting for electronic health records: http://www.aha.org/search?q=Electronic+Health+Record&site=redesign_aha_org (2011 - members-only); and Booz Allen Hamilton. (2009). Toward health information liquidity for Federation of American Hospitals (investor-owned hospitals and health systems): http://www.fah.org/fahCMS/Documents/On%20The%20Record/Research/2009/Booz_Allen_Toward_Hlth_Info_Liquidity.pdf

U.S. Agency for Healthcare Research and Quality (Privacy and security solutions, 2009).

Privacy matters to patients equally, if not more importantly, than access to their records. HIPAA emerged because Congress decided that the patchwork of state laws failed to protect patients' privacy and the security of their health information. The government initially limited providers to using and disclosing PHI in everyday situations only if patients gave consent (Solove, 2013). These circumstances included treatment from "direct" providers who interacted one-on-one with patients, coding and submitting claims for payment, and engaging in "healthcare operations" (e.g., quality assurance activities). Physicians and hospitals protested that the rule stymied them from working with PHI to enhance patient care. In turn, HHS modified the Privacy Standards to remove the consent mandate and give wider latitude to use and disclose PHI. Researchers also gained by having a "limited data set" of PHI that had to de-identify certain aspects of, but not all, patient information. However, gaps remained. Although HIPAA required covered entities to ensure by contract that their business partners, or "**business associates**," handled data responsibly, the law did not impose the same liability on such associates. Patient data **breaches** continued to occur after HIPAA took effect in 2002, while enforcement languished.[7]

In 2009, Congress strengthened the HIPAA privacy and data security regulations by enacting the HITECH Act. HITECH addressed PHI use and disclosure not only by health systems but also by their business associates. In 2013, HHS at last published a final rule to implement HITECH's provisions. Now, a more objective test exists for determining whether business associates that furnished services to providers qualify as "conduits" that have only incidental access to patient PHI, such as telephone companies or post offices (Shields & Hoffman, 2013). Conduits do not have to follow HIPAA's business associate requirements. In contrast, a service provider that routinely provides electronic communication services to an integrated health system, such as a billing company or a cloud company that stores patient health data, would constitute a business associate. The government will focus on how regularly a service provider handles PHI, not the type (if any) of access, in making a determination of whether it qualifies as a business associate (Shields & Hoffman, 2013).

---

[7] The privacy enforcement agency, HHS's Office for Civil Rights, had investigated only approximately 8000 of 33,000 complaints by 2008. Remarkably, it had not issued any fines. HHS officials defended the emphasis on education and voluntary compliance, stating that "HHS didn't want to play gotcha." Privacy advocates fiercely criticized the government's approach as wholly inadequate (Solove, 2013).

HITECH also extends the business associate mandates to "downstream contractors" of business associates, even if they do not actually view PHI. A health system has to enter into a business associate agreement with only its billing company, but the organization's business associate or downstream subcontractor must in turn obtain written "satisfactory assurances" from its immediate subcontractor that the latter will protect any PHI it receives (Shields & Hoffman, 2013). The final rule imposes direct obligations on business associates to limit the use and disclosure of PHI to the terms of the business associate agreement or the HIPAA Privacy Rule's requirements. Business associates also have the same legal duty to disclose PHI to HHS so the government may investigate the associates' HIPAA compliance (Shields & Hoffman, 2013).

The federal government likely will enforce HIPAA violations more consistently because it has unveiled a system of additional—and tougher—penalties. The penalties range from $100 to $500 fines for "did not know" violations to as much as $50,000 for violations in which a court or HHS decides that a health system executive willfully neglected HIPAA duties and failed to correct deficiencies (Shields & Hoffman, 2013). HITECH also authorizes enforcement of HIPAA by state attorneys general. HHS may investigate and directly enforce cases that establish a health system has willfully neglected HIPAA compliance. HHS will continue to informally resolve matters that do not involve willful neglect. Significantly, a health system or its business has "upstream vicarious liability" for the activities of a downstream contractor that faces HIPAA criminal or civil penalties. This determination applies if the organization or business associate had the authority to control—but did not control—its downstream contractor's conduct in performing a healthcare service.

Health systems must vigilantly monitor their transmission of PHI because the HIPAA rules under HITECH require them to notify affected patients and the government in the case of a breach of unsecured PHI. In certain situations, HITECH also mandates that covered entities notify the media of such breaches, regardless of whether they or their business associate committed the breach. "Breach" means any unauthorized acquisition, use, or disclosure of PHI that compromised the patient's privacy and security (*Federal Register, 79*[5566, 5695], 2013). The rules exempt unintentional acts or omissions that occurred within an employment or professional relationship with a covered entity or business associate (*Federal Register, 79*[5566, 5695], 2013). Inadvertent acts or omissions that did not result in further unauthorized use or disclosure also are exempt.

Case Study

A practical example might assist health executives to understand and solve HIPAA entanglements. Suppose a health system employs a physician who is a specialist. She provides care to patients whom primary care physicians refer under a contractual arrangement with the health system. One contractor incurs heavy financial losses and files for bankruptcy. The health system requests that the contractor satisfy its financial debts for the health care that its patients received. Bankruptcy law forces all creditors such as the health system to seek redress by filing claims with a bankruptcy trustee. An accounting assistant in the health system prepares and sends to the trustee's office invoices that detail the services that physicians rendered to patients. Unfortunately, the documents inadvertently contain PHI because they list patient names and addresses that were not secured through encryption or other comparable technology. Counsel for the bankruptcy trustee sends to the health system a "nasty gram" letter. It informs system executives that the organization has violated HIPAA and threaten to report it to federal authorities.

What do system executives do—and not do?

The federal HIPAA Privacy Standards permit covered entities—including physicians and their group practices—to disclose protected health information for payment purposes (U.S. Department of Health and Human Services, Office for Civil Rights, n.d.[b]). Does filing a claim for reimbursement through a bankruptcy proceeding qualify as an exempt "payment" activity? It arguably does, because the trustee is an authorized government agent who decides whether and how to disburse funds to the debtor's creditors, including funds for payment of healthcare services. The HIPAA rules generally require that health systems and their physicians disclose only the "minimum necessary" amount of PHI to accomplish their objectives. However, some exceptions to that minimum necessary standard exist. The Privacy Standards authorize a health system to use and disclose PHI as part of its "healthcare operations." Such operations include conducting or arranging for legal services that involve "covered functions," such as treatment or payment. Thus, the health system could assert that it is a party to a legal proceeding to disclose PHI for litigation purposes as part of its "healthcare operations."

In an answer to a HIPAA FAQ, the government lists as one example a situation in which a physician is a plaintiff in a lawsuit to obtain payment. Although the health system in the case study did not directly sue the contractor for which its employees performed patient care services, the system nonetheless sought payment within the context of a federal legal proceeding. This health system *must* work with its counsel in using the PHI. As HHS states:

> In most cases, the covered entity will share protected health information for litigation purposes with its lawyer, who is either a workforce member or a business associate. In these cases, the Privacy Rule permits a covered entity to reasonably rely on the representations of a lawyer who is a business associate or workforce member that the information requested is the minimum necessary for the stated purpose. See 45 CFR 164.514(d)(3)(iii)(C). A covered entity's minimum necessary policies and procedures may provide for such reasonable reliance on the lawyer's requests for protected health information needed in the course of providing legal services to the covered entity (HHS, n.d.).

The example health system would have to rely on its "minimum necessary" policies and procedures to guide how the lawyer handles PHI in this matter. Whether the system uses in-house or outside counsel, the lawyer may have to de-identify the PHI or remove its direct identifiers (HHS, n.d.). If that narrower scope of patient data cannot enter into evidence because it is not sufficiently relevant, the lawyer could seek a protective order (HHS, n.d.).

Does the system have to notify its patients, the government and/or the media of this breach? No, not necessarily. Healthcare organizations and their practitioners, when they inadvertently disclose PHI, can try to fit within a HIPAA regulatory exception. However, the new HITECH rules place the burden of proof on the system. Executives must conduct a risk assessment and demonstrate that there is a low probability that their systems have compromised PHI (*Federal Register, 78*[5566, 5641], n.d.). IT, corporate compliance, and risk management departments within health systems will have to work collaboratively in such a case. Health systems that experience significant PHI disclosures may have to engage external security experts to lend independent perspective to their due diligence. Only an informed and thorough risk assessment will satisfy the government if the system concludes it does not have to notify affected individuals, HHS, and even the media of a breach.

The health system in this case study will help its legal cause by promptly de-identifying PHI in the bankruptcy court's docket, thereby mitigating potential harm to patients. Certain PHI breaches, though, will compel systems to notify patients and the government, in addition to the media. HITECH's rules mandate how and when that process must occur (*Federal Register, 78*[5566, 5641], n.d., pp. 5648-5657). Whenever integrated health systems have to "self-disclose," they absolutely should consult with qualified counsel and other advisors.

CHAPTER SUMMARY

Health care continues to evolve, but always involves people helping people. Leaders of these complex enterprises continually seek innovative ways to deliver and finance their noble calling. Many health systems have determined that they should engage in integration because "bigger is (or should be) better." Other contributors to this text will caution, however, that integrating care will succeed only if diverse cultures can blend well. To harmonize cultures may represent what commentators have termed as a "wicked problem" (Jha & Lexa, 2014). Proud, independent hospitals and physicians will have to accept the case for integration as a business imperative—but the law will shape such change. Executives who stretch their horizons may benefit by learning about the legal opportunities and challenges ahead.

KEY TERMS AND CONCEPTS

Antitrust: Laws that prohibit business practices designed to restrain trade.

Breach: Any unauthorized acquisition, use, or disclosure of protected health information that compromises the patient's privacy and security.

Business associate: A company that furnishes services to healthcare providers and has only incidental access to patient protected health information, such as telephone companies or post offices.

Health Information Technology for Economic and Clinical Health (HITECH) Act of 2009: A federal law that contains major financial incentives for health systems and other providers that incorporate electronic health records. It also addresses use and disclosure of protected health information by health systems and their business associates.

Health Insurance Portability and Accountability Act of 1996 (HIPAA): A federal law that protects patients' privacy and the security of their health information.

Protected health information (PHI): Information about health care status, treatments or conditions, and payments that can be linked to a specific individual.

Shared Savings Program (SSP): A Medicare-sponsored program for accountable care organizations (ACOs), which authorizes an ACO to share in a portion of any savings it achieves by meeting particular quality performance standards.

Questions to Consider

1. What was the driving force behind the origination of antitrust law?
2. How does the government assess market conduct?
3. Describe why law is important to integration
4. Discuss the pros and cons of physicians banding together to become a union.
5. Why is it so important for healthcare managers to consider the medical liability for EHR technology?
6. How should healthcare managers evaluate the HIPAA implications of using patient data within integrated health systems?

REFERENCES

AMA: Meaningful use requirements and penalties discourage physician participation. (2014, May 14). *Modernhealthcare.com*. Retrieved from http://medicaleconomics .modernmedicine.com/medical-economics/news/ama-meaningful-use-requirements-and-penalties-discourage-physician-participate

American College of Radiology response to CMS' request for information regarding "Advancing Interoperability and Health Information Exchange" (CMS-0038-NC; 78 FR 14793). (2013, April 15).

Berlin, B. (n.d.[a]). Retrieved from http://www.ober.com/publications/2611-ftc -defeats-another-hospital-merger

Berlin, B. (n.d.[b]). FTC's success in St. Luke's challenge shows litigation risks to merging hospitals and physicians. Retrieved from http://www.ober.com/publications /2615-ftcs-success-st-lukes-challenge-shows-litigation-risks-merging-hospitals

Burns, L., Goldsmith, J., & Sen, A. (2013). *Advances in health care management*. In Goes, J. (Ed.), *Annual review of health care management: Revisiting the evolution of health systems organization* (Vol. 15, p. 13). Bingley, West Yorkshire, UK: Emerald Publishing.

Centers for Medicare and Medicaid Services. (n.d.). Accountable care organizations. Retrieved from http://www.cms.gov/Medicare/Medicare-Fee-for-Service-Payment/ ACO/

EHR's interoperability should be ONC's priority, vendors say. (2014, May 15). *Medical Economics*. Retrieved from http://medicaleconomics.modernmedicine.com/medical -economics/news/ehr-interoperability-should-be-onc-s-priority-vendors-say

Federal Register, 71(45110), August 8, 2006.

Federal Register, 78(79202, 79204), December 27, 2013.

Federal Register, 78(5566, 5641).

Federal Register, 79(5566, 5695), January 25, 2013. Retrieved from http://www.gpo .gov/fdsys/pkg/CFR-2013-title45-vol1/pdf/CFR-2013-title45-vol1-part164.pdf

Federal Trade Commission & Department of Justice. (2011, October 28). Statements of antitrust enforcement policy regarding accountable care organizations participating in the Medicare Shared Savings Program. *Federal Register, 76*.

Federal Trade Commission (FTC). (n.d.). The antitrust laws. Retrieved from http://www.ftc.gov/tips-advice/competition-guidance/guide-antitrust-laws/antitrust-laws

Flynn, J. (2014, March 26). *Meaningful use: Attestations, audits and appeals.* Presentation at American Health Lawyers Association Institute on Medicare & Medicaid Payment Issues.

Geisinger Health System. (2013). Marcellus Shale research initiative, http://www.geisinger.org/100/pdf/Marcellus_Shale_Research_Case_for_Support_2013.pdf See also Health Information Management Systems. (2013). Retrieved from http://www.himss.org/files/FileDownloads/2013-08_HIMSS%20CBI%20Population%20Health%20TF_Charter_FINAL.pdf The national health association will delve into population health data.

HHS. (n.d.). Retrieved from http://www.hhs.gov/ocr/privacy/hipaa/faq/minimum_necessary/705.html

Jha, S., & Lexa, F. (2014, May). Wicked problems. *Journal of the American College of Radiology, 11,* 437–439.

Kutscher, B. (2014, May 21). Vital signs. *Modern Healthcare.* Retrieved from http://www.modernhealthcare.com/article/20140520/blog/305209996&utm_source=AltURL&utm_medium=email&utm_campaign=mpdaily?AllowView=VXQ0UnpwZTVEL2FlL1RIZ0s4WHRlRU9zalV3ZEErOWI=

Magrabi, F., Ong, M., Runciman, W., & Coiera, E. (2011, October 22). Patient safety problems associated with healthcare information technology: An analysis of adverse events reported to the US Food and Drug Administration. *AMIA Annual Symposium Proceedings Archive.* Retrieved from http://www.ncbi.nlm.nih.gov/pmc/articles/PMC3243129/

Motion to Stay Judgment and Notice of Appeal, filed by St. Luke's Health System, Ltd. and St. Luke's Regional Medical Center, Ltd.; March 4, 2014; D. Idaho (Case No. 1:12-CV-00560-BLW).

National Association of ACOs. (2014, January). A request for improvement in the data partnership between CMS and ACOs. Retrieved from https://www.naacos.com/pdf/NAACOSDataTaskForceJanuary2014.pdf Cited in Barsky, T., Williams, J., & Murphy, D. (2014, March 27). *Medicare and commercial accountable care organizations: A retrospective and prospective view.* Presentation at American Health Lawyers Association Institute of Medicare & Medicaid Payment Issues.

New Mich. network must tread carefully to avoid antitrust scrutiny. (2014, May 16). *Modern Healthcare.com.* Retrieved from http://www.modernhealthcare.com/article/20140516/NEWS/305169965?AllowView=VDl3UXk1TzhDL0tCbkJiYkY0M3hlMGFvVVVZERPTT0=&utm_source=link-20140516-NEWS-305169965&utm_medium=email&utm_campaign=mpdaily&utm_name=top

Office of Inspector General; Final Rule; December 27, 2013.

Oversight of the enforcement of antitrust laws: Hearing before the Subcomm. on Regulatory Reform, Commercial and Antitrust Law of the H. Comm. on the Judiciary, 113th Cong. (2013). Statement of Edith Ramirez, Chairwoman Federal Trade Commission.

Patient Protection and Affordable Care Act, Public Law 111-48, 124 Stat. 119 (2010).

Privacy and security solutions for interoperable health information exchange: A report on state medical record access laws. (2009, August). Retrieved from http://www.healthit.gov/sites/default/files/290-05-0015-state-law-access-report-1.pdf

Robertson, J. (2013, June 25). Digital health records' risks emerge as deaths blamed on systems. *Bloomberg News.com*. Retrieved from http://www.bloomberg.com/news/2013-06-25/digital-health-records-risks-emerge-as-deaths-blamed-on-systems.html

Shields, B., & Hoffman, T. (2012, September). In law we antitrust. *ACR Bulletin*, 28–29.

Shields, B., & Hoffman, T. (2013, April). New HIPAA mandates. *ACR Bulletin*, 28–29.

Shields, B., & Hoffman, T. (2014, April). Court invalidates health system's acquisition of physician group. *ACR Bulletin*.

Showalter, J. S. (2012). *The law of healthcare administration* (6th ed.). Burlington, MA: Jones & Bartlett.

Solove, D. J. (2013, April). HIPAA turns 10: Analyzing the past, present and future impact. *Journal of AHIMA*, 22–28. Retrieved from http://library.ahima.org/xpedio/groups/public/documents/ahima/bok1_050149.hcsp?dDocName=bok1_050149

Statements of Antitrust Enforcement Policy, at 67029.

U.S. Department of Health and Human Services, Office for Civil Rights. (n.d.[a]). Health information privacy: Your medical records. Retrieved from http://www.hhs.gov/ocr/privacy/hipaa/understanding/consumers/medicalrecords.html

U.S. Department of Health and Human Services, Office for Civil Rights. (n.d.[b]). Frequently asked questions. Retrieved from http://www.hhs.gov/ocr/privacy/hipaa/faq/disclosures/266.html

Chapter 7

Managing Human Capital

—Salvador J. Esparza, RN, FACHE, DHA, and Sandra K. Werner

LEARNING OBJECTIVES

- Explain what human capital management is
- Describe how the Affordable Care Act increases the need for effective management of human capital
- Describe the process of human capital planning
- Understand the importance of laws and regulations, especially as they pertain to medical staff human capital relations
- Describe what the value chain is

INTRODUCTION

The U.S. healthcare industry is capital and labor intensive and highly regulated—both factors that complicate efforts to rapidly transform its **human capital**. Confounding this situation, the industry faces **talent management** challenges that demand new and distinctive knowledge, skills, and abilities; a workforce whose members think and operate differently; and health system leaders who are capable of managing in an ever-changing environment characterized by increased pressure to remain financially viable and meet high-performance expectations.

The Patient Protection and Affordable Care Act (ACA), often called simply the **Affordable Care Act (ACA)**, offers extraordinary challenges and opportunities for healthcare human capital. The opportunities present themselves in a variety of delivery system reforms and has expanded access to coverage for millions of Americans. The challenges lie in issues such as certain workforce shortages, fragmented and inconsistent workforce data methods, and mistrust between professional groups.

An innovative approach is required to plan for and manage human capital if the industry is to effectively respond to increased demand for services while also reducing costs and improving quality (Deloitte Center for Health Solutions, 2013). Human capital management (HCM) is an approach to employee staffing that perceives people as assets (human capital) whose current value can be measured and whose future value can be enhanced through investment.

An organization that supports HCM provides its employees with clearly defined and consistently communicated performance expectations. Managers are responsible for rating, rewarding, and holding employees accountable for achieving specific business goals, creating innovation, and supporting continuous improvement.

HEALTHCARE REFORM: HUMAN CAPITAL DEMANDS AND REQUIREMENTS

Healthcare systems both in the United States and globally are struggling to identify the appropriate mix of healthcare professionals necessary to meet the needs of current and future patient populations. Because of current reform efforts that are driving the movement to improve the **quality**, effectiveness, and efficiency of the healthcare system, coupled with national deficit reduction strategies, it is imperative that we take an informed approach to U.S. healthcare human capital management and workforce planning.

Effective planning requires a disciplined approach that includes external and internal analysis, and that is aligned with the mission, vision, values, and strategic objectives of the organization. Human capital or workforce planning is no exception. The external environment informs the health system what it "should do" and can include supply-side influences and demand-side workforce variables. Examples of supply-side influences include labor market factors such as access to the necessary professions, licensure requirements, and portability of skills, as well as structural issues such as aging of the workforce, participation levels, and lifestyle factors. Examples of demand-side issues include changing consumer expectations of health care, shifting utilization patterns, and evolving sociodemographic characteristics, including aging of the population, policy changes that may impact payment systems and pricing, access to insurance, and emerging service-delivery models (Deloitte Center for Health Solutions, 2013).

Internally, the health system must analyze its capabilities—that is, what it "can do"—from a values-based perspective. Any human capital or workforce planning effort must add value to the patient/customer/client in all three phases of the service delivery component: pre-service, point of service, and post-service. This goal cannot be achieved unless the organization's support service component (i.e., human resources, finances, culture, competencies, and leadership) adds value to the service-delivery component (Ginter, Duncan, & Swayne, 2013).

Lastly, the mission, vision, values, and strategic objectives inform the health system regarding what it "wants to do" and provide direction to the organization overall. As organizations make adjustments to their service delivery alternatives, some key provider needs must be determined.

Physicians

The ACA has created both an opportunity and a threat vis-à-vis human capital management and resources. Predictions of workforce need and shortages abound, particularly in the areas of primary care, which is expected to face increasing demand as more individuals obtain insurance coverage through a variety of vehicles (Ollove, 2014). For example, according to the Association of American Medical Colleges (2014), there will be a shortage of 45,000 primary care physicians and 46,000 surgeons and medical specialists by 2020, due in large part to the aging of the population. Specifically, a large number of baby-boomers will have entered or be entering retirement by this year. Another factor that will contribute to the anticipated shortage of healthcare providers is the addition of millions of Americans to the healthcare market, as they will gain access to health insurance via the government exchanges established under the ACA. These predicted workforce shortages are based on the assumption that no changes will occur in the way primary care is delivered today.

Some healthcare policy researchers have indicated that these shortages may be mitigated via alternative, team-based service delivery models such as *patient-centered medical homes* (PCMHs) and *nurse-managed health centers* (NMHCs), which rely on nonphysician, mid-level providers such as advanced practice nurses (APNs), also known as nurse practitioners, and physician assistants (PAs) for provision of primary care services (Auerbach, et al., 2013). According to Auerbach et al. (2013), if PCMHs increased from the current 15% to 45% of primary care providers, and if the NMHCs grew from the current 0.5% to 5%, then predicted primary care physician shortages could be cut in half by 2025 without training a single additional physician. These same researchers estimate that if medical homes could effectively handle 20% more patients—using coordination, technology, or other means—then the predicted shortage could be nearly eradicated.

Other researchers are not as optimistic. Although they generally agree that the infusion of APNs and PAs into the mix of the primary care physician workforce will have a positive impact, they suggest that without an adequate supply of skilled generalists and specialists, the fundamental goals of healthcare reform will be unachievable and the health of the nation may be at risk (Sargen, Hooker, & Cooper, 2011).

Nurses

As a result of the downturn in the U.S. and world economy in the past decade, the status of nursing supply and demand appears to be less certain, with some professional journals having indicated that the predicted nursing shortages have failed to materialize (Salka, 2014). However, the American Association of Colleges of Nursing (2014) contradicts these findings by citing critical nursing shortage indicators. For example, in a report released in 2012 by the Bureau of Labor Statistics, titled *Employment Projections 2010–2020* (United States Department of Labor, 2013), the registered nurse (RN) workforce was identified as the top occupation in terms of job growth through 2020. The number of employed nurses is expected to grow from 2.74 million in 2010 to 3.45 million in 2020, an increase of 26%.

Key findings of a 2013 Clinical Workforce Survey of healthcare executives include a persistent and current shortage of RNs and APNs, which is predicted to be exaggerated by the influx of millions of insured individuals as a result of healthcare reform efforts (AMN Healthcare, 2013). These findings were previously predicted by Juraschek, Zhang, Ranganathan, and Lin in 2012. In a state-by-state analysis conducted by the *American Journal of Medical Quality* (Juraschek, Zhang, Ranganathan, & Lin, 2012), the authors forecast the RN shortage to be most intense in the South and West. These findings are consistent with a 2013 report titled *The U.S. Nursing Workforce: Trends in Supply and Education* from the National Center for Health Workforce Analysis of the Health Resources and Services Administration (HRSA).

Clearly, the quantity of nursing resources will have a profound effect on the service delivery capabilities of healthcare systems and organizations.

Various studies have repeatedly reinforced the association between nurse staffing and patient care outcomes. For example:

- Tubbs-Cooley and colleagues (2013) observed that higher patient loads or assignments are associated with higher hospital readmission rates.
- Esparza and colleagues (2012) found that the more RNs present in providing patient care, the lower the incidence of urinary tract infections and shorten the length of stay.
- Blegan and colleagues (2012) observed that higher nurse staffing levels are associated with fewer deaths, fewer failure-to-rescue incidents, lower rates of infection, and shorter hospital stays.
- Needleman and colleagues (2011) found insufficient nurse staffing is related to higher patient mortality rates.
- Aiken and colleagues (2010) found that lower nurse–patient ratios on medical and surgical units are associated with significantly lower patient mortality rates.

Ironically, although the RN workforce grew by 24% in the past decade, the push to create more APNs may actually contribute to an ongoing shortage of RNs needed to mitigate the shortage of primary care physicians—a difficult balancing act.

Findings related to the other side of the coin—that is, education and quality of RNs—are equally compelling. In 2010, the Institutes of Medicine (IOM) released a landmark report titled *The Future of Nursing,* which called for increasing the proportion of baccalaureate-prepared nurses (BSN) in the nursing workforce to 80%. The rationale for this recommendation was derived from studies conducted over the last 10 years that have demonstrated an association between nurses' academic preparation and better patient outcomes. For example, as far back as 2003, Aiken and colleagues identified a clear link between higher levels of nursing education and surgical patients' survival advantage; studies published in *Health Services Research* (2008) confirmed findings of several prior studies that linked nursing education level and patient outcomes (Friese, Lake, Aiken, Silber, & Sochalski, 2008); and most recently, international studies by Van den Heede et al. (2009) found a significant association between BSN-prepared RNs on cardiac care units and lower in-hospital mortality.

These and other studies related to the nursing workforce have been conducted in earnest for the past 10 years or more, yet very few healthcare system executives are familiar with them and their findings. This disconnect has the effect of creating a situation in which decisions regarding human capital management and workforce planning may be made in somewhat of a vacuum.

Different Roles for Existing Providers

The focus of human capital management has clearly been on the presumed shortages of primary care physicians and registered nurses, yet any workforce planning models that are developed must take into consideration changes in practice patterns, funding and payment mechanisms, provider skills required by new team-based delivery methods, population health risk, nontraditional sources of care access, technology innovations, and ultimately, provider efficiency and effectiveness (Deloitte Center for Health Solutions, 2013). As most healthcare system executives know by now, health reform demands a transition from a focus on volume to a focus on value. This demand has brought about an evolution in traditional positions within the healthcare arena, and the human capital within the organization must be able to adapt to these changing roles.

Recently, many states have introduced legislative initiatives intended to expand or more fully utilize the knowledge, skills, and abilities of nonphysician providers, sometimes referred to as "mid-level" practitioners. The rationale for such action is the realization that there will not be enough primary care physician-providers to handle the large influx of both newly insured patients into the general healthcare market as a result of health reform efforts and the baby-boomer population into the Medicare program. For example, effective January 1, 2014, a law in California gave appropriately trained pharmacists the ability to independently provide additional services such as furnishing routine vaccinations, hormonal contraception, nicotine replacement medications, and some prescription drugs for travelers. In addition, the law created a new "advanced practice pharmacist" role that—with enhanced training and in collaboration with a primary care physician—will be allowed to assess and refer patients; start, stop, and adjust drug therapies; order and interpret drug therapy-related tests; and participate in the evaluation and management of health conditions and diseases (Jacobson, 2013).

Most health system executives are familiar with the various roles that APNs can fill. Nevertheless, with the increasing demand for primary care services, the emphasis is on nurse practitioners and their ability to practice independently. Nurse practitioners are graduate-trained individuals who are able to deliver front-line primary and acute care in community clinics, schools, hospitals, and other settings; they perform such services as diagnosing and treating common acute illnesses and injuries, providing immunizations, conducting physical exams, and managing high blood pressure, diabetes, and other chronic problems. These are the necessary components to successfully run NHMCs. While there is a great deal of resistance from organized medicine against further expansion of the role of nurse practitioners, it is important to know that in at least 45 states, advanced practice nurses can prescribe medications, while 16 states have granted APNs authority to practice independently without physician collaboration or supervision.

Public Health Mindset

Public health is defined as the science of protecting and improving the health of communities through education, promotion of healthy lifestyles, and research for disease and injury prevention. Public health professionals analyze the effect on health of genetics, personal choice, and the environment so as to develop programs that protect the health of populations (Association of Schools & Programs of Public Health, n.d.). Little, if any, knowledge is taught in medical school regarding population health, yet accountable care organizations (ACOs) and patient-centered medical homes require management of a defined population of patients. Management of public health is vastly different from individualized patient care management. For instance, public health focuses on a population, whereas clinical medicine focuses on the individual. Additionally, public health focuses on prevention, whereas medicine focuses on diagnosis and treatment. This differentiation is reinforced by the fact that most undergraduate and graduate medical education and training occur in hospital settings, one patient at a time. However, as distinct as they are, the fields of public health and medicine must work together to improve the health of the population being served.

Similarly, baccalaureate-prepared RNs have a large component of public health nursing as part of their curriculum, yet the majority of nurses take positions in hospitals that do not allow them to apply these concepts in practice. This must fundamentally change if healthcare organizations are to take full advantage of the knowledge and skill set learned by nurses to help improve the health of the populations they serve, and contribute to the quality of care and financial success of the alternative health delivery systems being created as part of health reform initiatives.

Public health professionals will play a key role in the success of health systems by utilizing their knowledge, skills, and abilities to the fullest extent. For large medical groups and alternative health delivery systems, public health experts can be a critical element of organizational success owing to their knowledge of epidemiology, biostatics, health education, and policy development. Human capital management demands that executives critically assess the potential contribution of these professionals for organizational success.

HUMAN CAPITAL PLANNING: ASSETS OR COMMODITIES

Human capital planning is a process used to measure the current value of employees and to project the investment needed to increase the value of those employees. Health system leaders are often quoted as saying, "People are our most important asset." However, in some organizations this statement is viewed cynically by employees because they experience decisions and policies in their daily work life that do not support such a belief. Traditionally, employees in many organizations have often been viewed as commodities—or worse yet, as costs. In economic terms, a commodity is a basic good that is interchangeable with other goods of the same type and is most often used as an input in the production of goods and services. Treating employees as commodities or costs means acquiring employees at the lowest price possible and exchanging them as needed without regard to individual effects. One rather infamous (but unsubstantiated) quote from an accountant is that "People are costs walking about on legs"—a perspective that reinforces the view of people as merely a headcount target for the purposes of minimizing costs.

In the human capital planning model, people are viewed as assets rather than commodities. Indeed, today's health care systems are knowledge-based organizations whose value is driven more by people rather than by any other factors (Mayo, n.d.). In economic terms, an asset is a resource with economic value that helps an organization generate income and, therefore, future value. If we view assets as value-creating entities in an era where knowledge and application are key to achieving competitive advantage, then we unavoidably arrive at the fundamental role people play within our organizations. Health systems often invest in their long-term assets like structures, buildings, and major equipment. Ongoing improvements of those assets are necessary to improve safety, keep up with technology, and ensure those resources are kept in complete working order. Investing in an asset is necessary to increase the value of that asset and to maintain it as a functioning part of the organization. Like other assets, when an organization can plan ahead to invest in its employees, it will increase the value of those employees and the work they are capable of doing.

A Strategic Point of View

Strategic planning is a structured process that guides an organization toward the achievement of its long-term goals. Typical measurements in a strategic planning process are often focused on financial data and the achievement of certain outcomes. Recently, human capital planning has emerged as an important element in the strategic planning process. Health systems are now recognizing that including human capital planning in their strategic plans requires a partnership with the human resources department and other functional areas of the organization; this partnership, in turn, enables the organization to develop an appropriate workforce that provides value to the patient/and thereby achieve the organization's strategic goals and objectives. It is the most effective way that an organization can assess its employees' current knowledge, skills, and abilities (KSA); determine the gaps in those KSAs; and obtain what is required to achieve the necessary outcomes for the success of the organization.

As mentioned previously, effective planning requires a disciplined approach that includes external and internal analysis, and its alignment with the mission, vision, values, and strategic objectives of the organization. This in-depth situation analysis allows health systems to determine the strengths, weaknesses, opportunities, and threats (SWOT) that face them. Human capital planning has the most profound effect on the internal aspects of an organization.

As adapted by Ginter, Duncan, and Swayne (2013), the **value chain** (**Figure 7–1**) provides a strategic thinking map that demonstrates how an organization can initiate and grow the partnership described previously. The value chain uses a systems approach and includes two subsystems—service

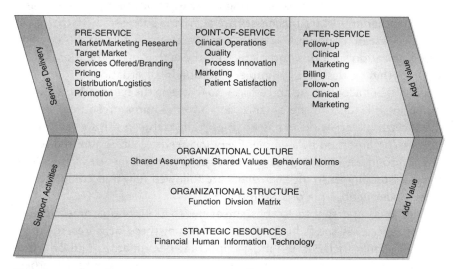

Figure 7–1 The value chain

Reproduced from Ginter, P. M., Duncan, J. W., & Swayne, L. E. (2013). *Strategic management of health care organizations* (7th ed.). San Francisco, CA: Jossey-Bass; and adapted from Porter, M. E. (1985). *Competitive Advantage*. New York, NY: Free Press.

delivery activities and support activities. Service delivery activities include the delivery of pre-service to customers, the delivery of point-of-service care to customers, and the delivery of after-service to customers. The factors that support these activities include organizational culture, organizational structure, technologies, and strategic resources. Human capital planning is part of the support activity system and more specifically is a critical strategic resource that adds value to the customer first and the organization as a whole.

Health system competitive advantage can be realized when human capital resource talent has the following characteristics (Ginter et al., 2013):

- Adds value to the delivery of high-quality patient care
- Is rare among competitors
- Is difficult to duplicate
- Can be sustained in the long run

Human Capital Management Planning Principles

Each specific human capital management plan is an individual process. It requires a careful analysis that will result in a plan designed to meet the identified needs of the organization. There are a few principles to consider that will apply once those needs have been outlined.

First, it is important to adopt best practices, but only as they relate to the organization's business. It is tempting to try to adopt best practices solely because other important businesses are achieving successes with them. Do extensive research and look at each best practice carefully, and then align the organization's actions and plans with those that make the most sense. Not everything is designed for implementation in all situations.

Second, put a lot of time and effort into fostering the partnership between the business leaders of the organization and the human resources teams. The success of the workforce is an important factor in the success of the business/organization as a whole. Everyone needs to be committed to the decision to invest in human capital. This commitment involves a high level of accountability, ensuring that plans are followed fully and completely at all levels throughout the organization.

Third, it is important to establish measures to monitor outcomes, including both successes and failures. While establishing these measures, the organization should focus on the most important key initiatives and prioritize them in order of importance. If the focus includes too many initiatives, there is a possibility of overextending the focus, resulting in multiple failures. In view of the limited resources that face all organizations, targeting those resources to the highest-priority areas will ensure the best success.

Lastly, remember that human capital management is not a one-time event. It is a purposeful commitment to invest in the workforce over time. This ongoing process will require planned updates as changes occur in the environment and in the workplace. Change will happen; it is unavoidable and being prepared to adjust to those changes is the key to success (Weyland, 2010).

Talent Management

The process of attracting, selecting, engaging, developing and retaining employees is known as talent management (Lockwood, 2006). Many industries and businesses stop in this process after the selection of an individual. The thinking is that the individual was hired to do a certain job and that is all that is needed. Continuing on with engaging employees, developing employees, and ensuring they stay in the organization will bring the best success.

Engaging employees involves cultivating the skills that each individual may have. This can be accomplished in many ways—for example, finding ways to include employees in decisions, ensuring employees are empowered to use the skills and knowledge they have, and giving employees a voice so they feel their contributions are valued.

Developing employees involves uncovering the potential for the growth or expansion of the skills, knowledge, and abilities of the workforce. It can be extremely expensive and time consuming to recruit new talent who can supply a missing skill in the organization. It is also possible that as employees retire from the workforce, gaps in the knowledge and skills necessary for the organization to succeed may appear. Planning to grow and develop the current employee base is a cost-effective way to maintain the high level of talent needed. As part of this development effort, an organization can plan for on-site education or can pay or reimburse for education obtained outside the organization. Either way, the investment made in the employees increases their value. Employees are highly valued assets: When investments are made in them, as in any other assets, the value of those assets increases the potential for high performance within the organization.

Retaining employees involves an intentional, purposeful cultivation of the possible talent that may exist in the workforce. This can be accomplished by providing opportunities both for personal growth and for promotion into management once the appropriate knowledge and skills have been mastered. Of course, it is always possible to recruit from outside your organization when filling management positions. However, when the organization can recognize the potential of its existing workforce and purposefully grow and promote that workforce into higher management, the result will be high-performing, empowered employees who are committed to the success of the organization.

Investing in employees by providing them with training and education can be expensive. While putting together talent management programs, it is important to identify the costs of such programs and ensure those costs are included in the budget planning process. Cultivating and developing talent is a purposeful, often expensive investment. However, such an investment will result in a positive return in the form of improved employee retention and increased loyalty and dedication.

COLLABORATIVE CARE: A TEAM SPORT

As healthcare financing moves from volume-based to value-based payment methods, clinicians will be required to work in interprofessional teams, coordinate care across settings, utilize evidence-based practices to improve quality and patient safety, and promote greater efficiency in care delivery (American Hospital Association's Physician Leadership Forum, n.d.). To support these changes, healthcare systems will need to adapt their human capital, acquire new competencies, and work more closely together than ever before.

Today's healthcare delivery processes include numerous exchanges and patient handoffs among multiple clinicians with varying levels of education and training. For example, in a 4-day hospital stay, a patient may interact with 50 different caregivers, including physicians, nurses, technicians, and others (O'Daniel & Rosenstein, 2008), thus making effective team collaboration essential to provision of high-quality care. Unlike multidisciplinary care, where each team member is responsible only for the activities related to his or her own discipline, collaborative care assumes that team members have complementary roles and cooperatively work together, sharing responsibility for problem solving and decision making, to formulate and execute plans for patient care.

According to the American Hospital Association (American Hospital Association's Physician Leadership Forum, n.d.), endeavors around building team-based care can be found in primary care, in inpatient hospital care. and in co-management of hospital service lines at organizations such as AtlantiCare Health System, Brigham and Women's Hospital, and Marquette General Health System. Increasingly, primary care practices are using **collaboration**-based service delivery models such as PCMHs to better serve their defined population.

A *team* is a group of people who are committed to achieving common objectives. The advantages of effective team performance include greater total experience, synergy, higher morale, greater personal retention, and increased flexibility. High-performing team-based care is now widely recognized as a critical tool for constructing a more patient-centered, coordinated, and effective healthcare delivery system (Mitchell et al., 2012). Naylor and colleagues (2010) have defined team-based care as follows:

> The provision of health services to individuals, families, and/or their communities by at least two health providers who work collaboratively with patients and their caregivers—to the extent preferred by each patient—to accomplish shared goals within and across settings to achieve coordinated, high-quality care.

Clinical Team Dynamics

With this information in mind and drawing from best practices of a variety of healthcare organizations, Mitchell and colleagues (2012) established five core principles of team-based care (**Table 7–1**). These principles—shared goals, clear roles, mutual trust, effective communication, and measurable processes and outcomes—form the basis of effective team-based care. Teams hold the potential to improve the value of health care, but to capture the full benefits of team-based care, institutions, organizations, governments, and individuals must invest in the people and processes that lead to improved outcomes. This investment has the potential to significantly transform the delivery of healthcare service in the United States.

Table 7–1 Principles of Team-Based Care

Shared goals: The team—including the patient and, where appropriate, family members or other support persons—works to establish shared goals that reflect patient and family priorities, and can be clearly articulated, understood, and supported by all team members.

Clear roles: There are clear expectations for each team member's functions, responsibilities, and accountabilities, which optimize the team's efficiency and often make it possible for the team to take advantage of division of labor, thereby accomplishing more than the sum of its parts.

Mutual trust: Team members earn each other's trust, creating strong norms of reciprocity and greater opportunities for shared achievement.

Effective communication: The team prioritizes and continuously refines its communication skills. It has consistent channels for candid and complete communication, which are accessed and used by all team members across all settings.

Measurable processes and outcomes: The team agrees on and implements reliable and timely feedback on successes and failures in both the functioning of the team and the achievement of the team's goals. These are used to track and improve performance both immediately and over time.

Modified from Mitchell, P., M. Wynia, R. Golden, B. McNellis, S. Okun, C.E. Webb, V. Rohrbach, and I. Von Kohorn. 2012. Core principles & values of effective team-based health care. Discussion Paper, Institute of Medicine, Washington, DC. www.iom.edu/tbc.

The Quality Imperative

In a 2005 study, the Agency for Healthcare Research and Quality (AHRQ) found evidence that team training improved patient safety and led to reductions in medical errors. AHRQ concluded that effective teams require team members' willingness to collaborate toward a shared goal, have strong communications skills within the team, and devote sufficient organizational resources to sustain the team's work. The researchers identified three types of human capital competencies that are critical for effective **teamwork**:

- *Teamwork-related knowledge:* Understanding the skills and behaviors needed for an effective team and how they are manifested in a team setting.
- *Teamwork-related skills:* The learned capacity to interact with other team members.
- *Teamwork-related attitudes:* Internal states that influence a team member's decision to act in a particular way.

In 2006, AHRQ launched the *TeamSTEPPS* (Team Strategies and Tools to Enhance Performance and Patient Safety) initiative. This program is an evidence-based framework to optimize team performance and teaches clinicians to understand one another's roles and responsibilities, including ways to collaborate to improve quality and patient safety. The training program focuses on four competencies—leadership, situation monitoring, mutual support, and communication—but it also goes beyond general healthcare team needs to include a set of tools for customizing the team performance based on the needs of the team.

LEGAL AND REGULATORY ISSUES

As health systems move increasingly toward employment models that include physicians as part of their human capital management plans, system executives must keep their eye on the regulatory ball to assure they maintain appropriate relationships with their medical staff and avoid any conflicts of interest. Although this topic is covered extensively elsewhere, it is instructive to summarize a few of the key laws and regulations that affect physician relations:

- *Federal Stark laws:* These laws have gone through several revisions, with many provisions and numerous guidelines. They govern physicians in terms of how they refer Medicaid and Medicare patients. The laws are intended to ensure that physicians do not self-refer patients to facilities in which they have personal financial ownership or interest. The Stark Laws are extremely detailed and need to be thoroughly studied to ensure full understanding and compliance.

- *Civil monetary penalties law:* This law authorizes substantial civil money penalties against an entity that engages in any of the following activities: (1) knowingly presenting a claim for services not provided as claimed or that is otherwise false or fraudulent in any way; (2) knowingly giving false or misleading information reasonably expected to influence the decision to discharge a patient; (3) offering or giving remuneration to any beneficiary of a federal healthcare program that is likely to influence the receipt of reimbursable items or services; (4) arranging for reimbursable services with an entity that is excluded from participation from a federal healthcare program; (5) knowingly or willfully soliciting or receiving remuneration for a referral of a federal healthcare program beneficiary; and (6) using a payment intended for a federal healthcare program beneficiary for another use (American Health Lawyers Association, n.d.).
- *Law of intermediate sanctions:* This law describes sanctions that can be imposed on excluded persons and organizations that receive a benefit greater in value than the economic value of the benefit. Examples of things included are benefits from compensation, purchasing or selling of goods or services, and renting or leasing properties.
- *Other laws:* Two more important sets of federal legislation include the federal religious tax exemptions laws, which exempt certain religious non-profit organizations from paying specific taxes, and federal antitrust laws, which are intended to prevent the monopolization of a certain industry.

Additionally, states have passed some laws that supplement or preempt certain federal laws. For example, state laws differ in terms of whether they allow a hospital to directly employ physicians to practice medicine. California and Texas are two states that currently do not allow such employment of physicians in hospitals; their laws restricting this ability are called "corporate practice of medicine" laws. The thought behind these laws is that they free the physician from undue administrative influence as a result of employment status, so that the physician can admit and treat patients based on the needs of each patient and not the needs of the employer. However, new payment models lend themselves more effectively to medical staff employment or virtual employment structures for aligned reimbursement and utilization performance targets.

A key position in any health system to assure the appropriate application of these laws and regulations is the compliance officer. This individual works directly with the executive management and governing body to ensure conformity with laws and regulations like those mentioned previously and to mitigate risk to the organization. Alternatively, health systems may contract with compliance specialists or in-house counsel to review all contracts and agreements regarding the relationship between physicians and the organization.

Is the Board on Board?

Besides its strategic role as a governing body in contributing to the development of a human capital management plan, the healthcare organization's board of directors must be acutely aware of the highly scrutinized relationship between the medical staff and the health system/organization, particularly in relation to the various laws and regulations to which the organization is subject. Regardless, the key to success in physician human capital management is the board's responsibility for creating trust, alignment, and collaboration between the health system and its medical staff. According to a brief written by the Walker Company (2009), a healthcare consulting company, health systems and organizations miss the mark with their physician partners when they fail to understand physicians' differing financial needs and pressures, more narrowly focused practice requirements, meaningful communication regarding interests, and inattention of the board to build a culture of collaboration.

To create an appropriate culture of collaboration, the Center for Healthcare Governance (2003) suggests three things the governing body can do to improve the relationship between health systems and their physicians:

- Move beyond an operational relationship into physician-based partnerships for system-wide services, governance, accountability, and incentives.
- Create an environment that encourages physicians to work on business development, quality of care, customer service, and simplifying internal systems.
- Build an entrepreneurial infrastructure based on collaboration that develops funding for investments, establishes a business strategy, develops new business opportunities, and publishes the results.

In addition, the Walker Company (2009) has identified nine steps the board can take to understand needs, align focus, and build bridges (**Table 7–2**). These board-driven steps are necessary to build trust, open lines of communication, and give physicians a real voice in the strategic direction of the organization.

Managing the Medical Staff

Health system executives know all too well that managing medical staff human capital in a traditional hierarchical manner is ineffective and runs counter to the very core of their training, problem-solving methods, and decision-making style. Nonetheless, organizations must strive to operate efficiently and effectively, while simultaneously engaging this human capital

Table 7–2 Steps for Improving Medical Staff Relations

1. Assess the service area	Gather market information, demographic profiles, economic data, community health status and risk, payer mix, and projected market trends.
2. Develop a medical staff profile	Conduct assessments of medical staff by age, specialty, affiliation, and admission patterns.
3. Obtain physicians' front-line point of view	Survey the medical staff regarding their viewpoints about the hospital, equipment, support needs, and other major issues facing physicians. Can also include ideas or concerns regarding community health issues, competition, and strategy.
4. Obtain nonphysician providers' front-line point of view	Survey the governing body and administrative team regarding similar issues for comparison.
5. Develop analysis of patient outmigration trends	Includes information regarding location by ZIP code and major diagnostic code or diagnostic-related group (DRG).
6. Conduct assessments of community perceptions of care	Survey residents' viewpoints regarding physician and hospital quality of care, availability of resources, barriers to access, and perceptions about unmet needs.
7. Identify gaps in community health needs and medical staff supply	Involve the medical staff in the assessment of the data and information to identify gaps and engage them in developing solutions.
8. Summarize findings and gap analysis	Collaborate to identify opportunities and threats in relation to the mission and vision of the organization, and utilize the information to project future medical staff development needs.
9. Reach consensus	Present information to hospital and medical staff leadership, and governance staff for deeper thinking, discussion, and strategic planning.

Modified from Walker, L. (2009). *Board brief: Building constructive hospital/medical staff relationships and alignment.* The Walker Company. Lake Oswego, OR: Author

in a manner that contributes to organizational success. Physicians, like most highly educated professionals, respond positively when a professional bureaucracy leadership style is adopted (Olden, 2012). Consequently, this is the method by which most organized medical staff structures are run.

In a professional bureaucracy, authority is based on highly specialized education, training, and expertise of professional workers. These professional workers (e.g., physicians) expect a great deal of autonomy without much managerial oversight. At times, this seems counterintuitive to how professional managers (health system executives) are trained and run their organizations. **Table 7–3** compares factors such as authority, decision

Table 7–3 Comparison of Managers and Physicians

Factor	Managers	Physicians
Authority	Bureaucratic, individual, and shared	Professional, individual
Responsibility	Individual and group	Individual
Work relationships	Hierarchical, bureaucratic	Peer, collegial
Allegiance, loyalty	To the organization	To patients, clients
Decisions	Deliberative, uses input from others, based on consensus	Quick, based on own judgment
Resources	Viewed as limited, must be used wisely	Assume resources will be available for patient care
Patient focus	Groups and populations of patients	Usually one patient at a time
Time frame	Ranges from now to years in the future	Now, today, this week, short-term
Dealing with uncertainty	Accepted as part of the job	Expects more certainty
Feedback	Sporadic, vague	Specific, frequent
Responsiveness	To patients, families, physicians, board members, employees, accreditors, other stakeholders	To patients, families, other physicians
Whom they help to survive	Organization	Patients
Compensation	Salary	Usually payment per patient or procedure

Reproduced from Olden, P. C. (2015). *Management of healthcare organizations: An introduction* (2nd ed.). Chicago, IL: Health Administration Press. Information from Gill (1987), Pointer (2006), and Welch (2010).

making, and responsiveness between managers and physicians. It is helpful to know the differences in how managers view certain factors versus how physicians view them for improved effectiveness.

HUMAN CAPITAL MANAGEMENT EFFECTIVENESS

All organizations focus on "the bottom line" in some manner, and healthcare systems are no exception. Every organization must emphasize staying within its budget, keeping costs down, and ensuring positive margins for organizational viability.

In health care, organizations also have a mission to heal, a mission to meet the health needs of their communities with high-quality care, and a mission to do this safely and efficiently. At times, the financial needs of the organization and the need to expend resources to achieve the mission would seem to be in direct conflict. The goal in the financial realm is to lower costs, and the result in achieving mission goals often includes adding costs.

James Shephard (2014), CEO and co-founder of AchieveMission, presents a unique view of the drive to accomplish the financial imperatives and the mission imperatives together through strong human capital management. Essentially, the focus is on "producing more mission for less cost." Investing in objectives that can affect the mission may cost money up front, but the return on that investment will result in lower overall costs for the organization.

Financially, organizations usually have goals that would enhance revenue generation and reduce operating costs. This can be accomplished with proper human capital investments. By recruiting, investing, and growing good leaders who are solid revenue producers, an organization will ensure it has a stable leadership team that will keep revenues coming in. In addition, human capital management can reduce operating costs. In human capital management plans, the priorities of the organization are clearly identified and aligned with the expectations of the leadership teams and the whole workforce. By maintaining this alignment, an organization can ensure that everyone stays focused on the goals, is held accountable for meeting goals, and is held accountable for satisfying strict productivity standards.

Solid human capital management will also increase the stability of the workforce. Creating pipelines, succession plans, and opportunities for advancement in an organization can eliminate the need to recruit outside candidates, which in turn will reduce the possibility of having the unfortunate experience of drastic hiring mistakes. A cohesive, focused workforce that is aligned with the goals and mission of the organization will achieve both the desired financial- and mission-oriented results (Shephard, n.d.).

ESSENTIAL MEASURES OF HUMAN CAPITAL MANAGEMENT

One of the most common mistakes made in establishing appropriate measurements to monitor the effectiveness of human capital management programs is to assume that there is a "best practice" list of measurements that will fit every organization. No such list exists, and the most current opinion is that no list should exist. Starting with a group of measures and working backward to fit them to the organizational goals is not effective at all. If any best practice exists, it is to start with the desired outcomes and establish appropriate, meaningful measurements that will demonstrate success or failure in achieving those outcomes (Becker, Huselid, & Ulrich, 2002).

Even though an exact list of required measures does not exist, three "types" of measurements should be part of any human capital measurement process: process measurements, leadership and organizational measurements, and strategy measurements (Shephard, n.d.).

- *Process measurements:* Examine an improved process to see if it achieved the desired outcome. An example might be a process to bring new employees on board quickly and efficiently, ensuring each employee is made aware of the mission, goals, and history of the organization. The purpose of this process could be to improve retention rates. The measurement is then the retention rate, and whether the process implemented affected the outcome in a positive manner over time.
- *Leadership and organizational measurements:* Assess the impact of improved processes on the leadership of the organization. An example might be a survey given to employees regarding the effectiveness of the leadership team, or comparison over time of positions that have identified successors who are being groomed for, or will soon be ready to take on, new leadership roles.
- *Strategy measurements:* Demonstrate whether an organization was able to achieve the desired goals. Examples of this type of measure might be financial targets or percentage of goals achieved. Strategy measures are the most important measures to demonstrate overall success.

CHAPTER SUMMARY

Human capital management views people as assets rather than as commodities. Like any asset, human capital should add value to customers (patients in the healthcare realm), which in turn adds value to the organization by generating revenues. Because of the rapidly changing healthcare environment and innovative delivery systems being created, shortages of certain types of human capital are projected, necessitating a reevaluation of the current roles of caregivers and development of means to allow them to practice to the fullest extent possible and deliver care in ways that incorporate public health concepts in a collaborative, team-based method.

Human capital planning is a critical element of the health system strategic planning process. Understanding the value chain and this type of planning's role within that chain is essential if the organization is determined to add value to its patient/customer base. Cultivating talent management methods and adhering to HCM planning principles will enhance the health system's chances for success.

Team-based, collaborative care will be the most efficient way to deliver care to a potentially increasing patient/customer base if managed appropriately, being mindful to keep one's eye on the quality imperative for effectiveness.

Governance and executive leadership attention to laws and regulations, especially as they pertain to medical staff human capital relations, is important to minimize risk to the organization and enhance those relationships when appropriate. Leadership will also need to play a critical role in creating an environment where physicians and mid-level primary care providers can work collaboratively to deliver care that is in the best interest of the patient/customer.

Finally, "what gets measured gets managed." Health system executives must find an appropriate balance between their financial imperatives and organizational mission. The use of current and evolving HCM measurements will be essential to ensuring the ongoing viability of the organization.

Key Terms and Concepts

Affordable Care Act (ACA): Formally, the Patient Protection and Affordable Care Act; federal legislation passed in 2010 that guarantees access to healthcare services for more Americans and creates incentives for medical practitioners to focus on better coordination and higher quality services.

Collaboration: In health care, a team-based effort in which team members have complementary roles and cooperatively work together, sharing responsibility for problem solving and decision making, to formulate and execute plans for patient care.

Human capital: People, who are perceived as assets, rather than commodities or costs.

Quality: According to the Institute of Medicine, "the degree to which health services for individuals and populations increase the likelihood of desired health outcomes and are consistent with current professional knowledge."

Strategic planning: A structured process that guides an organization toward the achievement of its long-term goals.

Talent management: An approach to employee staffing that perceives people as assets whose current value can be measured and whose future value can be enhanced through investment.

Teamwork: The outcome of group members' willingness to collaborate toward a shared goal, have strong communications skills within the team, and devote sufficient organizational resources to sustain the team's work.

Value chain: A strategic thinking map that demonstrates how an organization can initiate and grow a partnership with both its employees and its customers. The value chain uses a systems approach and includes two subsystems—service delivery activities and support activities.

Questions to Consider

1. How does the Affordable Care Act increase the need for effective management of human capital?

2. How can healthcare organizations prepare themselves for the pressures of the Affordable Care Act?

3. Describe the best and most efficient model for delivering care?

4. What is the manager's role in creating an environment where physicians and mid-level primary care providers can work together?

5. Explain how current job roles may be changing as a result of the Affordable Care Act.

REFERENCES

Aiken, L. H., Clarke, S. P., Cheung, R. B., Sloane, D. M. & Silber, J. H. (2003). Educational levels of hospital nurses and surgical patient mortality. *Journal of the American Medical Association, 290*(12), 1617–1623.

Aiken, L. H., Sloane, D. M., Cimiotti, J. P., Clarke, S. P., Flynn, L., Seago, J. E.,...Smith, H. L. (2010). Implications of the California nurse staffing mandate for other states. *Health Services Research, 45*(4), 904–921.

American Association of Colleges of Nursing. (2014). *Nursing shortage fact sheet.* Washington, DC: Author.

American Health Lawyers Association. (n.d.). *Health law resources.* Washington, DC: Author.

American Hospital Association's Physician Leadership Forum. (n.d.). http://www.ahaphysicianforum.org/

AMN Healthcare. (2013). *Clinical workforce survey: A national survey of hospital executives examining clinical workforce issues in the era of health reform.* San Diego, CA: Author.

Association of American Medical Colleges. (2014). *2014 Physician specialty data book.* Washington, DC: Center for Workforce Studies.

Association of Schools & Programs of Public Health (ASPPH). (n.d.). http://www.aspph.org/discover/

Auerbach, D. I., Chen, P. G., Friedberg, M. W., Reid, R. O., Lau, C., & Mehrotro, A. (2013). Nurse-managed health centers and patient-centered medical homes could mitigate expected primary care physicians shortage. *Health Affairs, 32*(11), 1933–1941.

Becker, B., Huselid, M., & Ulrich, D. (2002). Six key principles for measuring human capital performance in your organization. http://mgt.buffalo.edu/departments/ohr/becker/Publications/Six%20Key%20Principles.pdf

Blegen, M. A., Goode, C. J., Park, S. H., Vaughn, T., & Spetz, J. (2013). Baccalaureate education in nursing and patient outcomes. *Journal of Nursing Administration*, *43*(2), 89–94. doi: 10.1097/NNA.0b013e31827f2028

Center for Healthcare Governance. (2003). *Strategic resource allocation: The board's critical role*. Chicago, IL: Author.

Deloitte Center for Health Solutions. (2013). *The complexities of national health care workforce planning: A review of current data and methodologies and recommendations for future studies*. Washington, DC: Author.

Esparza, S. J., Zoller, J. S., Weatherby White, A., & Highfield, M. E. F. (2012). Nurse staffing and skill mix patterns: Are there differences in outcomes? *Journal of Healthcare Risk Management*, *31*(3), 14–23.

Friese, C. R., Lake, E. T., Aiken, L. H., Silber, J. H., & Sochalski, J. (2008). Hospital nurse practice environments and outcomes for surgical oncology patients. *Health Services Research, 43*(4), 1145–1163.

Ginter, P. M., Duncan, J. W., & Swayne, L. E. (2013). *Strategic management of health care organizations* (7th ed.). San Francisco, CA: Jossey-Bass.

Institute of Medicine. (2010). *The future of nursing*. Washington, DC: Author.

Jacobson, D. (2013). New law could expand role of pharmacists as health care providers. The School of Pharmacy. The Regents of the University of California. http://pharmacy.ucsf.edu/news/2013/11/new-law-could-expand-role-pharmacists-health-care-providers

Juraschek, S. P., Zhang, X., Ranganathan, V., & Lin, V. W. (2012). United States registered nurse workforce report card and shortage forecast. *American Journal of Medical Quality, 27*(3), 241–249.

Lockwood, N. R. (2006). *Talent management: Driver for Organizational Success*. Alexandria, VA: Society for Human Resource Management.

Mayo, A. (n.d.). The human value of the enterprise. *QFinance*. http://www.qfinance.com/human-and-intellectual-capital-best-practice/the-human-value-of-the-enterprise?full

Mitchell, P., Wynia, M., Golden, R., McNellis, B., Okun, S., Webb, E. C., ... Von Kohorn, I. (2012). *Core principles and values of effective team-based health care*. Washington, DC: Institute of Medicine.

National Center for Health Workforce Analysis. (2013). *The U.S. nursing workforce: Trends in supply and education*. Health Resources and Services Administration, Bureau of Health Professions. Washington, DC: Author.

Needleman, J., Buerhaus, P., Pankratz, V. S., Leibson, C. L., Stevens, S. R., & Harris, M. (2011). Nurse staffing and inpatient hospital mortality. *New England Journal of Medicine, 364*, 1037–1045. doi: 10.1056/NEJMsa1001025

O'Daniel, M., & Rosenstein, A. H. (2008). Professional communication and team collaboration. In R. G. Hughes (Ed.), *Patient safety and quality: An evidence-based handbook for nurses* (Vol. 2, pp. 271–284). Washington, DC: Agency for Healthcare Research and Quality.

Olden, P. C. (2012). *Management of healthcare organizations: An introduction*. Chicago, IL: Health Administration Press.

Ollove, M. (2014, January 3). Are there enough doctors for the newly insured? *Kaiser Health News*. http://kaiserhealthnews.org/news/doctor-shortage-primary-care-specialist/

Salka, S. (2014, March 5). Healthcare staff shortages? *AMN Healthcare*. https://www.amnhealthcare.com/industry-research/2147484673/1033/

Sargen, M., Hooker, R. S., & Cooper, R. A. (2011). Gaps in the supply of physicians, advanced practice nurses, and physician assistants. *Journal of the American College of Surgeons, 212*(6), 991–999.

Shephard, J. (2014). *Measuring the ROI of human capital management*. Boston, MA: Bridgespan Group. http://www.bridgespan.org/Publications-and-Tools/Leadership-Effectiveness/Lead-and-Manage-Well/Measuring-the-ROI-of-Human-Capital-Management.aspx

Tubbs-Cooley, H. L., Cimiotti, J. P., Silber, J. H., Sloane, D. M., & Aiken, L. H. (2013, May 7). An observational study of nurse staffing ratios and hospital readmission among children admitted for common conditions. *BMJ Quality & Safety*. [Epub ahead of print.] doi: 10.1136/bmjqs-2012-001610

U.S. Department of Labor, Bureau of Labor Statistics. (2013). Employment by major occupational group, 2012 and projected 2022. http://www.bls.gov/news.release/ecopro.t06.htm

Van den Heede, K., Lesaffreb, E., Diyab, L., Vleugelsa, A., Clarke, S. P., Aiken, L. H., & Sermuesa, W. (2009). The relationship between inpatient cardiac surgery mortality and nurse numbers and educational level: Analysis of administrative data. *International Journal of Nursing Studies, 46*(6), 796–803.

Walker Company. (2009). *Board brief: Building constructive hospital/medical staff relationships and alignment*. Lake Oswego, OR: Author.

Weyland, T. (2010). *10 principles for building an effective human capital plan*. San Leandro, CA: TriNet Group.

Chapter 8

The Role of Leadership in Healthcare Sustainability

—Carrie Rich, Seema Wadhwa, and Knox Singleton

LEARNING OBJECTIVES

- Understand what is healthcare sustainability
- Understand why healthcare leaders should care about sustainability
- Identify sustainability stakeholders and how their value systems align with sustainability
- Clarify the role of healthcare leader in creating and supporting sustainability programs

INTRODUCTION

Healthcare providers have the unique responsibility to "First do no harm," which is inextricably linked to being responsible stewards of the environment and surrounding communities. Leadership responsibility for environmentally sustainable healthcare is like spinach or broccoli— it is green, healthy, and the right thing to do. But just because leadership is responsible for healthy healing environments does not guarantee that outcome. This chapter moves beyond leadership responsibility to leadership commitment, meaning a personal involvement and strategic business investment.

Sustainability fosters the basic healthcare mission to provide safe, quality, compassionate, and cost-effective care resulting in patient health and well-being. Champions of healthcare sustainability call for treatment centers built without materials linked to cancer, cleaning systems free of chemicals that trigger asthma, and hospitals with healthy food, fresh air, and sunlight. **Sustainable care** means patient-centered care with the overarching objective that not only should the process contribute to the health of the patient, but also the setting where that care takes place, both in the healthcare facility and in the wider community. Absence of sustainability as a traditional component of business practice is incongruous with the mission of health care. Healthcare sustainability is a long-term solution that enhances the **triple bottom line** mission of ensuring fiscally, socially, and environmentally responsible operations (Rich, Singlton, & Wadhwa, 2013).

A hospital does not operate in isolation and is, in fact, dependent on many constituencies for its success. To simplify this concept, social entrepreneurs use the term "triple bottom line" to describe the business mission—to support people, the planet, and profit. A balance of economic viability, social responsibility, and environmentally sound practices is essential for healthcare sustainability success as measured by competitive advantage, allowing hospitals to compete more effectively, serve patients better, and build a stronger business.

Once the importance of sustainability in health care is established, the question then emerges: What is the role of a healthcare executive leader in creating value for an environmental sustainability program?

UNPRECEDENTED OPPORTUNITY

The healthcare industry is a significant consumer of resources and energy, and outpaces most other industries in waste production and associated hazards. The impacts of these practices yield a large, infrequently measured environmental footprint.

Until now, this concept has been too far "upstream" for us to consider placing it in the picture. However, the recent focus on healthcare delivery had made it abundantly apparent that the healthcare sector has both an opportunity and a responsibility to address environmental health realities by modifying practices and modeling behavior in ways that demonstrate an understanding of ecological health systems as related to public health and healthcare delivery systems. Ecological health embraces the deeply fundamental complex interrelationships that collectively influence human and environmental health.

Healthcare systems that embrace sustainability can produce lower long-term operational costs due to improved maintenance systems as well as recruiting and staff retention advantages. "**Going green**" is shifting from a moral prerogative to a business proposition, offering healthcare organizations the potential to realize cost savings in the form of "green dividends." Indeed, many healthcare leaders are responding to societal demands by looking for ways to address environmental concerns. Executive leadership has an unprecedented opportunity to be socially and fiscally responsible in ways that address environmental concerns. This five-step guide outlines the role of leadership in healthcare sustainability.

STEP 1: COMMIT

Many competing priorities can be found within healthcare organizations, but sustainability has not traditionally been included on this list. This section outlines reasons why sustainability is drawing more attention at healthcare organizations throughout the United States.

The sustainability agenda is here to stay. The role of the healthcare executive in sustainability is to emphasize the value of such an initiative by visibly demonstrating commitment to it. This commitment signals support for the organization in achieving its sustainability goals. Engaging employees and holding leadership accountable are key tactics for achieving culture change. Employee pressure, staff retention, and workforce engagement are key issues for executives in an already strained economic and political setting. Environmental sustainability is one method to engage the workforce, especially younger colleagues. Other drivers of environmental sustainability programs include strategies for operational cost containment and improved public relations. Healthcare sustainability offers an opportunity to "do good while doing well."

Beyond doing good, leadership is responsible for doing what needs to be done. Accreditation agencies, such as The Joint Commission, continue to develop and hold healthcare delivery systems accountable for meeting environmental sustainability standards. Violation of compliance with environmental regulations, such as those established by the Environmental Protection Agency (EPA), can lead to both heavy fines and negative media attention. Industry leaders, such as the American Hospital Association (AHA), are raising awareness about environmental stewardship through development of sustainability tools and an industry roadmap.

The ultimate sustainability program is not one that has prescribed elements of "being green," but rather one that creates a baseline **culture of sustainability**. Healthcare sustainability cannot be managed in the isolated silo of an environmental initiative; it plays a strategic role across departments and management directives. Executives have a unique vantage point for providing sustainability oversight, as this issue cuts across all aspects of the healthcare organization's business. Healthcare sustainability is everyone's responsibility, but executive leaders are especially responsible for translating the strategy from the board room to the front lines.

STEP 2: EDUCATE THE BOARD OF DIRECTORS

Healthcare leadership plays a key role in educating the board of directors. Upon recognizing the importance of healthcare sustainability to organizational success, the executive's next step is to translate this priority to terms that the board of directors will appreciate. The wise healthcare leader equips the board with the tools and information necessary to monitor a financially executable sustainability strategy. Metrics used to document success of sustainability strategies include the following:

- Financial savings (e.g., money saved from diverted medical waste)
- Community benefits (e.g., local landscape preservation)
- Environmental benefits (e.g., kilowatts of energy saved)

Establishment and review of corporate sustainability goals and indicators for tracking progress should be routine components of every healthcare board's agenda.

Case Study: Board Presentation

The sustainability program has been in place for a few years. The program has achieved well-established successes, including environmental benefits and cost savings. Although it had taken some time to gain support from all stakeholders, there is now great support for the program from the leadership team in the organization.

You have been given the opportunity to present information on the current state of the program to the board of directors. You are excited to share program successes. The board is made up of diverse leaders from the community. In researching the board members, you realize they are also members of the executive team for a manufacturing plant that has been violating emission standards and negatively impacting air quality. You had been preparing to share a study that highlighted impacts on increased asthma rates related to poor air quality owing to industrial emissions. How do you handle the content of the presentation?

STEP 3: CONVENE A GREEN TEAM

The purpose of a **Green Team** is to engage leadership across diverse departments, ensuring that sustainability initiatives permeate the entire organizational culture. Stakeholders assume accountability of Green Team initiatives for various reasons. While individual members may not initially embrace sustainability programs wholeheartedly, the Green Team is responsible for implementing the executive vision.

Motivators for Green Team participation may include any of the following factors:

- Opportunity to demonstrate leadership or act as a departmental liaison
- Personal commitment and passion
- Increase fiscal savings opportunity associated with sustainability
- Gain access to internal funding for sustainability projects
- No choice—assigned role

With an understanding of the motivators to be part of the Green Team, the question arises about which departments are ideally positioned to facilitate sustainability stewardship. The following leadership domains are key conduits of the sustainability vision:

- Administration
- Communications
- Community Affairs
- Design and Construction
- Engineering
- Environmental Services
- Facility Management
- Finance
- Food Services
- Materials Management
- Strategic Planning

Aligning strategic opportunities with key stakeholders creates opportunity for both horizontal and vertical integration of sustainability within an organization.

Sustainability initiatives are often deeply rooted in employees' interests in supporting a socially responsible workplace. In fact, engaging employees in sustainability initiatives may be used as an employee retention technique. This opportunity is especially significant in the healthcare setting, where workers will be scarce for the foreseeable future; effective recruitment and retention will continue to be critical to the success of healthcare systems.

For young professionals especially, but not exclusively, the environment is of particular interest. An employer's stance vis-á-vis earth-friendly policies and practices can be a satisfier for these workers—or just the opposite.

Hire a Sustainability Officer

Given the many competing priorities that healthcare leaders must address on a daily basis, sustainability initiatives need to be led by a dedicated resource. While Green Team leaders may be accountable for their individual departments, a sustainability officer often acts as the shepherd for the organization's comprehensive sustainability program. For Green Team members, sustainability is one more item on the to-do list. For the sustainability officer, the overall success of the sustainability vision is top priority.

Practice Greenhealth is a leading national healthcare sustainability nonprofit organization that emphasizes the importance of a sustainability officer. Likewise, leading healthcare delivery systems across the United States are implementing the role of a sustainability officer as part of their corporate strategic plans. Areas of focus for the sustainability officer are addressed next.

Energy Management

The healthcare industry currently ranks second among U.S. industry sectors in terms of energy consumption. Consequently, any sustainability program adopted by a healthcare organization should include energy conservation and energy reduction among its principal elements. While the triple bottom line of fiscally, socially, and environmentally sound operations applies to all aspects of sustainability programs, fiscal responsibility in terms of cost cutting and sustainable energy programs operate particularly well together. The financial benefits of reducing energy use by healthcare facilities include improved profitability, lower operational and maintenance costs, and reduced impact of changing energy prices. Other benefits include improved environmental performance, a reduced carbon footprint, healthier work environments, and healthier communities.

Reducing energy usage and energy waste can be achieved by streamlining processes within healthcare facilities and across the healthcare organization. Simple actions like turning off lights, unplugging unused electronics, and reducing energy waste through other common-sense methods have actual effects when measured using a tool like the Energy Use Index (EUI), which measures the amount of energy used by a building per square foot on an annual basis. The EUI can be a tool for identifying where opportunities exist to improve energy efficiency and establish measurable goals for energy use reduction. The EUI can also be a critical tool for communicating the institution's energy goals to shareholders and the public.

To implement simple actions like the ones described here on a meaningful scale, it is essential that employees be educated and engaged in the program and results. Communicating meaningful goals is one way to ensure **employee engagement** and, in turn, the success of the program.

Energy management can be dependent on the condition of the facilities used, and more significant energy conservation efforts may require financial outlays to update facilities to become more sophisticated and energy efficient. However, the long-term results of this investment, in both financial and environmental returns, can be significant. Additionally, organizations and institutions subject themselves to reputational and brand-related risks when they demonstrate an excess of energy wastage. Some states track energy usage by institution, and appearing among the highest leaders in terms of energy consumption may tarnish the name of the institution in the view of an increasingly energy-conscious public.

Water Management

Healthcare organizations and healthcare leaders share a professional imperative to work for the betterment of their communities. Not-for-profit hospitals and care organizations in the United States operate under a community charter through which the hospitals receive tax benefits in exchange for promoting the community's health. Within communities, water is a finite, essential resource. Healthcare organizations such as hospitals have a responsibility to ensure that they are not using excess water at the expense of the larger community, and particularly to ensure that they are not polluting or contaminating the available potable water.

Hospitals and other healthcare facilities use a great deal of water owing to the 24/7 nature of their operations. Water prices have gone up significantly in the last five years, and energy usage corresponds to water usage: The more water used, the more energy needed for storage, treatment, transportation, heating, and cooling. Thus, the more water used by a facility, the greater that facility's costs for water and associated energy.

There are many opportunities for healthcare organizations to manage water processes in a sustainable manner. Water contamination can be reduced by instituting processes to dispose of pharmaceutical and other waste according to EPA standards and by using technologies such as permeable pacers, bioswales, and rain gardens. Water can be conserved by updating operations and equipment, such as installing low-flow fixtures and irrigation systems and/or promoting closed-loop HVAC systems that eliminate once-through water use. Alternative water sources can also be utilized for nonpotable purposes. Such sources include rainwater and storm water harvesting, air conditioner condensate, foundation drain water, and treated wastewater (if there is an on-site system). To maximize the effect of these programs, the healthcare organization's leadership must engage the employees, patients, and visitors in a sustained, communal effort toward water sustainability by educating them about the importance of *water management* and the steps the healthcare organization is taking, and by encouraging all parties to act as responsible water stewards within the organization's facilities.

Waste Management

Waste management is one of the core elements of a sustainability program, and affects all three bottom lines—fiscal, social, and environmental. Waste management involves both correctly utilizing the waste created by a healthcare institution and improving institution processes, which reduces the amount of waste generated as a preventive measure. Improved waste management and leaner processes can boost efficiency, lower operating costs, and benefit both the community and the environment. Waste reduction strategies often act as a highly visible and collaborative starting point for implementing sustainability programs, bringing all members of the organization together, from the board of directors to the front-line employees, to innovate, implement, and operate waste management and process improvements.

A number of factors favor programs to ensure effective waste management, including financial considerations, federal regulation, public pressure, and institutional image. Medical waste is federally regulated, and hospitals lose money from the costs associated with creating and disposing of medical waste in an approved manner. In short, a healthcare organization that reduces its physical waste stream (particularly regulated waste) reduces its waste disposal costs.

Wasting less intrinsically means saving more (Rich & Wadhwa, 2010). The combination of waste reduction and prevention strategies saves millions of dollars at healthcare organizations across the United States. The increased public interest in environmentally sound practices and sustainability also increases expectations for medical organizations to have visible signs of waste management, such as recycling. Healthcare leaders who fail to implement these signs and programs run the risk of creating an unfavorable public image of the organization.

Waste management links sustainability goals to business values and fiscal aims in tangible ways. There can be questions, however, regarding how to implement a sustainability or waste management system. The most effective systems function across departments and facilities and encompass the entire organization and its functionalities, from beginning to end. Outside vendors and third parties may be hired to design a waste management program for the healthcare organization. The success of the program depends on the ability of the leadership to convey the importance of the new measures, and the degree to which employees—physicians, nurses, staff, and others—actively implement the sustainability programs as they go about their daily work. An organization can increase the effectiveness of its sustainability efforts by making it easy for employees and those on the ground to act on sustainability ideas, and to experiment with and implement new approaches to waste management.

Case Study: Waste Management

You have been learning about the various types of waste in healthcare facilities. Some of these waste streams include regulated medical waste, solid waste, recycling, sharps, hazardous waste, chemotherapeutic waste, and radioactive waste, among others. You have been working with your team to benchmark and understand how much of each type of waste is produced in your organization. In this process, you have discovered that each waste stream has different disposal costs as well as varying degrees of environment impact.

During a waste audit, you learn how the different waste types are managed. Regulated medical waste is generally treated by autoclaving—a process that includes applying steam for sterilization, physically shredding the waste, and sending the waste to specially designated landfills. Hazardous waste is treated by using specially designated incinerators with specific emission controls and adding the ash product to concrete for solid waste disposal in designated landfills.

During the audit, it was discovered that some of your organization's waste is being discarded as regulated medical waste rather than hazardous waste. While this is completely legal, best management practices recommend treating this waste as hazardous waste to decrease environmental impacts. The governing laws—both federal and state—allow this practice. Additionally, managing certain waste products as regulated medical waste rather than hazardous waste is less costly.

Your discoveries as a result of the audit highlight opportunities for better environmental management of some of the organization's waste. However, the organization is currently engaged in many initiatives focused on cutting costs. The additional expense for better environmental disposal is not accounted for in the budget. What are your recommendations?

Alternative Transportation

Transportation is an area where sustainability ventures have a direct impact on the health of employees and the community. Adopting or encouraging **alternative transportation** systems can improve employee engagement, increase energy efficiency and reduce costs, reduce air pollution (which brings significant health benefits), reduce supply chain and waste disposal costs, and improve the image and connectivity of the institution within the community.

Transportation concerns for healthcare organizations center on employee recruitment and retention, the trend toward transitioning patients to home and ambulatory care (which involves more services located in the home or community, instead of at the hospital), pollution and health concerns, and image and reputation within the community. Organizations with sustainable transportation systems can promote commuting alternatives, including providing shuttle options, improving bike racks, and making public transit more attractive by subsidizing costs. They can also create an infrastructure geared toward sustainable transportation by updating technology used in garages, building greener facilities, and leveraging parking-related programs.

Here are a few tips to facilitate the efficacy of sustainable transportation systems:

- Make it easy for employees and visitors to engage in alternative or sustainable transportation programs.
- Make a concerted effort to engage employees in taking ownership of alternative transportation options.
- Highlight public and alternative transportation such as biking and walking.

Each of these sustainable transportation alternatives accrue benefits to the healthcare organization by encouraging increased exercise among employees, which can significantly reduce the organization's health benefit costs. Simply put, active employees are more likely to be engaged, healthy employees.

Sustainable transportation initiatives involve more than just employee and visitor transportation, however. Supply chain transportation (getting supplies to the facilities and sending waste out) is an often overlooked part of an overarching sustainable transportation policy. Sustainable supply chain transportation can be achieved by updating the organization's fleet of vehicles to encourage the use of fuel-efficient or green vehicles. Labeling these vehicles to make the public and employees aware of their environmental benefits can have a positive impact on the image of the healthcare organization. The combination of encouraging alternative transportation, updating infrastructure, and using green vehicles can positively impact air quality, thereby providing health and environmental benefits to the community and employees alike.

Sustainable Foods

The healthcare industry is currently undergoing a shift in mission—instead of treating people only when they go to the hospital, the emerging goal is preventive, to contribute to the health and well-being of individuals so that they do not have to go to the hospital. This focus on health instead of illness overlaps strongly with the sustainability goals of medical organizations; both focus on long-term problem prevention and improved well-being.

Central to this focus on well-being is the role of **sustainable foods** within healthcare organizations. Research shows—and the public is increasingly aware—that nutrition is intrinsically linked to health. Curing a patient of an illness and then providing him or her with high-calorie, high-fat, high-sugar foods is counterproductive. Implementing a sustainable food initiative within healthcare organizations is one of the most effective health promotion tactics that such organizations can take.

Healthy, sustainable food in healthcare settings is based on a structure of purchasing local food grown and harvested in a sustainable manner with verified sourcing, then providing this food to patients, staff, and visitors. Local, fresh foods have the double benefit of lowering transportation costs (as compared to transportation costs of foods grown far away) and retaining more nutrients due to decreased travel and storage time. Implementing a sustainable food program within a hospital or similar institution depends on four things: food sourcing; connecting the use of sustainable food to the organization's core mission of health; educating patients, visitors, and caregivers on the importance of sustainable foods; and offering healthy, sustainable foods as the most attractive option in the cafeteria or other food-related locations within the organization's facilities.

In addition to increasing the well-being and health of patients, visitors, and caregivers, implementing a sustainable foods program can have a positive effect on patient and public perception of the institution. Food quality impacts patient health and perceived quality of care, and an institution that offers sustainable meals will benefit from the increased public awareness of the importance of healthy foods. Additionally, the community will benefit from the organization buying local produce, as the income generated goes into the local economy.

Environmentally Preferable Purchasing

Environmentally preferable purchasing (EPP) is the procurement of products and services that, throughout the entirety of the **product or service life cycle**, do not cause harm to the environment, patients, employees, or community, or cause less harm than the alternatives. This approach is an essential element of any sustainability program, as it acts to prevent harmful chemicals, products, and waste from entering the healthcare facility and community, thereby addressing the need to prevent environmental and health problems instead of dealing with them as they arise.

Environmentally preferable purchasing works via two avenues:- purchasing products that are environmentally sound throughout the entirety of their life cycle, and examining the **EPP profile** of suppliers. Purchasing environmentally sound materials begins with a **life-cycle analysis** of the products, which assesses the impact that the products have at every step along the supply chain. It is important that every step is examined, as many products are made abroad and may be subject to less stringent regulations in their originating countries than those manufactured domestically. Examining the EPP profile of suppliers is similar to running a sustainability background check. Buying from the more EPP-conscious suppliers is a significant step toward improving the healthcare organization's EPP profile. It is also possible to work with suppliers when negotiating new contracts or working within existing contracts to insert language and requirements regarding sustainability purchasing decisions.

EPP programs can begin by evaluating current practices across the organization, which allows the organization to identify areas where EPP programs and goals can be developed and implemented. Developing an EPP program based on the results of the evaluation allows healthcare organizations to target the low-hanging fruit, and expand the EPP program from there. It is important to maintain transparency in the EPP program and policies that are developed—transparency allows those involved to find areas for improvement and continually strive for greater success in the EPP program.

Cost is an often-cited concern when developing EPP programs. Short-term savings goals and sustainability often operate at cross-purposes. When developing and implementing an EPP program, however, a healthcare organization must make the decision to pursue long-term financial and health goals. All too often, short-term fixes are made at the expense of longer-term success. By comparison, operating according to a mission of wellness and long-term organizational sustainability and financial well-being will pay continual dividends that overshadow the short-term savings that could accrue from ignoring the potential of EPP programs.

Green Construction

A trend that is gaining steam both nationally and globally is **green construction**—that is, designing, building, and retrofitting sustainable and environmentally friendly facilities. Sustainable facilities are environmentally, socially, and financially responsible in the long term.

One of the most widely recognized sustainable building systems is **Leadership in Energy and Environmental Design (LEED)**, an international certification program for green buildings. The United States Green Building Council (the entity responsible for LEED standards) also designed LEED for Healthcare, which addresses sustainable design related to the specific needs of the healthcare industry. Building or renovating healthcare facilities according to LEED standards (or the standards of other sustainable building systems) is an important part of a broader sustainability program that reduces operational costs over the long term by conserving energy and water and reducing waste, reducing individual exposure to unsafe chemicals, improving patient outcomes and employee performance and satisfaction, and reducing the environmental footprint of the facility.

Among the many benefits of green construction is brand enhancement. In a competitive market, operating sustainable (particularly LEED certified) facilities can set a healthcare organization apart in a positive way and add value to its portfolio. Operating a green facility is a strong way to show that sustainability is one of the organization's values. The medium is the message.

Increased upfront costs are often cited as concerns when building or retrofitting greener facilities. In reality, not only will greener builds have lower operational costs that will at least partly offset the increased initial price, but the total value of the green building is also significantly higher than that of a nonsustainable building. When assessing value, one must include positive effects on productivity, employee satisfaction, patient wellness, brand value, and other intangibles in addition to the financial cost–benefit analysis. All of these items, taken collectively, indicate that sustainable facilities add significant value to the organization and its overall sustainability program.

Case Study: Reporting

Each year your team has produced a report to the community about your organization's sustainability efforts. This report, which highlights data on current performance, provides transparency for the community about the organization's efforts to be environmentally sustainable. Some of the information contained in the report includes quantities of waste, energy usage, water usage, dollars spent on local food, and other indicators of sustainability success.

Your department has been producing this report for a number of years. The data from the report are also used to develop internal and external goals. In addition, the public relations team highlights this report to draw media attention to the organization's success.

Historically, the publication of the sustainability report has been a shining moment showing continual success and improvement related to the organization's sustainability efforts. As the program has matured, the progress rate has slowed but still shows an increase each year. This last year was especially challenging to get the organization's employees to focus on sustainability due to the rollout of a new electronic health record (EHR). Looking at the data, the introduction of the EHR has been reflected in an increase in energy usage.

Knowing that the report to the community receives significant attention internally and externally, how do you address the indicators that have shown regression in sustainability success?

Case Study: Inova Health System

In 2008, Inova Health System hired a sustainability officer. In concert with Green Team participation and executive leadership, Inova demonstrated the return on investment for the sustainability program shown in **Table 8–1**.

Now the sustainability officer seeks to grow the division's efforts by hiring another staff member. How would you use the data provided to make a case for growing the sustainability team? Recognizing that sustainability efforts have impact across the healthcare organization, who on the leadership team would you, as the sustainability officer, pitch to for the purpose of gaining support to grow the sustainability team?

Table 8–1 Inova Health System: Returns from Sustainability Program

Area of Focus	Example Strategy	Environmental Benefit	Social Benefit	Fiscal Benefit
Energy management	Demand load response shedding	Curtailing energy use on high-energy days	Reduction in carbon footprint	More than $15,000 for a hospital
Water usage reduction	Sterilization equipment	1.2 million gallons saved annually	Water conservation	More than $60,000 annually
Waste management	Waste segregation through education	More than 750 tons recycled in 2009	Avoided use of landfills	More than $100,000 saved annually through recycling efforts
Alternative transportation	Employee fringe benefits	Reduction in carbon emissions from transportation	Reduction in carbon footprint and traffic impacts	Up to $2,200 pretax spending annually for employees partaking in the program
Sustainable foods	Community-supported agriculture	Reduction in carbon emissions from transportation	Supporting the local economy	More than $13,000 directly supporting a local farm from one hospital
Environmentally preferable purchasing (EPP)	Changed office supply products to environmentally preferable alternatives	Reduction in virgin material content use	More than 3,500 trees saved through use of recycled-content paper	$27,000 saved in 2009
Green construction	Lighting retrofits	Reduction in energy demand	Reduction in carbon footprint	Pending savings of $12,000 at a facility

STEP 4: CREATE A SUSTAINABLE CULTURE

When it is ingrained in people to waste less, it becomes an intrinsic preference to save more. Creating a culture of sustainability, therefore, is one of the most economical starting points for developing a sustainable workplace.

Executive involvement in the sustainability program highlights to employees that sustainability is an organizational value. Knowing the executive team cares about sustainability sends an unspoken message to employees that they, too, can and should embrace sustainability. Employees are more likely to get involved when they witness executive leadership in support of the sustainability program. This top-down, bottom-up approach is critical to the success of the sustainability program from the standpoint of cultural adoption. The executive team empowers employee leadership by encouraging employees to explore how to integrate sustainability into business strategy.

The more employees who support the organization's sustainability program, the more likely the organization will prioritize sustainability as a core element of its cultural identity moving forward. Awareness surrounding sustainable operations can be leveraged to entice employee behavior change. Behavior change in healthcare sustainability is directly linked to resource conservation; health systems, in turn, can use behavior change as a cost savings tool.

STEP 5: CELEBRATE SUCCESS

For sustainability to be an integral component of corporate DNA, sustainability success must be showcased. Recognition of sustainability success helps foster behavior change throughout the organization, not just where the success originated. Conversely, when colleagues do not share success stories, neither employees nor the public understands the importance of sustainability as a preeminent organizational value. Celebrating success maximizes opportunities to effect the greatest change.

Success stories are most prominent and powerful, both internally and externally, when they are showcased and endorsed by executive leadership. Executive celebration of success stories validates sustainability as an important organizational value.

CONCLUSION

This chapter has attempted to answer the question, What is the role of an executive healthcare leader in creating value for an environmental sustainability program? The five-step guide presented here outlines the role of executive leadership in healthcare sustainability:

1. Commit.
2. Educate the board of directors.
3. Convene a Green Team.
4. Create a sustainable culture.
5. Celebrate success.

The role of the healthcare executive in leading an environmentally sustainable organization continues to evolve. A strategic starting point for an executive is to align sustainability goals with a vision of being a socially responsible organization. The executive's commitment must be to develop a sustainability program that is integrated into the corporate culture, versus tacked onto the existing agenda. Executives have a unique role and responsibility in the future of sustainable health care.

CHAPTER SUMMARY

Healthcare providers have a responsibility to the health and well-being of both the environment and their surrounding communities. Part of this responsibility lies in implementing environmentally sustainable health care—that is, healthcare practices that pursue a triple bottom line of fiscally, socially, and environmentally responsible operations. Sustainable health care is not only environmentally responsible stewardship, but also brings long-term benefits in terms of lower operational costs, increased efficiency, better staff retention, and improved patient and employee well-being. Sustainable leadership in health care can be achieved via the following five steps:

1. *Commit.* This step involves making sustainability a priority and visibly demonstrating a commitment towards achieving sustainability goals.
2. *Educate the board of directors.* This step involves educating the board about the importance and benefits of developing a sustainability program, and equipping them with the tools needed to effectively monitor progress toward corporate sustainability goals.
3. *Convene a Green Team.* This step involves engaging employees across departments to create a management team responsible for implementing sustainability initiatives. A key component of this step involves hiring a sustainability officer who will make the success of those initiatives his or her top priority.
4. *Create a sustainable culture.* This step involves engaging leadership and employees in embracing sustainability as a central tenet of the organization's culture. Success in this step will ensure that the organization prioritizes sustainability long term.
5. *Celebrate success.* This step involves showcasing successes in sustainability programs to foster understanding of and enthusiasm for sustainability throughout the organization. Maximize opportunity to effect the greatest change by communicating the steps being taken and positive changes resulting from those efforts.

KEY TERMS AND CONCEPTS

Alternative transportation: Use of public or self-powered models of transportation instead of driving; additionally, the implementation of sustainable technologies in standard transportation.

Culture of sustainability: A corporate or organizational culture that embraces sustainability as one of its core tenets, and incorporates sustainability into everyday operations from the top down and bottom up.

Employee engagement: The degree of employee involvement and investment in the program, system, or action being promoted.

Energy management: Devising and implementing processes or systems to maximize energy efficiency and reduce energy waste.

Environmentally preferable purchasing (EPP): The procurement of products and services that, throughout the entirety of the product or service life cycle, do not cause harm to the environment, patient, employees, or community, or cause less harm than alternatives.

Environmentally preferable purchasing (EPP) profile: The degree to which suppliers or other companies adhere to environmentally preferable purchasing in their operations.

Going green: Taking steps to implement environmentally responsible processes and facilities.

Green construction: Designing, building, and retrofitting sustainable and environmentally friendly facilities.

Green Team: A team of leaders from across divisions who are responsible for implementing the executive vision of sustainability program(s).

Leadership in Energy and Environmental Design (LEED): An international certification program for green buildings, created by the United States Green Building Council.

Life-cycle analysis: Assessment of the impact that products have at every step along the supply chain.

Product or service life cycle: The process of product or service creation and use, from the initial material to the final waste product.

Sustainability: A method of operating that promotes the most efficient use of resources while minimizing the negative environmental effects of operations.

Sustainable care: Patient-centered care with the objective of promoting not only the patient's well-being, but also the well-being of the setting where care takes place, both in the facility and in the wider community.

Sustainable foods: Healthy, fresh local food grown and harvested in a sustainable manner, with verified sourcing.

Triple bottom line: A business goal that involves fiscally, socially, and environmentally responsible operations.

Waste management: Devising and implementing processes and systems that improve efficiency of resource use to reduce the amount of waste generated by a healthcare facility and appropriately dispose of waste generated.

Water management: Devising and implementing processes or systems to maximize the efficient use of water, including utilizing alternative water sources.

Questions to Consider

1. Why would a hospital or healthcare facility adopt a sustainability program?
2. How is environmental sustainability related to the mission of a healthcare organization?
3. What role does leadership play in creating and implementing a sustainability program?
4. What is the use of a culture of sustainability when implementing environmentally sustainable programs?
5. How would a sustainability program be developed by a healthcare organization?
6. How would a sustainability program be implemented by a healthcare organization?
7. What are the elements of a sustainability program, and why is each important?
8. How does the concept of a "triple bottom line" affect the healthcare organization's relationship to and perception within its community?

REFERENCES

Rich, C., & Wadhwa,. (2010). People, planet, profit. *Sustainable Healthcare & Hospital Development Magazine*.

Rich, C., Singleton, J. K., & Wadhwa, S. (2013). *Sustainability for healthcare management: a leadership imperative*. New York, NY: Routledge.

Rich, C., Collins, A., Messervy, J., & Wadhwa, S. (2013). Pathways to Leadership, Modern Healthcare. Transitioning to an environmentally, socially and economically sustainable model. Webinar.

Chapter 9

The Journey from Quality to Value

—John M. Shiver, MHA, LFACHE, FAAMA, and John Cantiello, PhD

LEARNING OBJECTIVES

- Understand the historical perspective of quality in healthcare
- Understand and evaluate the role of leadership in creating an organization focused on quality and value
- Understand the relationship between quality, safety and value

INTRODUCTION

Contemporary health care is focused on the quality of medical care, the quality of services, and cost considerations. This chapter addresses how this focus impacts providers, payers, and society overall, by introducing historical perspectives on healthcare quality and evolution of quality definitions in recent years. It also examines the history of health care from economic, quality, and **value** perspectives. Major legislative actions addressing cost and quality, such as the Affordable Care Act, are considered, along with the overall social implications and pressures accompanying them, and the advances that are resulting from increased technological capabilities. Each facet of the relationship has had an impact on healthcare delivery and advanced the quality and outcomes of medical care.

A BRIEF HISTORY OF QUALITY IN HEALTH CARE

Tradition has it that the phrase *"Primum non nocere"*—Latin for "First, do no harm"—was taken from the **Hippocratic Oath**; thus it might be thought of as the first and earliest code of quality in medicine. The Oath, one of the oldest binding documents, goes into greater detail but clearly lays out a formula for quality care. Hippocrates, considered the "father" of medicine, lived in a time when mythology still permeated Greek society. Medicine, for this philosopher, was a family affair. In fact, his family claimed lineage back to the god Apollo. To be an "Apollo Physician," then, was to associate with Hippocrates's heritage, a heritage winding back 19 generations. While quality may not have been a contemporary term at the time the Oath was originally penned, Hippocrates's focus on ethical and equitable care—a focus on quality care for all patients—is clear:

Classic Version of the Hippocratic Oath

I swear by Apollo Physician and Asclepius and Hygieia and Panaceia and all the gods and goddesses, making them my witnesses, that I will fulfill according to my ability and judgment this oath and this covenant:

To hold him who has taught me this art as equal to my parents and to live my life in partnership with him, and if he is in need of money to give him a share of mine, and to regard his offspring as equal to my brothers in male lineage and to teach them this art—if they desire to learn it—without fee and covenant; to give a share of precepts and oral instruction and all the other learning to my sons and to the sons of him who has instructed me and to pupils who have signed the covenant and have taken an oath according to the medical law, but no one else.

I will apply dietetic measures for the benefit of the sick according to my ability and judgment; I will keep them from harm and injustice.

I will neither give a deadly drug to anybody who asked for it, nor will I make a suggestion to this effect. Similarly I will not give to a woman an abortive remedy. In purity and holiness I will guard my life and my art.

I will not use the knife, not even on sufferers from stone, but will withdraw in favor of such men as are engaged in this work.

Whatever houses I may visit, I will come for the benefit of the sick, remaining free of all intentional injustice, of all mischief and in particular of sexual relations with both female and male persons, be they free or slaves.

What I may see or hear in the course of the treatment or even outside of the treatment in regard to the life of men, which on no account one must spread abroad, I will keep to myself, holding such things shameful to be spoken about.

If I fulfill this oath and do not violate it, may it be granted to me to enjoy life and art, being honored with fame among all men for all time to come; if I transgress it and swear falsely, may the opposite of all this be my lot.

—Classic version from the translation from the Greek by Ludwig Edelstein (1943)

"I will apply dietetic measures for the benefit of the sick according to my ability and judgment; I will keep them from harm and injustice." There is no doubt that Hippocrates valued quality care. In the time of Hippocrates, physicians may not have had access to the advances of modern medicine; however, they did have an exalted role in society. The Hippocratic Oath places significant responsibility on the shoulders of every physician and sets a very high standard of conduct. For its time, the Hippocratic Oath dictated the responsibility of every physician to provide the highest-quality medical care and to be cognizant of a social responsibility as well.

While not remembered for her passion for statistics and quantitative analysis in health care, in actuality Florence Nightingale was an early force for healthcare quality improvement. During the Crimean War of 1854–1856, she quantified and measured problems and initiated many medical and nursing practice reforms. She recorded outcomes of care, tracked death rates, and compared outcomes in Crimea care centers to outcomes for soldiers transported to England for treatment. Moreover, after instituting initial sanitary reforms, she was able to show a link between death rates and sanitation. Eventually, due to her research, Nightingale became concerned about the need for overall healthcare reform within the British Army. In 1858, she published a report titled *Notes on Matters Affecting the Health, Efficiency and Hospital Administration of the British Army Founded Chiefly on the Experiences of the Late* War—a report she threatened to release to the public unless the British government appointed a Royal Commission to make healthcare improvements across the board. The government listened to Nightingale:. A commission was established and Nightingale's detailed report was never made public. According to Duncan Neuhauser (2003), a professor at Case Western Reserve University, "She [Nightingale] was a 'passionate statistician', responsible for the most remarkable hospital quality improvement project ever carried out and, as shown by her careful quantitative documentation, of both the process and outcomes of care."

In the United States, significant historical milestones can be used to chart the evolving definition of quality in health care. One of the earliest milestones is found in the work of Ernest Codman (1869–1940), a physician who practiced at Massachusetts General Hospital and taught at Harvard Medical School. Recognized as a pioneer in outcomes management. Codman is credited with being the first American physician to track and study patient outcomes over a period of time. He advised that every hospital follow each patient long enough to determine whether a treatment was successful and then to inquire "if not, why not" to prevent similar failures in the future. Up until Codman's time, hospitals and physicians often remained unaware of the patient's final outcome, and no records were kept that could be used to discover outcome data. Prior to Codman's work, only Florence Nightingale had suggested such methods.

Initially, Codman created "patient end result cards" for each of his patients. On these cards, he tracked his patients' care and outcomes. Eventually, Codman coined the broader term "end results," a concept considered radical for his time. He wrote several papers on end results—papers that also included the idea of transparency through outcomes reporting. Hardly noticed by peers, his papers received some national attention and led to an important collaboration with a Philadelphia-based physician. At the time, transparency in medical care was not considered part of the ethos of medicine. Indeed, physicians were very protective of their treatment methods and the subsequent results of such treatment. Scientific medical studies were new and not yet considered mainstream. Given this milieu, Codman's methodology and broader recommendations were revolutionary.

During his career, Codman helped found the American College of Surgeons (ACS). Subsequently, his studies led to the creation of what eventually became the Joint Commission on the Accreditation of Healthcare Organizations, which is now called simply The Joint Commission. From the outset, this organization, which was originally named the Committee for Hospital Standardization, created basic guidelines for hospitals. For example, early guidelines called for ensuring that a medical staff was available and that members of the staff had graduated from a medical school. In addition, the committee asked that hospitals create records for every patient.

Codman's ideas are now threaded throughout the lexicon of healthcare providers and health systems, and they serve as the foundation for current quality reform. His vision for transparent outcome reporting may become a reality in the near future. In 2014, the ACS dedicated a memorial for Codman's grave, which reads: "Father of outcomes assessment and quality measurement: It may take 100 years for my ideas to be accepted."

Under the aegis of the Carnegie Foundation, in 1910, Dr. Abraham Flexner of Harvard and Johns Hopkins published the *Flexner Report*, which had major repercussions for the medical profession and medical training. At the time of its publication, there were 151 medical schools in the United States, all of which operated without any overarching standards for curriculum, quality, or degree requirements. The impact of Flexner's report was significant.

The number of medical schools decreased (151 down to 31), with schools such as Johns Hopkins, McGill, Michigan, Case Western, and Wake Forest receiving citations as examples of the best medical schools. The publication of the *Flexner Report* resulted in the development of minimum curriculum standards, state licensing and oversight, and the requirement for an adherence to strict scientific standards. In addition, all schools were subject to oversight by state medical associations.

In 1951, some 40 years after the publication of the Codman and Flexner reports, the Joint Commission on the Accreditation of Healthcare Organizations was founded. Furthering the work of Codman's Committee on Hospital Standardization, the Commission represented the first nationwide effort to create an ongoing and uniform method of overseeing and accrediting the quality and safety of hospitals and the physicians practicing in them.

In contrast, there was little significant involvement of the federal government in health care. Federal involvement began in the aftermath of World War II, when society as a whole was experiencing a sea change—one to which healthcare was not immune.

Health care in the United States today is moving rapidly toward a model called value-based service—a journey that has been decades, if not more than a century, in the making. Consider how little was known about medicine in the beginning, and how information was transmitted and aggregated. In the early days, there were few metrics beyond the mind of an individual physician. Consider also the context of medical care and how it has evolved over the years. In the early days of healthcare delivery in the United States, providers had very limited capability to deliver anything but the most rudimentary therapies. As recently as 1939, much of the country was provided with medical care from people not unlike Professor Marvel in *The Wizard of Oz*.

Until the World War II era, antibiotic treatment was limited to penicillin, and blood transfusion was a new technology. Today we have medicines that can cure diseases, which, just a decade ago, were fatal. Almost every day new technologies and medicines are introduced. While technology continues to influence and enhance medical care, it also contributes to the need for new standards in health care. Today's emerging electronic medical records allow for easier metrics, complex healthcare computer systems allow for increased access to best practices, and health systems can better track outcomes. Technology and value go hand in hand in modern health care. Through the application of ever more sophisticated information sharing as well as analysis, new methods and best practices are now shared around the globe. With all of these advances, life expectancy continues to extend and quality of life increase. The phrase "Sixty is the new forty" takes on significant meaning in relation to the recent advances of modern medicine.

THE GOVERNMENT'S ROLE

Healthcare financing and federal involvement in quality standards were essentially nonexistent until the mid-twentieth century. Health insurance, used for payment of hospital and physician fees, became commonplace only after World War II. Until then, health expenses were paid out of pocket or services were rendered through barter agreement. Because the medical therapies available were both few in number and rudimentary in nature, costs were also relatively inconsequential to the average consumer. Until the advent of modern medicine, there was little a physician could offer a patient except compassion and various potions created from hand-me-down remedies. Medical science was relatively nonexistent.

Infectious disease, in particular, was a scourge across the globe. **Figure 9–1** illustrates the dramatic decline in some of the most common

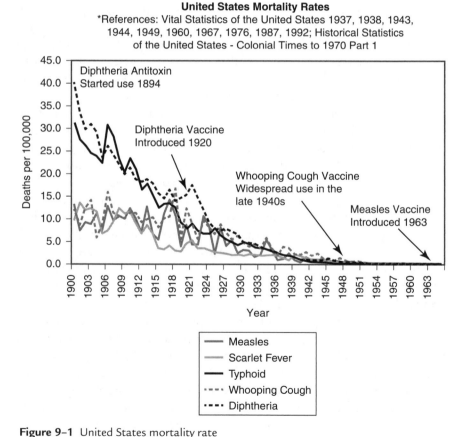

Figure 9–1 United States mortality rate

Reproduced from Roman Bystrianyk and Suzanne Humphries, MD. Dissolving Illusions. 2013.

infectious diseases over the past century. The most significant outcome of controlling the more common infectious diseases was a dramatic decline in the infant mortality rate, as shown in **Figure 9–2**, along with the extension of life expectancy from 47 years at the turn of the twentieth century to 76 years at the beginning of the twenty-first century—an astonishing 62% increase in just 100 years (**Figure 9–3**). These advances did not come for free, however: As medicine advanced and benefited society, the cost of providing this service rose.

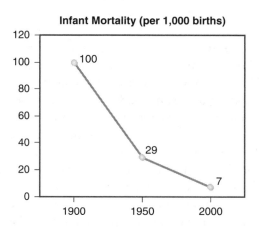

Figure 9–2 Infant mortality
Data from Centers for Disease Control and Prevention.

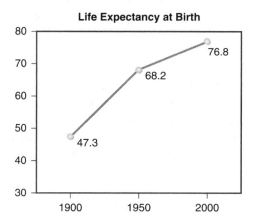

Figure 9–3 Life expectancy at birth
Data from Centers for Disease Control and Prevention.

Some of the greatest advances in medicine have been a by-product of great crisis. The most significant of such crises was World War II. As noted earlier, much of what defines "modern medicine" was an outgrowth of this mid-century conflict. To control the costs of the war, the government imposed a freeze on workers' wages. Companies competed for employees by offering health insurance as a compensation for the wage freezes, and by the end of the war health insurance became institutionalized as a common and expected benefit of employment. Thus a national awareness of the cost of health care developed for the first time.

If prior to World War II healthcare science was still relatively rudimentary, following the war it became gradually more complex and sophisticated. This sophistication led to the need for ever-larger and ever-complex systems for providing care and nationwide pressure for organizations to deliver more integrated health care than had been possible with an independent physician. With the end of World War II, the federal government shifted its focus from supporting a wartime economy to addressing multiple social issues. One of the more significant moves was the expansion of access to health care. The Hill-Burton Act, or Hospital Survey and Construction Act, was passed in 1946, sponsored by Sen. Harold Burton (Republican–Ohio) and Sen. J. Lister Hill (Democrat–Alabama). This act authorized grants to hospitals in exchange for hospitals providing free and charitable care to the needy. It resulted in a boom in construction of new and larger hospitals across the country, greatly expanding the capacity of the national health-care system to reach previously unserved communities. Ultimately the law financed a total of 10,490 healthcare facilities. The Hill-Burton program remains the largest piece of federal legislation to provide subsidies for the construction of nonprofit and local governmental hospitals: From July 1947 through June 1971, $33.1 billion was distributed through this act for the construction and modernization of healthcare institutions (Clark, Field, Koontz, & Koontz, 1980).

The expanded number of hospitals and hospital beds provided better access to care facilities throughout the United States. Coupled with the widespread availability of health insurance as a common benefit of employment, the utilization of these facilities grew. The combination of the means to pay for care as well as greater access to hospitals, which were capable of offering that care, created an atmosphere for utilization growth. **Figure 9–4** depicts the increase in healthcare costs that occurred right after World War II. Note that the expenditures have grown steadily since the mid-1940s, with only temporary dips, many of which are explained in the following paragraphs.

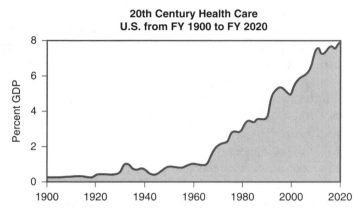

Figure 9–4 Twentieth century health care
Courtesy of www.usgovernmentspending.com.

The growing utilization of healthcare services, and the parallel rise in costs, highlighted a major social issue: the rise in poverty among the elderly. Because the elderly did not work and, therefore, were much less likely to have health insurance, medical costs for this group became the single largest cause of poverty in the United States. The Social Security Amendments of 1965 (Pub.L. 89–97, 79 Stat. 286), enacted July 30, 1965, resulted in the creation of two programs: Medicare and Medicaid, which were designed to address the healthcare crisis among the elderly and the poor. The legislation initially provided federal health insurance for persons older than age 65 and for poor families. Under this law, hospitals, doctors, and other providers were paid for medical care provided to these federal beneficiaries. With the passage of Medicare and Medicaid, the majority of Americans—though certainly not all—had some form of health insurance; that is, the employed had coverage as a benefit, the elderly under Medicare, and the poor under Medicaid.

In Figure 9–4, it is easy to see that the national cost of medical care grew dramatically after 1965. With healthcare financing mechanisms in place from employers (employee benefit) and for the elderly and the very poor (Medicare and Medicaid), providing healthcare became an attractive business arrangement. Thus, just a few short years after the end of World War II, the healthcare industry became a lucrative business in which financial success for participants was almost guaranteed. The rapidly growing national medical expenditures attracted the interest of the government, however, which in turn generated a number of programs aimed at retarding and reducing the rapidly rise in these costs. Such significant legislative efforts are discussed in greater depth later in this chapter.

On August 15, 1971, just six years after the inauguration of Medicare and Medicaid, President Richard Nixon announced Executive Order 11615, implementing a wage and price freeze, in an effort to control the then turbulent economy. It impacted the healthcare care delivery system by freezing federal reimbursement of healthcare costs. The immediate effect on the healthcare industry was to retard expansion of capacity or services. As a consequence, the public soon began to experience an increasing lack of access to healthcare. The executive order, while initially popular, became so unmanageable that Congress let it lapse in April 1974. The impact on the healthcare industry was temporary and produced only a transient decline in the growth of healthcare costs.

Healthcare costs continued to be a concern at the federal level, however. In 1974, the same year the Nixon price controls were lifted, Congress passed the National Health Planning and Resources Development Act (Public Law 93-641). It established a programmatic approach to managing the allocation of healthcare resources through a network of federal, state, and local reviews of healthcare capital expenditures. Under this program, states, within federal guidelines, established local Health Systems Agencies (HSA), which continue to operate in some parts of the country. Local HSA boards were tasked with reviewing and approving, subject to state review, all major capital expenditures on health care. This oversight resulted in the creation of significant barriers for any provider wishing to initiate a new capital program or enter a new market. At the same time, it created a system whereby every significant growth effort by a provider was now public knowledge. Competition was greatly reduced and market power became consolidated among fewer, but larger providers. As a purely economic tool, the National Health Planning and Resources Development Act made no pretense of addressing quality of care.

In 1973, Congress passed the Health Maintenance Organization (HMO) Act, which provided financial support for the creation of health maintenance organizations—yet another effort to gain control over rising healthcare costs. An HMO is an insurance program that is held financially responsible for providing a defined set of health services. This payer is at financial risk for the costs of providing care to a defined population; consequently, in theory, the HMO must tightly manage care to adequately control costs. An HMO moves both insurer and provider away from the fee-for-service reimbursement model and shifts financial accountability to providers. The HMO Act provided financial grants to encourage the creation of pioneer HMOs in the hopes that others would find the model attractive. While some HMOs have met with success— the most notable being Kaiser Permanente—overall the U.S. public rejected the idea of closely managed provider networks and the HMO movement stalled. However, a less restrictive iteration of the HMO did gain traction and is today the most common form of health insurance: the preferred provider organization (PPO), a model that is much less restrictive than the HMO and does not shift as much financial risk to providers.

A **prospective payment** system for the operating costs of inpatient hospital services furnished to Medicare beneficiaries, specified in Public Law 106-113, went into effect on October 1, 1983. Under this payment system, which continues today, hospitals and other inpatient providers are paid a prospectively determined fee set by the Health Care Finance Administration (HCFA), now known as the Centers for Medicare and Medicaid (CMS). This system was based on a fee schedule that uses diagnostic-related groups (DRGs); the fee is paid on a per-discharge basis, which depends on the admitting diagnosis. The intent of the law was to incentivize providers to reduce costs, primarily through reducing lengths of stay. The program represented a significant change in the fee-for-service payment system in that it capped the amount paid based on the patient's diagnosis. Interestingly, the DRGs were initially developed at Yale University in the 1970s as a way to catalog and track healthcare services so that researchers could study outcomes and quality. However, when adopted by the federal government, the system was used to primarily manage healthcare costs.

The Balanced Budget Act of 1997 instituted the outpatient prospective payment system (OPPS), which set proscribed payment rates for outpatient services. Because the emphasis of prior legislation had been on regulating inpatient costs, providers had begun to move more services into outpatient settings, where reimbursement was still based on a fee-for-service model. With the implementation of the OPPS, ambulatory care services were brought under a program similar to the inpatient payment system. In addition to setting rates in advance, the law mandated that certain services be reimbursed only when rendered in an ambulatory setting; it was all-inclusive, including drugs, equipment, and supplies within it scope. Again, the intent was to incentivize providers to create more cost-effective methods of delivering health care.

Numerous examples can be cited of healthcare providers who moved their practices to an outpatient setting immediately upon enactment of the OPPS. Cataract surgery is a good example. Inpatient cataract surgery had historically entailed about a week of inpatient treatment, during which time the patient was kept in a dark room, immobilized and blindfolded following surgery. The move to outpatient provision immediately reduced this treatment to a one-day-stay procedure. The only reason many hospitals had maintained the inpatient model for cataract surgery was the reimbursement mechanism; once that financial incentive was changed, the move to outpatient surgery was almost instantaneous.

THE BEGINNING OF QUALITY IMPROVEMENT IN HEALTH CARE

Hospitals and physicians have historically worked to review quality. This focus has included such efforts as credentialing healthcare providers, including physicians and nurses. These programs were generally internally based and carried out by peer review committees that utilized paper medical records to review care rendered within the organization. By their very nature, they reviewed only individual episodes of care; consequently, they were not very effective in studying or detecting patterns of care, or ascertaining more than individual incidents. While operating with the best of intentions, the limits of anecdotal data and the absence of scientifically derived best practice standards meant that these internal reviews were not terribly effective in raising the level of quality.

The Medicare Quality Improvement Organization (QIO) Program, formerly referred to as the Medicare Utilization and Quality Control Peer Review Program, was created by statute in 1982 to improve the quality and efficiency of services delivered to Medicare beneficiaries. This law established regional quality review organizations across the United States. Initially, they functioned by reviewing paper medical records, much in the same fashion as the quality care committees of individual hospitals. Over the years, the quality review organizations did raise awareness of the need for increasing quality standards and safety. At the same, they were hindered by their limited powers and the availability of only unwieldy, ad hoc, incidental data.

Quality improvement tools have been around for many decades. Walter A. Shewhart developed the first known control chart—the so-called Shewhart cycle—in 1924. This chart linked quality improvement and statistical approaches to management techniques (Best & Neuhauser, 2006; Handfield, 1989). The components of this plan–do–check–act cycle are used to help improve processes leading to a final product (Bisgaard & De Mast, 2006; Gupta, 2006; Tague, 2004). All four of these components of the cycle are linked and can be viewed as steps.

W. Edwards Deming expanded on Shewhart's work and brought quality improvement efforts into the business world. Following World War II, Japan's economy deteriorated as the country struggled to recover from the war. Deming was asked to teach Japanese businesses about quality improvement. In his "14 Points of Management," he emphasized that the work environment must uphold the idea of continued improvement not only individually, but also at the organizational level (Gupta, 2006; Lynn & Osborn, 1991). Deming demonstrated that employees from all levels and within all components of an organization must be involved in quality improvement efforts, not just leadership (Lynn & Osborn, 1991).

After Deming's success in Japan became widely known, other industries began to inspect and change their improvement efforts and quality processes. The earliest successes were documented in the utility industries; those successes were subsequently studied and replicated in the manufacturing and service industries, including information technology (IT) corporations. Key to the earlier efforts was a focus on eliminating top-down styles of leadership. The creation of teams at all levels of organizations—specifically, teams that studied processes and developed solutions for improvements— was a critical tenet in the Deming approach to quality improvement. "Total quality management" became a standard business term referring to this strategy, and entire departments were devoted to helping organizations evolve into quality businesses. In the early 1980s, leaders in the healthcare industry began to formalize similar quality improvement techniques to be specifically used in their industry.

QUALITY IMPROVEMENT AND VALUE ENHANCEMENT METHODS

Numerous quality improvement methods were originally used in the manufacturing industry, including **Six Sigma**, **Lean** methods, plan–do–study–act methods, flowcharts, and Ishikawa (fishbone) diagrams. All are crucial for executing improvement efforts. The Six Sigma and Lean methods were especially transformative when it came to improving and redesigning the way medical care is delivered in the United States.

Six Sigma was developed during the 1980s by Motorola, which had the goal of eliminating deficits in its processes (Aboelmaged, 2010). The objective of Six Sigma is to first define the problem, then to obtain process performance measurements, and finally to analyze the process and determine the cause(s) of the identified issue. These steps assist in determining whether the process in place should be redesigned or whether it can be further improved (Aboelmaged, 2010; Tague, 2004). The concept of Six Sigma of manufacturing was eventually replicated in the healthcare industry, where it was used to improve processes already in place and to create new processes for delivering care.

Lean methods were also developed in the manufacturing industry. The goal when employing Lean methods is to appropriately manage waste and variations that can occur during manufacturing. In health care, this concept is applied to improve customer satisfaction and to empower those involved in healthcare processes. At the same time, the Lean approach helps to eliminate wasteful steps and/or recourses that really have no importance to the successful delivery of high-quality medical care (Brandao de Souza, 2009; Tague, 2004).

Unlike the manufacturing realm, from which much of the quality improvement technology evolved, the healthcare industry was very slow in developing detailed costing information. The historical causes for this delay are many, based mostly on a lack of necessity: Because reimbursement was not calculated utilizing detailed costing analysis, little effort was invested in creating and tracking specific "production" costs. Value-based purchasing (VBP) reverses this relationship. Without detailed costing information to use as input to the value equation, determining the financial impact of decisions quickly becomes an exercise in guesswork.

Because of the exceptional complexity of healthcare delivery, the effort to create a viable costing methodology remains a major hurdle. This difficulty can no longer be an excuse for avoiding it, however; the imperative for having this information is no longer debatable. VBP mandates that if they are to survive, all providers must be able to include accurate costing data in their calculations.

TWENTY-FIRST CENTURY CARE

In the first two decades of the twenty-first century, healthcare costs have continued to rise—almost without abatement. One significant effort to address the issue at the national level was made at the end of the twentieth century. President Bill Clinton, during his first presidential run, campaigned on a platform that included healthcare reform. Upon taking office in 1993, he immediately launched an effort to enact legislation that would reform the U.S. healthcare system. The proposed Health Security Act mandated that every citizen be enrolled in a qualified health plan and not be allowed to drop that coverage until covered by another qualified plan. All health plans were to have mandated minimal benefits and limits on out-of-pocket expenses.

The Clinton administration's efforts at healthcare reform were opposed by almost every industry that touched the healthcare system. National advertising campaigns attacked the proposal from every angle. Provider, payer, vendor, and pharmaceutical organizations opposed the legislation. Conservatives and libertarians were united against it, and there was not enough Democratic party support to pass the legislation. Within a year of its launch, the effort was defeated in Congress.

In the years following the Clinton administration's aborted attempt, health-care reform took a backseat to other national agendas, and no significant effort in this area was launched until the 2008 presidential campaign. Upon taking office, President Barack Obama, who ran on a platform that included healthcare reform, almost immediately pushed the most far-reaching health-care legislation since Medicare and Medicaid through Congress. His success in enacting this legislation was due in large part to a combination of economic factors that caused the public, private industry, and the government to see an aligned benefit from the proposal. By the time President Obama took office, the country was in the most significant recession it had experienced in half a century. Healthcare costs were increasing at double-digit rates, and employ-ers were very concerned about the cost of healthcare benefits. The inflation rate for private healthcare costs exceeded by the rate of cost increases for government-funded health programs such as Medicare and Medicaid. In addition, Congress was then under the control of one political party. The stars were aligned for the next step, the passage of the Patient Protection and Affordable Care Act, more simply known as the Affordable Care Act (ACA).

Perhaps the most important piece of federal legislation since the passage of Medicare and Medicaid in 1965, the ACA (PL111-148) was signed into law by President Obama in March 2010. It created a number of new regula-tions and programs designed to manage the continued escalation of health-care costs. Portions of the act focus on quality and value-based purchasing.

The relationship of quality to value is a significant component of the Affordable Care Act and shifts any initial discussion of healthcare quality to the more complex context of quality, cost, service, and efficiency. For some time, government and private payers have sought to pay only for care that was of a high quality. There have been many experiments in defining and quantifying the term *quality*. For example, Don Berwick, founder of the Institute for Healthcare Improvement, has for many years been a leader in moving the medical profession toward the concept of high-quality and high-value medical care. While it is not universally true, many organizations have maintained the status quo because implementing cultural change within an organization and within professions is difficult, especially when there is no pressure to make the change. Historically, payment methods have been used to reduce costs for the payer, but with no incentives that would consider qual-ity improvement being built into the methodology. Until recently, payers left the issue of quality solely in the hands of providers. Many of the more recent studies, such as those undertaken by the Institute of Medicine, have pointed out the very close relationship between quality outcomes and reduced costs. As a consequence, today's payers and providers are more closely aligned in their mission to enhance quality while at the same time managing costs.

THE STAKEHOLDERS

Today everyone is a stakeholder in the U.S. healthcare system—patients, care providers, administrators, employers, the government, and insurance providers. This point was driven home on a national level with the November 1999 publication of the Institute of Medicine's seminal study, *To Err Is Human: Building a Safer Health System*. The impact of this publication is hard to overstate: It opened by highlighting 98,000 deaths due to medical errors in U.S. hospitals. The report shined a bright light into the darkest reaches of hospitals, and the public reaction was profound. There were calls for action at every level, and the focus on the issue was front-page news in every community. Hospitals were no longer thought of as a sanctuary for the ailing, but rather were perceived as dangerous and callous. Quality improvement could no longer be theorized; it was urgently moved to a front burner.

Two years later, in March 2001, the Institute of Medicine followed up *To Err Is Human* with a more focused report that called for restructuring the entire U.S. healthcare delivery system: *Crossing the Quality Chasm: A New Health System for the 21st Century*. This widely read study drove home the message that the U.S. healthcare delivery system was "broken." It recommended very specific changes in healthcare delivery to address fundamental challenges in this area:

- Reengineered care processes
- Effective use of information technologies
- Knowledge and skills management
- Development of effective teams
- Coordination of care across patient conditions, services, and sites of care over time

Quality in the healthcare industry today is no longer what it was almost two decades ago, when the Institute of Medicine's reports were first published. The ongoing impact of these reports on the U.S. healthcare system is now woven into the very fabric of all healthcare institutions. Perhaps even more important is how these reports have stimulated patients' active involvement with their care and interest in the healthcare industry. Pressure for transparency throughout the healthcare industry is growing. Quality improvement projects have proliferated in hospitals and other clinical settings. Both the quality of care and improved health system processes are the focus of numerous reports and projects.

Organizations such as the Institute for Health Care Improvement, the National Committee for Quality Assurance, The Joint Commission, and the National Quality Measures Clearinghouse, among others, are working together to improve quality in health care. Medical associations facilitate quality improvement by providing treatment recommendations and by setting standards for clinicians to follow. These organizations also provide a means of benchmarking, so that organizations can measure their own quality improvement efforts against existing data. Materials are circulated by these organizations that assist clinicians in better serving patients and in improving certain processes. Moreover, administrators are taking note of different approaches to ensuring quality outcomes and patient satisfaction. Many are involving patients in the quality process through the use of study groups, surveys, and boards.

THE ROLE OF LEADERSHIP

Health system leaders will play an increasingly critical role in creating the culture of quality and value that is essential to secure a successful future for the U.S. healthcare system. Along with clinicians, managers and other key stakeholders will lead the movement to implement quality and value enhancement improvement efforts. Leaders must be prepared to take the helm in setting in motion the adoption of the new culture of quality. Cultural change is never easy, nor is it simple. Health systems are perhaps the most complex businesses in the country, and creating change across the myriad of professional disciplines, social strata, financial constraints, and other vested interests found in these organizations will necessitate the highest quality of leadership. Leaders will have to rely on tested strategies and frameworks if they are to succeed. The creation of partnerships with other key stakeholders is critical, especially partnerships with clinicians. Finding common ground among key players and doing so at the correct time are key. Aligning interests among the various constituents is another key principle for moving an organization forward.

Creating a system with aligned interests takes time and focused effort. While time is of the essence for ensuring better value and outcomes, the timing itself is perhaps more important. Creating a sense of urgency and ownership is critical, but speed alone will not suffice to meet the overall goals. Trust among the various interest groups must be earned, often many times over. The role and value of the patient and the payer in the process cannot be ignored. Payers and their clientele are the lifeblood of a provider system, and the current market is very sensitive to changes that may not be immediately appreciated or understood. While not outright divergent, the interests of payers and patients may not always be perfectly aligned. For example, a payer may prefer to see patients utilize a less expensive provider. While that provider may have a perfectly good reputation, other factors may be of greater importance to the consumer—factors such as the availability of an even more prestigious provider, or a more convenient, equally well-qualified provider, or a provider with a particular expertise or knowledge base that is essential to the patient's care. When differences of this nature arise, the market may become contentious, with patients pressuring employers and insurers to accede to their demands.

Quality improvement efforts and value creation are critical at all levels: financial, strategic, and patient care. During this time of incredible change in the healthcare arena, healthcare leaders must guide their organizations to make sound, evidence-based decisions. The leader's role is to establish the most effective environment for an organization to create necessary and sustainable change—change that will then be enacted by the entire healthcare team and community. To create an environment for success, the leader must develop an organizational structure and provide tools that will help the entire team support and embrace the large shifts in culture and process. The healthcare industry of today, as in no time before, needs leaders who can embrace the concept of an empowered organization. The successful leader will be one who can empower those persons who own the necessary processes, adopt new methodologies, and provide the entire team with the wherewithal to implement change. Leadership has the potential to be a conduit for solutions generated by those who are most involved and affected by the work that they perform. In this era of great change, the realization of leadership that is rooted in evidence-based decision making is of utmost importance.

CHAPTER SUMMARY

In this chapter, the history and evolution of healthcare quality, cost, and value is reviewed. These related components of the United States healthcare system are important to understand, as they impact providers, payers, patients, and society overall. The current quality of medical care to society and legislative efforts to mandate quality, as well as the social repercussions of such efforts, are important considerations and key to understanding the quality improvement landscape in the United States. As such, these elements are discussed in this chapter. The focus on studying and measuring processes has increased in recent years. Consequently, we discuss the importance of scientific methodologies used to evaluate and improve processes.

The relationship between quality and cost of care is outlined and the growing importance of value is a key component of this chapter. Therefore the growing importance of healthcare value on the purchasing decisions of payers and government is considered and the future impact this new emphasis will have on providers is projected. In the future, healthcare purchasing decisions will be determined based on the value of the services provided and the outcome for the payer.

The role of the healthcare leader in creating a justifiable and documentable value case for the healthcare product or service will be of paramount importance as the industry evolves. To do this, the leader must be open to and be prepared to deal with significant change. He or she must be willing to adapt to a new healthcare landscape that is more transparent and focused on value. Leaders must also be able to create a culture of quality and value that permeates their organizations. The appropriate organizational structure and the availability of tools that allow the entire healthcare team to contribute are key to developing such a culture.

KEY TERMS AND CONCEPTS

Hippocratic Oath: The first and earliest code of quality in medicine.

Lean: A process improvement methodology that focuses on appropriately managing waste and variations. In health care, this concept is applied to improve customer satisfaction and to empower those involved in healthcare processes.

Prospective payment: A payment system under which hospitals and other inpatient providers are paid a prospectively determined fee; it is based on a fee schedule that uses diagnostic-related groups (DRGs) and the fee is paid on a per-discharge basis, which depends on the admitting diagnosis.

Six Sigma: A process improvement methodology that focuses on three steps—define the problem, obtain process performance measurements, and analyze the process and determine the cause(s) of the identified issue. These steps assist in determining whether the process in place should be redesigned or whether it can be further improved.

Value: An amount considered to be a suitable equivalent for something else; a fair price or return for goods or services. In healthcare it would be considered the fair price for a healthcare good or service taking into consideration the outcome of utilization of the good or service.

REFERENCES

Aboelmaged, M. G. (2010). Six Sigma quality: A structured review and implications for future research. *International Journal of Quality & Reliability Management, 27*(3), 268–317.

Best M., & Neuhauser, D. (2006). Walter A Shewhart, 1924, and the Hawthorne factory. *Quality Safety Health Care, 15*(2), 142–143.

Bisgaard, S., & De Mast, J. (2006). After Six Sigma: What's next? *Quality Progress*, *39*(1), 30–36.

Brandao de Souza, L. (2009). Trends and approaches in Lean healthcare. *Leadership in Health Services*, *22*(2), 121–139.

Clark, L., Field, M., Koontz, T., & Koontz, V. (1980). The impact of Hill-Burton: An analysis of hospital bed and physician distribution in the United States 1950-1970. *Medical Care 18*(5), 532–550.

Edelstein, L. (1943). *The Hippocratic Oath: Text, translation, and interpretation.* Baltimore, MD: Johns Hopkins Press.

Gupta, P. (2006). Beyond PDCA: A new process management model. *Quality Progress*, *39*(7), 45–52.

Handfield, R. (1989). Quality management in Japan versus the United States: An overview. *Production and Inventory Management Journal*, *30*(2), 79–85.

Lynn, M. L., & Osborn, D. P. (1991). Deming's quality principles: A health care application. *Hospital & Health Services Administration*, *36*(1), 111–120.

Neuhauser, D. (2003). Heros and martyrs of quality and safey. *Quality and Safety in Healthcare*, *12*(4), 317.

Tague, N. R. (2004). *The quality toolbox* (2nd ed.). Milwaukee, WI: ASQ Quality Press.

Chapter 10

Health Policy

—P.J. Maddox

- Define health policy and policy making authorities
- Discuss the politics and process of health policymaking
- Understand the drivers for health policy
- Identify the key actors in health policy
- Analyze the role of interest groups in policymaking
- Synthesize stewardship and leadership in health care policy

INTRODUCTION

Many believe the U.S. health system is too focused on disease treatment, and is overly complex, fragmented, unreliable, and too costly. Since the 1960s, federal and state **health policy** has sought to influence the organization and functioning of the health system, primarily to improve access to health services and/or slow the growth of health expenditures. U.S. politics and policy-making processes at all levels of government are complex, but add to this a patchwork of nuanced, rule-laden federal and state health policies and this specialized area of **public policy** becomes especially difficult to understand. Health policy is an important concern for all health executives, as it affects strategic planning and management of health services, impacting every individual, business entity, and community. It is also linked directly to the economic vitality of the country and every state. Health policy changes as a result of political agendas and in response to unmet public needs and problems. Conversely, the provisions and impact of health policies substantially affect strategy and operational considerations in the planning and management of healthcare organizations. For all these reasons, healthcare executives must have a working knowledge of the policy-making process and an understanding of the drivers for health policy formulation and change. They also need to understand the evolution of public policy that explains the need for healthcare **stewardship**.

Professional organizations that represent healthcare professionals and business entities that make up the health sector have all championed the importance of greater policy awareness and advocacy by healthcare clinicians and managers. As the evolution of practice standards, knowledge domains, and certification of healthcare executives indicates, there has been a call for more active involvement of health executives in the policy-making process (National Center for Health Leadership [NCHL], 2006). This chapter provides an overview and analysis of the U.S. policy-making process, discusses the key actors that are influential in setting the policy agenda and making health policy, and identifies important drivers and environmental factors shaping health reform. The chapter also discusses the evolving role of health executives as stewards of health policy, as these individuals are increasingly expected to be responsible for the allocation and use of limited/scarce healthcare resources. The information in this chapter is intended to be useful to health executives as they seek to understand the politics of health policy making, understand the role and function of the hospital executive in working effectively with policymakers, manage government relations or legislative affairs staff/consultants as part of the healthcare enterprise, and engage in advocacy related to health policy formulation.

BACKGROUND

The U.S. healthcare system is a collection of public and private entities that finance and provide healthcare services; develop, manufacture, and distribute healthcare supplies and technology; and regulate the entities that finance and provide health services. It is also the most costly health system in the world. According to the Organization for Economic Cooperation and Development (OECD, 2014), the United States spends more per capita on health care than any nation, despite not providing universal healthcare coverage. While the Patient Protection and Affordable Care Act of 2010 (often called the Affordable Care Act [ACA]) was designed to achieve a substantial increase in health insurance coverage, it did not guarantee universal coverage or access to care. As the implementation of the ACA has evolved, gaps have persisted as individuals have chosen not to comply with the mandate to purchase health insurance and some states have declined to participate in the Medicaid program expansion. Meanwhile, U.S. health expenditures continue to increase as the number of individuals eligible for government-funded health care through Medicaid and Medicare increases.

Although the U.S. health system is unique in the world, its challenges are similar to those faced by countries with very different health systems—namely, challenges dealing with rising healthcare costs and concerns about healthcare quality and effectiveness (Institute of Medicine [IOM], 2001). Indeed, our European colleagues are engaged in a variety of reform efforts designed to change the delivery of healthcare services, including developing new expectations about individual responsibility in accessing and using health systems and changing government roles and interventions to move beyond the care of individuals to manage population health. In the United States, recent state and federal policy has been directed at bringing about changes to integrate health insurance and payment with service delivery and more recently toward implementing value-based purchasing (paying for services that produce quality outcomes and withholding payment for services that do not meet quality metrics).

Although the United States does not have a national health system, there is a long-standing history of significant government involvement in shaping the country's health system and health care through health policy (Feldstein, 2006). Since 1965, when the Medicare and Medicaid programs were established, federal policy initiatives have profoundly shaped the structure and functioning of the U.S. health system. Selected important federal policies are highlighted in **Table 10–1**.

Non-health-related policies also influence hospitals and health systems. Notable among these are labor laws, merger and anti-trust laws such as the Sherman Anti-Trust Act and Clayton Anti-Trust Act, anti-kickback laws, and corporate ethics laws (Sarbanes–Oxley Act of 2002). While a discussion of these laws is beyond the scope of this chapter, the point is that health executives must be aware of policy changes that stem from a variety of sources (state and federal) and that focus on or extend to the management and operation of healthcare entities.

Fueled by growing concerns about escalating healthcare costs and unmet value for performance, policymakers' interest in health policy as a vehicle to change the health system will continue. The central question is which changes in U.S. policy will emerge, and which health reforms will be undertaken in the future.

Table 10–1 Selected Significant Federal Health Policies

Year	Federal Policy
1966	Comprehensive Health Planning Act: establishes state-level healthcare facility planning
1973	Health Maintenance Organization Act
1974	Employee Retirement Income Security Act
1983	Deficit Reduction Act of 1982: establishes the prospective payment system
1986	Emergency Medical Treatment and Active Labor Act: guarantees emergency medical treatment to anyone regardless of legal status or ability to pay
1989	Medicare prospective payment system is extended to physicians
1994	Social Security Act Amendments include the Stark Act: prohibits physician self-referrals
1995	Federally Supported Health Centers Assistance Act
1996	Health Insurance Portability and Accountability Act
1997	Balanced Budget Act: creates the Medicare + Choice program, extends prospective payment to nursing homes, and establishes the State Children's Health Insurance Program (SCHIP)
2003	Partial Birth Abortion Ban Act
2006	Medicare prescription drug benefit begins
2009	Obama executive order allows federal tax dollars for embryonic stem cell research
2010	Patient Protection and Affordable Care Act

Data from Patel K., & Rushefsky, M. (2014). *Healthcare politics and policy in America* (4th ed.). New York, NY: Taylor & Francis.

WHAT CONSTITUTES A HEALTH POLICY PROBLEM?

Health policy is a specialized type of public policy. Generally speaking, public policies are authoritative decisions made in the legislative, executive, or judicial branches of government, intended to direct or influence the actions, behaviors, or decisions of others (Longest, 2010). When public policies are related to influencing health and the diverse array of health-care providers and functions, they are considered "health policies." Health policy, like any public policy, is intended to serve the interests of "the public." While this may mean all residents or citizens, it calls attention to those who make their expectations or demands known to policy-making officials. Perhaps not surprisingly, legislators and government policymakers are most responsive to the demands of their voting constituents and funders (Patel & Rushefsky, 2014).

The most compelling reasons for policy interventions are related to solving recognized problems or addressing public needs. Public policy—that is, new laws or amendments to existing laws—is developed through the policy-making process, from the "interactions of diverse health related problems, possible solutions, and dynamic political circumstances that relate to the problems and to their possible solutions" (Longest, 2010, p. 59, para 3). At any given time, there may be many problems or issues, each with a possible set of solutions, some of which may be known or apparent to policy-makers but others not. According to Longest (2010), all problems have a variety of potential solutions, with each also having a set of "supporters and detractors." Whether a problem ever rises in importance to garner the attention of policymakers is determined by what Kingdon (1984) describes as a confluence of problems, consideration of possible solutions, and political circumstances to create a "**window of opportunity**" for policy making. Such a window of opportunity is viewed as a necessary condition for the drafting or formation of legislation (new laws or amendments).

There are three principal stages in the policy-making process: policy formulation, policy implementation, and policy evaluation (Longest, 2010). Before delving into the complexity of this seemingly simple process and the politics of health policy making, it is important to have an understanding of the types of policy and the policy-making structures and entities in state and federal government.

POLICY-MAKING STRUCTURE

The U.S. Constitution created a federal government that distributes political power and decision-making authority among three branches of government: legislative, judicial, and executive. The intent of the country's founders was to create a series of checks and balances so that no one entity could dominate the government. Generally speaking, in both federal and state governments, the legislative branch makes the law, the executive branch and its agencies implement the law, and the courts apply and interpret the law. Courts and judges are important in policy making indirectly and influence policy implementation through their interpretation of constitutions and statutory language at both the state and federal levels (Teitlebaum & Wilensky, 2013).

Public policy is made by both executive and legislative branches of government at federal, state, and local levels and by authoritative administrative entities in public agencies. Policy is also made (indirectly) by the judicial branches of government, primarily through the system of courts and judges. Although the executive and legislative branches of state government demonstrate more variability, the policy-making process and policy decisions themselves are similar whether they occur at the state or federal level (Teitlebaum & Wilensky, 2013).

Four types of policy exist: laws, rules and regulations, operational decisions, and judicial decisions. These types of polices may be further described based on their purpose and, therefore, their mechanism of action: allocative (distribution or redistribution of resources) or regulatory (Feldstein, 2006). The mechanism of action of health-related policies is illustrated by examples identified throughout this chapter.

State Policy Making

State governments vary widely in the authority and term limits given to the executive (governor), the frequency with which their legislative bodies are in session, and whether legislators serve on a full- or part-time basis. State legislatures may meet annually or biannually and have different budget cycles. Additionally, states differ in their budget requirements and tax authorities (many have at least some tax and expenditure limit rules), with most requiring a balanced budget.

State policy is particularly important for health care because states have authority over a variety of health-related matters that are not governed by federal law. For example, states have authority over scope of professional practice and licensure, accreditation of academic programs, and healthcare service providers. They regulate commerce and insurance (including health insurance) and determine public health roles and responsibilities, providing essential public health services as well as emergency and first response infrastructure. States also control the scope and operation of Medicaid programs after federal requirements are met (Teitlebaum & Wilensky, 2013).

If a healthcare entity or health executive is interested in being informed about or informing state health policy, it is important to know about the state's governing entities and legislative structure, be familiar with key public officials and elected representatives, and understand the legislative calendar in that state or jurisdiction.

Federal Policy Making

The executive branch of the federal government is the office of the president of the United States. The legislative branch of the federal government comprises two chambers, the House of Representatives and the Senate, each with unique governmental authority. The House includes 435 members, with state representatives allocated in proportion to the population in each of the

50 states. Congressional representatives serve four-year terms. The Senate has 100 members, two from each state, who serve six-year terms.

The leadership of each legislative body is determined by political party (elected by the members), with the majority party enjoying advantages such as the ability to determine when bills are introduced and voted upon. Both the House and Senate representatives do the majority of their work in working committees—that is, writing (drafting) and amending bills and managing the process that controls how those bills are considered. Legislators are appointed to serve on several working committees. There are 20 standing or working committees in the House of Representatives and 17 in the Senate.

Committees that have **"authorization jurisdiction"** have the authority to establish programs and agencies. As such, they are particularly influential. Committees that have **appropriation authority** are able to propose program and agency funding and are also very important (Teitlebaum & Wilensky, 2013). Eleven congressional committees have primary jurisdiction over legislation that is pertinent to hospitals and other healthcare institutions. In the Senate, these are the Budget Committee; Finance Committee; Homeland Security and Governmental Affairs Committee; Committee on Health, Education, Labor and Pensions; and Judiciary Committee. In the House, they are the Budget Committee, Committee on Education and Labor, Committee on Energy and Commerce, Homeland Security Committee, Judiciary Committee, and Ways and Means Committee (which has jurisdiction over health and legal issues affecting hospitals). The members and leadership of these committees are among the most influential legislators on Capitol Hill, and certainly the most important in matters related to health policy (American Hospital Association [AHA], 2011). As such, the representatives who serve as leaders and members of these key committees figure importantly in the policy-making process and are often the target of **interest groups'** opposition or support, depending on their position.

THE POLICY-MAKING PROCESS

The policy-making process informs the understanding or perception of a policy problem and the options to address it, thereby contributing to development of the political will and motivation to solve it (Paton, 2014). Policy process is the means through which policies are initiated, developed or formulated, negotiated, communicated, implemented, and evaluated. The conceptual model for public policy making involves three interconnected phases: policy formulation, policy implementation, and policy modification (Longest, 2010). The description of the central activities involved in the process are depicted in **Table 10–2**.

Table 10–2 Conceptual Model of Public Policymaking

Policy Process Phase	Process Activities
Policy formulation (including problem identification)	Includes activities that inform how the policy agenda is set and policies are developed, agreed upon, and communicated.
Policy implementation	Includes activities that specify how policy is implemented (who does what and how). This is particularly important because policies that are not implemented, or that are diverted or changed, will not achieve the outcomes sought.
Policy evaluation	Includes policy impact, monitoring, and evaluation (what happens when a policy is implemented, including how it is monitored to achieve its objectives) to determine whether there are unintended consequences. This process may lead to policies being changed or terminated and new policies being introduced.

Reproduced from Longest, B. (2010). *Health policy making in the United States* (5th ed.). Chicago, IL: Health Administration Press.

Those who wish to influence the development of legislation must become familiar with the timetable, calendar, process, and responsibilities associated with how legislation is proposed and ultimately becomes law. Extensive website resources are provided at the end of the chapter for those interested in learning more about the federal policy-making process and legislative actions.

COMPLEXITY OF HEALTH POLICY AND POLITICS: FEDERAL POLICY

The policy decisions and actions taken by elected representatives are complex and sometimes convoluted. The politics of health policy in particular is shaped by individual values (typically individual social and religious philosophies) and views about the proper role of government in policy making. It is influenced by what policymakers understand about problems and various policy options. Policy making is also ultimately influenced by what policymakers believe to be the political feasibility of pursuing a particular course of action and the influence (financial contributions and voter mobilization) of interest groups as they operate within the electoral cycle. A variety of factors also influence policymakers' views on policy-amenable problems and decision options, especially those related to business and economic trends, international conditions and events, population health and demographic trends, and trends or innovations related to science and technology (Paton, 2014; Smyrl, 2014). These factors are discussed in greater depth later in this chapter.

The process of raising funds and campaigning for reelection shapes the political reality of elected officials by creating the need for policymakers to produce immediate results to appease voters and earn reelection. For political expediency and other reasons, policies tend to be made incrementally and often coincide with the election cycle. Considering the iterative, interdependent steps in the policy-making process and the number of votes required to enact legislation, successfully navigating the legislative process necessitates lengthy negotiations, bargaining, and compromise. When there is a lack of agreement or unwillingness to compromise, the result is government gridlock and inaction (Frakes, 2012). This problem becomes even more pronounced when different political parties control the White House and the legislative bodies.

The Importance of Managing Agreement

The process of managing agreement to establish consensus is particularly important to the policy-making process. Whether at the state or federal level, the policy process often unfolds under circumstances where there is a lack of public agreement on what constitutes a policy-relevant problem and amidst disagreement about whether or how the problem should be addressed through government/policy interventions. In such circumstances, the political will to move forward is not guaranteed. Policymakers are much less likely to be influenced by scientific merit and more likely to be influenced by policy options that bridge or bring together conflicting and diverse interests. For this reason, comprehensive legislation to enact significant change can be derailed by disagreements that cannot be overcome in the policy-making process. Generally speaking, elected representatives are more likely to support and vote for a policy that is popular with their constituents than one that is not. Thus the management of disagreement reinforces the importance of public opinion and interest groups' influence as they shape policymakers' views about the political feasibility of a given policy option.

Amidst the wide variation in political and social views in the United States, one consistent area of public agreement is growing cynicism about perceived dysfunction in the federal policy-making process and criticism of the ineffectiveness of government interventions in actually solving difficult social and economic problems (Pew Research Center, 1998, 2014). This attitude is expected to figure prominently in the outcome of future elections.

U.S. health policy currently consists of a patchwork of public- and private-sector healthcare programs and policies that at times represent conflicting values and have demonstrated varying degrees of success in addressing problems and needs related to healthcare access and equity, quality of care, and efficiency. Ideally, health policy should be made based on objective scientific evidence and facts, after rational public debate about the nature of the problem and the most effective available policy alternative(s). Unfortunately, on a practical level this process tends to be highly emotional and is not always informed by credible information and facts. It is more typically made through what Kingdon (1984) describes as a process akin to making sausage.

While health policy is influenced and shaped by the constitutional, institutional, political, economic, ideological, and technological trends in the environment, it is the guarantees of the U.S. Constitution that give rise to differences in viewpoints (especially minority views), that ensure minority views are heard, and that give special interest groups a voice in the policy-making process.

HEALTH POLICY ACTORS AND INTEREST GROUPS

Interest groups influence public policy in several important ways—for example, by generating campaign contributions, distributing information, and mobilizing voters. As disseminators of specialized information, interest groups are influential with other voters and public opinion makers as well as elected representatives. These groups apply their economic resources and the influence of their constituents' votes to lobby for or against specific issues and may also fund background research and marketing materials to influence public opinion and the policy-making process (Stone, 2011).

The constitutionally guaranteed rights to freedom of speech, association, and petition make it possible for a variety of interest groups to promote policies for a variety of purposes (including for private profit) and engage in a variety of strategies to successfully defeat policies they perceive as harmful to their interests. Many interest groups promote what may be narrow, personal interests; some do so while claiming to represent the public's interest or the common good.

The key actors in the health policy-making process include a variety of public and private institutions and groups, such as healthcare providers, healthcare practitioners, healthcare purchasers, and health insurers as well as consumers. Health professionals and health executives have specialized, in-depth knowledge about the health system and understand the complexity of issues associated with or likely to be influenced by a particular policy intervention. As insiders, they often have credibility to inform policymakers' views (in all phases of the policy-making process) and may have access that enables them to communicate directly with large numbers of voters. As such, they are important political power brokers.

Every voter is also a consumer of health services, and each individual is likely to have personal experience with a health problem or illness that shapes his or her views about how well the health system is working and, in turn, his or her understanding of the merits of a particular health policy under consideration (Soroka, Maioni, & Martin, 2013). Voters view issues and policies in terms of perceived personal impact ("what it means to me") first. This perspective on the perceived impact of a particular policy option explains not only an individual's voting preference, but also the course of policy action and communication strategy an interest group may elect to pursue.

Associations that represent various interest groups may demand five types of legislation: legislation to increase demand, legislation to secure higher reimbursement, legislation to reduce the price and/or increase the quantity of complements, legislation to decrease the availability of and/or increase the price of substitutes, and legislation to limit increases in supply (Feldstein, 2006).

Healthcare professionals are insiders—experts who have recognized credibility to sway what the public and policymakers think. They are directly affected by policy and, therefore, are likely to exert extensive political leverage not only to inform an understanding of the problem(s), but also to weigh in on the merit or impact of policy options on specific individuals and the community at large. For similar reasons, hospitals and long-term care facilities also represent important and active interest groups. They, too, are key actors that influence health policy because of their engagement in the policy process and because they are the actual providers of care and services (especially to aged and disabled populations under the Medicaid and Medicare insurance programs). This said, almost every consumer of health services has expectations about hospitals as important providers of health services that are readily recognized as being needed by individuals. Thus, healthcare executives may be particularly influential in all phases of the policy-making process and in shaping policy change over time.

Financial Influence of Special Interests

As well as shaping public views, interest groups make direct contributions to political campaigns and use lobbyists to represent them in the political arena. They engage in marketing to influence public perception as well as policy officials' knowledge and views about issues and options throughout the policy-making process. In addition to campaign contributions to elected officials and candidates, interest groups spend billions of dollars each year to lobby for their causes, disseminating technical and political information to Congress and federal agencies. Because of the financial "influence" of lobbyists and their contributions in funding campaigns, these actors figure prominently in the policy-making process and are important in understanding special interest impact in election outcomes.

The Center for Responsible Politics (CRP) tracks campaign contributions and monetary giving to federal legislators—information that is relevant to understanding how interest groups operate. CRP publishes data on contributions made by individual, registered lobbyists by sector and type of organization; it also tracks giving by political action committees and analyzes the recipients of campaign contributions.

It is important for health executives to understand that health-sector entities and health professionals groups figure prominently as campaign contributors. According to the CRP, from 1998 to 2014, the health sector was the second highest campaign contributor (just behind the miscellaneous business sector), with giving that totaled $6,381,242,984. Within the health sector, the industry with the highest campaign contribution total was pharmaceuticals/health products, with $3,036,124,697. From 1998 to 2014, the hospital/long-term care industry ranked as the 10th highest giving entity, with $1,277,409,621; health professionals were ranked as 15th highest, with $1,148,654,336 in total giving.

Only four industries and retirees spent more money on political campaigns in 2012 than health professionals—a fact that elected officials certainly know. Health-related contributions totaled nearly $152.3 million in 2012, far more than the nearly $102 million given during the 2008 election (Vendituoli, 2013). Notably, the American Medical Association (AMA) spent more money ($16.5 million) on lobbying in 2012 than any other health professional group. Its generosity was followed by that of other physician groups: The American College of Radiology gave more than $3.5 million to elected officials, and the American College of Emergency Room Physicians gave $2.9 million. The contributions by all health professionals were distributed between both Republican candidates (58%) and Democratic candidates (42%). The breakdown of funds by source is also interesting: Individual contributors were the lead source with 48%, followed by political action committees at 44% and soft money at 9%. Not surprising, the top lobbying concerns expressed by health professionals in 2013 dealt with implementation of the ACA and physician compensation (Vendituoli, 2014).

Even when scientific evidence is available and compelling, it may fail to inform policy-making outcomes when it conflicts with societal cultural, moral, or religious values that resonate with the public or elected officials. More often than not, the science of policy making is trumped by the influence of the emotional side of deal making and the means by which political will is expressed. Health policies resulting from such deal making may turn out to be ineffective in addressing the problem of interest. To understand health policy in the United States, one must understand the health policy environment, including the underlying politics. Further, it is important to keep in mind that no single factor in the health policy environment influences and shapes health policy making; rather, health policy making is the product of a variety of complex and interrelated factors (Patel & Rushefsky, 2014). These factors constitute the environmental context for policy making.

The Importance of Environmental Context

The environmental context sets the stage for the policy-making process and helps identify what is resonating with voters and elected representatives to create political will. It is determined by complex, systemic factors (political, economic, and social factors at the local, regional, national, and international levels) that have an ongoing effect on health and health policy. Health executives need to understand that many factors far removed from the health system itself are important in the policy process (Moat, Lavis, & Abelson, 2013). For example, the following factors (some of which are interdependent) are instrumental in establishing the environmental context for health policy making (Leichter, 1979):

- *Situational factors:* Changing conditions or "focusing events" that serve to motivate policymakers and create broad public awareness about a problem and/or policy solution options.
- *Structural factors:* Population characteristics and social conditions such as demographic characteristics and economic conditions in a community. These factors influence the opportunities and motivations of individuals and organizations to participate in policy discussions and governance decisions.
- *Cultural factors:* The characteristics and values that dictate the norms of a nation, society, and community. Differences in ethnicity and language, in particular, may lead to certain groups being poorly informed about their rights (related to civic engagement and healthcare) or receiving services that do not meet their particular needs.
- *International factors:* Conditions that influence interdependence between states, and that influence sovereignty and international cooperation in health-related matters. Although many health problems are dealt with by local and national governments, some demand cooperation between national, regional, or multilateral organizations. For example, such collaboration is important when considering global mobility and its relationship to the spread or containment of infectious diseases.

THE IMPORTANCE OF ECONOMICS IN HEALTH POLICY MAKING

Because policy is often used to correct problems with market failures, an understanding of the importance of economic conditions that attract the attention of policymakers is important. The U.S. health system is defined by an imperfect economic market, where services are provided by private healthcare providers who are primarily paid by public and private insurance entities (Shi & Singh, 2014). Consumers have varying degrees of choice in selecting healthcare service providers, with this freedom typically being limited by the provisions of their health insurance coverage and the constraints of who is permitted to provide (supply) healthcare services. Even though the majority of health services in the United States are provided by private entities, health care is not a true free market. Those entities that influence demand for health services figure prominently in supplying them (creating a quasi-perfect or imperfect market). However, the U.S. health system is also influenced by principles consistent with both market justice and social justice principles, which sometimes conflict with one another, especially when considering how health services for the uninsured are financed (Shi & Singh, 2014). True free market (income-optimizing) forces that dominate the behavior of those who deliver and consume healthcare services do not exist. The overlaying income motivations, government regulation, and administrative costs associated with the health system and its various providers are viewed as restrictive and excessively influential.

As noted previously, concerns about U.S. healthcare costs, quality, and access, brought about by rising healthcare costs, inadequate access to limited healthcare resources, and wide variation in quality, have been key factors motivating the call for health reform. The healthcare component as a share of the nation's total gross domestic product (GDP) has been steadily increasing (standing at 16.9% in 2013), even as government efforts have attempted to decrease national health expenditures. Government policymakers, consumers, and payers of health services are demanding greater efficiency and quality from healthcare service providers and more value for the public's investment in health care. Medical price inflation is consistently higher than the annual changes in the consumer price index, and healthcare spending growth rates have consistently surpassed the growth rate in the general economy.

The complex interactions of many factors explain the ongoing rise in U.S. healthcare spending. Chief among these factors are the high costs of producing healthcare goods and services in the United States, which stem from numerous sources: higher and increasing wages and benefits; the cost of technology and supplies; regulation; excessive administrative costs; the cost of defensive medicine and medical practice variation; the cost of waste, fraud, and abuse; and demographic factors such as the aging of the population. In addition, the reliance on third-party payments for health care makes most consumers oblivious to the price of services and their costs. Moreover, the expectation that the latest available technology will be used and individual demand for particular goods and services make health care less "price sensitive" than other consumer markets. As such, public expectations are consistently high and sometimes unrealistic considering the cost relative to the benefit of particular services. Some economists also believe healthcare provider–induced demand leads to excessive utilization of limited resources. Thus, an imperfect healthcare market affects health resource utilization, supply, and demand.

The United States spends more money on health care than any nation. In 2012, U.S. spending on health care accounted for 16.9% of GDP—the highest share among all OECD countries (**Figure 10–1**). Moreover, the healthcare component of the nation's GDP continues to increase despite attempts to control expenditures and health care prices.

While U.S. policy efforts have succeeded in slowing the rate of health spending in recent years, costs continue to increase. National health expenditures (NHE) grew 3.6% to $2.9 trillion in 2013 ($9,255 per person), when they accounted for 17.4% of the GDP (Centers for Medicare and Medicaid Services [CMS], 2015); see **Exhibit 10–1**. NHE are forecast to reach

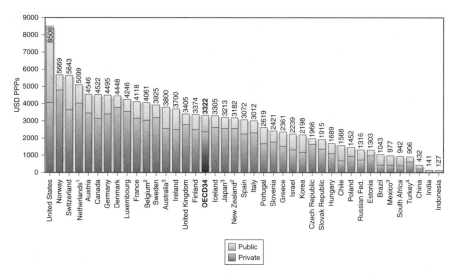

Figure 10–1 GDP share of health expenditures, public and private, in OECD Countries, 2011

Reproduced from OECD. (2013). Health at a glance 2013: OECD indicators. OECD Publishing. Available at: http://dx.doi.org/10.1787/health_glance-2013-en.

> **Exhibit 10–1** U.S. national health expenditures, 2013
>
> - Medicare: Grew 3.4% to $585.7 billion, accounting for 20% of total NHE
> - Medicaid: Grew 6.1% to $449.4 billion, accounting for 15% of total NHE
> - Private health insurance: Grew 2.8% to $961.7 billion, accounting for 33 % of total NHE
> - Out-of-pocket spending: Grew 3.2% to $339.4 billion in 2013, accounting for 12% of total NHE
> - Hospital expenditures: Grew 4.3% to $936.9 billion (slower growth than the 5.7% in 2012)
> - Physician and clinical services: Grew 3.8% to $586.7 billion (faster growth than the 4.5% in 2012)
> - Prescription drugs: Increased 2.5% to $271.1 billion (faster growth than the 0.5% in 2012)
>
> Reproduced from Centers for Medicare and Medicaid (CMS). (2015). National health expenditures 2013. Available at: http://www.cms.gov/Research-Statistics-Data-and-Systems/Statistics-Trends-and-Reports/NationalHealthExpendData/NHE-Fact-Sheet.html.

approximately $5.1 trillion by 2023 (CMS, 2015). With so many dollars at stake and given the size and influence of the health sector on the overall U.S. economy and its impact in local communities, the cost, quality, effectiveness, and value of health care will continue to be an important concern for policymakers, government agencies, voters and business entities alike.

Increasingly on the minds of policymakers are differences in U.S. health outcomes given the amount spent on health care. In 2011, OECD reported U.S. life expectancy was 78.7 years, lagging behind the average life expectancy of 80.2 years in other OECD nations. The shorter U.S. life expectancy is thought to be due to gaps in health insurance coverage, inadequate primary care, and poorer living conditions and health-related behavior for a significant portion of the U.S. population (OECD, 2014). Given the status of ACA implementation, the shortfall in state Medicaid expansion, the aging of the population and the increase in the number of Medicare-eligible persons (e.g., baby-boomers) in coming years, and the ongoing concerns about Medicare program solvency, this issue will no doubt continue to garner policymakers' attention in coming years.

Recent health reform efforts have also focused on government and health-care provider roles and responsibility for improving population health and for reducing health disparities. Elected policymakers and nonelected government officials alike are using payment policy to improve the cost, quality, and effectiveness of healthcare services by holding health professionals and healthcare organizations accountable for the results of the care they provide. Herein lies the basis of the implicit expectation of limited-resource stewardship for all health executives.

Large employers, labor, insurance companies, physicians, and hospitals make up the most powerful and politically active special interest groups that are represented before lawmakers by lobbyists, each with a different economic interest. Political observers see physicians, for example, as advocating policy that maximizes their incomes and minimizes any interference in the way they practice medicine; healthcare organizations seek to maximize reimbursement/payment (from both private and public payers); large employers are motivated to maximize health insurance costs as a business expense related to employee benefits; and both health insurance companies and healthcare organizations want to maintain their share of the healthcare insurance market. All the while, policymakers and government officials are motivated to seek policy that is oriented to influencing the price of health services so as to maintain or enhance benefits for selected population groups and simultaneously to reduce the costs of providing health care.

For policymakers in search of a ready, if not always easy, solution, the problem is that the interests of one group are often at odds with the interests of others. For example, while providers seek to maximize government reimbursement for services provided to Medicare- and Medicaid-covered consumers, government interests call for restraining cost increases, if not actually reducing reimbursements to healthcare providers over time. Similarly, employers dislike rising health insurance premiums, while health insurers (under pressure from employers to constrain rising premiums) face pressures from healthcare providers, who resent payment cuts that lead to a reduction in their incomes.

The self-interests of the various players produce countervailing forces within the system that keeps any one interest from dominating the policy arena. Each provider has a large stake in health policy, is motivated to protect its own self-interest, and would prefer to avoid comprehensive, system-wide changes. Consequently, the approach to U.S. healthcare reform is characterized as incremental or piecemeal.

OBJECTIVES OF HEALTH REFORM

The most recent health reform efforts are those associated with the passage of the Patient Protection and Accountability Act. Putting aside the politics of the ACA, the development, adoption, and implementation of this legislation have provided observers with numerous examples of stakeholder/interest group conflicts and countervailing self-interests and economic goals. The biggest challenge with the status of the legislation and health reform efforts moving forward is managing government interests and the policy goal of increasing insurance coverage while curtailing the rise of healthcare costs.

The conflict between achieving social objectives and economic principles complicates adoption of a cohesive set of values to guide health reform. That said, an evolving focus on population health reflects support for social justice values and goals over primarily economic principles and business focused goals. Thus evolving social and economic conditions are important to national policy goals of increasing access to health care and improving healthcare quality while decreasing costs. As such, they are among the key drivers that can be expected to shape health reform in the future.

The confluence of these factors can be observed in five specific socioeconomic trends that figure prominently in health reform and demands related to the management of scarce resources. First, it is widely recognized that the health status of a community significantly influences the utilization of available health services and healthcare costs overall. Second, future planning for health services must focus on population demographics and health status to reduce the social and economic burden of disease and disability. Third, there is evolving consensus among policymakers and providers alike that the effectiveness of healthcare systems and organizations should be based on their contributions and impacts not only on individual health outcomes, but also on the health outcomes of the population in a particular geographic area. Fourth, the challenge of making health care available to all Americans remains an ongoing and unmet goal and problem that will require the collective, ongoing efforts of healthcare providers, policymakers, and other stakeholders to tackle. Fifth, managers and policymakers alike understand that objective data and evidence from a variety of metrics (i.e., health status and financial performance) are relevant to evaluating health system performance and determining the effectiveness of existing policy. These metrics should likewise be utilized by policymakers and health care executives in planning future strategies, measuring progress, and identifying opportunities to discontinue ineffective or unneeded services.

STEWARDSHIP AND HEALTH POLICY

Socioeconomic and demographic trends reinforce the importance of healthcare executives having the knowledge and skills needed to manage complex systems and also influence health policy and public health outcomes that are dependent upon a loosely coupled system of professional providers, third-party payers (government and private insurance), and employees, in an environment characterized by shrinking reimbursements, while improving the safety, quality, and value of healthcare services. As the management of increasingly scarce resources increases in importance, so does the role of health executives as stewards of healthcare resources.

The ACA's requirement for nonprofit hospitals [IRS section 501(r)(3)] to undertake community health assessments and provide documented community benefit programs aligned with improving public health overall is not a coincidence (Internal Revenue Service [IRS], 2011). The basic elements of the legislation provide for expanded access, cost sharing and subsidies, changes to the tax code, health insurance exchanges, changes in Medicare and Medicaid payments, and federal regulation for health insurance benefit design; the ACA also standardizes private insurance through federally determined stop-loss ratios. While the legislation provides for state Medicaid expansion, as of February 2015 only 28 states had opted to do so, after the U.S. Supreme Court struck down this mandate for states. In addition, the ACA provides funds for innovations in cost containment and strategies for improving quality and performance along with prevention and wellness (Department of Health and Human Services [HHS], 2014).

While the ACA provides for major changes in the U.S. healthcare system, it is also notable for what it leaves unchanged. After more than four decades of rising costs, health inequalities, and healthcare insecurity, the ACA provides resources to improve the living standards of low-wage workers and their families and increases economic protection for the middle class. It is widely agreed that the most important objective of the law is to change how health insurance works and to make it affordable. That said, the ACA does not change how medical care is delivered and it may not change the long-term trajectory of health spending.

Effective healthcare stewardship in the future depends on the ability of health systems and organizations to identify solutions to the endemic problems of high cost, limited access, and variable—if not poor—quality of health (Travis, Egger, Davies, & Mechbal, 2002). Stewardship functions require healthcare executives to be comfortable in the management of scarce resources and to have the ability to understand the interrelationships of these complex factors so that they can develop health policies to manage stakeholder expectations and improve the performance of the imperfect market in the healthcare sector.

Definition of Stewardship

The World Health Organization (WHO, 2001) has identified four functions that all health systems carry out, regardless of how they are organized:

financing, resource generation, service delivery, and stewardship. Expanding on the WHO definition, "stewardship" is the careful and responsible management of resources to maximize the well-being of the population (including population health). As they pertain to the health system, the functions associated with the stewardship role of health executives are concerned with managing resources and system performance to reconcile market inefficiencies and potential public-sector (policy) failures.

The following functions are associated with the role and performance of healthcare stewardship:

- Generation of intelligence
- Formulation of strategic policy direction
- Ensuring tools for implementation (authority/power, incentives, and sanctions)
- Building coalitions and partnerships
- Ensuring fit between policy objectives and organizational structure and culture
- Ensuring accountability (Buse, 2012)

"Stewards distinguish themselves first by accepting responsibility, and then by acting on that responsibility to preserve, protect, and nurture something precious, through recurrent threats, for the purpose of delivering that precious thing to future generations" (Nichols, 2009, p. 30). The most important concept here is that stewardship of the healthcare system by health executives involves working to ensure that the system and available resources are used efficiently. "That is what stewardship is... leaders have to take care to set rules and make key choices to prevent imbalances that would lead to unacceptable outcomes... Political, economic, and health system leaders... must make sure that our system serves all of us at a basic level (and not just all Americans, but all residents and visitors)... At the same time, rules and choices must be made so that the system will be sustainable over time, and thus able to serve all of us in the future" (Nichols, 2009, pp. 31–32).

The responsible management of the health system involves the promotion of health and the well-being of its constituents, consistent with the principles of good government and some measure of social justice (Jansen, 2013). When government or health executives fail to use limited resources efficiently, that failure has a deleterious impact on those we care for (e.g., leading to preventable deaths and disability). Health systems are charged with using data and evidence to monitor performance and establish procedures to address the financial health of the populations they serve, and with reducing inefficient and ineffective care and services so as to reduce unnecessary health expenditures. Stewards must provide the necessary leadership to establish the rules by which all the stakeholders behave to achieve resource management and service delivery performance that reflects the interests of both the public and private sectors and health policy requirements (Buse, 2012). Health policy is an important tool to achieve this goal.

CONCLUSION

Many believe the U.S. health system is too focused on disease treatment, and is overly complex, fragmented, unreliable, and too costly. Since the 1960s, federal and state health policy has sought to influence the organization and functioning of the health system, primarily to improve access to health services and/or slow the growth of health expenditures. Fueled by growing concerns about escalating healthcare costs and unmet value for performance, policymakers' interests in health policy as a vehicle to change the health system will continue.

Health executives must understand the politics of health policy making as well as the role and function of the hospital executive in working effectively with policymakers as part of their duties in leading and managing the healthcare enterprise. Moreover, their expertise and fiduciary responsibilities make them suitable to serve as healthcare stewards. As federal health reform continues to evolve and greater accountability and value are not only expected but specifically linked to reimbursement, the management of resource efficiency must be understood as having a broader community impact. For health executives as community leaders and stewards, advocating for health policy that contributes to the greater good while meeting public expectations and ensuring the success of the healthcare enterprise is the new norm.

CHAPTER SUMMARY

Health policy is a specialized type of public policy. Generally speaking, public policies are authoritative decisions made in the legislative, executive, or judicial branches of government. The policy-making process informs the understanding or perception of a policy problem and the options to address it, thereby contributing to development of the political will and motivation to address problems/needs. Policy process is the means through which policies are initiated, developed or formulated, negotiated, communicated, implemented, and evaluated. The inter-connected phases of the public policy process involves: policy formulation, policy implementation, and policy modification (Longest, 2010).

U.S. health policy has evolved over time through complex policy-making processes (administrative and judicial actions that have created a patchwork of nuanced, rule-laden federal and state health policies). Health policy directly affects every individual, business entity, and community and is linked to the economic vitality of the country and every state. Health policies change as a result of political agendas, and in response to public health, unmet needs and problems. Views about public policy action and needs are in turn shaped by individuals and entities that participate in the policy-making process

The scope and impact of health policies and economic conditions substantially affects the planning and management of healthcare services organizations. For these reasons, healthcare executives must have a working knowledge of the policy-making process and an understanding of the drivers for health policy formulation and change. They also need to understand the evolution of public policy and the goals and impact of policy in allocation and management of limited resources. Challenges in managing health service organizations efficiently and effectively given local health needs explains the importance of the stewardship role and function of health executives.

While environmental context sets the stage for the policy-making process, that context evolves over time, determined by complex, systemic factors (political, economic, and social factors at the local, regional, national, and international levels). These factors influence population health on-going, and in turn iteratively influences the public policy process, the regulation and financing of health systems. Health executives need to understand that many factors far removed from the health system itself are important in the health policy making process. Effective healthcare stewardship depends on the ability of health systems and organizations to identify solutions to the endemic problems of high cost, limited access, and variable—if not poor—quality of health.

Recent health reform efforts have focused on government and healthcare provider roles and responsibility for improving population health and for reducing health disparities. Elected policy makers and nonelected government officials alike are using payment policy to improve the cost, quality, and effectiveness of healthcare services and by holding health professionals and healthcare organizations accountable for the results of the care they provide. Herein lies the basis of the implicit expectation of limited-resource stewardship for all health executives.

Key Terms and Concepts

Appropriation authority: A legislative committee that has the authority to propose program and agency funding.

Authorization jurisdiction: A legislative committee that has the authority to establish programs and agencies.

Health policy: Public policy that is related to influencing health and the diverse array of healthcare providers and functions.

Health policy process: The means through which policies are initiated, developed or formulated, negotiated, communicated, implemented and evaluated. It involves three interconnected phases: policy formulation, policy implementation, and policy modification.

Interest groups: Groups who use their economic resources and engage in a variety of strategies to successfully promote or defeat policies they perceive as harmful to their interests.

Key health policy actors: A variety of individuals and entities such as public and private institutions and groups such as healthcare providers, healthcare practitioners, healthcare purchasers, and health insurers as well as consumers who influence public health policy.

Public policy: An authoritative decision made in the legislative, executive, or judicial branch of government, intended to direct or influence the actions, behaviors, or decisions of others.

Stewardship: The careful and responsible management of resources to maximize the well-being of the population (including population health). In regard to health systems, the functions associated with the stewardship role of health executives are concerned with managing resources and system performance to reconcile market inefficiencies and potential public-sector (policy) failures.

Window of opportunity: The necessary conditions (confluence of problems and consideration of possible solutions, and political circumstances) that create the motivation and political will to stimulate the drafting or formation of legislation (new laws or amendments).

REFERENCES

American Hospital Association (AHA), Legislative Committees on Health. (2011). http://www.aha.org/content/00-10/09congresshealthcommittees.pdf

Buse, K. (2012). *Making health policy: Understanding public health.* New York, NY: McGraw-Hill International.

Center for Responsive Politics. (n.d.a) https://www.opensecrets.org/lobby/

Center for Responsive Politics. (n.d.b). Ranked by industry/year. https://www.opensecrets.org/lobby/top.php?indexType=i&showYear=2014

Center for Responsive Politics. (n.d.c). Ranked by top contributors (individuals)/ year. https://www.opensecrets.org/lobby/lobby_topcontribs.php

Center for Responsive Politics. (n.d.d). Ranked by spending/year. https://www.opensecrets.org/lobby/top.php?indexType=s&showYear=2012

Centers for Medicare and Medicaid (CMS). (2015). National health expenditures 2013. http://www.cms.gov/Research-Statistics-Data-and-Systems/Statistics-Trends-and-Reports/NationalHealthExpendData/NHE-Fact-Sheet.html

Department of Health and Human Services (HHS). (2014). Affordable Care Act summary. http://www.hhs.gov/healthcare/facts/timeline/index.html

Feldstein, P. (2006). *The politics of health legislation: An economic perspective* (3rd ed.). Chicago, IL: Health Administration Press.

Frakes, V. L. (2012). Partisanship and (un)compromise: A study of the Patient Protection and Affordable Care Act. *Harvard Journal on Legislation*, 49(1), 135–149.

Institute of Medicine (IOM). (2001). *Crossing the quality chasm: A new health system for the 21st century.* Washington, DC: National Academy Press.

Internal Revenue Service (IRS). (2011). Summary: ACA community health assessment rule. http://www.gpo.gov/fdsys/pkg/USCODE-2011-title26/html/USCODE-2011-title26-subtitleA-chap1-subchapF-partI-sec501.htm

Jansen, L. (2013). Between beneficence and justice: The ethics of stewardship in medicine. *Journal of Medicine & Philosophy*, 38(1), 64–81.

Kingdon, J. (1984). *Agendas, alternatives and public policies.* Boston, MA: Little, Brown.

Leichter, H. (1979). *A comparative approach to policy analysis: Health care policy in four nations.* Cambridge, UK: Cambridge University Press.

Longest, B. (2010). *Health policy making in the United States* (5th ed.). Chicago, IL: Health Administration Press.

Moat, K. A., Lavis, J., & Abelson, J. (2013). How contexts and issues influence the use of policy-relevant research syntheses: A critical interpretive synthesis. *Milbank Quarterly*, 91(3), 604–648.

National Center for Health Leadership (NCHL). (2006). Healthcare leadership competency model v2. http://www.nchl.org/Documents/NavLink/NCHL_Competency_Model-full_uid892012226572.pdf

Nichols, L. (2009). Stewardship: What kind of society do we want? In M. Crowley (Ed.), *Connecting American values with health reform* (pp. 30–32). Garrison, NY: The Hastings Center. http://www.thehastingscenter.org/uploadedFiles/Publications/Primers/stewardship_nichols.pdf

Organization for Economic Cooperation and Development (OECD). (2014). Health statistics. http://www.oecd.org/els/health-systems/health-data.htm

Patel, K., & Rushefsky, M. (2014). *Healthcare politics and policy in America* (4th ed.). New York, NY: Taylor & Francis

Paton, C. R. (2014). The politics and analytics of health policy. *International Journal of Health Policy and Management*, 2(3), 105–107.

Pew Research Center. (1998), How Americans view government. http://www.people-press.org/1998/03/10/how-americans-view-government/

Pew Research Center. (2014). Cure for national political divisions. http://www.people-press.org/2014/12/11/few-see-quick-cure-for-nations-political-divisions/

Shi, L., & Singh, D. (2014). *Delivering healthcare in America: A systems approach* (6th ed.). Burlington, MA: Jones & Bartlett Learning.

Smyrl, M. E. (2014). Beyond interests and institutions: US health policy reform and the surprising silence of big business. *Journal of Health Politics, Policy and Law*, 39(1), 1–4.

Soroka, S., Maioni, A., & Martin, P. (2013). What moves public opinion on health care? Individual experiences, system performance and media framing. *Journal of Health Politics, Policy and Law, 38*(5), 893–920.

Stone, D. (2011). *The policy paradox: The art of political decision making* (3rd ed.). New York, NY: W. W. Norton.

Teitlebaum, J., & Wilensky, S. (2013). *Essentials of health policy and law* (2nd ed.). Burlington, MA: Jones & Bartlett Learning.

Travis, P., Egger, D., Davies, P., & Mechbal, A. (2002). *Towards better stewardship: Concepts and critical issues.* Global Programme on Evidence for Health Policy Discussion Paper, No 48. Geneva, Switzerland: World Health Organization.

Vendituoli, M. (2014). Health professional background analysis in influence and lobbying. https://www.opensecrets.org/industries/background.php?cycle=2014&ind=H01

World Health Organization (WHO). (2001). *Report on WHO meeting of experts on the stewardship function in health systems.* Document HFS/FAR/STW/00.1. Geneva, Switzerland: Author.

WEBSITE RESOURCES

Political Contributions

- Center for Responsive Politics: https://www.opensecrets.org/lobby/

Federal Government

- Legislative Information: http://thomas.loc.gov
- *Roll Call*: http://www.rollcall.com
- Code of Federal Regulations: http://www.access.gpo.gov/nara/cfr/cfr-table-search.html
- How a bill becomes a law: http://www.usconstitution.net/consttop_law.html
- Legislative branch of government: http://www.whitehouse.gov/our-government/legislative-branch
- Executive branch of government: http://www.whitehouse.gov/our-government/executive-branch
- Judicial branch of government: http://www.whitehouse.gov/our-government/judicial-branch
- Federal rule-making process: http://www.uscourts.gov/RulesAndPolicies/rules/about-rulemaking.aspx
- Kaiser Family Foundation, summary of the Affordable Care Act: http://kff.org/health-reform/fact-sheet/summary-of-the-affordable-care-act/
- Look up federal representatives, offices, and committee leadership: http://www.contactingthecongress.org/

Government Agencies

- Centers for Medicare and Medicaid Services: http://www.cms.gov
- Centers for Disease Control and Prevention: http://www.cdc.gov
- Health Resources and Services Administration: http://www.hrsa.gov
- National Institutes of Health: http://www.nih.gov
- National Library of Medicine: http://www.nlm.nih.gov
- National Center for Health Statistics: http://www.cdc.gov/nchs/
- National Technical Information Service: http://www.ntis.gov
- Substance Abuse and Mental Health Services Administration: http://www.samhsa.gov
- Agency for Health Care Research and Quality: http://www.ahrq.gov
- Government Printing Office (Congressional reports): http://www.gpo.access.gov/congress
- Medicare Payment Advisory Commission: http://www.medpac.gov
- U.S. Office of Rural Health Policy: http://www.hrsa.gov/ruralhealth
- Bureau of Health Professions: http://www.bhpr.hrsa.gov
- Agency for International Development: http://www.info.usaid.gov/
- U.S. Census Bureau: http://www.census.gov/hhes/www/hlthins.html
- U.S. Department of Health and Human Services: http://www.hhs.gov
- U.S. Food and Drug Administration: http://www.fda.gov
- Congressional Budget Office: http://www.cbo.gov
- General Accounting Office: http://www.gao.gov

State and Local Government

- State and local government: http://www.piperinfo.com/state/states.html
- National Conference of State Legislatures: http://www.ncsl.org
- National Governors Association: http://www.nga.org
- National Academy for State Health Policy: http://www.nashp.org
- State coverage initiatives: http://www.statecoverage.net
- State constitutions and laws: http://www.law.cornell.edu/statutes.html#state
- National Council of State Boards of Nursing: http://www.ncsbn.org
- Federation of State Medical Boards: http://www.fsmb.org
- Pennsylvania Health Care Cost Containment Council: http://www.phc4.org
- Association of State and Territorial Health Officials: http://www.astho.org

Healthcare Professional and Advocacy Organizations

- Academy Health: http://www.academyhealth.org
- Alliance for Health Reform: http://www.allhealth.org
- American Enterprise Institute: http://www.aei.org
- American Association of Health Plans (managed care plans): http://www.aahp.org
- American Health Care Association: http://www.ahcancal.org
- American Psychiatric Association: http://www.psych.org
- American Psychological Association: http://www.apa.org
- Catholic Health Association of the United States: http://www.chausa.org
- Center for Health Care Strategies: http://www.chcs.org
- Children's Defense Fund: http://www.childrensdefense.org
- Health Consumer Alliance: http://healthconsumer.org/
- Families USA: http://www.familiesusa.org
- Insure Kids Now: http://www.insurekidsnow.gov
- National Coalition on Health Care: http://www.americashealth.org
- National Health Council: http://www.nhcouncil.org
- Center for Medicare Advocacy: http://www.medicareadvocacy.org
- Center for Medicare Education: http://www.medicareed.org
- Medicare Rights Center: http://www.medicarerights.org
- Healthcare Leadership Council: http://www.hlc.org
- Health Insurance Association of America: http://www.hiaa.org
- Health Research and Education Trust: http://www.hret.org
- American Association of Retired Persons: http://www.aarp.org
- World Health Organization: http://www.who.org
- American Public Health Association: http://www.apha.org
- American Nurses Association: http://www.ana.org
- National Rural Health Association: http://www.NRHArural.org
- National Association of Community Health Centers: http://www.nachc.org
- National Association of Public Hospitals and Health Systems: http://www.naph.org
- Society for Healthcare Consumer Advocacy: http://www.shca-aha.org
- American Academy of Nurse Practitioners: http://www.aanp.org
- American Association of Colleges of Nursing: http://www.aacn.nche.edu
- American College of Nurse Midwives: http://www.acnm.org
- American College of Nurse Practitioners: http://www.acnpweb.org
- American Academy of Physician Assistants: http://www.aapa.org
- Association of American Medical Colleges: http://www.aamc.org

- American Medical Association: http://www.ama-assn.org
- American Hospital Association: http://www.aha.org
- American Dental Association: http://www.ada.org
- American Dental Education Association: http://www.adea.org
- Joint Commission on Accreditation of Healthcare Organizations: http://www.jcaho.org
- National Committee for Quality Assurance: http://www.ncqa.org
- American Quality Health Association: http://www.ahqa.org
- Pan American Health Organization: http://www.paho.org

Health Policy Resource Centers

- Center for Health Care Strategies: http://www.chcs.org
- Center for Budget and Policy Priorities: http://www.cbpp.org
- Center for Studying Health System Change: http://www.hschange.org
- California Healthcare Foundation: http://www.chcf.org
- Robert Wood Johnson Foundation: http://www.rwjf.org
- Urban Institute: http://www.urban.org
- Heritage Foundation: http://www.heritage.org
- National Academy of Social Insurance: http://www.nasi.org
- Institute of Medicine: http://www.iom.edu
- Institute for Health Policy Solutions: http://www.ihps.org
- Kaiser Family Foundation: http://www.kff.org
- Kaiser Family Foundation, State Health Facts Online: http://www.statehealthfacts.kff.org
- National Health Information Resource Center: http://www.nhirc.org
- Policy News and Information Service: http://www.policy.com
- Employee Benefits Research Institute: http://www.ebri.org
- Dartmouth Atlas of Health Care: http://www.dartmouthatlas.org
- University of Maine: http://www.muskie.usm.maine.edu/research
- Project Hope: http://www.projhope.org
- National Health Policy Forum: http://www.nhpf.org
- North Carolina Rural Health Research and Policy Analysis Program: http://www.schsr.unc.edu
- Association for the Care of Children's Health: http://www.acch.org
- National Clearinghouse for Alcohol and Drug Information: http://www.health.org

- University of California, San Francisco Center for the Health Professions: http://futurehealth.ucsf.edu
- Public Broadcasting Service: http://www.pbs.org
- The Commonwealth Fund: http://www.cmwf.org

Other Resources

- Glossary of Policy Terms: Frequently used health system/policy terms from the Academy Health website: http://www.academyhealth.org /Training/content.cfm?ItemNumber=1657

Chapter 11

The Ethics of Healthcare Reform: Coordinating Rights with Commoditization

—Keith William Diener, PhD

LEARNING OBJECTIVES

- Understand the historical and global perspective of ethics and health care
- Recognize the theoretical background of health care as a commodity and a human right
- Understand the importance of coordination in healthcare management to promote ethical decisionmaking
- Identify the ethical issues incorporated in and implicated by the Affordable Care Act

INTRODUCTION

Healthcare management requires a commitment to coordinating constituents and resources so as to satisfy the increasingly complex legal and moral obligations arising from and persisting beyond full implementation of the Affordable Care Act (ACA).[1] Much literature has examined whether the ACA is morally justified. This chapter sidesteps the justificatory debate by

---

[1] The Affordable Care Act (ACA), as defined herein, incorporates both the Patient Protection and Affordable Care Act (Pub. L. 111–148), which was enacted on March 23, 2010, and the Health Care and Education Reconciliation Act of 2010 (Pub. L. 111–152), which was enacted on March 30, 2010.

accepting the ACA as setting certain boundaries for permissible legal action and obliging citizens to act or refrain from acting under the law. It acquiesces to the ACA by identifying key components of the ACA's consequent ethical challenges and explaining how **coordination** may aid in satisfying these obligations.

This chapter contends that the ACA creates a paradigm within the United States whereby health care is perceived as both a human right and a commodity. The ACA moves beyond the traditional dichotomous argumentation pertaining to health care as a right versus **health care as a commodity** by fashioning an environment in which managers must balance recently expanded healthcare rights with profit-motivated indicia of the commoditization of health care. This chapter first examines health care as a right, then discusses health care as a commodity. Next, an argument is made that coordination is imperative to satisfying the increasingly complex obligations spurred by the ACA. The chapter concludes by analyzing ethics issues that will persist beyond full ACA implementation.

HEALTH CARE AS A RIGHT

Liberal egalitarians often identify **health care as a human right**. According to liberal egalitarians, barriers to access to health care must be removed to ensure that all people have access to health care (Lachman, 2012, p. 249). In pursuit of the removal of these barriers to healthcare access, a multitude of international agreements specify rights to "health" and "health care" as fundamental human rights—for example, *The Universal Declaration of Human Rights* (Article 25), *The International Covenant on Economic, Social, and Cultural Rights* (Article 12), *The Convention on the Rights of the Child* (Article 24), *The Convention on the Elimination of All Forms of Racial Discrimination* (Article 5), *The Convention on the Elimination of All Forms of Discrimination Against Women* (Articles 12 and 14), *The American Declaration on Rights and Duties of Man* (Article 11), and *The Convention on the Rights of Persons with Disabilities* (Article 25). All of these agreements incorporate guarantees aimed at ensuring the removal of barriers to the rights to health and/or health care.

The International Covenant on Economic, Social, and Cultural Rights (ICESCR) includes what is perhaps the most comprehensive article stating what constitutes the right to health. Article 12 of ICESCR provides that:

1. The States Parties to the present Covenant recognize the right of everyone to the enjoyment of the highest attainable standard of physical and mental health.

2. The steps to be taken by the States Parties to the present Covenant to achieve the full realization of this right shall include those necessary for:

a. The provision for the reduction of the stillbirth rate and of infant mortality and for the healthy development of the child;
b. The improvement of all aspects of environmental and industrial hygiene;
c. The prevention, treatment and control of epidemic, endemic, occupational and other diseases;
d. The creation of conditions which would assure to all medical service and medical attention in the event of sickness.

The ICESCR provides for the universality of the right to both physical and mental health and indicates the steps that states shall take to ensure the right to health is fully satisfied. These steps include alteration of environmental conditions to ensure medical services are provided to those in need, reduction of child deaths, and control of various diseases. The ICESCR provision provides a pathway for states to ensure the right to health across national boundaries.

The National Economic and Social Rights Initiative (NESRI, n.d.) maintains a list of human rights standards and procedural principles entailed in the right to health. The human rights standards include universal access, availability, acceptability and dignity, and quality. The procedural principles include nondiscrimination, transparency, participation, and accountability. State governments embracing the right to health may utilize these standards and principles when developing internal and external policies promoting the right to health. In so doing, they should strive for the "highest attainable" standard of health which they can achieve.[2] The obligation to protect and promote the right to health, under most international agreements, extends to the state governments, but it is also imperative that the general population take steps to promote the right to health of others.

In 2000, the United Nations' Committee on Economic, Social, and Political Rights published *General Comment Number 14*, which defines and interprets the right to health. According to the committee, the right to health should be broadly construed to entail both freedoms and entitlements. In other words, the right to health includes the freedoms to control one's body and to be free from torture and simultaneously the entitlement to a system aimed at protecting equality of opportunity in health. The right to health

---

[2] *The Convention on the Rights of Persons with Disabilities* (Article 25).

also includes the "underlying determinants of health," such as conditions necessary to live a reasonably healthy life (e.g., clean drinking water) (*General Comment*, para. 14). The *General Comment* provides a detailed explication of the right to health, all it entails, and its close relationship with other core human rights.

The policy underlying the ACA reinforces the right to health care as an entitlement. It suggests that all persons should be capable of availing themselves of the right to health care. The ACA removes previous barriers to health care, such as those imposed by insurance companies attempting to lower their risk by refusing coverage to certain classes of individuals. For example, section §1101 of the ACA aims to give immediate insurance access to uninsured individuals with preexisting conditions; section §2716 aims to prevent certain discrimination in group health plans arising from income discrepancies. The ACA progresses toward ensuring more-universal access to health care within the United States, and to promoting health care as an entitlement. It moves the country toward the removal of barriers to health care for classes that have traditionally found it difficult to attain coverage.

HEALTH CARE AS A COMMODITY

Some libertarian and free market advocates view health care as a commodity to be exchanged on open markets without governmental interference (Lachman, 2012, p. 249). Free market advocates, such as Milton Friedman, frequently oppose governmental regulation of private business activities. Health care, for many free market advocates, constitutes a private business activity that governments should avoid regulating. Some proponents of health care as a commodity consider scarcity as the underpinning reason for this categorization (Tanner, 2009). Like most commodities, health care is inherently scarce due to financial constraints and a limited number of suppliers, such as doctors and hospitals. From a pragmatic standpoint, health care is often considered a commodity without questioning whether it normatively should be categorized as such.

Views that health care is solely a commodity dovetail with antiregulatory streams of thought. The arguments typically follow the same pattern: By allowing the invisible hand of the market to function and by reducing governmental interference with private economic activity, free competition will emerge within which individuals are motivated to provide better health care, to be innovative, and to consistently try to improve to stay competitive. Perceiving health care as anything other than a commodity may lead to issues of externalization of costs and failure to economize. According to these commentators, when the visible hand begins governing health care, it reduces the motivation of innovators to consistently provide new and better health care.

The profit-oriented hospital developed relatively late in human history. Even in the early nineteenth century, most hospitals were founded in religious institutions and supported mainly by charitable contributions (Welzien, 2011, p. 21). Several developments led to the shift away from charity and toward profit-making enterprises in hospital settings. New advances in medical technology, and the mounting costs of implementing these technologies, triggered the transformation of hospitals from centers for caring for the poor to profit-oriented businesses. Physicians realized that money could be made by providing their services, and eventually hospitals began courting patients to subsidize the costs of caring for the poor, culminating in some hospitals becoming solely for-profit institutions (Welzien, 2011, pp. 21–22). The transformation continued into the twentieth century, when increasingly more hospitals began to focus on profit as their underlying rationale.

The establishment of third-party payers in the 1960s further caused shifts in the profit orientation of many hospitals (Welzien, 2011, p. 22). The advent of Medicare and Medicaid in 1965 and the increasing prevalence of private insurance led many nonprofit hospitals to compete with for-profit hospitals for a piece of the government funding and insurance payouts. In 1969, the Internal Revenue Service (IRS) changed the requirements for hospitals to attain nonprofit status under Section 501(c)(3) of the tax code. In 1969, the charitable care requirement, which mandated a nonprofit hospital to provide for the poor "to the extent of its financial ability," was removed after Medicare and Medicaid were initiated, as these programs were seen as taking on the mission of providing for the poor (Welzien, 2011, p. 22). The IRS initiated a less stringent standard, the community benefit standard, which did not require nonprofit hospitals to care for the poor, but instead only to benefit the community (through a fairly broad measure of community benefit ranging from holding seminars to creating clinics) (Welzien, 2011, p. 22; The Tax Exempt Hospital Sector, 2005). The establishment of Medicare and Medicaid, along with the changes to the tax code that followed, resulted in further shifts toward profit motivations in hospital settings.

The community benefit standard remained the primary standard until the ACA added further requirements for hospitals desiring to maintain tax-exempt status. Under the ACA, 501(c)(3) "charitable hospital organizations" must satisfy a much more stringent set of criteria to maintain their tax-exempt status. To be tax exempt as a charitable hospital, §9007 of the ACA requires that hospitals meet these criteria:

- Hospitals must conduct community needs assessments and implement strategies to meet those needs. Such assessments must take into account a broad array of interests represented by the community and be made widely available to the public.
- Hospitals must develop a written financial assistance policy that includes eligibility criteria for assistance and specifies any discounts, the basis for calculating charges to patients, and the method for applying financial assistance. They must also publish a policy or statement pertaining to measures taken in the event of nonpayment; each hospital must widely publicize this policy within the hospital's community. Finally, the hospital must have a written policy that satisfies the Emergency Medical Treatment and Active Labor Act (EMTALA).
- Hospitals must limit the amount charged to the eligible uninsured (who fall within the financial assistance policy) to be no greater than the amount charged to the insured for the same service, and must prohibit gross charges.
- Hospitals must not engage in extraordinary collections actions before making "reasonable efforts to determine whether the individual is eligible for assistance under the financial assistance policy.[3]

Each hospital aiming to be tax exempt as a charitable hospital must satisfy these four requirements, including all of their subrequirements. Through its new requirements, the ACA assures health care for certain financially eligible patients while simultaneously acknowledging the costs associated with its provision.

COORDINATING HEALTH CARE AS A RIGHT AND AS A COMMODITY

The ACA creates a regime that portrays health care as both a right and a commodity. Coordination is crucial to navigating the new obligations arising from the ACA while simultaneously adhering to the basic ethical principles of mankind. Coordination involves utilizing practical reason (practical wisdom)—what the ancient Greeks called **"phronesis"**—to successfully balance obligations to various constituents, and to determine and take morally

---

[3] ACA §9007.

correct action in complex scenarios. Coordination further involves the "three Cs" of cognizance, communication, and capabilities:

- *Cognizance:* The ability to identify and analyze the everyday problems that inevitably arise in business settings.
- *Communication:* The ability to gather and relay information from and to others.
- *Capabilities:* The means to execute the action decided upon through cognizance and communication—the capacity to complete such action.

Healthcare managers should utilize the three Cs of coordination to ensure their actions satisfy ethical precepts. By embracing phronesis and utilizing reason to make decisions about daily actions, healthcare managers will more effectively contribute to their organizations.

The ACA moves beyond traditional dichotomous notions of health care as a right versus health care as a commodity by portraying health care as *both* a right and a commodity. Through its mandates, this act attempts to mitigate the negative effects of both vantage points while simultaneously embracing the positives of each. Although health care should normatively be available to those who genuinely need it, the industry cannot escape a minimal economic component. Whether in the provision of services through doctors, nurses, and physician's assistants, or in the form of the inescapable costs of medical devices, equipment, and medicine, economics will always play some role in the provision of health care. Even in the early days of religious hospitals that cared for the poor, such hospitals relied heavily on charitable contributions to fund their noble missions. These economic considerations, however, are largely bound by ethical concerns. As Joshua Perry (2012) argues, "A physician's business of treating patients should similarly be understood as an enterprise with ethical boundaries that requires monitoring by legislators, policy makers, and government regulators" (p. 371). The ACA infuses ethical considerations, such as community care, broad access, and responsibility, into hospital administration and industry.

The ACA prohibitions on insurance companies' exclusion of many classes of individuals from coverage reflect the premise that health care is both a right and a commodity. ACA §2704 provides that a "group health plan and health insurance issuer offering group or individual health insurance coverage may not impose any preexisting condition exclusion with respect to such plan or coverage." Prior to the ACA, such exclusions were commonly cited to prevent coverage of individuals with preexisting conditions. The Department of Health and Human Services estimated that "[a]s many as 129 million Americans under age 65" may have been subject to preexisting condition exclusions (Goldstein, 2011). The ACA, however, recognizes the commoditization of health care while removing barriers to access for many classes of individuals.

Healthcare managers embracing coordination should recognize the dual nature of health care as both a right and a commodity. By doing so, they will be better equipped to deal with the challenges they face. The scope and extent of the right to health care in light of the costs of health care recurrently raise thorny questions for hospital administration. Since the EMTALA came into effect in 1986, hospitals have been prohibited from "refusing acute care to any individual who could not afford to pay" (Lachman, 2012, p. 249). This requirement led to cost shifting, in which patients who could afford to pay were forced to pay for those who could not afford to pay. It is estimated that cost shifting raises the yearly health insurance premium by approximately $1000 for each insured family (Menzel, 2009). Part of the justification for the **individual mandate** of the ACA is to prevent such cost shifting by requiring individuals to maintain health insurance or pay a penalty tax. The constitutionality of the individual mandate was affirmed by the U.S. Supreme Court in 2012 in a controversial 5-4 opinion, *NFIB v. Sebelius*.[4] Given this decision, the cost-shifting problems are projected to decline as previously uncovered citizens attain health insurance in the future.

The libertarian and free market concerns that forcing individuals to purchase a commodity infringes on liberty and freedoms have persisted beyond the *Sebelius* decision. Yet individuals are free to violate the individual mandate so long as they are willing to pay the penalty for doing so. According to libertarian thought, despite the mandate's potential for promoting efficiency and distributive justice, because it impinges on individual liberties, it should be avoided. Within the new healthcare paradigm created by the ACA, many freedoms remain protected, including choice of insurance plans, choice of doctors (or networks), and choice of whether and when to seek medical care. In other words, the ACA ensures that everyone may have access to health care, but when and whether to exercise the right to health care resides with each individual. Even in the post-*Sebelius* environment, when and with which provider to expend money on the commodity of health care remains within the ambit of individual choice, despite the reality that most persons must purchase insurance or pay a penalty.

Traditional concepts of virtue ethics may aid the healthcare manager in efforts to coordinate the dual nature of health care in an effective manner. The balance between right and commodity, between extreme viewpoints

---

[4] *National Federation of Independent Business et al. v. Sebelius*, 132 S. Ct. 2566 (2012).

in combination, allows for a middle way to be identified—a mean between two extremes. As Aristotle suggested, **arete** (often translated as "virtue" or "class") is sought by embracing the mean between two extremes. Only through embracing this middle way through reason can one ultimately attain **eudaimonia** ("happiness" or "well-being"). In each circumstance, a health-care manager may similarly balance rights with commoditization through coordination to find the middle way. By exercising coordination, healthcare managers will more effectively navigate the ethically laden terrain that is management.

Aside from virtue ethics, traditional principles of healthcare ethics also influence coordinating efforts. Kurt Darr (2011, pp. 26–33) discusses how principles often link ethical theory and action. Coordination similarly requires a link between abstract ethical theory and a course of action. These links may be formed through cognizance of ethical principles such as (1) **respect for persons**, (2) **beneficence**, (3) **nonmaleficence**, and (4) **justice** (pp. 26–33).

Respect for persons is largely rooted in Kantian ideology, and particularly the second formulation of his categorical imperative. Respect for persons is a key component of human dignity. It is broadly accepted as an integral principle of ethics that may require considerations of autonomy, honesty, confidentiality, and fidelity (Darr, 2011, pp. 26–33). Healthcare managers should recognize that the core value of respecting human dignity qua human dignity underpins many ethical considerations.

The principle of beneficence is broadly accepted in many ethical theories, and may guide healthcare managers to appropriate action. Beneficence is rooted in the Hippocratic Oath, and includes acting for the benefit of patients, with both charity and kindness. Beneficence requires a positive duty of acting to benefit patients and, according to some commentators, to balance the benefits and harms within patient care (Beuchamp & Childress, 1989, pp. 169–170). Although positive action is required to satisfy the principle of beneficence, this principle is rarely impartially applied, but rather is very fact specific and contextually motivated. Although generally healthcare managers, doctors, and other constituents should act to benefit patients with charity and kindness, the scope of this requirement varies situationally.

Nonmaleficence, in contrast, generally involves a duty to refrain from performing certain acts and generally should be abided by impartially. Beuchamp and Childress define the principle of nonmaleficence as involving an "obligation not to inflict harm on others"; it is closely related to the maxim *Primum non nocere* (Above all, do no harm) (Beuchamp & Childress, 1989, p. 113). Nonmaleficence underpins many arguments against permitting physician-assisted suicide and euthanasia. It is a generally accepted moral principle that is consistent with most ethical theories.

Finally, the principle of justice is defined in many different ways, and entails a variety of elements. The Preamble to the United States Constitution provides that, among its purposes, it is intended "to establish justice," yet the meaning of justice is not explicated in this document. John Rawls associates justice with fairness. Aristotelian justice harps on equality. David Schmidtz (2006) contends that justice involves elements of reciprocity, equality, desert, and need. Healthcare managers frequently face decisions requiring determinations of justice—and often distributive justice—in the administration, clinic, resource allocation, and human resources. Distributive justice itself is said to underlie many arguments in favor of healthcare reform (Sade, 2007, pp. 1429–1431).

Healthcare managers should utilize the four traditional principles of healthcare ethics when coordinating rights with commoditization. If these principles are used in conjunction with virtue theory and the three Cs of coordination, healthcare managers may more easily identify and execute morally correct actions.

ETHICS ISSUES PERSISTING BEYOND FULL IMPLEMENTATION OF THE ACA

Only through time, practice, and interpretation will the exact scope of the ethics issues resulting from the ACA become fully manifest. This section nevertheless highlights five situations that are particularly likely to require ethical deliberation by healthcare managers in an ACA-governed environment. Following this section is a brief conclusion that suggests that exercising coordination may aid managers in these, and other, difficult situations.

Three ACA Mandates

The ACA entails three highly controversial mandates that create a terrain fraught with ethical landmines: the individual mandate, the **employer mandate**, and the **contraception mandate**.

The individual mandate requires most U.S. citizens to maintain insurance, or pay a tax penalty. As of 2014, several exceptions existed that exempt some members of the population from having to pay a penalty for not having insurance: being incarcerated, being a member of a Native American tribe, being an undocumented immigrant, having an income level below that required to file taxes, being part of a religion that opposes receiving health insurance benefits, or having health insurance costs that exceed 8% of one's household income (taking into account tax credits and employer contributions) (Kaiser Family Foundation, 2013). Moreover, coverage by Medicare, Medicaid, Tricare, veterans' health program insurance, employer-sponsored insurance, purchased Bronze-level insurance, or a grandfathered health plan will satisfy the health insurance requirement of the individual mandate (Kaiser Family Foundation, 2013). Questions of individual liberties aside, in the post-ACA implementation environment, due to the exceptions and choice that some individuals will make not to get insurance (and to instead pay the penalty), healthcare managers will continue to face concerns associated with treating the uninsured.

The employer mandate requires employers with 50 or more employees to provide affordable health insurance coverage. This requirement exempts approximately 96% of U.S. businesses, as the vast majority have fewer than 50 employees (Luhby, 2014). "Affordable insurance means that a worker doesn't have to spend more than 9.5% of his income on premiums for employee-only coverage. (The health reform law does not consider the affordability of family coverage.) And the policy must cover an array of essential health benefits, such as prescriptions and maternity care" (Luhby, 2014). The employer mandate requires healthcare managers to make difficult decisions regarding staffing and compensation.

The contraception mandate was not explicitly part of the ACA as enacted in 2010, but was added via a list developed by the U.S. Department of Health and Human Services (HHS) on August 1, 2011 (National Women's Law Center, 2011; Rice, 2011). The rule encapsulating the contraception mandate was published in the *Federal Register* on July 2, 2013.[5] The rule has two purposes: (1) to "provide women with access to contraceptive coverage without cost sharing," and (2) to do so "in a narrowly tailored fashion that protects certain nonprofit religious organizations with religious objections to providing contraceptive coverage from having to contract, arrange, pay, or refer for such coverage."[6] Despite the attempts at narrowly tailoring the contraception mandate, in 2014 the U.S. Supreme Court held that the contraception mandate "substantially burdens the exercise of religion," and that "as applied to closely held corporations, violates RFRA [Religious Freedom Restoration Act of 1998]."[7] Following this Supreme Court decision, HHS proposed new rules governing contraception. Public support for the contraception mandate is high, with 69% of survey responders supporting it (Fox, 2014; Kaplan, 2014; Moniz, Davis, & Chang, 2014). Despite the apparent

---

[5] 39872 *Federal Register*, Vol. 78, No. 127 (July 2, 2013). http://www.gpo.gov/fdsys/pkg/FR-2013-07-02/pdf/2013-15866.pdf

[6] 39872 *Federal Register*, Vol. 78, No. 127 (July 2, 2013).

[7] *Sebelius v. Hobby Lobby Stores, Inc.* (13-354) (June 30, 2014); and *Conestoga Wood Specialties Corp. v. Sebelius* (13-356) ("Sebelius" was ultimately replaced with "Burwell").

public support, healthcare managers face the particularly challenging task of balancing religious toleration with legal obligation. The three ACA mandates create difficult ethical queries for managers.

Resource Allocation

Questions of resource allocation post ACA arise in at least two generalized contexts: the provision of care and the pilot **bundled payments** program.

A shortage of doctors compounded by an increase in the insured population is expected to cause a higher demand for an already struggling U.S. healthcare industry. There is already a shortage of qualified primary care physicians and waning interest among doctors in pursuing careers in primary care (Biola, Green, Phillips, Guirguis-Blake, & Fryer, 2003; O'Connell & Wright, 2003; Winslow, 2014). The Association of American Medical Colleges estimates that there is currently a shortage of 20,000 doctors in the United States; moreover, with almost half of the current doctors approaching retirement age, this shortage is expected to increase (Christensen, 2013). Compounding the problems in the already busy healthcare industry, the 48 million people who were uninsured prior to the ACA are expected to reap the benefits of their insurance by seeking medical care (Christensen, 2013). Following full ACA implementation, it is estimated that the United States will need almost 52,000 more primary care physicians by the year 2025 (Peterson et al., 2012). The sheer quantity of patients may lead to ethical dilemmas if the quality of care cannot be maintained, or if doctors are forced to refuse treating patients due to volume concerns.

The ACA also created a pilot bundled payment program that is expected to create the potential for unique issues of conflicts of interest (Hsieh, 2014). The bundled payment program is a temporary, experimental program that may or may not be the first step toward full national implementation. Initially, it will be implemented in only a small number of states (up to eight).[8] The program is intended to study the evidence for "providers of services and suppliers to improve the quality of care furnished to Medicaid beneficiaries while reducing total expenditures under the State Medicaid programs selected to participate."[9] Although the aim of the program is noble, some commentators express reservations about the ethics implications of bundled payments. As one commentator explains, in a bundled payment system, "Hospitals and doctors would receive a fixed sum for treating a patient's condition (e.g., pneumonia or stroke), regardless of what it costs the providers. If the hospital and doctors treat the patient for less than the bundle, they keep the

---

[8] ACA §2704.

[9] ACA §2704.

excess. But if their costs exceed the bundled payment, they must absorb the loss. In theory, bundled payments eliminate incentives to overtreat patients. But they can also create dangerous incentives to undertreat" (Hsieh, 2014). Although currently just an experimental program, bundled payments have the potential to give rise to a variety of ethics issues, as do other questions of resource allocation such as those embedded in the provision of care.

Patient Privacy

Various provisions of the ACA support or even require the utilization of electronic health records. These requirements give rise to significant privacy and confidentiality concerns, particularly given the slew of electronic data breaches experienced in the twenty-first century. Despite genuine privacy issues, the American Recovery and Reinvestment Act (ARRA) did little to modify the contemporary privacy institution, but rather tends to "reinforce its flaws" (Gostin, 2009). To date, the $20 billion invested in health information technology has done little to mitigate the risk of privacy breaches (Gostin, 2009). These privacy concerns will be expanded in light of the likelihood that patients in the future will carry their own health records in electronic devices and access them online (Lachman, 2012, p. 250). As the use of electronic health records increases, healthcare managers must ensure proper precautions are taken to guarantee informed consent and patient privacy in the electronic age. The safekeeping of electronic health records persists as a major ethics issue beyond ACA implementation.

Palliative Care Services

Although many provisions of healthcare reform bills pertaining to **palliative care** were ultimately not adopted into law, the ACA nevertheless enables the integration of palliative care and hospices (Meier, 2011). According to Diane Meier (2011),

> Palliative care focuses on achieving the best-possible quality of life for patients and their family caregivers, based on patient and family needs and goals and independent of prognosis. Interdisciplinary palliative care teams assess and treat symptoms, support decision making and help match treatments to informed patient and family goals, mobilize practical aid for patients and their family caregivers, identify community resources to ensure a safe and secure living environment, and promote collaborative and seamless models of care across a range of care settings (i.e., hospital, home, and nursing home). In the United States, palliative care is provided both within and outside hospice programs.

The ACA's explicit incorporation of hospice quality reform stretches to allow for palliative care measures.[10] Despite the lack of a mandate for palliative care in the ACA, the law does create potential for the integration of such services (Meier, 2011). Healthcare managers may influence the scope and extent of palliative care offerings in their hospitals.

Preventive Care Services

On the opposite side of the treatment spectrum is **preventive care**. The ACA requires that marketplace plans and many other insurance plans provide a broad range of preventive care services without a copayment or coinsurance, but most services are in the form of diagnostics and screenings as opposed to education and counseling. Some circumstances do permit counseling: For example, obesity and diet, breast cancer risk, sexually transmitted infections, alcohol misuse, and tobacco use all have a counseling component to their preventive care (Preventive Health Service for Adults, n.d.). All of the preceding have a screening component as well as do a variety of other services, including type 2 diabetes screening, depression screening, cholesterol screening, and a variety of other screening services for adults, women, and children (Preventive Health Service for Adults, n.d.). Immunization vaccines are also provided as part of preventive care services (Preventive Health Service for Adults, n.d.). Healthcare managers must aid in accommodating the likely increase in preventive diagnostics and counseling by the masses that now have access to these services without a copay or coinsurance.

This early in the implementation of the ACA, the scope of the ethics issues surrounding these five situations has yet to be fully gleaned. Nevertheless, ethical deliberation and coordination will aid healthcare managers and executives as they navigate this ethically challenging terrain.

CONCLUSION

Utilizing coordination in everyday decision making will assist healthcare managers and executives in assessing and taking morally correct actions. The ACA creates a new paradigm of health care within the United States and, in doing so, creates new ethical issues and allows other dimensions of ethics to persist beyond its implementation. Healthcare managers must recognize that health care is both a right and a commodity when coordinating the various

---

[10] ACA §3004.

obligations to patients and other organizational constituents. The ACA creates new legal and moral obligations that will affect the entire healthcare community. Coordination is crucial to understanding and executing those obligations effectively.

CHAPTER SUMMARY

Two traditional notions have cast health care as either a right or a commodity. The Affordable Care Act moves beyond this dichotomy by recognizing health care as *both* a right and a commodity. Although the ACA makes progress toward removing barriers to health care within the United States, it does give rise to a variety of new legal and ethical obligations. Coordination will be necessary to address these challenges, including the various situations that will persist beyond ACA implementation and are fraught with ethics questions. By exercising coordination, healthcare managers and executives will be able to more effectively navigate this ethically laden terrain.

KEY TERMS AND CONCEPTS

Arete: Virtue; class.

Beneficence: Acting for the benefit of patients, with both charity and kindness.

Bundled payment: A payment system in which healthcare providers receive a fixed sum for treating a patient's condition, regardless of what it costs the provider.

Contraception mandate: Arising from the Affordable Care Act, the requirement that certain employers provide health insurance with free contraceptive coverage to their employees.

Coordination: Use of practical reason to successfully balance obligations to various constituents, and to determine and take morally correct action in complex scenarios.

Employer mandate: Within the Affordable Care Act, the requirement that employers with 50 or more employees provide affordable health insurance coverage.

Eudaimonia: Happiness; well-being.

Health care as a commodity: The libertarian and free market advocate view that health care is a commodity to be exchanged on open markets without governmental interference.

Health care as a human right: The liberal egalitarian notion that health care is a human right, and barriers to access to health care must be removed to ensure that all people have access to health care.

Individual mandate: Within the Affordable Care Act, the requirement for most U.S. citizens to maintain health insurance, or pay a tax penalty.

Justice: A broad notion encompassing fairness, reciprocity, equality, desert, and need.

Nonmaleficence: The duty to refrain from performing certain acts; the obligation not to inflict harm on others.

Palliative care: Care that is focused on ameliorating symptoms, rather than effecting a cure; care directed toward "achieving the best-possible quality of life for patients and their family caregivers, based on patient and family needs and goals and independent of prognosis" (Meier, 2011).

Phronesis: Practical wisdom.

Preventive care: Care that is focused on preventing disease, rather than treating disease after it develops.

Respect for persons: A key component of human dignity; an integral principle of ethics that may require considerations of autonomy, honesty, confidentiality, and fidelity.

Questions to Consider

1. Do you think that health care should be treated as a right, a commodity, or both? Do you agree that the Affordable Care Act incorporates health care as both a right and a commodity?

2. Which measures might you take to ensure privacy and confidentiality of electronic patient records?

3. Should hospitals integrate palliative care services into their treatment portfolios? Why or why not?

4. Which other types of educational preventive care services might hospitals try to initiate aside from counseling?

REFERENCES

Beuchamp, T., & Childress, J. (1989). *Principles of biomedical ethics* (5th ed.). New York, NY: Oxford University Press.

Biola, H., Green, L. A., Phillips, R. L., Guirguis-Blake, J., & Fryer, G. E. (2003). The U.S. primary care physician workforce: persistently declining interest in primary care medical specialties. *American Family Physician, 68*(8). http://www.ncbi.nlm.nih.gov/pubmed/14596434

Christensen, J. (2013). Doctor shortage, increased demand could crash health care system. *CNN.* http://www.cnn.com/2013/10/02/health/obamacare-doctor-shortage/

Committee on Economic, Social and Cultural Rights. (2000). *General Comment 14: The right to the highest attainable standard of health* (Twenty-Second Session, 2000), UN Doc. E/C.12/2000/4 (2000). Reprinted in *Compilation of General Comments and General Recommendations Adopted by Human Rights Treaty Bodies*, UN Doc. HRI/GEN/1/Rev.6 at 85 (2003). http://www1.umn.edu/humanrts/gencomm/escgencom14.htm

Darr, K. (2011). *Ethics in health services management* (5th ed.). Baltimore, MD: Health Professionals Press.

Fox, M. (2014). Most support birth control mandate, survey shows. *NBC News.* http://www.nbcnews.com/health/womens-health/most-support-birth-control-mandate-survey-shows-n86766

Goldstein, A. (2011, January 17). Study: 129 million have preexisting conditions. *The Washington Post.* http://www.washingtonpost.com/wp-dyn/content/article/2011/01/17/AR2011011704481.html

Gostin, L. (2009). Privacy: Rethinking health information technology and informed consent. In M. Crowley (Ed.), *Connecting American values with health care reform* (pp. 15-17). Garrison, NY: Hastings Center.

Hsieh, P. (2014). How Obamacare creates ethical conflicts for physicians and how patients can protect themselves. *Forbes.* http://www.forbes.com/sites/paulhsieh/2014/01/28/how-obamacare-creates-ethical-conflicts-for-physicians/

Kaiser Family Foundation. (2013). The requirement to buy coverage under the Affordable Care Act beginning in 2014. http://kaiserfamilyfoundation.files.wordpress.com/2013/04/requirement_flowchart_3.png

Kaplan, K. (2014). Nearly 7 in 10 Americans say health plans should cover birth control. *LA Times.* http://www.latimes.com/science/sciencenow/la-sci-sn-birth-control-mandate-obamacare-support-20140422,0,2520891.story

Lachman, V. (2012). Ethical challenges in the era of health care reform. *Ethics, Law, and Policy, 21*(4), 245, 248–250.

Luhby, T. (2014). Obamacare employer mandate eased. *CNN.* http://money.cnn.com/2014/02/10/news/economy/obamacare-employer/

Meier, D. (2011). Increased access to palliative care and hospice services: Opportunities to improve value in health care. *Millbank Quarterly, 89*(3). http://www.ncbi.nlm.nih.gov/pmc/articles/PMC3214714/

Menzel, P. (2009). Justice and fairness: Mandating universal participation. In M. Crowley (Ed.), *Connecting American values with health care reform* (pp. 4-6). Garrison, NY: Hastings Center.

Moniz, M., Davis, M., & Chang, T. (2014). Attitudes about mandated coverage of birth control medication and other health benefits in a US national sample. *Journal of the American Medical Association, 311*(24), 2539–2541. doi: 10.1001/jama.2014.4766

National Economic and Social Rights Initiative (NESRI). (n.d.). https://www.nesri.org/programs/what-is-the-human-right-to-health-and-health-care

National Women's Law Center. (2011). Contraceptive coverage in the new health care law: Frequently asked questions. http://www.nwlc.org/sites/default/files/pdfs/contraceptive_coverage_faq_11.9.11.pdf

O'Connell, P., & Wright, S. (2003). Declining interest in primary care careers. *Journal of General Internal Medicine, 18*(3). http://www.ncbi.nlm.nih.gov/pmc/articles/PMC1494827/

Perry, J. (2012). Physician-owned specialty hospitals and the Patient Protection and Affordable Care Act: Health care reform at the intersection of law and ethics. *American Business Law Journal, 49*(2), 369–417.

Petterson, S., Liaw, W., Phillips, Jr, R., Rabin, D., Meyers, D., & Bazemore, A. (2012). Projecting US primary care physician workforce needs: 2010–2025. *Annals of Family Medicine, 10*(6). http://www.annfammed.org/content/10/6/503.full.pdf+html

Preventive Health Service for Adults. (n.d.). https://www.healthcare.gov/what-are-my-preventive-care-benefits/#part=1

Rice, S. (2011). HHS oks birth control with no co-pay. *CNN.* http://www.cnn.com/2011/HEALTH/08/01/free.birth.control/

Sade, R. (2007). Ethical foundations of healthcare system reform. *Annals of Thoracic Surgery, 84,* 1429–1431.

Schmidtz, D. (2006). *Elements of justice.* New York, NY: Cambridge University Press.

Tanner, M. (2009). Healthcare is a precious commodity that must be used wisely. http://www.usnews.com/opinion/articles/2009/08/10/healthcare-is-a-precious-commodity-that-must-be-used-wisely

The Tax Exempt Hospital Sector. (2005). Hearing before the Committee on Ways and Means, U.S. House of Representatives, 109th Congress, First Session (Serial No. 109-17). http://www.gpo.gov/fdsys/pkg/CHRG-109hhrg26414/html/CHRG-109hhrg26414.htm

Welzien, A. (2011). Balancing EMTALA's duty to stabilize hospital inpatients and CMS's regulations in the midst of a struggling hospital industry. *Health Lawyer, 23*(6), 21–34.

Winslow, L. (2014). Physician shortage spurs universities to try to attract students to healthcare. http://www.tulsaworld.com/business/finance/physician-shortage-spurs-universities-to-try-to-attract-students-to/article_ef1f24d3-575d-5359-864d-64cc4a0121ab.html

Chapter 12

Health Care in Rural America

—Renee Brent Hotchkiss, MHA, PhD, and David Schott, MSPH

LEARNING OBJECTIVES

- List examples of public health interventions in rural areas and why they are important
- List potential barriers to healthcare and public health in rural areas
- Describe the relationship between insurance and rural hospitals
- Understand what happens to the health delivery systems infrastructure as a population ages and why the problem is worse in rural areas

INTRODUCTION

Caregiving in Rural America

Public health and the provision of medical services in rural areas have been overshadowed for many years by interventions targeted at urban areas. Approximately 20% of the U.S. population lives in rural areas but, only about 9% of the physicians practice in rural areas (Rosenblatt & Hart, 2000). The population in rural America is typically older and less affluent than the population in urban areas. The differences in demographics between these two populations are largely the result of economic factors, but they have repercussions for the health of the population in both rural and urban areas. Residents of rural counties, especially those living in counties that border only other rural counties, are less likely to have health insurance than residents of more populated areas (Bailey, 2004). Even those individuals in rural areas who are insured may not have access to required healthcare services for a variety of reasons, as discussed in this chapter. While health services are available in rural areas, there are typically coverage gaps due to the geographic barriers associated with rural areas.

Geographic Barriers

The practice of health care and public health in rural areas faces many challenges. The biggest difference between urban and rural health systems practice pertains to the geographic barriers that are present in rural areas. Traveling across a city or downtown from the suburbs to visit the dentist or receive medical care can be an "inconvenience" in urban areas. Traveling to the next county to visit the dentist or receive medical care can be impossible in a rural area. For those readers from urban areas, it may be hard to understand the lack of access to care in rural areas. Thus, to better illustrate this problem, we will look at rural Georgia as an example (**Figure 12–1**).

According to the Georgia Rural Health Association, in 2013 there were 6 counties in the state without a family physician, 63 counties without a pediatrician, 79 counties without an obstetrician/gynecologist, 78 counties without a psychiatrist, and 115 counties without a neurologist. Clearly, most types of specialized care will not be located near individuals living in rural areas of Georgia.

This situation also holds true for rural areas throughout the United States to varying degrees. Some areas have access to all services; others have access to none. The **uneven distribution** of medical and public health workers in rural areas also contributes to the inaccessibility of care in rural areas. As will be discussed later in the chapter, one way in which health professionals deal with this issue is by going to the patients either in person or with **telehealth services**.

In addition to the uneven distribution of resources, providing care in rural areas can be complicated by the terrain. In mountainous rural areas, such as Alaska, or states with very large rural areas, such as Wyoming, going to patients is not always practical. Indeed, in some cases physicians and other health workers have to access areas via small airplanes. Rural areas may also lack the telecommunication infrastructure required to support modern healthcare tools such as electronic medical records or telehealth.

Lack of Insurance

Perhaps because of the lack of provided services and greater travel distances, the economy in rural areas is primarily made up of small businesses and self-employed individuals. In the United States, the number of small businesses

State of Georgia Rural Counties

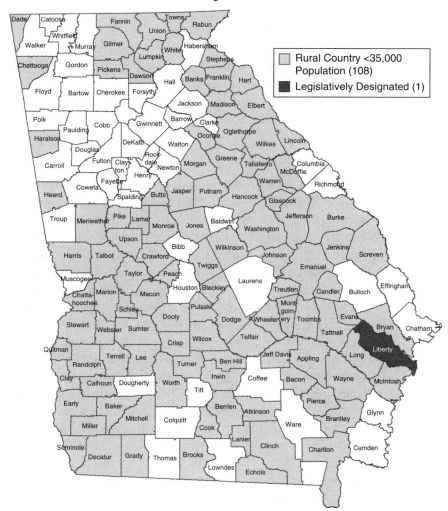

Figure 12–1 Georgia's rural counties
Courtesy of State Office of Rural Health, Georgia Department of Community Health.

and self-employed individuals in rural areas has increased by more than 240% since the late 1960s (Goetz, 2008). Traditionally, self-employed individuals have had higher rates of being uninsured. The personal insurance mandate (also called the **individual mandate**) specified in the Patient Protection and Affordable Care Act of 2010 (i.e., the Affordable Care Act [ACA]), however, should lead to a greater number of people being insured. The insurance mandate in the ACA requires individuals to show that they were insured throughout the year or pay a fine on their taxes. In the first year it became effective, the fine was $95 or 1.0% of family income, but it will rise to $695 or 2.5% of family income in 2016. It is thought that this increasing penalty for being uninsured will encourage individuals to obtain coverage. If the rates of insured individuals in rural areas increase, it could lead to the opening of new **critical access hospitals** in underserved rural areas because the newly insured population would provide a paying customer base for their services.

Change Is on the Horizon

Health care is a rapidly evolving field; many innovations appear every year, including new treatments, new ways to provide services, and policy changes. To stay competitive, healthcare organizations need to be aware of which changes are being implemented currently and what could be coming in the future. Some examples of recent changes to the healthcare system are briefly mentioned here and discussed in more detail later in the chapter. Technological advances are allowing for primary care, dentistry, and more advanced procedures to be performed in rural areas using telehealth techniques. Recent policy changes, such as the passage and implementation of the ACA, are fundamentally changing the way health care is delivered in rural areas and across the United States. As rural demographics change, so do the needs of the population. Currently, the rural population has a larger percentage of older adults than urban areas. This shift in the average age of the population is also changing the healthcare needs of rural areas.

BARRIERS

A key component of the ACA is its acknowledgment that prevention is much less costly than treating disease when it arises. Under the ACA, **community needs assessments** are required to be initially completed as a benchmark and then conducted again in three years to document progress. The first round of community needs assessments conducted by rural hospitals documented many barriers to improving the health of rural communities. Some of the major issues discovered are outlined here in addition to previously known issues related to workforce and **practitioner bias**.

Workforce Issues

Rural areas often see a shortage of physicians, nurses, and allied health workers resulting from too few applicants for these positions. Other workforce issues related to rural areas include **workforce turnover** and uneven distribution of existing workers. Workforce turnover measures the rate at which employees leave their current job. The uneven distribution of workers in rural areas is primarily caused by individuals choosing to work in larger towns or familiar areas. Later in the chapter, we will discuss some strategies for recruiting healthcare workers to more remote areas.

Practitioner Shortages

The uneven distribution and relative shortage of healthcare workers in rural areas has long been acknowledged as one of the most difficult challenges to public health in rural areas (United States Administration on Aging, 2007). Over the period 1975–1985, the number of physicians per 100,000 residents grew almost three times faster for the entire United States than for rural areas, despite overall growth in supply (Kindig & Movassaghi, 1989). In an effort to provide care to more individuals in rural locations, there have been changes in governmental policy, encouragement of network development, and the increased use of telehealth. While these changes have brought relief in some rural areas, overall the uneven distribution of healthcare workers still leads to shortages in areas where they are needed most (Ricketts, 2000).

In rural areas where public health and primary care networks do exist, they often struggle to retain qualified workers and recruit new talent. Physicians are often much more interested in entering into high-paying specialties or running their own practice in an urban area. This shift away from rural care is often encouraged by the large debt load shouldered by recent medical graduates. There are also additional challenges to retaining rural physicians that are different for primary care and specialist physicians.

For the past 20 years, primary care has been declining in popularity as a specialty among medical students. Currently, it is expected that between 16% and 18% of all medical students will work in primary care (Schwartz, Durning, Linzer, & Hauer, 2011). A perception also exists that primary care physicians in rural settings have poor work–life balance, largely because in the past most rural physicians worked alone and were typically on call on a 24/7 basis. The declining interest in primary care combined with the perception of longer hours for equal or less pay in rural areas tends to push primary care physicians toward urban areas. The shortage of specialists in rural areas reflects the reality that, in many cases, there simply is not a sufficient patient base to support their practice. An additional challenge to retaining physicians in rural areas is the shrinking number of physicians relative to the demand for health care. The Association of American Medical Colleges (AAMC, 2010) predicts that by 2025, there will be a shortage of nearly 65,000 physicians nationwide, with a substantially higher shortage in rural areas than in urban settings.

There are, however, several ways to encourage physicians and healthcare professionals to practice in rural areas. These methods are discussed later in the chapter.

Lack of Prevention Education Leading to Service Misuse

The lack of preventive services in rural areas is a large barrier to improving the health of rural communities. Treating health issues once they occur is much more costly than providing preventive care and ultimately reduces the quality of life for individuals in the community.

Practitioner shortages and lack of prevention education may also lead to a misuse of hospital emergency room services. This problem exists in urban areas as well, but it is magnified in rural settings where critical access hospitals (hospitals with fewer than 25 beds) are struggling to keep up with the high demands on their emergency rooms and other resources. Compared to their larger counterparts, critical access hospitals generally have worse measured processes of care and higher mortality rates for chronic conditions such as pneumonia, acute myocardial infarction (AMI), and congestive heart failure (CHF) (Joynt, Harris, Orav, & Jha, 2011). This disparity is due to the critical access hospitals' inability to take advantage of **economies of scale** due to their size. Unfortunately, this creates an intensifying cycle where the hospitals' resources are being used to treat more chronic conditions instead of acute conditions. The most viable solution for this situation is to build up the public health infrastructure in the community, such as primary care offices and transition clinics to manage and reduce chronic disease rates.

An Aging Rural Population

The percentage of older people living in rural areas is 25% greater than the percentage in the nation as a whole. In 2007, nearly 15% of all persons living in rural areas were age 65 or older (Reinertson-Sand, 2014; U.S. Administration on Aging, 2007). By 2030, the population older than 65 years is expected to double as the baby-boomer generation gets older. As individuals enter their elderly years, they experience a greater incidence of chronic disease, which in turn requires more resources to manage.

Despite having insurance coverage, a large portion of seniors living alone are unable to obtain necessary health services due to a lack of transportation. The challenges posed by individuals not having access to transportation to care can be particularly difficult in rural areas due to the large distances between towns. Transportation has become an especially important issue when working with an aging population. Every year, older drivers across the country stop driving and become dependent on others for transportation. In a study by Foley, Heimovitz, Guaralnik, & Brock (2002), the researchers found that male drivers, on average, were dependent on alternative sources of transportation for approximately the last 7 years of their lives and female drivers were dependent on alternative sources of transportation for approximately the last 10 years of their lives. Given that advanced age is typically when chronic health conditions need to be closely managed, this lack of transportation can create a situation in which individuals are forced to use emergency medical services (EMS) when they become sick and need to visit the hospital. Such reliance on EMS for transportation to the hospital for medication adjustments or basic care (instead of visiting a primary care physician) puts a large amount of stress on the already over-leveraged rural healthcare system.

Socioeconomic Barriers

Generally, income levels are lower in rural areas than in urban areas, both in the United States and worldwide (Idriss, Mohiuddin, & Panuccio, 1992). The main reasons for this inequality are lack of infrastructure and insufficient access to **markets**. The term *market*, when used in economics, refers to a place where there is an exchange of goods and services. When this key infrastructure is not available, people will not stay in these areas—a trend that can be seen by reviewing U.S. Census data. In 2010, 19.3% of the U.S. population lived in rural areas, compared to 20.8% in 2000 (U.S. Census Bureau, 2012; U.S. Department of Transportation, Federal Highway Administration, 2012). With increasingly fewer people residing in rural areas, any market pressures to bring new infrastructure to rural areas diminish each year. These economic conditions perpetuate the lower wages in rural areas and feed into the 240% increase in self-employment seen in U.S. rural areas since the 1960s.

Technological Barriers

As medicine and public health become more complex, new technologies are adopted that quickly become the "standard" used in the field. A current example is the move to electronic medical records (EMR). These systems work well in urban areas that have readily available high-speed Internet access and cellphone service. However, there are still large coverage gaps with regard to these services in rural areas. The lack of high-speed access to the Internet also limits the use of telehealth services in these areas. Where such access is available, many critical access hospitals lack the funding to implement new systems. It is not uncommon for a critical access hospital to struggle to make payroll due to the low Medicaid reimbursement rate for care providers and low numbers of privately insured individuals in some rural areas. Facing the increased costs of caring for an aging population, the misuse of emergency room services due to lack of preventive services, and requirements to modernize their systems, critical access hospitals in rural areas are closing because they are unable to pay their bills. When these facilities close down, it simply intensifies the disparities between rural and urban areas.

DISPARITIES IN RURAL VERSUS URBAN AREAS

As noted earlier, many physicians prefer to practice in urban areas. This preference can create the perception that those physicians who were not able to practice in urban areas may not be as good as those physicians who were able to do so. In turn, these perceptions can lead to community members not using available services.

In 1999, a well-cited study was published that concluded most rural communities were at a relatively low stage of readiness with regard to implementing drug use prevention programs (Plested, Smitham, Jumper-Thurman, Oetting, & Edwards, 1999). Ten years later, in 2008, a similar study was conducted in rural Georgia. This second study concluded that barriers existed to preventive services including the perception of need, access, service availability, perception of racism, and ability to pay (Strickland & Strickland, 1996). This is just one example where the need for a rural public health program, similar to those found in urban areas, was identified and little was done to prepare communities for its implementation over a 10-year time frame.

Lack of Resources for Rural Areas

When designing health intervention programs, such efforts are often targeted where the intervention can improve the lives of the most people. Urban areas have traditionally been the popular choice for interventions because of their higher population density as compared to rural areas. Since the time of John Snow and the Broad Street pump, the combination of better sanitation, better understanding of disease etiology, and public health programs have transformed cities into what we know today, but in many ways rural areas have been left behind.

The desire to reach the largest number of individuals possible instead of looking for the greatest need and the negative perceptions regarding rural healthcare providers have traditionally worked together to maintain the current low levels of services in rural areas. Recently, rural public health has become the target of more research and funding due to the great disparity between rural and urban areas. Unfortunately, increases in staffing and programing funding open the door to another kind of barrier—namely, practitioner bias or **program design errors**.

Practitioner Bias and Program Design Errors

In areas with appropriate staffing and programs with approved funding, a key barrier to successful interventions may be practitioner bias. The quickest way to have a public health program fail is for its practitioners to enter a community uninvited by the residents, appear to discount the views of the population, and proclaim themselves to be the experts with all the answers to the residents' problems. Sadly, this story is all too common with public health interventions in rural areas. While some communities may not have the knowledge or motivation to effect change on their own, it is important to recognize where a community exists relative to the community members' readiness for change. In areas where individuals are not sure where their next meal will come from, chronic conditions such as diabetes may just be an annoyance to residents rather than their primary concern.

When designing an intervention, it is important to work with the community to develop goals and measures for the program. If the program goals are important to the community. then the community members are more likely to participate in the program (Sanoff, 2000).

OPPORTUNITIES

Workforce Improvement

A recent study that addressed the issues of public health workforce turnover in rural areas suggested that a comprehensive **retention strategy** implemented within the first year of employment in a rural area would reduce worker turnover significantly (Chisholm, Russell, & Humphreys, 2011). It has also been suggested that monitoring data from sources such as exit interviews can help determine the reasons employees leave a particular rural area, so that the externalities factoring into their decisions can be addressed if possible.

Reviews of the literature regarding the selection and training of physicians for rural areas suggest that identifying students with an interest in rural health care early in their pre-medicine career is important. Once identified, these individuals can be given additional formal training, with the goal of having physicians be more likely to start a career in rural health and less likely to leave in the future for an urban area (Brooks, Walsh, Mardon, Lewis, & Clawson, 2002).

Telehealth

The uneven distribution of healthcare workers in rural areas can be addressed, in part, by the use of telehealth services. Telehealth services entail the use of technology and information to support long-distance clinical health care, education, and public health activities. Adoption of telehealth is rapidly increasing in rural areas and is expected to continue to grow, especially as new payment policies are adopted to accommodate this new type of delivery (Adler-Milstein, Kvedar, & Bates, 2014). While telehealth programs can help fill in coverage gaps and provide care to those who would not otherwise be able to receive it, there are considerable **startup costs** associated with purchasing the required equipment.

POLICY

The ACA and Rural America

The ACA includes many provisions that will have a positive impact on the healthcare system in rural communities. Initially, the creation of high-risk pools to distribute risk, allowing children to stay on their parent's health insurance plans until they reach age 26, and small business tax credits helped expand care to some individuals. The creation of tax credits for small businesses, which is intended to encourage them to offer health insurance to their employees, seems like a program that is targeted equally at both rural and urban areas. However, this provision has a larger impact on rural areas because of the higher level of self-employment and small-business employment in rural areas as compared to urban areas.

In late 2013-when the ACA-mandated insurance exchanges were first opened through the first quarter of 2014 and during open enrollment in 2015, 11.4 million Americans signed up for insurance through the Health Insurance Marketplace (DHHS, 2015). The original model providing coverage for all individuals included expanding Medicaid to individuals between the ages of 18 and 64 earning up to 133% of the federal poverty level. The cost for this expansion was to be paid completely by the federal government for the first three years, with the federal government continuing to pay at least 90% of the cost after that period ended. The ACA also provides for a tax credit for individuals making up to 400% of the poverty level to help them purchase insurance on the health exchanges.

While the Medicaid expansion was ruled to be voluntary on a state-by-state basis, many of the individuals making up to 100% of the federal poverty level in some states did not qualify for Medicaid under their states' current rule, but also did not qualify for the federal health insurance subsidy

(Centers for Medicare and Medicaid Services, 2013). This situation created a coverage gap—a problem that has not yet been rectified.

The initial impact of ACA will probably not be seen until the beginning of 2016, because the penalty for not having health insurance was assessed for the first time on taxes due April 15, 2015. For this reason, 2014 and 2015 are critical years for advocacy and promotion of the health exchanges in an effort to sign up as many individuals as possible before the deadline.

Advocacy and Promotion

To encourage physicians to practice in rural areas, financial incentives are sometimes offered in the form of tuition repayment. These programs have been successful in addressing short-term recruitment goals, but often the physicians leave the rural community as soon as all of their loans have been repaid/forgiven (Sempowski, 2004).

Another potential solution to the practitioner shortage in rural areas, and an alternative to financial incentives, is **compulsory service programs**, which are used in more than 70 countries. Compulsory programs typically consist of mandatory service with compensation, mandatory service with no compensation, or voluntary service with compensation (Frehywot, Mullan, Payne, & Ross, 2010). While these programs ensure that there is staffing in these rural areas, they fail to address physician turnover after the participants' contracts expire. Another potential issue with this model is the possibility of lowering the quality of care relative to incentive-based programs if the physicians feel coerced to practice in the rural area with no perceived benefit to themselves.

Through the ACA, physicians in rural areas of the United States are granted geographic practice cost indices (GPCIs), which are payment adjustments designed to encourage physicians to practice in rural areas. A primary feature of the GPCIs is a payment increase of 10% for provision of primary care services to Medicaid patients, but only if those primary care services account for at least 60% of the physician's total billing. This may unintentionally punish those rural providers who offer more services than prevention, such as critical access hospitals. Currently, many critical access facilities are in the process of closing their doors, and the GPCI payment structure, combined with the decreased disproportionate share hospital (DSH) payments, is a contributing factor in the closings. The decreased federal funding for critical access hospitals creates an especially difficult burden for these facilities because at the same time federally qualified health centers (FQHC) are seeing increased subsidy rates (almost $3 billion in 2015). This situation creates a definite opportunity for a policy change to provide increased support for all rural providers—not just those who have Medicaid billings that account for 60% of their practice or those who qualify as a federally qualified health center (FQHC).

The ACA also provides increased support for long-term acute care (LTAC) facilities. Increasing funding for these facilities is especially important for rural areas, which are already home to a larger percentage of the older population, as this segment of the population is most likely to require the services of an LTAC facility. To assist with this provision of care, the ACA created a new federal office that deals with coordinating state and federal policies related to Medicare and Medicaid policies.

Collaboration and Integration

The ACA also increases the emphasis on public health programs through Title IV. This part of the law contains provisions that will help local efforts that focus on community—as well as individual—health. Title IV also provides for a new public health–related fund that is designed to support the implementation of community-based public health programs. Some other interventions within Title IV include a national campaign focusing on health promotion and disease prevention, community transformation grants, school-based health centers, small business programs, research on public health disparities, and programs designed for individuals in their mid-50s to mid-60s (Coburn, Lundblad, MacKinney, McBride, & Mueller, 2010).

There is much opportunity for collaboration and integration of services in rural areas. Critical access hospitals and FQHC serve the same segment of the population but typically view each other as competition instead of stakeholders in the overall health of the community. Through collaboration and cooperation, these facilities—particularly those serving the same or similar communities—can better meet the needs of the community, enhance each other's roles, and stabilize and expand the range of services provided to the local community (U.S. Department of Health and Human Services, Health Resources and Services Administration, Office of Rural Health Policy, 2010).

THE FUTURE

Will the Opportunities Overcome the Barriers?

Thankfully, the opportunities can address the barriers if full advantage is taken. Health disparities due to lack of resources in rural areas can be combatted through the use of telehealth services to provide care in areas with no other options. There is an opportunity for rural advocacy groups and financial incentives to physicians to encourage practice in rural areas. If enough physicians are encouraged to practice in these rural areas, then the workforce issues in rural areas will be overcome.

Unfortunately, some of the challenges related to rural health care will probably not be resolved anytime soon. The issues related to the demographics of rural areas are not likely to change, for example. In fact, when census data are compared over time, it becomes clear that the population in rural areas includes more elderly individuals than the population of urban areas. If the trend of the population growing older in rural areas continues, support for LTAC facilities will increase in importance in the coming years.

Is There More That Needs to Be Done?

In this chapter, we have outlined both opportunities for improving rural health and barriers preventing the improvement of health services in rural areas. The ACA goes a long way toward improving health disparities in rural as well as urban communities. However, there is still room for improvement with regard to Medicaid reimbursement rates for providers such as critical access hospitals. The passage of the 2010 healthcare law, along with a gradual shift in public perception regarding the status of health care in rural areas, has brought the subject into the forefront. As time goes on, additional challenges will be discovered with regard to the provision of care in rural areas. As these issues arise, they should be addressed individually to provide the best possible outcome for the population.

Can We Anticipate Improvements in the Future?

In the future, the ACA will likely be used as a tool to strengthen healthcare services in rural areas. The law contains provisions that encourage physicians to practice in rural areas and supports training for various types of practitioners in rural areas. Many of the loan repayment programs for physicians are also being extended to the allied health professions. It is hoped that these changes will be enough to offset the increase in demand that will stem from the newly insured population. If this is not the case, and a supply shortage in the healthcare marketplace persists, than additional support will need to be offered to providers to encourage them to practice in rural areas.

CHAPTER SUMMARY

Residents of rural counties suffer from healthcare access issues due to low socioeconomic status, lack of health insurance coverage, workforce issues, practitioner shortages, few preventive services, and other geographic barriers. The lack of care is even more pronounced when discussing health-care specialties. Even in instances where rural residents have access to care the quality of that care may be subpar. Furthermore, the rural population is disproportionately older than its urban counterparts and therefore is likely to require more healthcare services.

Despite these barriers, technological and policy changes are expected to help alleviate the rural access issue. Medical students with an interest in rural care are being identified early in their studies to improve the rural healthcare and public health workforce. The adoption of telehealth services is allowing service needs to be virtually satisfied. The ACA is diminishing the number of uninsured in rural areas through the healthcare insurance marketplace. It is also helping to build the necessary infrastructure for long term acute care and public health services.

In order to fully overcome the barriers to the delivery of health care in rural America more work needs to be done. Future policies must include mechanisms such as loan repayment programs, payment adjustments, or compulsory service programs that would help incentivize physicians to practice in rural areas. A greater emphasis on funding streams meant to increase the use of telehealth services is needed. Preventive services targeting the elderly should be implemented and transportation issues ought to be addressed. Finally, as additional challenges are identified they should not be ignored but rather should serve as an indicator that more needs to be done.

Key Terms and Concepts

Community needs assessments: Under the ACA, assessments of community health and unmet needs that are required to be initially completed as a benchmark and then conducted again in three years to document progress.

Compulsory service programs: Programs for physicians that require mandatory service with compensation, mandatory service with no compensation, or voluntary service with compensation; they are often used to provide healthcare services in remote and rural areas.

Coverage gaps: Areas that do not have high-speed Internet access and cellphone service.

Critical access hospitals: Hospitals with fewer than 25 beds.

Economies of scale: The relationship in which costs decline as the scale (of services or production) increases.

Individual mandate: Within the Affordable Care Act, the requirement for most U.S. citizens to maintain insurance, or pay a tax penalty.

Market: A place where there is an exchange of goods and services.

Practitioner bias: Practitioners' tendency to discount the community's self-knowledge and to assert that their own goals and interventions are appropriate.

Program design errors: Design of healthcare interventions that fail to recognize where a community exists relative to the community members' readiness for change.

Retention strategy: Measures to reduce workforce turnover.

Startup costs: Costs associated with purchasing the equipment required to support a healthcare service.

Telehealth services: The use of technology and information to support long-distance clinical health care, education, and public health activities.

Uneven distribution: Workforce imbalances caused by individuals choosing to work in some areas, but not others—for example, in larger towns or familiar areas rather than in remote rural areas.

Workforce turnover: The rate at which employees leave their current job.

Questions to Consider

1. How is practicing health care and public health different in rural areas than in urban areas?
2. What do you think would be the most effective way to retain healthcare workers in rural areas?

REFERENCES

Adler-Milstein, J., Kvedar, J., & Bates, D. W. (2014). Telehealth among US hospitals: Several factors, including state reimbursement and licensure policies, influence adoption. *Health Affairs*, *33*(2), 207–215.

Association of American Medical Colleges (AAMC). (2010). The impact of health care reform on the future supply and demand for physicians: Updated projections through 2025. https://www.aamc.org/download/158076/data/updated_projections_through_2025.pdf

Bailey, J. (2004). Health care in rural America. *Center for Rural Affairs Issue Brief*, *1*, 1–7.

Brooks, R. G., Walsh, M., Mardon, R. E., Lewis, M., & Clawson, A. (2002). The roles of nature and nurture in the recruitment and retention of primary care physicians in rural areas: a review of the literature. *Academic Medicine*, *77*(8), 790–798.

Centers for Medicare and Medicaid Services (CMS). (2013). Is my state expanding Medicaid coverage? https://www.healthcare.gov/what-if-my-state-is-not-expanding-medicaid/

Chisholm, M., Russell, D., & Humphreys, J. (2011). Measuring rural allied health workforce turnover and retention: What are the patterns, determinants and costs? *Australian Journal of Rural Health, 19*(2), 81–88.

Coburn, A. F., Lundblad, J. P., MacKinney, A. C., McBride, T. D., & Mueller, K. J. (2010). Patient Protection and Affordable Care Act of 2010: Impacts on rural people, places, and providers: A first look. http://www.rupri.org/Forms /Health_PPACAImpacts_Sept2010.pdf

Foley, D. J., Heimovitz, H. K., Guralnik, J. M., & Brock, D. B. (2002). Driving life expectancy of persons aged 70 years and older in the United States. *American Journal of Public Health, 92*(8), 1284–1289.

Frehywot, S., Mullan, F., Payne, P. W., & Ross, H. (2010). Compulsory service programmes for recruiting health workers in remote and rural areas: Do they work? *Bulletin of the World Health Organization, 88*(5), 364–370.

Goetz, S. J. (2008). Self-employment in rural America: The new economic reality. *Rural Realities, 2*(3), 1–13.

Hart, L. G., Salsberg, E., Phillips, D. M., & Lishner, D. M. (2002). Rural health care providers in the United States. *Journal of Rural Health, 18*(5), 211–231.

Idriss, J., Mohiuddin, A., & Panuccio, T.; International Fund for Agricultural Development. (1992). *The state of world rural poverty: An inquiry into its causes and consequences.* New York, NY: New York University Press.

Joynt, K. E., Harris, Y., Orav, E. J., & Jha, A. K. (2011). Quality of care and patient outcomes in critical access rural hospitals. *Journal of the American Medical Association, 306*(1), 45–52.

Kindig, D. A., & Movassaghi, H. (1989). The adequacy of physician supply in small rural counties. *Health Affairs, 8*(2), 63–76.

Plested, B., Smitham, D. M., Jumper-Thurman, P., Oetting, E. R., & Edwards, R. W. (1999). Readiness for drug use prevention in rural minority communities. *Substance Use & Misuse, 34*(4–5), 521–544.

Reinertson-Sand, M. (2014). Rural Assistance Center: Aging. http://www.raconline .org/topics/aging

Ricketts, T. C. (2000). The changing nature of rural health care. *Annual Review of Public Health, 21*(1), 639–657.

Rosenblatt, R. A., & Hart, L. G. (2000). Physicians and rural America. *Western Journal of Medicine, 173*(5), 348.

Sanoff, H. (2000). *Community participation methods in design and planning.* New York, NY: John Wiley & Sons.

Schwartz, M. D., Durning, S., Linzer, M., & Hauer, K. E. (2011). Changes in medical students' views of internal medicine careers from 1990 to 2007. *Archives of Internal Medicine, 171*(8), 744–749.

Sempowski, I. P. (2004). Effectiveness of financial incentives in exchange for rural and underserviced area return-of-service commitments: Systematic review of the literature. *Canadian Journal of Rural Medicine, 9*(2), 82–88.

Strickland, J., & Strickland, D. L. (1996). Barriers to preventive health services for minority households in the rural South. *Journal of Rural Health, 12*(3), 206–217.

U.S. Administration on Aging. (2007). Statistics on the aging population. http:// www.aoa.gov/AoARoot/Aging_Statistics/index.aspx

U.S. Census Bureau. (2012). Frequently Asked Questions. https://ask.census.gov/faq.php?id=5000&faqId=5971

U.S. Department of Health and Human Services, Health Resources and Services Administration, Office of Rural Health Policy. (2010). Manual on effective collaboration between critical access hospitals and federally qualified health centers. http://www.hrsa.gov/ruralhealth/pdf/qhcmanual042010.pdf

U.S. Department of Health and Human Services, HealthCare. (2015). By the numbers: Open enrollment for health insurance. http://www.hhs.gov/healthcare/facts/factsheets/2015/02/open-enrollment-by-the-numbers.html

U.S. Department of Transportation, Federal Highway Administration. (2012). U.S. population living in urban vs. rural areas. http://www.fhwa.dot.gov/planning/census_issues/archives/metropolitan_planning/cps2k.cfm

Chapter 13

The Challenge of Integrative Medicine in Healthcare Systems

—James Yang, MD, MPH, and Andrew Heyman, MD, MHSA

LEARNING OBJECTIVES

- Develop an understanding of integrative medicine as a ubiquitous cultural phenomenon.
- To clearly define alternative, complementary, and integrative medicine.
- Develop an understanding of functional and integrative models of medicine, including the return of integrative physicians to biomedical medicine.
- Examine the clinical intersection of allopathic and integrative medicine.
- Develop a comprehensive understanding of the increasing emergence of integrative models in health systems.

INTRODUCTION

Integrative medicine, also known as **complementary and alternative medicine (CAM)**, is a ubiquitous part of healthcare consumption by consumers in the United States. Data from the 2007 National Health and Nutrition Examination Survey (Barnes, Bloom, & Nahin, 2008) found that nearly 4 out of 10 Americans used some form of CAM in the last 12 months, with the highest rates (44%) found among people aged 50–59. Most users of CAM therapies utilize them as an adjunct to standard care, with only a small minority excluding conventional care altogether (Astin, 1998). In 2007, nearly $34 billion in out-of-pocket dollars was spent on CAM, accounting for 1.5% of total U.S. healthcare expenditures and 11.2% of out-of pocket health expenditures (Barnes et al., 2008). The total number of annual visits to CAM providers has been estimated at 425 million, a number that exceeds the total number of visits to all primary care physicians combined (Eisenberg et al., 1993).

The spread of interest in integrative and complementary therapies has been driven by widespread exposure to these therapies in TV and other popular media. One of the most well-known TV physician personalities is Dr. Mehmet Oz, a cardiothoracic surgeon who presents complementary and alternative medicine topics to his nearly 2.3 million viewers per show. Even former President Bill Clinton famously turned to Dr. Mark Hyman, an integrative and **functional medicine** doctor, when despite the best cardiovascular care available, he still had "well over 90% blockage" of some of his heart arteries, requiring a quadruple heart bypass surgery in 2004 (Nichols, 2004). Under Hyman's treatment, President Clinton lost an estimated 30 pounds and his daughter, Chelsea Clinton, noted that he had improved his cardiovascular health by more than 10 years (Chozick, 2014).

When looking at the natural products market more broadly, the *Nutrition Business Journal* reported that U.S. consumer sales of nutrition products— which include the product categories of organic foods, functional foods, and supplements—reached $117 billion in 2010. This included supplement sales of $28 billion and $39 billion in sales of functional foods (foods made with health-associated additives) that were sold and marketed based on labeled health claims.

The spread of integrative medicine has led to the institutionalization and adoption of integrative services within healthcare systems as well. The American Hospital Association's 2010 survey reported that as many as 42% of hospitals are offering CAM services (Ananth, 2011). These facilities include all of the top 18 hospitals on the *U.S. News and World Report*'s "America's Best Hospitals" list (Comarow, 2008). In academic medicine, the Consortium of Academic Health Centers for Integrative Medicine (CAHCIM) boasts 57 academic medical centers and affiliate institutions, including Harvard University, Yale University, Duke University, Mayo Clinic, and Stanford University. Within the U.S. healthcare system, a study published in *Health Services Research* found that 76% of healthcare workers and 83% of doctors and nurses personally used CAM, compared with 63% of the general population (Johnson, Ward, Knutson, & Sendelbach, 2012).

While integrative approaches and concepts are ubiquitous in television programs, magazines, social media, and even medical education today, their formal entrance into healthcare delivery systems is often challenging. Professional resistance to integrative medicine by physicians and administrators is common. Questions of safety, efficacy, and scientific rigor are typical flashpoints in the debate.

DEFINITIONS OF INTEGRATIVE, COMPLEMENTARY, AND ALTERNATIVE MEDICINE

The National Center for Complementary and Alternative Medicine (NCCAM) of the National Institutes of Health (NIH), which was established by Congress in 1998, has been a leader in advancing research in therapies and modalities that fall broadly under the umbrella of complementary and alternative medicine. NCCAM gives a very broad definition of CAM: "CAM is defined as a group of diverse medical and health care systems, practices, and products that are not generally considered part of conventional medicine" (NCCAM, 2012). NCCAM classifies CAM therapies into five categories or domains:

- Alternative medical systems, or complete systems of therapy and practice
- Mindbody interventions, or techniques designed to facilitate the mind's effect on bodily functions and symptoms
- Biologically based systems, including herbalism
- Manipulative and body-based methods, such as chiropractic and massage therapy
- Energy therapies (CAM, 2003)

These therapies include natural products and supplements, diet-based therapies, mind–body practices such as meditation and yoga, and traditional medicine practices such as Ayurvedic medicine from India, traditional Chinese medicine, homeopathy, and naturopathy.

While much of CAM care is delivered by nonphysician providers (e.g., massage is delivered by a massage therapist), integrative medicine physicians, trained in allopathic or osteopathic medicine, have received further training in the use of CAM in clinical practice. The practice of integrative medicine is defined by the Consortium of Academic Health Centers for Integrative Medicine (2009), a group of 57 university and academically based practices, as follows:

> Integrative Medicine is the practice of medicine that reaffirms the importance of the relationship between practitioner and patient, focuses on the whole person, is informed by evidence, and makes use of all appropriate therapeutic approaches, healthcare professionals, and disciplines to achieve optimal health and healing.

Within this broad definition, integrative medicine practitioners have historically adopted an approach to medicine that emphasizes the role of complementary modalities. This model of integrative health, combining conventional medicine with CAM modalities, has been the dominant model of integrative care. The NCCAM similarly defines integrative medicine as the use of complementary and alternative medicine by a healthcare practitioner.

FUNCTIONAL AND MODERN INTEGRATIVE MEDICINE MODELS: THE RETURN OF INTEGRATIVE PHYSICIANS TO BIOMEDICAL MEDICINE

Significant changes in the model of integrative medical care have occurred since the initial introduction of CAM into the world of medicine and the establishment of the CAM paradigm. With **complementary medicine**, physicians used their conventional medical training as a foundation for evaluation and treatment and added CAM therapies that they believed had sufficient research or clinical evidence to improve their patients' outcomes. Integrative medicine, however, has begun to change from the "add-on therapy" of CAM to a revision of the basic biomedical paradigm of conventional medicine. A focus on the etiology of disease, "root cause" analysis, emerging physiological pathways, interconnectiveness of body systems (e.g., the gut–immune–brain axis), and the biological consequences associated with lifestyle choices have refocused the biomedical lens of medicine and changed the way physicians evaluate their patients.

Most of the largest and well-respected physician training organizations in integrative medicine, such as the Institute for Functional Medicine (IFM), the American Academy of Anti-Aging Medicine (A4M), the American College for the Advancement in Medicine (ACAM), and the George Washington University School of Medicine Graduate Program in Integrative Medicine, instruct physicians on a model of medical care, both in evaluation and treatment, that reflects this emerging but influential movement within integrative medicine. A recent survey of 30 different integrative medicine clinics that are affiliated with academic health centers found that one out of three clinicians practiced functional medicine (Ehrlich, Callender, & Gaster, 2013). While we do not have space to discuss in detail the specifics of this paradigm shift, some of the common tenets of these approaches include the following:

- Person-centered medicine (versus disease or organ-based medicine)
- Upstream medicine: Evaluations based on identifying the genetic, biochemical, physiological, emotional, psychological, spiritual, and sociological causes of an individual's condition

- Use of functional laboratory evaluations to identify biochemical and physiological imbalances that reflect dysfunction or disease
- Integrating lifestyle medicine concepts, including stress, sleep, diet, environmental exposures, and exercise, in the pathogenesis and treatment of chronic disease
- Incorporation of complementary and alternative treatments as indicated

While the use of complementary and alternative treatments still exists, the emphasis and rationale for using these treatments has changed. Functional and integrative medicine is a personalized approach that uses basic and epidemiological science to investigate and evaluate a patient's condition. Comprehensive risk factor analysis and tests that evaluate the physiological ability of the body to perform basic bodily functions are conducted to identify factors that may be involved in mediating a patient's disease. Treatments aimed at addressing the underlying etiological and biochemical basis of disease may use all appropriate therapies, whether traditional medications or CAM.

THE CLINICAL INTERSECTION OF ALLOPATHIC AND INTEGRATIVE MEDICINE

Conventional Medicine

Modern-day medicine has strongly institutionalized the importance of research-based treatment approaches. Given that most large clinical trials are expensive and the pharmaceutical investment necessary to bring a single new drug to market has been estimated at $4–11 billion (Herper, 2012), it is not surprising that the best evidence-based medicine is pharmaceutical medicine. In today's clinical marketplace, third-party payer pressures have led to "problem-based/chief complaint" medical visits that generally last 15.7 minutes and attempt to address an average of six topics (Tai-Seale, McGuire, & Zhang, 2007). In general, a prescription for a synthetic pharmaceutical drug is given to deal with the condition. Noninfectious conditions are treated with medications, most of which are generally given over the lifespan under a chronic disease model; evidence-based medicine rarely ventures upstream to tackle sickness at its source. While lifestyle counseling is recommended in most chronic disease guidelines, current medical practices tend to focus on pharmacologic management. Chronic disease management has become the largest sector in healthcare spending, and about half of the U.S. population has one or more chronic health conditions (Centers for Disease Control and Prevention [CDC], 2014).

The Role of Integrative Medicine

From the perspective of integrative practitioners and dual-trained integrative physicians, the intersection of allopathic and biologically based medicine with integrative principles is seamless. Patient-centered integrative care of the whole patient, addressing the mind, body, and spiritual needs in a comprehensive evaluation, has been suggested as a potential solution to the U.S. healthcare crisis (Maizes, Rakel, & Niemiec, 2009). The strong focus on lifestyle medicine in integrative care practices is the foundation for reversing and managing chronic conditions.

Despite patients' expectations, only 16% of somatic complaints in primary care lead to an organic etiology; 84% remain unexplained, and conventional treatments are often ineffective (Kroenke & Mangelsdorff, 1988). For integrative practitioners who add CAM practices to their patient care, these modalities provide much-needed tools for the treatment of stress, chronic pain, fatigue, somatic complaints, and other conditions that have limited treatment options in conventional medicine or require treatments that have significant adverse effects.

A study of 1150 patients found that 85% of patients expect their primary care physician to refer them to CAM when appropriate as well as have updated knowledge about CAM (Ben-Arye, Frenkel, Klein, & Scharf, 2008). Basic knowledge of integrative medicine is required to meet patients' expectations, given these therapies' widespread use. Patients oftentimes present with multiple problems that statistically would be improbable based on common epidemiologic prevalence if they were not somehow interconnected. The recognition that a person is in a state of poor health, not just unluckily subject to a multitude of unconnected health conditions, begs for a holistic approach that attempts to address the underlying causes of their symptoms. Integrative approaches provide noninvasive options for these patients.

Evidence for CAM and Integrative Medicine

From a health administrative perspective, therapies with evidence of clinical benefit, patient safety, and patient satisfaction are important considerations for a successful and ethical medical system. Yet, the significance of having a strong evidence base for clinical practice—defined and idealized in the modern era as the existence of multiple, supportive, randomized controlled trials—has never been a clear requisite for ethical and effective care. Very few surgical procedures have been tested using the gold standard, the randomized controlled trial, yet few people would claim that the fields of surgery and all of its subspecialties are quackery. Perhaps more striking is the fact that of the thousands of recommendations published in formal "evidence-based clinical guidelines" by the American College of Cardiology and the American Heart Association, only 11% are supported by quality clinical trials (Tricoci, Allen, Kramer, Califf, & Smith, 2009). Similarly, only 16% of the recommendations found in the Infectious Disease Society of American (ISDA) guidelines are supported by high-quality controlled studies (Khan, Khan, Zimmerman, Baddour, & Tleyjeh, 2009). For guidelines in oncology, only a paltry 6% of recommendations are based on "level 1" evidence (Pooncha & Go, 2011).

The poor evidence across almost all fields of medicine highlights the fact that the era of modern scientific medicine has only just begun. It will take time to build a mature, clinical database of evidence for conventional and integrative therapies. For behavioral, dietary, herbal, and mind–body therapies, the millions of dollars needed to conduct large clinical trials may not be feasible for all conditions. There is a lack of funding for researching treatments that cannot be patented or made profitable. For personalized medicine approaches, where the same disease is treated differently based on the results of a complex array of individualized tests, large, rigorous clinical studies are often very challenging to conduct.

In the 2005 Institute of Medicine (IOM) report on CAM, the authors stated that hundreds of systematic reviews have evaluated specific CAM therapies, and some have shown a clear benefit of CAM (p. 145). Acupuncture, for example, is very effective, and studies consistently find it more effective than placebo (Kawakita & Okada, 2014). However, it is only modestly more effective than sham acupuncture (Kawakita & Okada, 2014). From a patient's perspective, pain relief is pain relief, whether the needles are working neurologically, through endogenous endorphins, through the power of placebo, or through ancient *qi* principles. When measures of patient satisfaction and subjective outcomes are examined, CAM therapies are usually effective ways to treat and improve patient experience.

A comprehensive review of economic studies on CAM by Herman, Poindexter, Witt, and Eisenberg (2012) concluded that "results of the higher-quality studies indicate a number of highly cost-effective, and even cost-saving, CAM therapies." From a health systems perspective, a large data set from a Dutch health insurer was used to compare costs and mortality for patients seen by 1913 conventional general practitioners compared with 79 general practitioners who had also been trained in integrative medicine or CAM (Kooreman & Baars, 2012). The researchers found that patients whose general practitioner had additional CAM training had between 0 and 30% lower healthcare and mortality rates depending on the patient age group and the type of CAM services used.

Another study looked at insured patients with back pain, fibromyalgia, or menopause symptoms in Washington state and found "that CAM users had lower average expenditures than nonusers. ... The largest difference was seen in the patients with the heaviest disease burdens among whom CAM users averaged $1,420 less than nonusers" (Lind, Lafferty, Tyree, & Diehr, 2010). Overall, research evaluating CAM and integrative medicine's cost-effectiveness has been promising, although more research is needed to evaluate specific therapies for specific conditions, as well as to understand which models of integrative care in general are cost-effective.

While clinicians wait for researchers to provide guidance on which treatments are most efficacious, integrative medicine practitioners commonly use the idea of a sliding scale when thinking about evidence: The greater the potential of a treatment to cause harm, the stricter the standard of evidence it should be held to when assessing efficacy. For treatments like Reiki, a form of hands-on energy work, which has impressive program evaluation research (Marcus, Blazek-O'Neill, & Kopar, 2013) and no known negative side effects, how many studies are needed before it is offered, for example, to cancer patients as a way to improve relaxation, anxiety, mood, sleep, pain, and appetite?

THE INTERSECTION OF ALLOPATHIC AND INTEGRATIVE MEDICINE IN EMERGING HEALTH SYSTEMS

Increasing Integration into Healthcare Systems

The 2005 IOM report on CAM addressed the growing integration of CAM and conventional medicine:

> A distinct trend toward the integration of complementary and alternative medicine (CAM) therapies with the practice of conventional medicine is occurring. Hospitals are offering CAM therapies, health maintenance organizations (HMOs) are covering such therapies, a growing number of physicians use CAM therapies in their practices, insurance coverage for CAM therapies is increasing, and integrative medicine centers and clinics are being established, many with close ties to medical schools and teaching hospitals. (p. 218)

In 1998, the American Hospital Association found that only 6% of hospitals offered CAM services. By 2001, that rate had doubled to 15%. The most recent AHA report (2010) suggests that as many as 42% of hospitals are offering CAM services (Ananth, 2011). According to a Landmark

Healthcare (1999) report, 67% of all HMOs offered at least one form of CAM in 1999, with the most common of these services being chiropractic (65%) and acupuncture (31%).

Hospital administrators in the American Hospital Association survey were strongly supportive of integrative therapies, citing patient demand and clinically observed efficacy as drivers of their integration into hospital-based healthcare systems. They noted that physician resistance was often cited as a potential barrier. While the relationship between physicians and complementary care providers can be strained, most research suggests that physicians and other clinicians are not only major consumers of complementary therapies (Johnson et al., 2012), but, across multiple specialties, are supportive and open to CAM. Most rheumatologists, for example, express favorable attitudes toward most categories of CAM practices relevant to the care of patients with chronic back pain or joint pain, with 70% supporting bodywork, 64% supporting meditation, and 54% supporting acupuncture for their patients (Manek, Crowson, Ottenberg, Curlin, Kaptchuk, & Tilburt, 2010). Similar research on infectious disease specialists found that 75% believe integrative modalities are useful and more than 50% believe CAM can directly affect the immune system and disease processes (Shere-Wolfe, Tilburt, D'Adamo, Berman, & Chesney, 2013). In another study, 71% of pediatricians indicated that they would consider referring patients to CAM practitioners (Sawni & Thomas, 2007).

The introduction of complementary and integrative practices into healthcare institutions generally requires a "motivated champion" of this model of care. In a study of integrative physicians in healthcare institutions, Keshet (2013) notes that effective change leaders were generally senior physicians, whose status enabled them to initiate and champion new practices. Recent changes in insurance reimbursement for CAM services may also decrease the barriers to CAM and integrative medicine.

Opportunities in Third-Payer Coverage: The Affordable Care Act

The 2010 Affordable Care Act (ACA) Section 2706(a), titled "Nondiscrimination in Health Care," became effective on January 1, 2014. This amendment to the ACA, proposed by Sen. Tom Harkin of Iowa states, "A group health plan and a health insurance issuer offering group or individual health insurance coverage shall not discriminate with respect to participation under the plan or coverage against any health care provider who is acting within the scope of that provider's license or certification under applicable State law." It is widely acknowledged that the intent of the law was to create affordable access to CAM providers. For states that license nonphysician providers who might treat back pain, such as massage therapists, chiropractors, and acupuncturists, the ACA provision means that insurance companies cannot discriminate against these state-licensed providers as long as they are practicing within the scope of their licenses. Significant controversy exists in the interpretation and implementation of the law, however, as the guidance issued by federal agencies differs from a report issued by the Senate Committee on Appropriations (Moore, 2014). It remains to be seen how the ACA will affect access to integrative care.

Envisioning an Integrated System: The Case of the Cleveland Clinic

The Cleveland Clinic is one of the most respected academic medical health systems in the world. While it is a leading medical health system renowned for cardiovascular care, it is also one of the leaders in implementing integrative care in a major healthcare system. The position of "chief wellness officer," which was filled by integrative medicine physician Michael Roizen, was created under the leadership of the Cleveland Clinic's chief executive officer, Toby Cosgrove. The creation of the Cleveland Clinic Wellness Institute, which is responsible for advocating healthy living and lifestyle medicine, has in turn led to the creation of a number of progressive programs and initiatives:

- Integrative medicine consults, lifestyle medicine consults, a Chinese herbal therapy clinic, and disease reversal programs were implemented.
- In September 2014, reflecting the importance of functional medicine, the Cleveland Clinic entered into a full partnership with the Institute for Functional Medicine (IFM), creating the Center for Functional Medicine on its main campus; the Center is led by the chair of IFM, Dr. Mark Hyman, and by IFM's chief medical officer, Dr. Patrick Hanaway.
- All employees in the Clinic's health plan must maintain health goals through its wellness program, and improvements in their health are reflected by changes in their insurance premiums.
- The Clinic banned smoking on its campus in 2005 and stopped hiring smokers.
- Healthy foods are offered on the hospital campus; almost every deep-fryer was taken out, sugared sodas were banned, and trans-fats have been eliminated.
- The health system offers free Weight Watchers meetings, free gym memberships and yoga classes, and free smoking cessation programs.

These initiatives have produced real results: In 2012, the Cleveland Clinic reported that over the last 4 years, fitness clubs usage had increased from about 2,500 hours per month to 25,000 hours per month, and employees had collectively lost 330,000 pounds. The percentage of workers who self-reported being smokers to physicians declined from 15.4% to 6.8%. Overall, the organization saved $15 million in employee healthcare costs.

In the Cleveland Clinic, a large healthcare system, the values of integrative medicine and its emphasis on wellness have become part of the organizational character and culture. Through a robust offering of integrative medicine wellness programs and unprecedented community engagement, the Cleveland Clinic has produced a vision of health, combining world-class medical care and quality wellness programs, for both its patients and its staff.

CHAPTER SUMMARY

Complementary, alternative, and integrative medicines have traditionally been mainstream approaches to health and wellness in the United States; however, their introduction into physician-based and institutionalized healthcare systems is a relatively recent phenomenon. Current data indicate that the initial integration of CAM into healthcare systems is high, but widespread application of the holistic and person-centered tenets of integrative medicine by physicians in these systems remains limited. Significant evidence supporting the use of integrative therapies exists; however, neither conventional nor integrative medicine can meet the idealized vision of using only evidence-based practices when treating patients. An integrative physician, with expertise in conventional medicine as well as training in the scientific evidence and clinical application of CAM therapies, is best able to make the clinical judgments necessary to improve patient care. With the rising prevalence of chronic diseases—more than 70% of the U.S. population will develop cardiovascular disease, 25% will develop diabetes, 40% will be diagnosed with invasive cancers, and one in five will live with chronic, persistent pain (Kennedy, Roll, Schraudner, Murphy, & McPherson, 2014)—an approach to medicine that focuses on prevention, takes into account the whole person, considers and actively addresses possible lifestyle causes of disease, and utilizes pharmacologic as well as complementary therapies may be one of the solutions for controlling the increasing epidemic of chronic diseases in the United States.

KEY TERMS AND CONCEPTS

Alternative medicine: Therapies used as replacements for conventional medicine.

Complementary and alternative medicine (CAM): "A group of diverse medical and health care systems, practices, and products that are not generally considered part of conventional medicine" (NCCAM, 2012).

Complementary medicine: Therapies used as adjuncts to conventional medicine.

Functional medicine: A personalized approach to health care that uses basic and epidemiological science to investigate and evaluate a patient's condition; it relies on risk factor analysis and tests that evaluate the physiological ability of the body to perform basic bodily functions, with the goal of identifying factors that may be involved in mediating a patient's disease.

Integrative medicine: "The practice of medicine that reaffirms the importance of the relationship between practitioner and patient, focuses on the whole person, is informed by evidence, and makes use of all appropriate therapeutic approaches, healthcare professionals, and disciplines to achieve optimal health and healing" (Consortium of Academic Health Centers for Integrative Medicine, 2009).

Questions to Consider

1. What is complementary and alternative medicine?
2. What is integrative medicine?
3. How widespread is the use of complementary and alternative practices by patients?
4. What are the different categories of complementary and alternative practices according to the National Center for Complementary and Alternative Medicine?
5. How are functional medicine models of integrative care different from models that add CAM therapies into current healthcare systems?
6. What is the status of evidence in current conventional medicine?
7. Is there evidence for integrative medicine?
8. How do integrative medicine practitioners consider the weight of the evidence before using treatments that are generally considered safe versus treatments that may increase the risk of harm?
9. How integrated are complementary and alternative practices into current health systems?
10. Which factors have been cited as important for the integration of CAM into healthcare systems? Which potential barriers are there?

REFERENCES

Ananth, S. (2011, September). *2010 Complementary and alternative medicine survey of hospitals: Summary of results.* Chicago, IL: Health Forum (American Hospital Association) and Samueli Institute.

Astin, J. A. (1998). Why patients use alternative medicine: results of a national study. *Journal of the American Medical Association, 279,* 1548–1553.

Barnes, P. M., Bloom, B., & Nahin, R. L. (2008). Complementary and alternative medicine use among adults and children: United States, 2007. *National Health Statistics Reports, 12*, 1–23.

Ben-Arye, E., Frenkel, M., Klein, A., & Scharf, M. (2008, January 16). Attitudes toward integration of complementary and alternative medicine in primary care: Perspectives of patients, physicians and complementary practitioners. *Patient Education and Counseling, 70*(3), 395–402. doi: 10.1016/j.pec.2007.11.019

Centers for Disease Control and Prevention (CDC). (2014). Chronic disease prevention and health promotion. http://www.cdc.gov/chronicdisease/overview/index.htm

Chozick, A. (2014, April 11). He tells the Clintons how to lose a little. *The New York Times.* http://www.nytimes.com/2014/04/13/fashion/dr-mark-hyman-clintons-health.html?_r=1

Comarow, A. (2008, January 9). Top hospitals embrace alternative medicine. http://health.usnews.com/health-news/managing-your-healthcare/pain/articles/2008/01/09/embracing-alternative-care

Consortium of Academic Health Centers for Integrative Medicine. (2009). About us. http://www.imconsortium.org/about/home

Ehrlich, G., Callender T., & Gaster, B. (2013). Integrative medicine at academic health centers: A survey of clinicians' educational backgrounds and practices. *Family Medicine, 45*(5), 330–334.

Eisenberg, D. M., Kessler, R. C., Foster, C., Norlock, F., Calkins, D., & Delbanco, T. (1993). Unconventional medicine in the United States. *New England Journal of Medicine, 328*, 246–252.

Herper, M. (2012, February 10). The truly staggering cost of inventing new drugs. http://www.forbes.com/sites/matthewherper/2012/02/10/the-truly-staggering-cost-of-inventing-new-drugs/

Institute of Medicine (IOM). (2005). *Complementary and alternative medicine.* Washington, DC: National Academies Press.

Johnson, P. J., Ward, A., Knutson, L., & Sendelbach, S. (2012). Personal use of complementary and alternative medicine (CAM) by U.S. health care workers. *Health Services Research, 47*, 211–227.

Kawakita, K., & Okada, K. (2014). Acupuncture therapy: Mechanism of action, efficacy, and safety: A potential intervention for psychogenic disorders. *Biopsychosocial Medicine, 8*(4). http://www.bpsmedicine.com/content/8/1/4

Kennedy, J., Roll, J., Schraudner, T., Murphy, S., & McPherson, S. (2014). Prevalence of persistent pain in the U.S. adult population: New data From the 2010 National Health Interview Survey. *Journal of Pain, 15*(10), 979. doi: 10.1016/j.jpain.2014.05.009

Keshet, Y. (2013) Dual embedded agency: Physicians implement integrative medicine in health-care organizations. *Health (London), 17*, 605. doi: 10.1177/1363459312472084

Khan, A., Khan, S., Zimmerman, V., Baddour, L., & Tleyjeh, I. (2010). Quality and strength of evidence of the Infectious Diseases Society of America clinical practice guidelines. *Clinical Infectious Diseases, 51*(10), 1147–1156.

Kooreman, P., & Baars, E. W. (2012). Patients whose GP knows complementary medicine tend to have lower costs and live longer. *European Journal of Health Economics, 13*(6), 769–776.

Kroenke, K., Wood, D. R., Mangelsdorff, A. D., Meier, N.J., & Powell, J. B. (1998). Chronic fatigue in primary care. Prevalence, patient characteristics, and outcome. *Journal of the American Medical Association, 260*(7), 929–934.

Landmark Healthcare. (1999). *The Landmark report II on HMOs and alternative care.* Sacramento, CA: Author.

Lind, B. K., Lafferty, W. E., Tyree, P. T., & Diehr, P. K. (2010). Comparison of health care expenditures among insured users and nonusers of complementary and alternative medicine in Washington state: A cost minimization analysis. *Journal of Alternative and Complementary Medicine, 16*(4), 411–417.

Maizes, V., Rakel, D., & Niemiec, C. (2009). Integrative medicine and patient-centered care. *Explore (NY). 5*(5), 277–289. doi: 10.1016/j.explore .2009.06.008

Manek, N. J., Crowson, C. S., Ottenberg, A. L., Curlin, F. A., Kaptchuk, T. J., & Tilburt, J. C. (2010). What rheumatologists in the United States think of complementary and alternative medicine: Results of a national survey. *BMC Complementary and Alternative Medicine, 10*, 5.

Marcus, D., Blazek-O'Neill, B., & Kopar, J. (2013). Symptomatic improvement reported after receiving Reiki at a cancer infusion center. *American Journal of Hospice and Palliative Medicine, 30*(2), 216–217.

Moore, A. (2014, January 31). ACA prohibits discrimination against licensed providers. http://www.insidecompensation.com/2014/07/31 /aca-prohibits-discrimination-against-licensed-providers/

National Center for Complementary and Alternative Medicine (NCCAM). (2012). What is complementary and alternative medicine? http://nccam.nih.gov/sites/nccam .nih.gov/files/D347_05-25-2012.pdf

Nichols, B. (2004, September 5). Bill Clinton bypass surgery successful. *USA Today.* http://usatoday30.usatoday.com/news/nation/2004-09-05-clinton-bypass_x.htm

Poonacha, T., & Go, R. (2011). Level of scientific evidence underlying recommendations arising from the National Comprehensive Cancer Network clinical practice guidelines. *Journal of Clinical Oncology, 29*(2), 186–191.

Sawni, A., & Thomas, R. (2009). Pediatricians' attitudes, experience and referral patterns regarding complementary/alternative medicine: A national survey. *BMC Complementary and Alternative Medicine, 7*(18). http://www.biomedcentral .com/1472-6882/7/18

Shere-Wolfe, K. D., Tilburt, J. C., D'Adamo, C., Berman, B., & Chesney, M. A. (2013). Infectious diseases physicians' attitudes and practices related to complementary and integrative medicine: Results of a national survey. *Evidence-Based Complementary and Alternative Medicine, 294–381.* doi: 10.1155/2013/294381

Tai-Seale, M., McGuire, T., & Zhang, W. (2007). Time allocation in primary care office visits. *Health Services Research, 42*(5), 1871–1894.

Tricoci, P., Allen, J., Kramer, J., Califf, R., & Smith, S. (2009). Scientific evidence underlying the ACC/AHA clinical practice guidelines. *Journal of the American Medical Association, 301*(8), 831–841. doi: 10.1001/jama.2009.205

Chapter 14

Population Health

—James S. Zoller, PhD

LEARNING OBJECTIVES

- Provide a definition of population health
- Explain why there is now an increased focus on population health
- Distinguish between population health and public health
- Identify ways that healthcare leaders can improve population health
- Describe how improvements in the health of a community can impact the overall cost of care
- Interpret measures of population health status

INTRODUCTION

Population health seemingly emerged as a distinct discipline in the United States in the 2000s. Nevertheless, a widely accepted definition of "population health" still does not exist. A definition proffered by Kindig and Stoddart in 2003 described this concept as "the health outcomes of a group of individuals, including the distribution of such outcomes within the group." The first School of Population Health in the United States, which was established at Thomas Jefferson University in 2008, suggests the definition of population health as "a systematic approach to coordinating the preventive and chronic care needs of patients:

efficiently manage risk, promote full transparency of information, lower costs and improve health outcomes. We do this through active program interventions based on strong patient data analysis and the cultivation of close ties with community and social service organizations, professional groups—especially primary care providers—as well as hospitals and other institutions directly responsible for care, in both the acute and ambulatory settings."

Population health is distinguished from **public health**, which was first defined as "the science and art of preventing disease, prolonging life and promoting health and efficiency through organized community effort" by Winslow in 1920. Population health includes public health but extends well beyond that.

The Institute for Healthcare Improvement (IHI), in its Triple Aims initiative, operationalizes population health by using the following set of measures:

- Health/functional status: Single-question (e.g., from CDC HRQOL-4) or multidomain (e.g. SF-12, EuroQol).
- Risk status: Composite health risk appraisal (HRA) score.
- Disease burden: Summary of the prevalence of major chronic conditions; summary of predictive model scores.
- Mortality: **Life expectancy; years of potential life lost**; standardized **mortality rate**. Healthy life expectancy (HLE) combines life expectancy and health status into a single measure, reflecting remaining years of life in good health (IHI, 2009).

What consistently distinguishes population health from public health is the incorporation of all determinants of health. These determinants, as defined by the World Health Organization (WHO, 2014), include the following factors:

- *Income and social status:* Higher income and social status are linked to better health. The greater the gap between the richest and poorest people, the greater the differences in health.
- *Education:* Low education levels are linked with poor health, more stress, and lower self-confidence.
- *Physical environment:* Safe water and clean air, healthy workplaces, safe houses, communities, and roads all contribute to good health.
- *Employment and working conditions:* People who have employment are healthier, particularly those who have more control over their working conditions.
- *Social support networks:* Greater support from families, friends, and communities is linked to better health.

- *Culture:* Customs and traditions, and the beliefs of the family and community all affect health.
- *Genetics:* Inheritance plays a part in determining lifespan, healthiness, and the likelihood of developing certain illnesses.
- *Personal behavior and coping skills:* Balanced eating, keeping active, smoking, drinking, and how we deal with life's stresses and challenges all affect health.
- *Health services:* Access to and use of services that prevent and treat disease influences health.
- *Gender:* Men and women suffer from different types of diseases at different ages.

Foremost in clarifying population health is understanding the concept of population. A population is the entirety of individuals who possess a particular grouping characteristic. The most typical characteristic for defining a population is geographic residency—for example, the population of the United States. However, populations may be defined using other characteristics, such as age (e.g., Medicare beneficiaries), religion (e.g., Jewish), or race (e.g., African American). The premise of population health is that the status of the group as a whole is of consequence as opposed to any one individual. Of course, the health of a population is derived as the sum or average of the health of its individual members.

Likewise, the definition of health is important in conceptualizing population health. The accepted WHO definition of health is "a state of complete physical, mental and social well-being and not merely the absence of disease or infirmity" (WHO, 1948). This definition is so broad as to include almost all aspects of a person's life. This is appropriate in the context of population health as we consider the range of determinants of health cited above.

Thus the distinguishing feature of population health, especially pertaining to the health administration practitioner, is the inclusion of a wide array of influences on individual health that must be integrated to maximize the overall health of a group of individuals. To illustrate further, based on the work of County Health Rankings (2014), the clinical care system is said to contribute 20% of the impact on the health of a community, while health behaviors contribute 30%, social and economic factors contribute 40%, and the physical environment contributes 10% (**Figure 14-1**). This suggests that to truly have an impact on population health, a myriad of efforts must be effectively integrated to produce large-scale improvements.

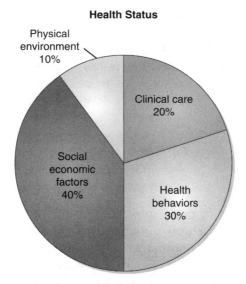

Figure 14-1 Factors affecting health status

Data from County Health Rankings. (2014). Our approach. Available at: http://www.countyhealthrankings.org/our-approach.

MEASURES OF POPULATION HEALTH

A crucial aspect of using measures of population health is the ability to make meaningful comparisons, either between populations or over time for a specific population. In either case, it is necessary that the calculation be made consistently. Following is a listing of commonly used measures of population health with their respective definitions and limitations:

Life Expectancy

Life expectancy is the average number of years of survival from some point in life. The most commonly expressed life expectancy is the expected number of years of survival from birth. The calculation starts with age-specific mortality rates, which are modeled using a Gompertz sigmoidal function, which is particularly suited for modeling certain time-series situations, or other appropriate statistical function. This is probably the most commonly used overall measure of population health. Of course, the higher the life expectancy value, the healthier the population (at least in theory). Because life expectancies are averages, some individuals will inevitably live longer than the expected lifespan, and some will die before the expected number of years.

Table 14-1 lists the life expectancy by sex for 21 countries (the top 10, the bottom 10, and the United States). The highest value is 86.5 years of life from birth for the country of Monaco; the lowest value is 47.5 years of life from birth in Sierra Leone. Notice that the United States ranks number 35, with a life expectancy at birth of 79.8 years.

One may surmise that there exists a relationship between the economic status of a country (e.g., per capita income, gross domestic product [GDP] per capita) and life expectancy. In fact, a model developed by Samuel Preston in 1975 displays such a relationship (**Figure 14-2**). Notice the bottom 10 countries are socially and economically underdeveloped, especially when

Table 14-1 Life Expectancy, by Sex, for Selected Countries

Overall Rank	Country	Overall Life Expectancy	Male Life Expectancy	Female Life Expectancy
1	Monaco	86.5	83	90
2	Japan	84.6	82	87.2
3	Andorra	84.2	80.8	87.6
4	Singapore	84	82	87
5	Hong Kong	83.8	82	85.6
6	San Marino	83.5	82	85
7	Iceland	83.3	81.4	85.2
8	Italy	83.1	80.4	85.8
9	Australia	83	80.5	85.5
10	Sweden	83	81.4	84.6
35	**United States**	**79.8**	**77.4**	**82.2**
184	Angola	52	51	53
185	Chad	51	50.5	53.5
186	Mali	51	50	53
187	Lesotho	51	50	52
188	Guinea Bissau	50	48	52
189	Swaziland	50	49	51
190	Somalia	50	48	52
191	Democratic Republic of the Congo	49.5	48	51
192	Central African Republic	48.5	47	50
193	Sierra Leone	47.5	47	48

Data from WHO Life Expectancy, 2013. Exact methods of calculation can be found at http://apps.who.int/gho/indicatorregistry/App_Main/view_indicator.aspx?iid=65.

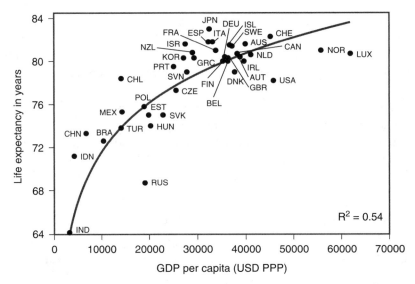

Figure 14–2 Scatter-diagram of relations between life expectancy at birth (e_0^0) and GDP per capita, 2009 (or nearest year).

Reproduced from OECD (2011), Health at a Glance 2011: OECD Indicators, OECD Publishing. Available at: http://dx.doi.org/10.1787/health_glance-2011-en.

compared to the top 10 countries. But then compare the United States which is widely considered to be one of the richest countries in the world and certainly the most advanced in healthcare technology. The relatively poor life expectancy in the United States emphasizes the complexity of influences on the overall health status.

Health Expectancy

Health expectancy is a modified version of life expectancy considering various health states. "A health expectancy figure is the combination of a life expectancy figure with a concept of health which makes it possible to calculate the number of years lived in the different health states" (Robine, Romieu, & Cambois, 1999). "The observed prevalence life table method" (**Table 14–2**) is probably the most common method of calculating health expectancy (Robine et al., 1999). This method incorporates some consideration of quality of life or years of life without disease or disability. It is reasonably hoped that increases in life expectancy do not consist solely of additional years in an unhealthy state.

Table 14–2 Health Expectancies at Age 65 According to the Different Concepts of Health, China, 1987–1992 (years)

	Male		Female	
	1987	**1992**	**1987**	**1992**
Life expectancy	12.6	13.0	15.0	15.6
Disability-free life expectancy	9.0	—	10.2	—
Active life expectancy	9.6	11.9	11.5	13.7
Life expectancy in good perceived health	9.4	10.2	10.7	11.7
Life expectancy without disease	—	4.2	—	4.4

Reproduced from Robine, J. M., Romieu, I., & Cambois, E. (1999). Health expectancy indicators. *Bulletin of the World Health Organization*, 77(2), 181–185. Data from Qiao X. (1997). Health expectancy of China. In: 10th Work-group meeting of REVES, International Research Network for Interpretation of Observed Values of Healthy Life Expectancy, Tokyo, (REVES Paper No. 305, available from REVES).

Potential Years of Life Lost

Years of potential life lost (YPLL) is an accepted measure of premature deaths (**Figure 14–3**). As a measure of premature mortality, it is helpful in assessing preventable deaths, especially among younger populations. It can serve as a good indicator of where prevention efforts may have the greatest impact in increasing overall life expectancy and lost economic productivity.

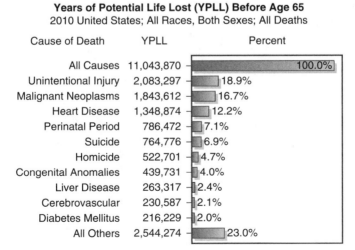

Years of Potential Life Lost (YPLL) Before Age 65
2010 United States; All Races, Both Sexes; All Deaths

Cause of Death	YPLL	Percent
All Causes	11,043,870	100.0%
Unintentional Injury	2,083,297	18.9%
Malignant Neoplasms	1,843,612	16.7%
Heart Disease	1,348,874	12.2%
Perinatal Period	786,472	7.1%
Suicide	764,776	6.9%
Homicide	522,701	4.7%
Congenital Anomalies	439,731	4.0%
Liver Disease	263,317	2.4%
Cerebrovascular	230,587	2.1%
Diabetes Mellitus	216,229	2.0%
All Others	2,544,274	23.0%

Figure 14–3 Years of potential life lost (YPLL) before age 65
Courtesy of CDC, WISQARS, 2014.

Disease Burden

Incidence

Incidence is the rate of new cases of a disease. It is calculated as the number of new cases divided by the number of individuals at risk for the disease over a period of time (**Table 14–3**).

Table 14–3 Cancer Incidence and Death Rates* by Site, Race, and Ethnicity, US, 2007–2011

Incidence	White	Black	Asian/Pacific Islander	American Indian/Alaska Native	Hispanic
All Sites					
Male	529	594.4	322	320.1	422
Female	424.4	398.5	283.4	269.2	331.4
Breast (female)	123.9	120.4	85.8	67.9	91.9
Colon & Rectum					
Male	48.8	60.6	39.8	35.4	46
Female	36.8	44.8	30	28.8	31.7
Kidney & Renal Pelvis					
Male	21.5	23.5	10.7	20.2	20.6
Female	11.3	12.6	5	12	11.6
Liver & Intrahepatic Bile Duct					
Male	9.8	15.8	21.2	13.2	19.1
Female	3.3	4.6	8	5.8	6.9
Lung & Bronchus					
Male	78.1	93.4	48	53.1	45.3
Female	56.2	50.6	28	40.1	26.5
Prostate	131.9	215.7	72.4	75.2	120.6
Stomach					
Male	8.4	15.2	15.2	8	13.9
Female	4	8	8.6	4.4	8
Uterine Cervix	7.5	10	6.4	6.6	10.6

*

Data from U.S. Cancer Statistics Working Group. United States Cancer Statistics: 1999–2011 Incidence and Mortality Web-based Report. Atlanta: U.S. Department of Health and Human Services, Centers for Disease Control and Prevention and National Cancer Institute; 2014.

The challenge of determining incidence is the actual identification of new cases. This is most commonly achieved through disease registries that actively seek to identify new cases. It is also critical that the denominator contains only those individuals at risk of the disease. New cases may also be identified through survey methods asking respondents whether they contracted a disease during a defined period of time.

Incidence is particularly useful in assessing the effects of treatments and interventions. Trends in incidence can also provide healthcare providers with information about the number of cases they might expect in the future.

Prevalence

Point prevalence is the number of cases of a disease state that exist at a point in time. This indicator is calculated by dividing the number of existing cases by the population at that point in time. For example, the CDC Behavioral Risk Factor Surveillance System (BRFSS) survey asks, "Have you been told by a doctor that you have diabetes?" In the 2009 survey, of 422,210 respondents, 52,386 responded yes to this question; thus the point prevalence was 9.10% or 91 per 1000.

Period prevalence is the number of cases that exist over a period of time divided by the population over that period of time (**Figure 14–4**). The denominator may be the average population over the period of time or the population at the midpoint of the period. Prevalence of conditions can also be a useful indicator of healthcare utilization.

Prevalence and incidence are clearly related, but are influenced by a third variable—**duration** of the disease or condition (**Figure 14–5**). Duration is either how long the disease lasts until recovery or time until death. For example, as the incidence rate of human immunodeficiency virus (HIV) infection has decreased, the prevalence has increased, because individuals are now living longer with HIV. As depicted in Figure 14–5, as incidence fills the container, duration/mortality empties the container. The contents of the container represent prevalence.

$$\text{Low birth weight prevalence} = \frac{\text{Number of infants weighing} <2500\,\text{g born during the reporting period}}{\text{Population during the same time period}} \times 100$$

$$\text{Example: } \frac{5807}{62,441} \times 100 = 9.3\%$$

Figure 14–4 Calculation of period prevalence
Courtesy of CDC, 2014.

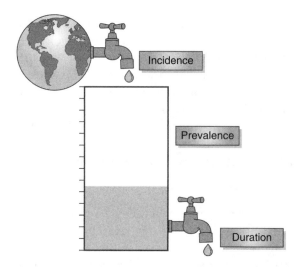

Figure 14–5 Relationship between prevalence, incidence, and duration

---

Exhibit 14–1 Health status

Health status is frequently measured using an interview instrument that asks questions related to functioning and well-being. The Patient-Reported Outcomes Measurement Information System (PROMIS) questions used in the National Health Interview survey are a good example of this type of measurement. The PROMIS survey uses four questions:

1. In general, how would you rate your physical health?
   (a) Excellent
   (b) Very good
   (c) Good
   (d) Fair
   (e) Poor
   (f) Refused
   (g) Don't know

2. To what extent are you able to carry out your everyday physical activities such as walking, climbing stairs, carrying groceries, or moving a chair?
   (a) Completely
   (b) Mostly
   (c) Moderately
   (d) A little

(e) Not at all

(f) Refused

(g) Don't know

3. In the past 7 days, how would you rate your fatigue on average?

(a) None

(b) Mild

(c) Moderate

(d) Severe

(e) Very severe

(f) Refused

(g) Don't know

4. In the past 7 days, how would you rate your pain on average? Use a scale of 0–10, with 0 being no pain and 10 being the worst imaginable pain.

(a) _____

(b) Refused

(c) Don't know

Courtesy of CDC/National Center for Health Statistics.

The scored responses to these four questions yield a measure of overall physical health. More specifics about this instrument can be found at http://www.nihpromis.org/?AspxAutoDetectCookieSupport=1#1. Of course, the responses are self-reported and subject to some bias, but as a valid measure the National Health Interview survey is a good way to monitor trends and make relative comparisons.

Mortality

All-Cause Mortality

Mortality rates are calculated as the number of deaths during a period of time divided by the average population over that same period of time. In the United States, deaths are routinely reported to health departments, and the numbers of deaths in a geographic area are readily available (**Table 14–4**). Despite some problems with the accuracy in causes of death, mortality data are a reliable indicator for measuring health of a population. They are especially valuable in making comparisons between regions if standardization methods are employed. Mortality rates can also be valuable in identifying

Table 14–4 Mortality Data: U.S. Deaths, 2000–2010

	2000	2009	2010
U.S. all-cause deaths per 100,000 population, age-adjusted	869.0	749.6	747.0

trends that indicate changes in health status. They can also be calculated by cause, allowing the same indicators to be used for certain conditions of interest, such as cancer.

Infant Mortality

Infant mortality is a special mortality indicator that can point to particular problems in the health of a population (**Figure 14–6**). It is calculated as the number of deaths of infants (younger than one year of age) divided by the number of live births during the same period. Births are typically reported accurately in most developed countries; therefore infant mortality can be a meaningful indicator. Infant mortality also can be a surrogate measure of certain social determinants of health such as poverty level.

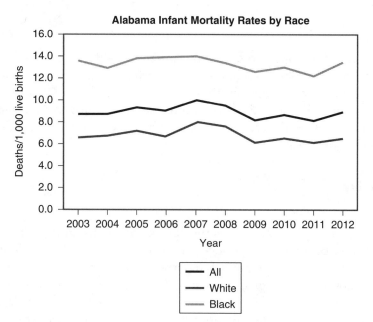

Figure 14–6 Alabama infant mortality rate

Data from Infant Mortality, Alabama 2012. Alabama Department of Public Health, Center for Health Statistics.

Standardization

To compare mortality rates across populations, it is necessary to adjust for structural differences in the respective populations. The most common characteristic used as the basis for adjustment is age, which clearly has implications for death rates. We would expect, for example, that a population with a higher proportion of elderly people would naturally have a higher death rate.

Direct adjustment allows comparisons while removing the impact of the age distribution in the respective populations. Adjusted mortality rates are statistically constructed rates and so cannot be used for making projections, but they can be used for comparison purposes. For example, **Table 14–5** demonstrates that while one community has a higher raw mortality rate, the age-adjusted rates show that same community has a lower mortality rate.

Age-adjusted rates using the direct method require data on age group-specific mortality rates and use the same age groups as a reference population. The reference population used is only important to the extent that each population to be compared uses the same reference. The expected deaths are the number of deaths calculated by multiplying the actual death rate times the reference population; in other words, if the community rate is applied to the reference population, then it would yield the expected number of deaths.

Morbidity

Morbidity is the occurrence of deviation from optimal health and well-being. It is usually measured by occurrences of events that require

Table 14–5 Example: Age-Adjusted Mortality Rates

Age Groups	Standard Population	Crude Death Rate in Community A per 100,000	Crude Death Rate in Community B per 100,000	Expected Deaths Community A	Expected Deaths Community B
Under 1	6000	15.0	20.0	0.90	1.20
1–14	23,000	1.0	0.5	0.23	0.12
15–34	41,000	1.0	1.0	0.41	0.41
35–54	30,000	4.0	5.0	1.20	1.50
55–64	15,000	15.0	20.0	2.25	3.00
Over 64	35,000	80.0	90.0	28.00	31.50
Total	150,000	35.6	17.4	32.99	37.73
Adjusted death rate per 100,000				21.99	25.15

healthcare interventions, such as clinic visits, hospitalizations, or sick days. These indicators are calculated by dividing the number of occurrences of the event (e.g., hospitalization or hospital discharge) by a population.

As an example, **Figure 14–7** shows the rate of hospital discharges per 1000 Medicare beneficiaries by county. The more darkly colored service areas have a higher rate of discharge (hospitalization), indicating possibly a less healthy population.

Morbidity has clear implications for healthcare providers as well as community economic conditions. High morbidity may or may not affect mortality, but it will affect productivity and healthcare expenses.

As a surrogate for these direct measures, when data are unavailable, indirect measures such as risk factor prevalence may be used. Factors such as smoking rates, obesity rates, and substance abuse rates, which have strong associations to disease conditions, are most commonly employed for this purpose. For example, because it is associated with multiple disease states, the smoking rate is a key indicator of health. It is presumed that decreases in smoking will reduce morbidity and mortality, leading to a healthier community population (**Figure 14–8**).

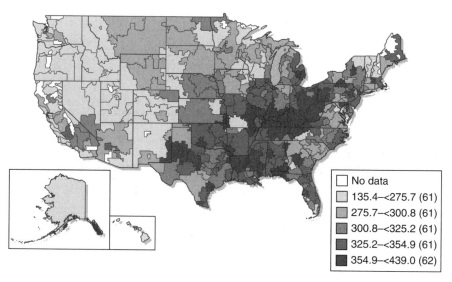

No data
135.4–<275.7 (61)
275.7–<300.8 (61)
300.8–<325.2 (61)
325.2–<354.9 (61)
354.9–<439.0 (62)

Figure 14–7 Rate of hospital discharges per 1000 Medicare beneficiaries by county

Reproduced from the Dartmouth Atlas of Health Care. Courtesy of the Dartmouth Institute for Health Policy and Clinical Practice. Available at: http://www.dartmouthatlas.org/data/topic/topic.aspx?cat=19.

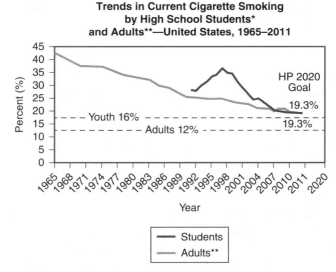

Figure 14-8 Trends in current cigarette smoking by high school students and adults—United States, 1965-2011

Courtesy of CDC, 2014.

HEALTHY PEOPLE 2020

Healthy People 2020 is the current extension of the 1979 Surgeon General's report, *Healthy People: The Surgeon General's Report on Health Promotion and Disease Prevention*. The *Healthy People* program defines national goals and objectives addressing the health of the country in 10-year increments (http://healthypeople.gov/2020/default.aspx). It is replete with metrics for monitoring the health of populations. It also provides a framework for communities to use in addressing community health priorities and progress. *Healthy People 2020* contains 42 topic areas with more than 1200 objectives. A smaller set of 26 leading health indicators within 12 topic areas have been selected to communicate high-priority health issues.

FOCUSING ON POPULATION HEALTH IMPROVEMENTS

Hospitals and other healthcare delivery organizations must decide which population health perspective they will adopt and how they will apply that perspective. Influencing the health of a population can be an overwhelming goal when so many confounding factors exist. Using the measures described earlier can help establish priorities for the investment of resources.

First, the organization must define the population which it wishes to influence. Definition using geopolitical boundaries is probably the most common and easiest approach. However, an organization may further define the target population using demographic characteristics, such as Medicaid beneficiaries or children. Next, compare measures for the defined population to other benchmark populations (e.g., the state, the nation). This comparison identifies areas of deficiency that warrant attention or opportunities for improvement.

Consider the greatest strengths of the organization. These areas may be those with the largest amount of devoted resources (volume utilization), greatest expertise, or best efficiency. Areas of strength may be centers of excellence (e.g., women's health) or specialization (e.g., heart care). This determination will help decide which population health initiatives are most likely to be successful.

Identify partners in the community that can complement initiatives. Improving population health needs to be a community-wide effort to achieve maximum effectiveness. Health departments can help identify and contact the segments deemed at risk. Medicaid agencies can identify persons at risk based on service use outside the hospital. Community organizations interact with diverse persons facing challenges with the social determinants of health. The broader inclusion of community resources results in a higher likelihood of achieving success. Community organizations and leaders have close contact with the population and, therefore, may be well suited to provide guidance on their needs and wants. No community initiative will succeed if the target population does not understand the value or need. Clinical need must translate into actual demand.

Set long-terms goals. Making improvements in the health of populations is a slow process and will take years, especially when efforts target factors influencing chronic disease. Organizations must be willing to invest the necessary resources over the long term to realize a return on their investment in the form of improvement of population health measures. How long will it take for a reduction in the smoking rate to translate into a commensurate reduction in lung cancer incidence? How long will it take for a reduction in the obesity rate to produce a commensurate reduction in heart disease? How long will it take for a reduction in hypertension prevalence to yield a commensurate reduction in stroke incidence?

Some initiatives may yield relatively short-term results. For example, mass immunization campaigns can be particularly effective at reducing incidence of infectious diseases. Similarly, changes in policies or regulations such as helmet laws or speed limits may reduce mortality or morbidity from highway accidents.

Ultimately, the goal of population health initiatives is to prevent or ameliorate population-wide disease and infirmity so as to improve the aggregate quantity and quality of life. Ostensibly, these efforts may also reduce the demand for traditional medical care services. All things being equal, a very successful healthy lifestyle adoption program (i.e., reduce obesity, improve diets, increase exercise habits) may reduce the need for cardiac services as the incidence of heart disease declines. Considering the reality of limited resources, organizations must make decisions about undertaking initiatives that will yield the greatest return on investment as measured by population health indicators.

The cost-effectiveness of smoking cessation programs is well documented (Cromwell, Bartosch, Fiore, Hasselblad, & Baker, 1997). Many other prevention strategies have also been found to be cost-effective. The combination of cost-effectiveness and population health benefits makes undertaking such activities a worthwhile endeavor.

EXAMPLES OF POPULATION HEALTH INITIATIVES

California Health Cities Project

Pasadena, California, began participating in the California Health Cities Project in 1989 with the goal of improving quality of life among its citizens. The hallmark of Pasadena's effort was development of a quality of life index, which includes 20 broad health indicators. The Pasadena Healthy Cities Program Steering Committee included 20–25 community partners, such as the health department, healthcare facilities, senior centers, and other community organizations, in implementing its program. Community leaders identified quality-of-life indicators to guide community groups and agencies in developing initiatives. This effort created common themes and coordination that maximized results.

Some indicators of health status changes in the Pasadena community include the following (Healthy Pasadena, 2014):

- The age-adjusted death rate due to cancer decreased from 144.4 deaths/100,000 in 2006–2008 to 138.2 deaths/100,000 in 2008–2010.
- The age-adjusted death rate due to diabetes decreased from 60.3 deaths/100,000 in 2006–2008 to 55 deaths/100,000 in 2008–2010.

- The age-adjusted death rate due to coronary heart disease decreased from 149.3 deaths/100,000 in 2006–2008 to 124.2 deaths/100,000 in 2008–2010.
- The percentage of self-reported general health assessment of good or better increased from 78.6% in 2003 to 80.5% in 2011–2012.

Minnesota State Department of Health: Statewide Health Improvement Program

The Minnesota State Department of Health's Statewide Health Improvement Program (SHIP) was established in 2008 as part of the state's Vision for a Better State of Health. That program was founded to "help Minnesotans live longer, healthier lives by preventing the leading causes of chronic disease: tobacco and obesity" (Minnesota Department of Health, 2014).

A specific example of the SHIP effort is the PartnerSHIP4Health program implemented in Becker, Clay, Otter Tail, and Wilkin counties. This program is a collaboration among a variety of health organizations, including schools, worksites, and healthcare facilities. The program claims to be (1) leveling the increasing rate of obesity, (2) reducing the rate of smoking and exposure to second-hand smoke, and (3) increasing the availability of good nutrition.

Partners Healthcare Population Health Management

Partners Healthcare of Boston. Massachusetts, has developed a program it calls Population Health Management (PHM). The program's goal is "improving the health of our patients while lowering the overall cost of care" (Partners Healthcare, n.d.).

Steps to Health King County, Seattle

The Steps to Health King County was initiated in the Seattle area in 2003 with the following goals:

- Reduce the impact of chronic diseases through preventing and controlling asthma, diabetes, and obesity
- Promote a comprehensive approach that coordinates actions at the individual, family, clinical, school, and community levels and integrates interventions addressing multiple chronic conditions
- Reduce health disparities due to chronic illness by reaching social and ethnic groups that are disproportionately affected

A hallmark of the program is its enlistment of more than 75 organizations as partners, including community-based organizations, hospitals, clinics, schools, and others.

Some of the outcomes realized over the term of the program (which lost funding in 2008) were as follows:

- A 9.5% per year reduction in hospitalizations for childhood asthma
- A 40% reduction in emergency department visits
- A 38% improvement in diabetes control

Genesys Health Works

The operations of Genesys Health System, which is located in mid-Michigan, encompass medical campuses, outpatient facilities, primary care practices, and ancillary providers. It is this continuum of care network that led Genesys Health System to develop HealthWorks, a model of care addressing the IHI's Triple Aims. "The Genesys HealthWorks model of care embodies the Triple Aims' unifying 'macro-integrator' function through three key elements that emphasize the importance of primary care, health promotion, and patient self-management support" (Commonwealth Fund, 2010):

- Engaging community-based primary care physicians in a physician–hospital organization that emphasizes the importance of primary care and makes more efficient use of specialty care
- Promoting health through the deployment of health navigators, who support patients in adopting healthy lifestyles to prevent and manage chronic disease
- Partnering with community organizations to extend the goals of the model to the entire local population

The system has demonstrated reductions in the use and costs of care (by 26% in some settings). The health navigator program has improved diet, physical activity levels, smoking rates, and medication compliance among a segment of at-risk patients.

CHAPTER SUMMARY

Population health is the intersection of public health, medical care, socioeconomic influences and behavioral health and relates to the health outcomes of a group of people. The concept includes all determinants of health such as income and social status, education, physical environment, employment and working conditions, social support networks, culture, genetics, personal behavior and coping skills, health services, and gender. A widely accepted definition for population health does not exist. A definition proffered by Kindig and Stoddart in 2003 described this concept as "the health outcomes of a group of individuals, including the distribution of such outcomes within the group."

One way to understand the concept of population health is to examine measures that indicate its status. We described measures of Life Expectancy, Health Expectancy, Potential Years of Life Lost, Disease Burden, Mortality, and Morbidity. Additional health indicator metrics are available through the *Healthy People 2020* program.

Finally, suggestions for how an organization may approach population health goals are presented along with descriptions of some successful programs.

Key Terms and Concepts

Duration: Either how long the disease lasts until recovery or time until death.

Health: "A state of complete physical, mental and social well-being and not merely the absence of disease or infirmity" (World Health Organization, 1948).

Health expectancy: A modified version of life expectancy considering various health states.

Incidence: The rate of new cases of a disease; the number of new cases of a disease divided by the number of individuals at risk for the disease over a period of time.

Infant mortality: The number of deaths of infants (younger than one year of age) divided by the number of live births during the same period.

Life expectancy: The average number of years of survival from some point in life.

Morbidity: The occurrence of deviation from optimal health and well-being.

Mortality rate: The number of deaths during a period of time divided by the average population over that same period of time.

Period prevalence: The number of cases that exist over a period of time divided by the population over that period of time.

Point prevalence: The number of cases of a disease state that exist at a point in time; it is calculated by dividing the number of existing cases by the population at that point in time.

Population: The entirety of individuals who possess a particular grouping characteristic.

Population health: "The health outcomes of a group of individuals, including the distribution of such outcomes within the group" (Kindig & Stoddart, 2003). A wide array of influences on individual health must be integrated to maximize the overall health of a group of individuals.

Public health: "The science and art of preventing disease, prolonging life and promoting health and efficiency through organized community effort" (Winslow, 1920).

Years of potential life lost (YPLL): An accepted measure of premature deaths.

Questions to Consider

1. How can public health be a part of community population health initiatives?
2. Given the multiple influences on the health of populations, which role(s) can the community hospital best play in effecting improvements?
3. What is the best measure of the health of a population?
4. How can improvements in the health of a community impact the overall cost of care?

REFERENCES

Centers for Disease Control and Prevention, Web-based Injury Statistics Query and Reporting System (WISQARS), 2014.

Commonwealth Fund. (2010). Genesys HealthWorks: Pursuing the Triple Aim through a primary care-based delivery system, integrated self-management support, and community partnerships. http://www.commonwealthfund.org/publications/case-studies/2010/jul/genesys-healthworks

County Health Rankings. (2014). Our approach. http://www.countyhealthrankings.org/our-approach

Cromwell, J., Bartosch, W. J. Fiore, M. C., Hasselblad, V., & Baker, T. (1997). Cost-effectiveness of the clinical practice recommendations in the AHCPR guideline for smoking cessation. *Journal of the American Medical Association, 278*(21), 1759–1766.

Healthy Pasadena. (2014, January 1). http://www.healthypasadena.org/index.php

Institute for Healthcare Improvement (IHI). (2009). Concept design. http://www.ihi.org/Engage/Initiatives/TripleAim/Documents/ConceptDesign.pdf

Kindig, D., & Stoddart, G. (2003). What is population health? *American Journal of Public Health, 93*(3), 380–383.

Minnesota Department of Health. (2014). SHIP frequently asked questions. http://www.health.state.mn.us/divs/oshii/ship/faq.html

Partners Healthcare. (n.d.). Population health management. https://www.partners.org/Innovation-And-Leadership/Population-Health-Management/Default.aspx

Preston, S. H. (1975). The changing relation between mortality and level of economic development. *Population Studies, 29*(2), 231–248.

Qiao X. Health expectancy of China. In: 10th Work-group meeting of REVES, International Research Network for Interpretation of Observed Values of Healthy Life Expectancy, Tokyo, 1997.

Robine, J. M., Romieu, I., & Cambois, E. (1999). Health expectancy indicators. *Bulletin of the World Health Organization, 77*(2), 181–185.

Winslow, C. E. A. (1920). The untilled fields of public health. *Science, 51*(1306), 23–33.

World Health Organization (WHO). (1948). Preamble to the Constitution of the World Health Organization as adopted by the International Health Conference, New York, 19–22 June, 1946; signed on 22 July 1946 by the representatives of 61 States (Official Records of the World Health Organization, no. 2, p. 100) and entered into force on 7 April 1948.

World Health Organization (WHO). (2014). Health impact assessment: Determinants of health. http://www.who.int/hia/evidence/doh/en/

Quality Care Is Good Business

An Interview with David Bernd, Chief Executive Officer of Sentara Healthcare

A man of few words, David Bernd is unabashed in his passion for the employees and physicians of Sentara Healthcare. Raised in Virginia's Tidewater area, Bernd did his undergraduate work at the College of William & Mary and received his master's degree in hospital and health administration from the Medical College of Virginia in Richmond. When he graduated, he knew that his professional career lay in the Tidewater area with what is now Sentara. Willing to sacrifice salary and title to work at the organization he felt best fit his long-term goals, Bernd started as an administrative assistant to the company's president. That early ability to envision a long-term career at Sentara has now, more than three decades later, translated into powerful visionary skills. Today Bernd maintains the same dogged commitment to the Tidewater community as he did at the outset of his career.

As CEO of Sentara Healthcare, a $5 billion integrated health system with 10 acute care hospitals, a health plan with 436,000 covered individuals, a 618-provider medical group, and a medical staff of 3,680 physicians, headquartered in the Tidewater region of Virginia, Bernd has surrounded himself with fellow executives who share his extraordinary vision for the organization. Howard Kern, Sentara's president and chief operations officer, joined Sentara seven years after Bernd, and their senior vice president and chief information officer, Bertram Reese, joined a year later. Reese describes their dream team in this way: "Dave envisions it; he gives us the rudder underneath it. I do the details and Howard keeps me on track."

Bernd was ahead of his time. In 1992, before other health organizations were tackling comprehensive IT design work, Bernd developed a vision of "Build once, roll many." But health technology was not yet as advanced as his vision, and there was no existing software to meet the company's needs. Bernd and his team were forced to table their design goals for 10 years.

By the time the software had caught up with Bernd's vision, Bernd and his team had developed a comprehensive plan for improving health processes, streamlining routines, and creating a computerized order management system to complement the overall IT design. The electronic health record (EHR) and clinical communications system, named Sentara eCare, was rolled out in 2009. Sentara eCare was expected to offer a $17 million return on its investment in its first year. But the return on investment far exceeded company executives' hopes, providing $12 million more than they had expected. Bernd's integrated vision included a well-designed and seamless communication system that connects Sentara's hospitals, pharmacies, physicians, nurses, radiologists, long-term care providers, and medical transport resources; it also included a 10-year plan for reengineering and consulting hours. In 2005, when the system was first proposed, EHR systems cost approximately $67 million. The overall cost that Bernd pitched to his board: $250 million. Once again, his vision was far-reaching—and successful.

"He doesn't think like a traditional healthcare provider executive," an old friend and colleague said of Bernd when asked to describe him. "He never has, never will. In other words, he doesn't think like a classically educated hospital administrator, but rather thinks about populations and their health ... he thinks in much broader terms—outside the box—outside the stratosphere. He thinks way ahead of everyone else."

Bernd is reserved—some might characterize him as shy—and modest. When the spotlight is shined on his success as Sentara's top executive, he is quick to reflect on his leadership team and the employees of Sentara. His vision for Sentara has included not only a world-class organization for its patients, but also a world-class organization for its employees and their families. For instance, Bernd has established community grant programs for families needing financial help with healthcare costs, and financial programs for Sentara employees and their families in the event of unexpected illness or other hardships.

The paper trail on Bernd is limited. He keeps a low-profile publicly, but those who know him speak of his humor, his willingness to volunteer in the community and with students at his alma mater, the College of William & Mary, and the times he refused to wear a tie to class in graduate school, despite the fact that wearing a tie was the dress code at the time. As it turns out, he may have been on to something before anyone else at the time: It is a rare thing these days to see graduate students wearing ties to class. Bernd is a trendsetter—an executive outside the traditional mold who developed a unique vision for health systems before the rest of his healthcare management peers.

Here is what Bernd had to say about his career, Sentara Healthcare, and the future of healthcare management.

1. **As one of the foremost leaders in health care, where do you find inspiration for your vision for running Sentara?**

   My biggest source of inspiration comes from Sentara employees and the many examples of their dedication to our mission of improving health. And I find inspiration from our patients and customers, who face and overcome adversities every day.

2. **Talk about the steps you have taken to create a culture in which Sentara has become one of the most integrated health systems in the country.**

   Our culture was established by my predecessor, Glen Mitchell, and has existed for some 30 years. I'm proud to carry forward and foster the environment he created, which values innovation and risk taking and promotes personal accountability and responsibility. This culture is found throughout every level of the organization, from the corporate executive suite straight through to our bedside caregivers.

   Can you take us into some concrete examples of how that works?

   Some of the Sentara business innovations that are most impressive would not have been successful without involvement and understanding from everyone within the organization. Implementing the first electronic ICU in the world and achieving Level 7 HIMSS integration of electronic health records—the first hospital system in the United States to do that in the first year of implementation—are two great examples.

   How, when implementing these initiatives, did you involve people at all levels of the organization?

   As leaders, we set global goals and strategic direction for the organization and ask our employees to fill in the specifics of their particular business line to follow the high-level strategic plan.

   Do you have focus groups? How does the information filter on up to you to make sure that you have it right?

   It filters up to me both formally and informally through meetings, interaction with managers, our strategic planning processes, and many other ways.

3. **Throughout the growth of Sentara, you have maintained strong partnerships with physicians. Tell us about this strategy and what you have learned over the past 30 years.**

It used to be that physicians and hospitals could remain in separate silos and success was not dependent upon cooperating very much. Today an integrated, seamless approach to health care is required to achieve real success for patients. Physicians need to be involved in all aspects of the patient care experience—from leadership and decision making to bedside care and beyond. We have a number of full-time physician executives with numerous responsibilities in the organization to help us achieve our goals of improving care and better managing populations of patients.

So, some of the physicians are involved in the business side of it and then others are more focused on patient care?

Yes, I think the key to success is to have physicians involved in both.

4. **Healthcare delivery and access and financing can sometimes be at odds with one another. How have you balanced delivery with access and financing?**

I believe that health care and financial success come from providing a seamless, efficient, effective, high-quality product. So finances, clinical quality, and patient satisfaction all go hand in hand. I don't see them as disparate or different. Quality care is good business.

5. **Sentara has received the designation as one of the top 10 "most wired health systems" for the past 10 years. Talk about Sentara's eCare Health Network and the importance of an electronic health system in today's healthcare world.**

We've been able to demonstrate through independent third parties that not only do we have clinical payback from our investment and electronic health records, but also a financial payback. So whenever we put in a new software system, it's a joint effort between our operations, clinical staff, and our IT system. It's seen as the total organization's responsibility to make it successful—both clinically positive and [delivering] financially greater returns. Unfortunately, very few organizations in our industry do that.

How exactly did you do that? Take us into the concrete. What would these graduate students need to understand about your approach?

When we decided, for instance, to implement an EMR [electronic medical record], we set up a steering committee that was composed of clinicians, line managers, senior executives, IT professionals, and physicians. This team was responsible for the selection of the software, the design of the product, the implementation of Sentara eCare, and future system updates. Everybody was involved. We put together a group of independent physicians out in the community, both in Sentara Medical Group and in private practice, who met with us on a monthly basis and actually helped us write the particular protocols for their practices. This was done over a three- or four-year period of time. We reengineered 16 key care processes through a period of 16 months before we implemented the EMR, so that it was not a matter of "garbage in, garbage out." In other words, we designed the EMR to work for the clinical staff in the most efficient manner rather than just automate the processes that predated technology. All of that together made for a successful project.

6. **As a leader of a large health system, how do you balance the needs of an individual patient who visits his or her provider for a personal health concern with the larger concerns of running a large not-for-profit business?**

   I don't see any conflict at all. I think our business is to take care of the individual needs of the patient. If we can do that better by standardization, by concentrating on managing populations and doing a more efficient, effective job, it helps the organization and the individual patient to get a better result.

7. **Under your leadership, it's been written that Sentara has focused on the values of *quality*, *patient safety*, and *delivery of care*. Talk about how you have implemented this three-pronged strategy.**

   Again, going back to what I've said in response to the earlier questions, the concentration on clinical quality ... There's been a feeling in the industry for years that better clinical quality is more expensive, and I think that we've proven through the years that better clinical quality, reductions in variations of outcomes, and standardizations lead to lower costs. Together they bring about better results, both financial and clinically. This philosophy is strongly embedded in our organization. Twenty years ago we put clinical quality indicators into our variable pay plans for our senior nonclinical executives. We were reinforcing the idea that quality was everyone's responsibility. I think we're one of the first organizations in the country—if not the first—to do that.

How about delivery of care? Do you see that as wrapped up in quality? Do you see them as integral within each other?

Yes.

8. **Sentara has a strong community partnership. Tell us about Sentara's Community Benefits and the Sentara Foundation.**

The community involvement starts with our board of directors, which is made up of community volunteers who serve without pay and represent the communities we serve throughout the state of Virginia and North Carolina. About 10 years ago, our board of directors approved management's suggestion that we set up a foundation under the auspices of Sentara with a $15 million grant. Every year we give out about $500,000 in grants to medically related charities that provide everything from free dental clinics to free care to mammography screenings, to support people who don't have medical insurance in our communities.

About eight years ago, the Sentara Foundation created the Hope Fund with an initial donation from Sentara Healthcare. The Hope Fund is an employee-supported program that provides grants to our fellow employees who have financial difficulties. For instance, if an employee has a fire in his or her home and needs temporary financial support to relocate, or a serious illness in a family, we give out grants to support the employee. We've raised more than $1 million in eight years just to help our own employees. All of these activities are proud examples of how we take care of the community and our own healthcare family at Sentara.

9. **Innovation is a word that often follows your name. How do you define innovation?**

Innovation really starts with a culture of risk taking in an organization. If you don't have a culture in which people are comfortable taking risks, you're not going to be innovative. You've got to have the freedom to experiment, the freedom to fail, the freedom to succeed, and to know that if you do what's best for the organization—even if it's a failure—that you're not going to be punished for it.

Along with risk taking needs to be the discipline of smart business planning. When you do try a new product or a new service, you need to have a strong business plan around it, and you need to have an exit strategy if it's not successful. I find a lot of healthcare organizations that innovate and bring in new programs, but they don't monitor them or they don't follow a business plan. They also do not close them down if they are not successful. If you have several of those running and you don't deal with them in the way they're prescribed, then people stop innovating.

Talk about the importance of innovation in today's world of health care.

I think that with what's going on with the outside pressures on health care, innovation is more important than it's ever been. It gives you a chance to differentiate your organization or differentiate your products. Maybe it gives you an advantage over your competitors or provides a better-quality product and a better financial return.

10. What do tomorrow's health systems leaders most need to know?

I think probably more than ever that they need to take basic business and finance courses offered out of a traditional business school. I think there needs to be more emphasis on MBA-type courses rather than healthcare-oriented courses. If they are at a university that offers both, I would suggest that they get a lot of courses in the MBA program. Also, when they look for employment, concentrate on the organization, the culture of the organization, and a mentor in the organization who will hire them and foster their career, rather than job titles or pay. In this day and age, the differential between organizations that are successful and those that will not be successful is widening, so they need to make sure that they join the right type of organization that has capital reserves, is innovative, and has the right culture to succeed.

You talked a little bit at the beginning of the interview about how you inherited this culture, this organization, from your predecessor. Was your predecessor a mentor to you?

Yes, he was. And he gave me a lot of opportunities. I made my fair amount of mistakes. He supported me through that and I learned from it.

Where did you start when you first entered the organization? What was your first position?

I was an administrative assistant to the president of the medical staff. Sentara did one of the first hospital mergers in the United States back in the 1970s, and the hospitals merged before the medical staffs did. I was the administrative assistant to the president of the medical staff, helping to merge the two medical staffs, which gave me a good foundation for the career that has followed.

I might add that I was the lowest-paid graduate of my graduate school class, but I took a job with the organization and the individual I thought would be good for my long-term career.

TAKE AWAY NOTES

1. Leaders set global goals and strategic direction for an organization; employees then fill in the specifics of their particular business line to follow the high-level strategic plan.
2. Physicians need to be involved in all aspects of the patient care experience—from leadership and decision making to bedside care and beyond.
3. Quality health care and financial success come from providing a seamless, efficient, effective, high-quality product—finances, clinical quality, and patient satisfaction go hand in hand.
4. Designing an EMR system to work for the clinical staff in the most efficient manner makes for a successful IT project.
5. A healthcare executive's business is to take care of the individual needs of the patient.
6. Quality is everyone's responsibility in healthcare organizations. Better clinical quality, reductions in variations of outcomes, and standardizations lead to lower costs.
7. Innovation starts with a culture of risk taking in an organization, which includes the freedom to experiment, the freedom to fail, and the freedom to succeed.
8. Strong business plans include exit strategies.
9. In today's healthcare environment, innovation offers the chance to differentiate an organization or differentiate its products.
10. When weighing future employment opportunities in health care, choose an organization that has capital reserves, is innovative, and has the right culture to succeed. Keep an eye out for a strong mentor.

RESOURCES

Before they were famous. (2010, June 14). *Modern Healthcare.*

http://insidebiz.com/powerlist25-2012/david-bernd

http://www.beckershospitalreview.com/hospital-ceo-cfo-profiles/ceo-david-bernd-riding-the-waves-of-reform-at-sentara-healthcare.html

http://blog.wmschoolofbusiness.com/dinner-with-an-expert-david-bernd-71-the-ceo-of-sentara-healthcare/

http://www.sentaranewsroom.com/sentara-executive-bios

Better Care, Better Health, Lower Costs

An Interview with Don Berwick, MD, MPH

In his first job, Don Berwick worked as a golf caddy. Later, during medical school, he worked for a blood bank—an experience he says first gave him an insider's view of families dealing with chronic illness or surgery. One might see a connection between Berwick's first job as a golf caddy and his later healthcare career. A good caddy, much like an administrator, shoulders a lot of weight. A good caddy is sensitive to the needs of the golfer, much as a physician is sensitive to the needs of a patient. And a good caddy finds and washes lost golf balls that have gone off course, much like a healthcare quality expert finds broken business processes and creates new and improved ones in their place.

Today Berwick is a national healthcare leader who has received numerous international awards and honors: the Ernest A. Codman Award, the Alfred I. DuPont Award for excellence in children's health care, the American Hospital Association Award of Honor, the Fellowship of the Royal College of Physicians in London, the Honorary Knight Commander of the Most Excellent Order of the British Empire, the Purpose Prize for care reform and improvement, the 13th annual Heinz Award for Public Policy, and the Honorary Fellowship of the Royal College of Physicians of Ireland.

Berwick, the son of a family practice physician, grew up in the small town of Moodus, Connecticut. He received his undergraduate degree from Harvard College, his medical degree from Harvard Medical School, and his master of public policy degree from Harvard's Kennedy School of Government. Berwick worked as a pediatrician and practiced at both Boston Children's Hospital and the Harvard Community Health Plan, where he served primarily underprivileged children from communities of color, and he has served on the faculty of the Harvard Medical School and Harvard School of Public Health. In 1991, Berwick founded the nonprofit Institute for Healthcare Improvement (IHI) and, in his role as founding president, grew the organization to its current international stature.

Berwick has led initiatives around the world that have been credited with saving hundreds of thousands of lives, the most famous of which was the 100,000 Lives Campaign, which involved nearly every hospital in the United States. He left his role as president at IHI to accept President Barack Obama's request to oversee the Medicare and Medicaid programs. Disillusioned by the political climate in Washington, DC, at the time, he resigned after 17 months.

According to Berwick, health care is at a turning point. Increased data collection, more rigorous application of quality improvement business management principles, soaring healthcare costs, and shifting ideas about healthcare paradigms contribute to this turning point. Berwick says, "Turning the lights on will take us through a period—hopefully not that long of a period—of conflict and pushback." He experienced this pushback while administrator of Medicare and Medicaid. His ideas of health care for all and transparency made some parties uncomfortable in Washington. "Health care is a human right, unequivocally so," he says. The country as a whole, however, is still debating this very point.

Berwick's true north has always been that "It's all about the patient." This philosophy has guided him as a physician, teacher, writer, and quality expert. To date, he has authored or co-authored more than 150 scientific articles and 4 books. In 2013 Berwick ran unsuccessfully for governor of Massachusetts. His primary slogan: "Bold Goals." He hoped to apply the same framework of bold, innovative leadership in health care to politics. In this interview, Berwick shares his leadership philosophy, his thoughts on the Triple Aim approach to healthcare reform, and more. In this time of upheaval and change, only leaders, Berwick says, "can set in place the context, the support, encouragement, insistence, the vision, the regular attendance that allows improvement in complex systems to occur."

We've built cathedrals to sick care, but not enough focus on healthy communities.

—Don Berwick

1. **In the span of your career, you have moved from practitioner to administrator and educator, and have become a recognized leader in health care. Which skills do you feel your past experience brings to your style of leadership?**

   My experience includes a combination of experiences. I'm trained as a physician, so I think that has a lot to do with skills in listening and in thinking systematically to diagnose problems. My leadership style is very much one involving listening very carefully to people and trying to understand their perspectives and what they have to contribute to a situation. I also got very interested in the field of quality years ago, 30 years ago, and modern views of quality and quality improvement. It involved incorporating, mobilizing, and enabling staff—the workforce—to actually use their minds and their hearts to help contribute to making work better and making products and services better. That sort of thing certainly informs everything that I think about in my leadership work. You want to really help the workforce and empower them instead of controlling them. That's a very strong theme in my leadership work. A lot of my career has been spent working with patients and families of disadvantage. My aims in leadership have a lot to do with helping people who need help.

2. **I have heard you speak about global thinking as a necessary skill for leaders of the future. Can you expand on that a little? On a global scale, what do you see for the future of health care?**

   Well, we're one world. It's true that people who are struggling to solve problems in health care—like patient safety or patient-centered care or cost reduction as examples—are doing this all over the world. And it's myopic to think that we're the only people—any particular country or any particular organization—that have a lock on the answers. Modern organizations and modern organizational leaders have what we call global brains. They're asking the question, "Who in the world, the entire world, has faced this kind of problem, and what have they done to solve it?" That enriches the array of good ideas to draw upon to solve a problem.

3. **The political seems inseparable from health care these days. In fact, you served as the CMS administrator and you campaigned for Massachusetts governor. Medicare and Medicaid are major sources of revenue for health systems. Do you think the political can be separated from healthcare solutions of the future?**

   I think health care in any nation is a major investment of both public and private resources, and it needs to be accountable for its use of those resources. I would say it's not just political; it just has to do with accountability. After all, dollars that go into health care are dollars that don't go elsewhere. The health of the nation is a very important issue of public policy. I would say, it's not just inevitable, it's important for health care to feel and be accountable to the greater society that it's a part of.

As a former physician, what do you think healthcare providers most want to see in healthcare administration of tomorrow?

Clinicians, doctors, nurses, pharmacists, therapists of all types—most of them want to be able to focus on the needs of the patient. That's why they went into their fields, and that's what gives them pride and joy in their work. So, they hold things back from the organizations that they work in and from the leaders that they depend on, so that they are given the opportunity to help people. The ability to focus on the needs of the patient is the major hope of the clinical workforce.

4. **You've been quoted as saying that we're in the midst of a healthcare restructuring, moving away from a paradigm that included revenue growth, specialization, professional dominance, and a hospital-centric model. Can you talk more about this restructuring? What is the healthy structure of the future?**

As I've written and talked about, a healthy structure of health care will be directed at what I call the Triple Aim. The Triple Aim is three goals at once: better care for individuals, better health for populations, and lower costs [achieved] by improving care and care processes. The way you do that is complex, but it mainly has to do with the integration of care. So we build healthcare treks: hospitals, doctor's offices, laboratories, clinics, and how Mrs. Jones needs her care. You need to take care of a patient over space and time. A restructured healthcare system would focus on continuity, coordination, and a lot about home—helping people stay home where they really want to be, instead of cycling in and out of hospitals. It's one oriented more around health than about waiting for someone to get sick. So a properly restructured system would really be reaching upstream for the causes of illness, and helping people thrive.

5. **You have written that cutting waste is integral to the future of health-care systems. What can we do now? What is on your elimination list, and what are the low-hanging and obvious fruits to eliminate?**

I wrote an article on this called "Eliminating Waste in Health Care" in *JAMA* [*The Journal of the American Medical Association*] in April 2012.

There are six categories of waste that my co-author and I designated as very good areas to target. They are:

- Overuse and use of care that doesn't really help people at all.
- Failures of coordination, where because we don't hand off care properly, patients get lost and complications go up and costs go up.
- Failures of reliability—we actually *do* know what to do scientifically for many patients, and sometimes we don't deliver that reliably.
- Administrative implementation, we have a lot of extra paperwork, totals that don't help anybody in health care. Eliminating bills would save money.
- Pricing failures, which has to do with competitive markets for goods and services in health care that are essentially interchangeable. Right now, we don't really have effective competition for a lot of products and services.
- And, finally, fraud. There's fraud in health care. It's quite expensive. Very few people engage in it, but those who do, they need to be stopped.

Those six categories by our estimates add up to over 30% of the total healthcare bill. So that's a lot of money we could get if we could reduce waste.

6. **What do you most want to say to the next generation of health-care leaders?**

   If they focus on patients and patients' needs and families and communities, always keeping the patient at the center, then the correct answers will surface. What goes wrong in health care goes wrong when we forget that we're there for the patient, that the needs of the patient come first. If the healthcare system was organized around the needs of the patient, fundamentally we'd be more capable of achieving the Triple Aim: better care, better health, and lower costs.

TAKE-AWAY NOTES

1. Developing skills in listening and systematic problem solving is important to strong leadership.
2. Modern healthcare leadership requires a "global brain"—leaders who have the ability to ask who in the world might be facing this kind of problem and how they solved it. Global leadership offers a larger array of good ideas to solve problems.

3. The health of a nation is an important issue of public policy. Health care should be accountable to the greater society.
4. Clinicians most want to focus on the needs of their patients.
5. The integration of care includes better care for individuals, better health for populations, and lower costs achieved by improving care and care processes.
6. Restructured systems will focus on continuity, coordination, and keeping patients home rather than cycling in and out of hospitals.
7. Cutting waste is integral to the future of healthcare systems.
8. A focus on the patient and the needs of the community will lead to necessary solutions.

Conveners, Collaborators, and Facilitators: Leaders of the Future

An Interview with Teri Fontenot, FACHE, Chief Executive Officer, Woman's Hospital, Baton Rouge, Louisiana

It has been said that part of Teri Fontenot's charm is her modesty. As CEO of Woman's Hospital, the only independent, community-owned women's and children's nonprofit hospital in the United States, she places the highest value on teamwork in her organization. She attributes her *Healthcare* magazine designations as one of 25 most influential women in health care (2005, inaugural) and one of the 100 most influential people in health care (2011, 2012) to the hard work and commitment of Woman's Hospital employees.

Born in Jackson, Mississippi, Fontenot received, with honors, a BBA in accounting from Ole Miss and an MBA from Northeast Louisiana University. She began her career as an accountant and never intended to go into health care. She wanted to be a tax lawyer, but when she found herself a divorced mother with a daughter while in her mid-twenties, she knew she would never be able to afford law school. Working for a hospital never crossed her mind.

In 1982, while working for a lumber and building supply co-op in Monroe, Louisiana, Fontenot met an IBM salesman who told her about an opening at the St. Francis Medical Center. The sister who hired her as the hospital's comptroller promised to teach Fontenot everything she knew about hospital operations. By the time Fontenot left St. Francis, she had served as comptroller, vice president of finance, and, in the end, chief financial officer. She went on to serve as CFO at Southwest Florida Regional Medical Center and Opelousas General Hospital before taking the same position at

Woman's Hospital in Baton Rouge in 1992. In 1996, she became CEO and president, and still holds that position today—the longest-running term of any CEO and president at Woman's Hospital.

Under Fontenot's leadership, the hospital has grown to a 350-bed (Level III regional referral) facility, and has consistently shown net margins higher than national averages; it has beaten the odds for most small, independent hospitals. It is easy to see how the culture of Woman's Hospital stems from Fontenot's vision. In addition to seeing the hospital staff as a team, with everyone interdependent with everyone else, Fontenot keeps the vision of "strengthening families" front and center in her management decisions. Woman's Hospital is a hub for women's health care in Baton Rouge and provides services such as obstetrics, on-site and mobile mammography, breast cancer care and treatment, gynecologic surgeries, bariatric surgeries, colonoscopies, orthopedic care, and fitness and rehabilitation (Woman's Center for Wellness). After Hurricane Katrina, Baton Rouge saw a 25% increase in population and Woman's Hospital played an important role helping evacuees adjust and thrive; Fontenot made sure that their medical and mental health needs were considered. In 2012, Fontenot oversaw the development of and transition to the $340 million replacement campus that exists today—a campus with room to grow.

To what does Fontenot attribute the success of Woman's Hospital? A strong balance sheet, a high level of loyalty and commitment from employees and physicians, a flattened organizational structure with only five levels between entry-level employees and herself, fewer executives and directors, and strong communication and trust among the leadership. Her strategy must be working. For five years running, *Modern Healthcare* has designated Woman's Hospital one of the top 100 places to work in health care.

Teri Fontenot speaks with a deep southern accent. Admixed with her southern charm is her obvious concern for Woman's Hospital families and her strong business sense, all of which have enabled her to become an unstoppable force in health care. With her usual modesty, she credits her career success to the understanding and support of her husband and daughters, important assets for every executive.

Fontenot served as the 2012 Chair of the American Hospital Association (AHA) Board of Trustees, the first chair to be elected from the state of Louisiana and the fourth woman to hold the position. The chair is the highest elected position at the AHA. In addition, she has served as chair of the Louisiana Hospital Association, has held a six-year appointment on the National Institutes of Health's Advisory Council of Women's Health Research, served for six years on the Sixth District Board of Directors of the Federal Reserve Bank in Atlanta, has served as the chair of the AHA Health

Forum (for-profit subsidiary), chairs the Board of Directors of the Louisiana Hospital Association Insurance Trust Fund, and is a member of the AHA Board of Trustees, an ex officio member of the Executive Committee, Chair of Operations Committee, and a member of the Governing Council for the Section for Maternal Child Health. In 2012, Fontenot was named by *Becker's Hospital Review* as one of the 40 most powerful people in health care; in 2011, she was inducted into Louisiana State University's E. J. Ourso College of Business Hall of Distinction.

In this interview, Fontenot opens up about running Woman's Hospital, the importance of female leadership in health care, and keeping an eye on the balance sheet, while improving value.

1. **Your background is in accounting, yet you have grown an impressive organization around your community of patients at Woman's Hospital. How have you balanced your attention to the numbers with the needs of the patients?**

   Our mission is to improve the health of women and infants. As an organization that's focused on creating and maintaining healthy families, we must have the financial resources in order to do that. I find them to be very compatible strategies. If we don't have the financial resources, then we're not able to provide the level of care and the scope of services that our patients deserve and need. On the other hand, as we focus more on outcomes, it's interesting to see how quality really can be measured. I can remember early in my career that people said that you couldn't measure quality, but we're seeing more and more evidence that not only can you measure quality and outcomes, but also organizations that benchmark learn from each other and improve the care of their patients.

2. **Your organization is patient specific, focused on women's health. How have your business decisions been affected by your patient population?**

   At Woman's, inpatient care is limited to women and newborns. Our wide array of outpatient services is available to women, men, and children of all ages. Initially, we focused on the needs exclusive to women. Now we have branched out into other areas where the use is predominantly by women. For example, we have an orthopedic service at our facility now. But it's focused on shoulders, feet, and ankles, because women predominantly suffer from those kinds of problems. We perform colonoscopies now, and we really believe that women need to stay healthy. If we can provide gastroenterology services in a setting that is more attuned to women, then that's how we differentiate. For colonoscopies, we provide a private room with a private bathroom pre and post procedure, which is very different than most digestive health centers and ambulatory surgery units, where the patients are separated by curtains and share bathrooms.

For care exclusive to women, we offer a tertiary level of care and a broad scope of services for those particular illnesses or diseases. We also look at a one-off situation and if it's something that improves the health of women and is predominantly a need of women or can be done in a way that focuses on women's needs, then we look at it that way. We're now moving into preventive and wellness care to improve access. An example is our fitness club. We've had it for over 20 years and the all-female membership is now at 3,000 (see Appendix 1). The women who are members of the health club are there because they want to be healthier. The center includes an indoor Olympic-size swimming pool. We offer classes geared to women in their prenatal and postnatal periods. It has a childcare center that's free and a quarter-mile indoor walking track. It's a different type of fitness club and women love it because they don't feel like they have to get dressed up and put on makeup to work out. And if they're out of shape, they're not intimidated.

So is it a membership club? Do you have revenues coming in from membership?

Yes. We don't do it to make a profit; it's not what we would consider a profit center. But certainly we need to be sure that the fees cover the cost.

3. **Talk about your continuum of care model—aside from the financial benefits, how else has this model benefited your organization?**

The ACA [Affordable Care Act] provides for and expects hospitals to be more involved in the care continuum. What I mean by that is being actively involved in keeping people healthy through preventive care, wellness, and chronic disease management. If patients do need acute medical care, hospitals are now actively involved in their postdischarge care—making sure that they take their medications, that they understand their illness, and if it's a chronic condition like diabetes or congestive heart failure, that they monitor and proactively treat them to prevent a readmission. So the traditional definition of a hospital is quickly changing from one where you go when you are sick and need an acute level of care, to being accountable to a community for the health of that community in a way that encompasses much more than the medical side of health care.

4. **Woman's Hospital has a strong Web presence and attention to patient satisfaction. Tell us about your decision to create such an interactive online presence. How does this benefit your organization?**

   Our patient population is primarily women of childbearing years—obstetrics and GYN. That age cohort uses social media and the Internet so much more than the traditional [media] methods of newspapers, radio, and TV. We are reaching our target audience based on the modalities that they tend to use. And we've been very pleased with the results. Our website is under major renovation right now so that we can make it even more accessible and desirable for patients.

5. **Do you involve any of your patients in the design decisions?**

   Absolutely. We use focus groups for our advertising campaigns, and for new programs and services. We moved into a new hospital a year ago, and we used several different patient groups and parent groups for the newborns to advise us on making the facility easy for them to use, meet their needs, and receive high-quality care in a setting that's going to be very compassionate, but with professional service.

6. **I read that by integrating the feedback from patients and staff on the new hospital's design that you were able to reduce the cost of the new building. How much did you save?**

   The original facility design was based on volume and a model of care from 2005. When we broke ground in 2008, we were seeing a lot of change. Technology, for example, had improved the length of stay for hysterectomies to 23 hours instead of two days. We were doing some things to reduce the number of early elective inductions for nonmedical reasons. That effort alone reduced our NICU admissions by 30%. There were a number of other things that we were doing by practicing evidence-based care and trying to incorporate them into the design of our facility. As we saw the care model evolving, we had the opportunity before we got too far into construction to modify some of the plans that we'd made three years earlier. In addition, we had already contracted for all of the various components of the new facility. In late 2008 to early 2009, when the recession hit, we renegotiated a lot of those contracts and reduced the cost. So it was a combination of rethinking—in particular, the number of beds in combination with renegotiating contracts.

7. **You've spoken in the past about hospitals, physicians, and patients sharing in the responsibility of lowering healthcare costs and sharing risk. How do you see this working in the future? How will this look for future administrators in terms of sharing in the responsibility of lowering the costs?**

I think it's always been a shared responsibility; it's just not necessarily been acknowledged as such. Administration felt like their responsibility was to grow patient volume, so they could add beds. Physicians historically have just wanted a place where they could work that was hassle free. They were looking for a hospital to be a place where they could do procedures, and admit their patients who needed a higher level of care than what they could provide in their offices, and they wanted to be able to get in and out quickly. Now, the focus is on wellness and prevention, as well as follow-up care for disease management. So physicians and hospitals have got to share data and work collaboratively. In some parts of the country, there already is a shared payment system, but in many parts, it doesn't exist—the physicians get paid based on their volume and the hospitals get paid on their volume, so you structure your service based on how you're going to be paid.

In the future, there is going to be less payment based on volume and more based on value. In order to get the value out of every dollar that is spent, it is going to require physicians and hospitals to work together. Hospital administrators will have to be more data driven, evidence based, and transparent, not only in cost, but also in quality and outcomes. Physicians train as scientists, so they respond to data. Hospital administrators are going to have to be sharper in providing objective data in order to improve care and outcomes.

8. **Female hospital CEOs make up only 18% of hospital administrators. What do you see as the role of female CEOs in the rapidly changing landscape of health care? How has your gender negatively or positively affected your career?**

I was CFO at four hospitals before I became CEO at Woman's Hospital. Maybe I'm in the minority, but I never really felt like my gender was an impediment to being able to move into the C-suite in health care. I do think that in health care gender is less of an issue than in banking, manufacturing, or other male-dominated business sectors. Health care is a predominantly female profession, and generally 80% of the employees are female. So I think that having females in the C-suite is probably not as stark of a contrast as it might be in some other business sectors.

Even though there's only 18%, I suspect that number has increased over the past 5 or 10 years. Women have a management style that is generally more nurturing and collaborative, and as a result, based on the model of care required today, working with others rather than supervising [is a trait] in high demand. As a result, I think women are well positioned for the future.

9. **How do you see the role of leaders in health systems of the future?**

I think that healthcare leaders in the future, particularly in hospitals, have got to be conveners, collaborators, and facilitators. They also have to have a strong understanding of data and an ability to persuade—not dictate—others to focus on the long-term vision of creating healthy communities.

TAKE-AWAY NOTES

1. The focus on outcomes allows for quality to be measured.
2. Benchmarking allows organizations to learn from one another and improve care.
3. The traditional definition of a hospital is changing to include the health of a community and encompasses more than the medical side of health care.
4. It is important to be clear about which media outlets are used by the target audience.
5. Focus groups consisting of patients can be used to determine design, thereby affecting the quality of care and ensuring the facility is easy for patients to use and meets patients' needs.
6. Evidence-based care can be incorporated into the design of a facility.
7. Physicians and administrators need to share data and work collaboratively.
8. Hospital administrators should be data driven, evidence based, and transparent about costs as well as quality and outcomes.
9. Administrators today need the skills of collaboration, persuasion, and facilitation. They should be able to bring people together.

APPENDIX 1

Woman's Hospital Woman's Center for Wellness offers audiology, physical therapy, outpatient services, occupational and speech therapy, fitness classes, cooking classes (including grocery shopping assistance), and weight loss programs, personal training, dietician counseling. The center includes a track, gym, pool, spa, and gift shop that sells workout clothing and accessories. Memberships are available only to women.

RESOURCES

http://www.womans.org/

Flexible Care Models and the Value of Relationships in Health Care

An Interview with Jeff Goldsmith, PhD, President of Health Futures Inc.; Associate Professor, University of Virginia

The trajectory of Jeff Goldsmith's career in health care has been anything but traditional. Graduating with degrees from Reed College in psychology and classics, Goldsmith went on to receive a doctorate in sociology from the University of Chicago in 1973. He worked as a fiscal and policy analyst in the Illinois governor's office and as special assistant to the state budget director. It was his experience in policy and state government that would set the course of his career in health care.

Goldsmith speaks with a wry, dry tone, not holding back on his thoughts and opinions, which have been shaped through years of teaching, writing, and researching the business of health care and healthcare policy. You get the sense that he revels in bucking the system and speaking his mind, whether his views are politically correct or not. Goldsmith's background in sociology gives him a highly effective lens through which to examine health systems; his early career in politics gave him a unique vantage point from which to interpret the complex relationships involved in health policy.

Goldsmith, a native of Portland, Oregon, currently lives in rural Albemarle County, Virginia, at Ricochet Farm, a rolling piece of property with stunning views of the Blue Ridge Mountains. He serves as Associate Professor in Public Health Sciences at the University of Virginia. Before arriving in Virginia, Goldsmith served as national advisor for health care for Ernst & Young, while also providing strategy consultation to a variety of healthcare systems, health plans, and supply and technology firms. He is a former lecturer in the Graduate School of Business at his alma mater, the University of Chicago, where he lectured on health services management and policy, and a past lecturer at the Wharton School of Finance, Johns Hopkins University, Washington University, and University of California, Berkeley.

Goldsmith is currently president of Health Futures, Inc., which he established in 1982. His organization offers health industry analysis on corporate strategy, trends, health policy, and emerging technologies. Goldsmith is highly regarded as a lecturer on topics pertinent to health care, finance, and technology in the United States and overseas. In addition, you can find Goldsmith's prolific writings on topics such as "The Tragedy of Healthcare Reform," "Slouching Toward Value: The Future of Health Care Payment," "Is the Health Cost Dragon Dead or Sleeping?", "The Future of the Hospital," "The Future of Medical Practice: What Does It Look Like?", and more on his website (see Appendix 1).

Known for sifting through and adeptly analyzing healthcare policy and trends in an often over-saturated market of opinions, Goldsmith strives to uncover the most significant numbers and necessary change, and to provide forecasts for the future. Here's what he had to tell us in a recent interview from his office in Virginia.

1. **You have had an unusual career path. Can you tell us how sociology uniquely positioned you to become an expert in the field of health care?**

   I studied sociology, the professions, complex organizations, and politics of developing nations. The large urban hospital, Peter Drucker said decades ago, is perhaps the most complex human institution. I was interested in the bureaucratic part of what healthcare organizations did, as well as how [healthcare] professionals fit into bureaucracies. Because they don't fit into bureaucracies—they just don't fit. They tend to be very much "one patient at a time, one problem at a time" kind of people. I entered through healthcare politics, not through academia. My first job out of graduate school was as a policy analyst for the governor of Illinois. I entered health care as a lobbyist and a policy person. I was the Medicaid and Medicare desk officer of a huge urban academic health center, and eventually became its first marketing officer. I really entered health care through policy.

   Does health care now need to have a global, international approach?

   I think that a culture and society have a great deal to do with how a health system operates and that cultures and societies differ massively. The power of professionals in those societies differs massively.

Whenever I hear people say, "Well, geez, the people in Sweden have a great health system," I say, "They have a great society and the health system fits that society and its values." We've got a lot to learn from other countries, but when I hear people say, "We need to have the German health system here," I kind of say, "Well, yeah, fine—what we really have to do is find the health system that fits our social values and that solves our society's problems."

2. **You've written that health cost growth needs to slow in relation to the growing number of people (insured or not) who cannot afford to use the health system. What does this mean for the future of health care?**

Well, what I said is that healthcare cost needs to be markedly reduced or an increasing percentage of Americans will not be able to afford to use the health system. That's a very different statement than what you said. If you take out inflation and the cost of inputs and population growth, our health system is pretty close to a dead stop. Right now, total cost is growing at 3.8%. Eight-tenths of a percent of that is population growth; inflation of inputs is probably 2% to 2½%. So the issue isn't slowing down the cost growth—the cost curve is already bent. The real problem is that half the country can't afford to use the health system without massive public subsidies, and unless we take out a huge amount of the cost—not just bend the cost curve, but also markedly reduce the cost of care—we're going to have serious problems as a society. That's a considerably more threatening policy problem than reducing the cost curve, isn't it?

Just since 2007, our health system has added over 1,558,000 jobs, even though the demand for care in every major sector of the health system has shrunk or leveled off. Is it sort of like, "Didn't management get the memo?" Well, they didn't. They've inured themselves to the idea that health care just gets more complicated and we have to staff up for that complexity. There's lip service given to improving efficiency and operational effectiveness and quality and all the rest of it. I think that's just what it is—lip service.

3. **How do you see the role of cash-strapped families in healthcare reform?**

Well, there are going to be a lot more of them. I mean, you look at the bronze and the second-tier silver plans—they leave anywhere from $2,500 to $5,500 of cash out-of-pocket exposure. Now some people are protected from cost sharing by ACA's cost-sharing limits and subsidies, but I think those fade out at family incomes more than twice that of poverty. All the growth in health plan enrollment both inside and outside the exchanges is going to be in high-deductible health plans. They've already quintupled since the beginning of the crash; I think they'll triple yet again in the next five years. The result: We're going to have a huge number of people who just flat out cannot afford to use the health system at the front end. And we're sort of gambling that you can put $4,000 or $5,000 of front-end cost in front of them and of course they're going to make the right choices. I don't believe it.

In terms of reform, what is this growing group of people who are cash strapped—how are they going to muscle more reform? How do you see them influencing it?

I'm not sure I do. I think there's a big political risk here for the health system. There are 48 million [people] without health insurance until January 2014; 35 to 40 million people more who have insurance, but no cash, so they can't afford to use the benefit; and 53 million people on Medicaid, who are facing shrinking networks and shrinking access—that's half the country. And all health reform is going to do is take maybe 20 million of those 48 million uninsured and move them into one of those two other categories. We're either going to put them on Medicaid or we're going to put them on high-deductible plans where they're nominally insured. And if they get into an auto accident, someone will pay most of the bill, but they're going to have $4,000 or $5,000 of front-end cost exposure. So they're not going to get their prescriptions filled, they're not going to see the primary care doc—they're going to be skimping on care in the front end. They're going to be self-managing instead of engaging the care system. I think the benefits design that we're headed into is not defensible in the long term. It's a broken model.

4. **What does a healthy consumer choice payment reform model look like?**

I've argued that we need to pay for care differently. Population health is one of the current buzzwords that everybody is convinced is the future of health care. I don't think it is at all, because I don't think most providers are going to be able to do it. I say, let's fix the functional relationships inside health care that are presently broken. I think we need to pay for relationships between patients and the care system. Relationships: Not visits, not tests—relationships.

And when someone is diagnosed with a problem requiring acute intervention, we need to pay for a complete clinical solution to that problem. Not 20 streams of payment, but one adjusted payment to cover the entire range of services required to get that person back to functioning again. And I think if you add them together, they are probably 40% of total health cost. But it's two things we're doing badly now, not counting the chronic disease management issues. You don't get to population health management unless someone takes ownership of the risk and partners with the patient/family to manage it.

So how do you do that? Well, you don't provide everybody with the same model of care—not everyone needs a medical home—but you do provide them with connectivity and with a care system that is geared toward the risk or risks that the individual is facing at the moment.

5. **You have written about the primary care physician shortage that will be created by baby-boomer physicians retiring. Some have advocated for shorter visits and increased patient loads, but you advocate for something different, something that includes a new way of practicing: reduction in "unnecessary" visits by leveraging texting, email, social media outlets. Tell us how you see this benefiting the patient and the provider.**

The core of an effective clinical relationship is a really good, two-way flow of communication. And it doesn't necessarily have to be between a doctor and a patient—it's between a care team and a patient, or a care team and a family if the patient isn't able to self-manage. So it's creating those information loops in real time. Not "Oh, make an appointment and see the doctor in three weeks"—that's not what we're talking about here at all. We're talking about, "I've just lost all feeling in my right hand. What do I do?" and to have somebody that knows enough about the patient's circumstances to be able to say, "Well, okay, here's what you do." That might be an emergency room visit or an MRI scan of the neck. What are missing right now are the tools that help someone navigate through the care system and manage their risk. That's what we need to get right.

That is a full-time job for patients right now, navigating.

Well, it's outsourced to family members, and the sicker the patient, the more that family is responsible for managing the patient's risk. We hang the family out to dry.

With this model, I understand how it benefits the patient, but how does it benefit the provider?

That's not the challenge. The challenge is to make better use of society's resources. Providers need to adapt to what society needs.

6. **Documentation is often a focus of reform. Electronic records have been touted as a time saver, but many patients find that their physician spends more time on the laptop than with the patient. What do you see as the solution for record keeping and maximizing the patient–physician relationship?**

For me, the answer is to dramatically reduce the number of payment transactions in the health system. The idea that you pay for a relationship, not a visit—that's where the idea comes from. You're not documenting every single encounter. You're essentially paying for a bundle of services on a monthly basis. So you're dramatically reducing the transactional density of the payment stream. And I would say the same thing with the "complete clinical solution." My big problem with a lot of the innovation center experiments is that they're laying the accountable care organization or the bundled payment or the medical home on top of fee-for-service. They're adding another layer of documentation, another tangle of "core measures," instead of saying, "Here's a healthy relationship. Here's how we judge that relationship." And the same with the federal bundled payment demonstration, BPCI. You've still got all of that fee-for-service nonsense playing in the background. It needs to go away. In other words, new payment models need to substitute for, rather than lay on top of, the existing fee-for-service system. So, my argument is that you don't get rid of fee-for-service to contain costs; you get rid of FFS to reduce the documentation time demands and overhead costs for caregivers.

About 10 years ago it became popular for some physicians to have people pay, for instance, $2,500 for unlimited services for a year. Is this similar to what you're talking about?

No, not at all. Very different. That solved the provider's problem; that provides the provider with a steady stream of income and a smaller group of people to work with. But it doesn't necessarily solve the patient's problem. I mean, if half of the country can't afford the healthcare system that we have, how many have an extra $2,500 to spend on concierge medicine? Most of these concierge practices haven't grown. Even elegantly designed direct-pay practices that don't have an annual fee, like Qliance in Seattle and GreenField

Health in Portland, Oregon, have had trouble growing, because there aren't enough patients with the free cash flow to be able to pay for it beyond their existing health benefit and they cannot use their HRA/HSA funds to pay the monthly subscription fee.

So is this something where we need to look more deeply at insurance? For instance, would it be something where someone would have *x* amount of dollars from their employer toward whatever type of health care they want, whatever model they want. So if they wanted one of those boutique clinics or direct-pay practices, they could have the choice to put their insurance money there?

I think there ought to be flexibility in how these relationships are financed. They shouldn't just be out of pocket. Medicare and Medicaid should pay for them. The payment system needs to be catholic enough to say, "All right, this is what the person needs; we're going to pay for it that way."

7. **What would you most like to say to the next generation of health-care administrators?**

If you're really going to make changes in our healthcare system, you're going to need to learn a lot more about how professionals are motivated and how they influence and direct organized care. Healthcare managers and professionals are joined at the hip. If I had a criticism of a lot of the MHA and MBA programs, it's sort of assuming that it's technical skills, like those of a classic MBA, that are missing. Managing professionals is really hard. Understanding what professionals do is really hard. If you can't create a collegial framework, communicate clearly, and motivate professionals who you work with to do a better job, you're not going to get anywhere in your job.

8. **When asking another healthcare expert what he would most like to hear from you, he replied, "Ask him what's on his mind today." Your progressive solutions continue to break new ground. What *is* on your mind today?**

I'm really worried about what's going to happen to the 40% of practicing physicians in the United States who are over the age of 55. They're completely burned out, and I think are going to be leaving practice, many of them, really angry about what has happened over the course of their career. A lot of these are 70-hours-a-week folks. Many of them were willing to get up in the middle of a Thanksgiving dinner to take care of us if something was wrong. They're going to quit and we're going to replace them with 35-hours-a-week docs who want to be home at 4 o'clock for their kid's soccer practice. And at the same time, 76 million boomers join Medicare. I just can't make those numbers work.

I'm very concerned about this generational transition that's taking place in medicine and the fact that we haven't created the flexible care models that we're going to need to make the limited number of professionals who we do have go further. We're squandering person power by really inefficient payment systems and care models.

TAKE-AWAY NOTES

1. Health systems should match a society's values and solve the society's problems, not simply replicate systems that exist in other cultures.
2. The cost curve in health care is already bent; the cost of care must be reduced.
3. Demand for care in every sector of health care has shrunk or leveled off, while jobs in health care have continued to grow.
4. The risk of high-deductible plans, for those above poverty level, is that consumers will not seek out timely and necessary care; they will skimp on care because of high front-end, out-of-pocket costs.
5. Goldsmith advocates for a healthcare model in which patients pay for relationships with care providers and complete clinical solutions.
6. Population health management cannot effectively happen unless someone takes ownership of the risk and partners with the patient and family to manage it.
7. Not everyone needs the same model of care, but patients do need connectivity with a care system that is geared toward the risk or risks that the individuals are facing at the moment of need.
8. Better use of resources, providers adapting to what society needs, and the creation of tools to help patients navigate the care system and manage risk are all essential in health care today.
9. Getting rid of fee-for-service payments is not necessary to contain costs; rather, it is essential to reduce the documentation time demands and overhead costs for caregivers. Bundled payments that reflect the relationship model are a necessary solution.
10. "The payment system needs to be catholic enough to say, 'All right, this is what the person needs; we're going to pay for it that way.'"

11. "Healthcare managers and professionals are joined at the hip." Managing professionals requires a collegial framework, clear communication, and strategies to motivate the professionals.
12. The generational transitions taking place in health care right now require flexible care models to make the limited number of professionals whom we do have go further.

APPENDIX 1

See Jeff Goldsmith's prolific writings on health care at the Health Futures, Inc., website: http://www.healthfutures.net/p-w.php

A Great Opportunity to Change the World, to Make the World a Better Place

An Interview with Sister Carol Keehan, DC, RN, MS, President and Chief Executive Officer, Catholic Health Association

One in six people who enter an American hospital today seeks care at a Catholic hospital. Catholic health care can claim in its history a long tradition of service to the poor and the sick, as well as one of the oldest hospitals in the country: New Orleans's Charity Hospital. From the beginning, religious orders have made care for the sick and the poor one of the primary focuses of their calling—a calling that Sister Carol Keehan, president and CEO of the Catholic Health Association (CHA) of the United States, has built her career upon. "Faith is the bedrock of my life," Sr. Carol says in a video profile by the Opus Prize.

Born in Washington, DC, Sr. Carol grew up in southern Maryland during World War II. She remembers when her Catholic school, motivated by Catholic social justice teachings and before the *Brown v. Kansas* ruling, made the decision to integrate. "My father never drove us to school. We rode the bus. But on that day, he drove us to school. Looking back now, I think many of the other fathers had rifles in their trucks and cars. Now, nothing happened. But those were the times." Even at a young age, Sr. Carol was acutely aware of social justice.

She almost did not attend college. In fact, like many bright students, she found school boring. But when she discovered nursing, and therefore a purpose, she found academic focus. Eventually she joined the Catholic order, Daughters of Charity, and at age 25, she helped to found the Sacred Heart Children's Hospital. As the hospital's first nursing director, Sr. Carol devoted herself not only to providing clinical care, but also to creating new and innovative programs that benefited the community, including an obstetric program for the poor.

Sr. Carol's administrative ascension was fast. Her first position was at St. Ann's Infant and Maternity Home, a position that deeply affected her because of her exposure to women with histories of abuse and poor health care. After leaving there, she served in many leadership positions, such as at Sacred Heart Hospital (Maryland) and Sacred Heart Children's Hospital and Regional Perinatal Intensive Care Center (Florida). It was these positions that spurred her pursuit of an advanced degree in finance so that she could become a more effective administrator. She then returned to Washington, DC—and the hospital where she was born, Providence Hospital—to serve as vice president for nursing, ambulatory care, and education and training. In the 15 years before she joined the CHA, Sr. Carol served as president and chief executive officer of Providence Hospital, which includes Carroll Manor Nursing and Rehabilitation Center. The key to Sr. Carol's success has been her ability to frankly assess the strengths and weaknesses of programs, while at the same time considering the impact of new care programs on patients and staff.

Niagara University, the College of the Holy Cross, St. John's University, Catholic University of America, Marymount University, and DePaul University have all awarded Sr. Carol honorary doctoral degrees. She earned her bachelor of science degree in nursing from St. Joseph's College, where she graduated magna cum laude, and her master of science degree in business administration from the University of South Carolina, from which she received the School of Business Distinguished Alumna Award in 2000. The latter institution has also honored Sr. Carol as an outstanding alumna who goes beyond what is required in her job or profession.

Sr. Carol serves on boards of various universities and healthcare associations, as well as finance committees and human rights organizations. Her awards include, but are not limited to, the following honors: the American Hospital Association's Trustee Award; the Pro Ecclesia et Pontifice bestowed by Pope Benedict XVI; the LCWR 2011 Outstanding Leadership Award, Leadership Conference of Women Religious; the 2009 Vision Award from Catholic Charities USA; and the Friend of Children Award from Children's National Medical Center. In 2010, Sr. Carol was named one of *Time* magazine's "100 Most Influential People in the World," and she has been on *Modern Healthcare*'s list of "100 Most Influential People in Healthcare" for several years, topping the list in 2007 as number one.

Sr. Carol's constant vision of social justice in health care is rooted in the tradition of her faith and religious order. When new immigrants from Catholic countries began to inhabit crowded urban centers in the United

States, Daughters of Charity opened homes for orphaned children and care centers for the sick. In fact, the history of hospitals in the United States can be traced directly to these early centers created by religious orders. The business of health care has changed dramatically since the days of those early immigrant-focused centers, but the mission of Catholic health care and, more specifically, of the religious order members who work in health care, has not changed. Sr. Carol never loses sight of the "sick, the vulnerable, and the poor."

CHA's involvement in and deep commitment to the most recent healthcare reform, and eventual legislation, led to many criticisms and often character assassinations of Sr. Carol—criticism fueled by political polarization. But she never wavered in her commitment to seeing the poor represented in healthcare reform.

For her interview, we sat together at a shiny mahogany table in her office on K Street, in the heart of the business district of Washington, DC. The glass windows overlook a busy street, and the sounds of sirens and car horns broke through our conversation often. Sr. Carol was dressed in her standard navy blue suit, white button-down blouse, and sturdy, black, lace-up shoes. Her gray hair was cut short, and she was fighting a cold that required her to take cough drops at regular intervals. But even her hoarse voice and sore throat could not stop her from expressing the passion she has for equity in health care. What she is most proud of, in the CHA offices, is a glass case that holds one of 20 pens awarded by President Barack Obama—pens he used to sign the ACA into law. In the center of the case is an image of President Obama signing the bill in the Oval Office. A young boy stands to his left watching the historical signature at the famous presidential desk. Two pictures flank either side of the central image: one of Sr. Carol standing with U.S. Vice President Joseph Biden and former Secretary of Health and Human Services Kathleen Sebelius, and the other of President Obama shaking Sr. Carol's hand. Sr. Carol does not easily share the important role she had in the creation of the ACA—but she was an important force, an important mind behind the bill. What she does share easily and openly is her pride in finally seeing a bill pass—one that is a step forward in equity of care, that takes care of the sick, the vulnerable, and the poor. What follows is our conversation.

1. **Tell us a little bit about your background. Why did you choose the Daughters of Charity, St. Vincent de Paul order? When did you know you wanted to be a nun and why did you choose nursing as a profession?**

   Well, I was a nurse before I was a Daughter of Charity. I wasn't a particularly diligent high school student—because I was bored—so it sure took a lot of patience on my parents' part to believe that I was doing my best, which I wasn't. I was just so incredibly bored. The reason to do better was so you could get into college, where I thought I'd be even more incredibly bored.

I went to nursing school, and I wasn't in nursing school two weeks when I found I was in love with nursing. Everything about the hospital, everything about nursing, was just so incredibly wonderful. And then, of course, you understand the biggest problem was not whether I knew what I should know, it was not that I'd fail a test, but the biggest problem was that I could really hurt somebody. So really knowing, getting it down pat, getting it right became very important. And, I liked it. I wasn't necessarily thinking I wanted to be a sister, by a long shot. In fact, I was thinking that I didn't want to be a sister.

Now, to tell you the truth, the first time I came to the Daughters of Charity community, I stayed six days and left. The nursing students who were in my class used to call it Keehan's six-day retreat. But I continued to believe that was what our Lord wanted me to do, and truthfully, I have to say, it has been an incredible journey, an absolutely incredible journey. I couldn't even have imagined the happiness of my vocation. And I couldn't have imagined the sense of being able to live a life that had meaning and fulfillment.

And so, in many ways it was more God's choice than my choice. I would have to say that it's been an incredible journey, one I wouldn't have traded for anything.

2. **Your background is in nursing and business administration. Can you tell us a little bit about how your nursing background informs your perspective as a healthcare executive?**

It's why I chose to go ahead and be a healthcare executive. I really loved clinical nursing. For me, clinical nursing is what I like to do. As much as I love this job, I still miss the blood and guts of health care. You know, looking at what a new treatment will do, or looking at a different way of managing a disease, or dealing with a crisis in which we all have to mobilize to "get this done and fix it." And I miss walking the halls with people who are taking care of patients every day. But—as a young sister in nursing, running a children's hospital and a perinatal center that was part of a big hospital complex—it became clear to me that many, many times things that needed to be done and care that needed to be offered to the people who needed it, not just the people who could afford it, could often get stopped in its tracks by people who understood money and could say, "That would be nice, *but*... ." So it became really clear to me that if I did not get a good handle on money, I would not be effective as an advocate for the patients and for the staff who cared for them.

That's why I did the preliminary work to get into a master's in healthcare finance [program]. Because the money could stop every good work in its tracks, but if you understood the money, you could say, "Well, yes, there will be some challenges to overcome, but they can be met by this and this and this." And you could be even more successful if you did the darn thing right.

When I was a healthcare executive, I could look at a decision, say in a budget that wasn't balanced, and say, "All right, this has the potential to call forth the best in people. We've got to work together to find a better way to do this that is economically tangible and economically realistic." Or, "This suggestion has the potential to carve out the poor. That's not going to do." And, "This suggestion has the potential to put the staff under such inordinate pressure that it will be counterproductive, both in the quality in care and the complications in care, and the turnover in care, which is the most expensive thing you can have in a hospital. So it's counterproductive." Also, you can intervene when people say, "Well, we could do this, and we could skip this step or two steps, such as running without a unit secretary or with a second checker, or we could cut people in central supply who clean the instruments by one person, and get away with it and we could make it work." But then you say, "Wait, when you're driving, you can pass on the curve sometimes and get away with it. But you pass on enough curves and you're going to get smashed up and you're going to hurt yourself and you're going to hurt other people." We don't have the right to make those kinds of choices.

So a combination of a nursing degree and a master's in finance helps me to understand safe and ethical ways of making choices that are tough choices. Can we put off renovating the waiting room? Probably for a year or so. Can we do other things that make it more warm and inviting that don't cost money? Yes. Can we put off upgrading the autoclave that we're not sure works 100%? Probably not—even though buying the new autoclave doesn't get you a lot of splash out there, or upgrading the generator, or the staffing, or whatever. So it really helps me to understand the impact on patient care, on staff, as well as on the economics.

So you never forget your experiences as a nurse and the patient relationships—that's where everything stems from ...

Exactly.

Even with your overlay of finance and business understanding...

You never forget it, and also you learn to still seek it out. By the time I finished my master's in finance, I had 20 years of clinical experience. In medicine, in just five years, you can say, wait a minute, that's a new procedure. Whereas when I was a nurse in the OR, I knew what it took to set up for a colectomy. I could tell you the timing and the instruments. But wait—today we're not doing a colectomy with a big incision; we're doing it with three or four small incisions, we're using robotics, we're using optics with a little tiny tube in there, we're going to have a video screen and a robotic screen. That's a whale of a lot more technology than I was dealing with. [Or think about] what we can do today with heart attacks: We're now in the ER talking about 30 minutes from the front door to the cath lab, or to administering clot-busting drugs.

So let me talk to those people in the trenches before we finalize a decision. Don't let me read what some expert, who has less clinical experience than I have and is certainly not going to deign to talk to these folks, determines what can be done in terms of staffing or equipment cuts or things like that. Let me talk to the people who deliver care. You never forget how important that is.

3. **What do you feel are your unique challenges as the CEO and president of a religious health system?**

    I think they're the same challenges that everyone has who wants to run an excellent healthcare system, with an additional challenge in that you have the responsibility and you have a long history and a commitment—not just because The Joint Commission says you have to deliver this level of care—you've committed in the name of Jesus Christ, in the name of His church, to giving a level of quality of care, a level of respect for the person who is the patient, the persons who are family members, and the persons who are staff members, that reflects the way that Christ looked at the poor and sick. That's a huge, huge issue. And it says that while you can't take care of everybody, you can't turn your back. And you have to always be pushing to make sure that you're doing the best you can to reach as many people as you can. To be as fair and in so many ways to treat the staff who are working with you, the way that Christ would treat them. To respect the contributions they are making. Not just, "Well, I pay them, I give them continuing education benefits, they have a pension, and they have a vacation." No, no, no. You *owe* them all those things. That's not a charitable deed; you owe them all those things. More profoundly, you owe them the respect [of recognizing] their inherent dignity, as a child of God created in the image and likeness of God. That's a big deal. And that big deal says that I will always try—and sometimes to some people it seems like you're always pushing the envelope—but I will always, always try, and I will profoundly regret when I fail to treat people the way they deserve to be treated. And [I will try] to respect the God-given dignity in them, no matter whether they're the staff member or a patient.

Today you often hear Pope Francis saying, "The Lord never tires of forgiving." As an administrator, I have to be that person who can't forgive mistakes over and over again by a staff member that are out of sloppiness or lack of caring. I can't say, "Oh sure, sweetie, God made you, so keep on being the RN." I have to say, "There are consequences to those mistakes. You're not being careful, you're not getting continuing education, you're not treating the patients the way you need to treat them. So you can no longer be part of this. We've tried to work with you. But, I am telling you this is not your best self. So while I cannot keep you on here as an employee, I have to tell you go and find your best self. Go and find your best self." And so my goal in that is I have to act on behalf of the patient; I have to act on behalf of fellow staff members. But I also have to say, "It's not your best self. You're called to be somebody else, and something much more." That's an important thing.

It's also important to be a witness who says that people are more than a disease. They are a whole person.

You need to talk about things that are not respectful of the dignity of people, such as rules—whether rules from an insurance company, rules from Medicare or Medicaid—that don't respect the dignity of people, that don't meet their needs. You always want to be able to find that there are things in your facility that recognize the whole person, whether that's pastoral care, palliative care, psych care—all of those things. You need to be about making choices that are what people need, not just the services that are the most lucrative. You need a bottom line so you can rebuild, so you can have the best, so you can pay just wages, et cetera, et cetera. But you need to be committed to finding ways to provide the care and services to the people who need it.

We have these tragedies, such as the tragedy of the Congressman from Virginia [Creigh Deeds, November 2013]. His son kept going to the emergency department and being released. There were no beds. They'd say, "Well he does need to be admitted, but there are no psych beds." Well, psych [care] is not well funded. And so the young man attacks his father and kills himself. It's not like this parent wasn't trying. Families, even wealthy families, find it difficult to cope. It's important that you see all those choices out there and it's important, I think, that your hospital reflects the spiritual, that it says to people, "You're more than an organism." That gives hope, whether it's hope because you struggle with a disease or whether it's hope when you're on your final journey to God. You've got to be able to do that. Whether it is a person of the Muslim faith or Hindu faith or Jewish faith or Christian faith or no faith, we [the healthcare system] have as much as we can have in place. And certainly if the person is of the Catholic faith, we have the sacramental system in place so that they have it and so that the family that surrounds them has that. Those are really important things. That's probably more than you wanted to know about Catholic health care.

4. **With Catholic social doctrine at the core of your ministry, you often speak of the poor, the vulnerable, and the marginalized. Could you talk more about those populations and how you feel health administrators can best serve them?**

Let me first say to you that the poor, vulnerable, and marginalized are often economically all of those things. But they're often not just the economically poor, particularly when you look upon the elderly. I was just talking to someone who went to visit an aunt who has plenty of money, but she is so incredibly vulnerable and marginalized. I know when I was running a hospital and a nursing home here in the city, there were times when we would take in—most of my patients in the nursing home were Medicaid [beneficiaries], because that was the section of the city we built the nursing home in, and we focused it on being there and being able to give Medicaid patients quality nursing care, a private room, a beautiful chapel, a swimming pool for rehab, great physical therapy, in a section of the city where I knew the bulk of my patients would be Medicaid—but there were times when we took in, because somebody knew me and asked me to do it, a person who had really significant wealth, but was so alone, so vulnerable.

And so we have what St. Vincent de Paul used to call the "bashful poor." They can be economically poor or they can be just vulnerable because of the poverty of their family life, the poverty of nobody cares for them, or the poverty of people only caring about getting their wealth and so they get more and more withdrawn, or the poverty because they have become paranoid, so they're afraid of everybody. They don't have a son or a daughter who wants to take care of them; they're alienated or they never had kids. It is really important that our systems of health care are able to understand: You think, well this person has this kind of wealth, you just send them home and they get whatever they need—no, they're as isolated as that low-income person and often more isolated. So it's having a heart and caring about that, and creating that sense in our staff, creating mission-focused programs with our staff, and giving our staff the tools and the liberty to care.

Providence here in Washington attracts a lot of people who are very poor—people off the streets who've been in the same clothes for weeks. When they would get ready to go home or we were going to transfer them to the drug treatment center, the ER folks would call the sisters in pastoral care and they would say, "They don't have anything to wear." Well, the sisters had this huge clothes room and people would give them secondhand clothes that were clean and nice. The sisters would never allow secondhand underwear or socks, but a nice pair of trousers, a nice shirt that was laundered and maybe a little worn, but quite nice. You prayed for people to grow out of it quicker than wear it out! But to have those kinds of programs where they come down with clothing—the nurses used to tease, "Now sister, let me give you my size as well"—to have the availability of food for the poor, or to have connections with the local food pantry or vans that go and pick up people because otherwise they'll never make the follow-up appointment for their doctor. They may be prescribed PT [physical therapy] three times a week and Medicare may pay for it or pay for part of it, but they'll never come in to get that unless you go pick them up. They'll never get their prescriptions filled.

Would you say that this requires health administrators to really understand their population?

Understand the population and understand the systems that are needed to prevent the population from falling through the cracks. Help their staff understand it; empower their staff to have the tools.

Because it doesn't do any good to say, "Well now, make sure they get back for physical therapy," if the staff can't do anything but say to the patient, "Now be sure you get back for physical therapy." Connect them with the van service so that they'll get back, or give them the number so they can call. It's those kinds of things, those millions of little things that never get the same publicity that an MRI turnover does.

5. **In 2007, you were quoted in *Modern Healthcare* as saying, regarding healthcare reform, "We can get the job done when we want to get it done." Have we really reached that critical point as a nation yet?**

I would say we are about 60% to 65% there. We've come a long way in the last year, or in the last three years. Part of it was a huge piece of the nation had to be convinced. I think this is what killed Hillary Clinton's initiative: People were convinced if we gave everyone care, they would get less care themselves. Now we have convinced a lot of people in this country, who have legitimate concern about their own health care and the health care of their children, of the fact that not only in the current system was it hard to continue to keep their health care, but also that it was eroding a huge piece of their personal economics. They had less disposable income every year. So they were convinced. A new system had to be developed, and the economics of the nation and individuals would be better if everyone was covered.

6. **While conducting interviews for this text, I have continued to hear that health care has been on a high-speed train heading toward a collision for a long time. Yet somehow there is a disconnect between average consumers, many of whom are religiously affiliated, under-standing the stark reality of health care in this country—for instance, the need for reform, those most affected, our outpaced spending and poor outcomes. What contributes to this disconnect?**

The myths. We create myths a minute in health care to prevent effec-tive action, and part of the reason is that a lot of people have a stake in the healthcare dollar. Never ever forget that. A lot of people have a stake in the healthcare dollar. And so you mobilize panic. We keep people petrified of having something taken away from them; we keep American businesses petrified that this is backbreaking. Also, there are businesses in this country that can outsource—they've done a huge amount of that outsourcing. But there are certain businesses you can't outsource. So you have to say, "I don't have the luxury of outsourcing, so I'm stuck with healthcare costs that are rising and rising and become a bigger part of our GDP every year. I have more cost shifting every year from people who don't have health care." It's just impossible.

I used to marvel at watching people on hospital boards who were titans of industry, from businesses and banks, major companies. They would come on a hospital board, tons of business expertise, and they would pull their hair out when they'd try to get their arms around healthcare costs. They would say, "I've never seen anything harder to deal with." And you'd sort of laugh and say, "Welcome to my world, sweetie." And for financial success, never mind if you add the components of quality and sensitivity to the vulnerable, we had competing incentives over and over. And we only made it worse every time we went to fix it.

Now, the smart thing about the Affordable Care Act—people don't want to say anything smart about the ACA. Believe me, I am not someone who thinks the ACA was a perfect bill. We have never in the history of our country passed a perfect bill, okay? Get real. We have never, ever passed the perfect bill. We didn't [create] a perfect Constitution; we have amendments to our Constitution. Why we are demanding perfection of a healthcare bill is another whole issue. But the first things that it started to do were things that were good for people who already had insurance, people who had not perfect health security, but a heck of a lot more than the poor. Kids during the recession could not get a job out of college, they were over 21, and now parents can keep them on their insurance. Many, even in the economically middle and upper incomes [brackets], had the lowest level of coverage. They now have, in the under-65 [market], the highest percent of coverage because they can stay on their parents' insurance until they are 26. We have the elderly who had a great plan except for the pharmacy piece, and that doughnut hole got closed, too.

We suddenly had people who had a pretty decent plan if they were sick, but had copays and deductibles that got bigger and bigger and bigger. So, you rallied and got that deductible and spent it if somebody said, "You've got a lump in your breast that needs looking at" or "You have a problem and you really do need a cardiac surgeon." But to get preventive care, they would put it off and put it off, particularly if you considered yourself middle class but you didn't have a lot of disposable dollars. And so you put it off, the things you thought, "We could put that off for another couple of months." Now with the ACA, you can get all the preventive care you need without a copay and deductible.

Another important change was that previously your insurance company could charge whatever the market would bear. And the market was really favoring insurance company stockholders, not policyholders. Under the ACA, if insurance [companies] didn't spend 85% of what they charged, they have to pay it back. Billions have already been paid back to American families by insurance companies. It might be $75 to you, $100 to someone else, or $50 to someone else. Now it's not what the market will bear, because insurance has to pay back the consumer, and business is going to close in. You need to change what care is going to cost.

So it helped people who had some health security, but didn't have as much as they wanted before the ACA, and it began to help the poor. All these people got these benefits, and now we're helping the poor as well. A lot of people who had an insurance policy that I would say was marginally miserable, when they went into the marketplace, they found themselves with a lot more coverage for a lot less money.

7. **You've served as a national leader on healthcare reform. What have you learned about politics, health systems, and medicine?**

It happened in the most polarized time, I think, in the modern history of our country. I recognize we had in the early history of our country Congressmen who ended up having duels—pistol duels. But in the modern history of our legislative branches, this is the most polarized time. It was just downright abusive and a sense that this was the issue that most divided the two parties. I would say that the really important thing to do, and this is where it helped us, was to say, "What's our vision? What are our principles?" We worked really hard with the people in Catholic health care and with others, but first with the people in Catholic health care, so that we had a document that laid out our vision. And we said clearly, "When it comes to our principles, we'll not compromise our principles. We'll compromise preferences, but not principles." So I think it's important to know what's a principle and what's a preference when you are negotiating.

I think it's also important to examine why you're doing something. To step by step say, "What's the integrity of what I'm going after? Am I going after this simply because I don't want to worry so much about budgeting? Because I want being a healthcare CEO to be not quite so difficult and more financially rewarding?" All of us would like that. "But am I really also at the forefront in my commitment to this nation and the integrity of its healthcare system? [Am I] building a system that works for everybody?"

Maybe you have a nicer house than somebody else, but everybody has safe housing. Or [maybe] you will never be able to eat lobster on food stamps, but at least you're not going to starve. All of us want to work and we want a country where you have the ability to get ahead so you can have lobster when you want lobster, or you can have an extra patio on your house if you want it. But the truth of the matter is we also want a country where nobody lives in squalor and in starvation, and the same should be true of our healthcare system.

8. **In a 2012 speech you gave in Cleveland, you spoke about a set of principles for a health system that serves everyone, a vision statement for a new system that CHA developed. Can you talk about these principles and how your organization arrived at them?**

We took about a three-year journey. It was before Obama was elected. We said, "The Clinton initiative failed. What did we learn from that? When's the next moment and will we be ready when the moment comes?" That sounds like a Viagra commercial! But we needed to say that. We spent a lot of time even when we knew the White House and Congress were not ready for healthcare reform. What would it look like? [We spent time] talking to people about what it would look like—working in coalitions, working with different groups that cared as we cared, and sharing our thoughts and learning from their thoughts. And then learning from people at the grassroots levels, the nurse caring for patients, the admitting clerk who when someone called to make an appointment for an MRI that their doctor had ordered said, "Your copay and deductible is $400," and having the patient say, "I can't find $400. There's no way." Not only people on the clinical side, but also people on the financial side. What did we learn from people who were frequent flyers to the emergency room?

And so we spent a lot of time. What did we learn from the people in pastoral care who listened? What did we learn from people in Catholic Charities? And then we came out with a vision statement and we tested it. We built posters that looked at one piece, one principle in the vision, quarter by quarter for a year or two. So people could articulate: *Respect life from the moment of conception to the moment of natural death*. And so it said clearly we're not in this and we're not going to partner with people who are into euthanasia and abortion. The next one would be: *Health care for everyone*. Now, we might not get everyone with the first bite, but we weren't going to settle for a bite that brought in 5000 more people and spent almost every dime on making it better for people who already had health insurance.

So it was those kinds of things.

Health and Prevention. We knew that we couldn't keep a sick care system going. We wanted quality and transparency. Then we could sit down there and say, "This is how we see quality being measured, and transparency." And maybe the Congress could come back and say, "No, we see quality being measured like this." Well, could we get to this, could we get to that? Yes. And that's the way we worked.

9. **You often remind others of the individual stories of consumers, diverging from the common political rhetoric and ideology. Do you feel that healthcare administrators can reach their communities with stories? Is this a new public relations element in the role of the administrator that may not have been necessary in the past?**

I think it was always necessary. I think that the most successful healthcare administrators knew the people they were caring for.

You know, [imagine] if you run a restaurant business and you don't know what your customers like about your menu, or whether they think your service is good, or whether you reservation system works—and the same is true whether you sell cars or toothpaste or whatever. You know, we can just look at the recent past with the sales pitch that JCPenney had. I mean [the CEO] made a fortune and [the company's stock] was traded on Wall Street, but [the strategy] was away from what the consumer wanted: "We're never going to have sales. We're always going to have a good low price. We're not going to have coupons." Well, can you compete with 30% off and a coupon for another 20% off? "I feel like I could have gotten the same quality at JCPenney as I could have at Macy's. I feel really good about 30% off and a 20% coupon." They didn't know their customers.

10. ***Modern Healthcare* magazine named you "The Most Powerful Person in Health Care" in 2007. With power comes a lot of responsibility and often burdens. What is your response to this designation? How do you define your power in the healthcare industry?**

I think that if you have a voice, you say, "Who do I use that voice for?" I made a commitment to using any resources that I have, whether they are financial resources or talent or influence, for people who need service, particularly those who are poor and vulnerable.

While people who are poor will never get to see the leader of the Senate, I can introduce them to the leader of the Senate—maybe not physically, but their situation. And I can make sure that he or she has heard their perspective. You know I'm not the only one who can do that. But [the important thing is] to always, always remember them—that they're in the boardroom, that they're in the hearing room in Congress. And whether it's the elderly person, whether it's the bashful poor, or whether it's the poor and vulnerable who just happen to be born in a really rotten, miserable family situation—or lack of family situation: Whose agenda am I advancing?

It sounds like when you walk into those rooms of power, you still have your nurse's uniform on and you have just been on the floor hearing the stories of the everyday patient.

And the caregiver. We can't make it impossible for people who take care of the sick and elderly to do so with dignity—and without feeling like, "I haven't been able to do a really good job because we're so tightly staffed, or we don't have the resources that we need."

11. **You've been described as a dynamic leader, a consensus builder, and as having an uncanny ability to look at the big picture. Are these essential ingredients for a successful healthcare executive? Would you add more ingredients to the mix?**

   I've been described other ways, too! I think everybody has talents. I think it's important to look at your natural gifts and develop those and to look where you don't have natural gifts. If you can develop them, and they're needed, develop them. If you can't, supplement them by working with people who do have them. Build a team. Partner with people. Nobody has it all. Nobody got us healthcare reform all by themselves.

12. **You are one of a minority of female CEOs in health care. What do you see as the role of women in healthcare executive administration?**

   I think women have a very bright future in healthcare administration. I see more and more women in it. I think it's really, really important. I think it's really important that we not only see women in it, but also that we help make sure that we don't make leadership in any meaningful role in our country or in our church, one in which if you really want to give your family the time and attention they need, that you can't do it and be successful.

   I take great pride in the leadership that's been shown in this country by women religious in health care. At a time when women didn't leave the convent, at a time when people didn't educate women, at a time when no women—much less nuns—had leadership roles, the sisters built the largest and most successful healthcare system the world has known. But we're in a different world and we're not an immigrant church anymore, and we don't need to be an immigrant church. But we do need the talent of women, just as much as we needed the talent of women when we were an immigrant church, but now we need it a little bit differently.

And we need to tap the talent, particularly as we live longer lives and have more productivity in lives; we need to be sure that we tap the talent of all women. And we never, ever talk about the importance of children, the importance of family life, the importance of relationships between husband and wife. And then to only have careers that if you're not willing to sacrifice most of that, you're never going to be successful—that's the wrong thing to do.

13. What would you most want to say to the next generation of healthcare administrators?

You have a great opportunity to change the world, make the world a better place. Make the world of your community, the world of your state, of our nation, a better place. [Make] our world a better place. But you also have the opportunity to make individual worlds such a much better place.

We just had here, last Friday, a couple of people locally who did a presentation to our elderly care committee. Now the committee is made up of people who have been leaders in elderly care from across our nation—people who are really doing great things. And one of the people who presented to them was a woman who had worked with me at Providence Hospital and at Carroll Manor Nursing Home there. She had just helped that nursing home to achieve Magnet status as a nursing home. There are only four nursing homes in the nation that have Magnet status. She had just been chosen in the last year as the "Black Nurse of the Year." You know that's a wonderful thing. To have been able to have worked with her, to see her talents go from being a staff nurse in the hospital to being the director of nursing, the "Black Nurse of the Year" in the area, helping this nursing home for Medicaid patients achieve Magnet status and then to see her present and have people just enchanted by her presentation—that is change that improves many people's worlds.

It's important to change individual worlds and the world of your hospital or your facility or the world of your community, and your state's world—to make your state better and your nation better. And the world is getting so small; many of us can do things in places like Haiti, Rwanda, the Philippines. There's a wonderful, wonderful opportunity out there to do so much good and to have an incredibly good time going through it. You will not be able to do it without a lot of hard work, often heartbreak, and often a lot of people slamming you. But the truth of the matter is that you need to decide what's important in your life.

14. **If you could wave a magic wand and create all the change you'd like in health care, what would you wish for?**

I'd work for a much more streamlined system of healthcare financing and delivery.

A single-payer system?

A single-payer or even a more streamlined one—single payer would be one way if it was done well, whether it'd be Medicare for all or another. But with the complexity of the healthcare system, it's too counterproductive [to have] incentives—perverse incentives. I would look for a much better, more streamlined approach. We'd spend our healthcare dollar better.

TAKE-AWAY NOTES

1. A strong handle on a health system's money and communication with the people who deliver care will give the administrator the opportunity to better advocate for patients and staff.
2. Healthcare administrators of religiously affiliated systems face unique challenges. Healthcare administrators in all types of systems should remember that people are more than a disease, and services should reflect what the patients need, not what is lucrative.
3. Successful health systems create a sense of mission and purpose in the staff, by creating strong programs and giving staff the tools and liberty to care about the programs and patients. Programs such as food for the poor, transportation assistance, clothing assistance, and connections to other community programs and resources are critical.
4. Understand the population and understand the systems needed to prevent the population from falling through the cracks.
5. Health systems now have to change what care is going to cost, because, due to the ACA, charging what the market will bear is a thing of the past.

6. As a healthcare administrator, it is important to examine motives and the integrity of choices.

7. The Catholic Health Association created coalitions that included multidisciplinary groups such as nursing care, administrative staff, and other care and community organizations, so as to develop a cohesive vision. Using a systemic approach, it tested key principles of that vision through a quarterly poster campaign. This approach allowed for development of a clearly defined vision and purpose that better prepared the organization for later national reforms.

8. The most successful administrators know the people they care for.

9. Influence and power in health care come with the responsibility to bring the most vulnerable populations into the boardrooms and political chambers.

10. Work with people who have those talents you do not have or cannot develop. Build a team. Partner with people. Nobody has it all.

11. Women have a bright future in healthcare administration. It is important to tap the talents of all women, including those reentering the workforce or who work part time while raising a family.

12. Healthcare administrators of the future have the opportunity to make their communities, their state, their nation, and our world a better place. They have an opportunity to change the world as well as the opportunity to make individual worlds a much better place.

Telehealth as Part of the Continuum of Care

An Interview with Alex Nason, Vice President of Clinical Care Services, Specialists on Call

Alex Nason solves problems—problems in the healthcare industry that can be addressed by technology. With an eye on innovation, Nason has built a unique career in health care by developing an expertise in telemedicine belied by his strong background in and understanding of research, as well as experience in political, clinical, academic, and consulting environments. Whether it has been a tele-ICU pilot, a tele-translation service, an international tumor board, a global second-opinion service, or the launch of an e-learning platform, Nason has had his hands in some kind of innovation in medicine.

Nason received his master of business administration and master of health administration degrees from the University of Pittsburgh; he also holds a bachelor of arts in biology from Tulane University. Currently he serves as the vice president of clinical care services for Specialists on Call, a company that provides highly trained board certified specialists directly to patients' bedsides during critical times of need. Specialists on Call has delivered more than 100,000 acute clinical telemedicine consultations—more than any other organization in the United States. Before joining Specialists on Call, Nason created telehealth solutions at Johns Hopkins University and consulted on telehealth implementations and installations. His experience in the healthcare arena spans nearly three decades and includes both a domestic and a global understanding of complex health issues and the ways in which technology can play a role in augmenting traditional healthcare delivery.

Telemedicine encompasses services, equipment, or capabilities within health care. By its very nature, telemedicine demands agility and forward thinking. At the same time, it presents unique business challenges such as cultural considerations, reimbursement hurdles, licensing restrictions, technology infrastructure needs, and customs and shipping for telemedicine products and equipment. Nason's experience positions him well to understand the inherent complexities in the healthcare business model, while searching for innovative ways for technology to bridge existing healthcare gaps—gaps in areas such as physician shortages, acute response, or chronic disease management.

Inevitably, Nason says, new technology creates a buzz of excitement, something he refers to as a "technology trigger." After the trigger comes inflated expectations, followed by disillusionment, and finally, utilization and a plateau of productivity. Nason approaches each technology trigger with an open-minded curiosity grounded by a pragmatic cynicism, and this combination has led to his many successful ventures in telehealth.

Nason is the first to say that telemedicine fills in gaps—that it merely supports and improves existing health systems. In this interview, he takes the time to share his thoughts on the future of telemedicine—telehealth—and the potential obstacles that new administrators may have to overcome to utilize the best that technology has to offer.

1. **Talk about telehealth—its beginnings and its accomplishments so far.**

   I think it's important to first define, What is telehealth? Everyone has different views on it and might have different interpretations. Different industries have different definitions for it, but, as a whole, telehealth is the utilization of technology to hook up distant pieces of the healthcare sector via technology. And "distant" doesn't necessarily have to mean far distances or geographically huge distances. For instance, it can mean when a physician and a patient are not next to each other, or a physician and another physician, or a patient and a specialist... Telehealth also gets into distance education: physicians training other physicians at a distance, administrative tasks, leadership, or managing other healthcare facilities at a distance.

   Telemedicine is the clinical focus of that broader umbrella of telehealth. So again physician-to-physician interaction, physician-to-nurse, patient-to-physician, patient-to-nurse, and all the other combinations out there. It's been around for a long time, because we've been using phones forever and physicians have been sharing ideas via technology, but it just happened to be through the basic communication tool of a phone. Of course, then it moved to the fax machine. The healthcare industry is probably the only industry keeping the fax machine in business, because we still, for whatever reason, rely upon that as a communication tool with information and data—which is actually a bit embarrassing!

When most people think of telemedicine, they think of the ability of individuals to access data and also engage with their colleagues, their peers, [and] their patients through the use of video technology. For many people, the majority of telemedicine—if you look at the transactions out there—includes teleradiology, teledermatology, [and] telepathology, where the actual physician never ever sees the patient. He or she just happens to be viewing something that has come to him or her in image form, or clinical data, and is communicating back on that information and documentation.

Is there is a risk with that—when the patient is completely uninvolved? Are there hidden hazards?

No. Not at all, especially for those particular disciplines. [In] radiology, you never really meet your radiologist. You never really meet your pathologist; they just have a cell sample that was sent to them. So those disciplines are very easy to work with. In the case of dermatology, there is obviously an opportunity for communication with the patient around what may be happening and also the explanation about risk factors that could impact dermatologic health. For example, many communities have access to primary care, but that primary care physician might not like a spot on the patient, so the opportunity to take that picture, transmit it digitally to a specialist wherever [he or she] might be sitting, and for that individual physician to give an opinion either back to the primary care physician or back to the patient is an important one. It could be, "Yeah, the rash is fine, no big deal," or it could be much more involved: "You know I really don't like that," and it's now worth traveling to a next level of care for additional evaluation—whether that next level of care is to a community hospital or a tertiary hospital, or whatever that might be.

2. **What are the primary benefits of telehealth in terms of health system management?**

In health care, we have a sector—we don't have a system—first and foremost. Some of the challenges we have in health care are because there is no connectivity, there is no connection, at least not a very good connection, between the patient's health and primary care, primary care to community hospital, community to specialty, specialty to rehab, and then back home again. There's very little system-ness, although obviously some of the models that are starting to be created through some of the financing mechanisms are starting to drive some of the system-ness. But telehealth, I think, brings that opportunity around to a sort of system of care that can really start with the patient, right where the patient is. The biggest thing in systems of care is—and we all know this—there are more and more patients and not enough doctors, not enough access to services. And yet our service model of how we deliver care is very archaic given some of the new available technologies. Our current system of care is just not sustainable, nor scalable. It's not sustainable given the current financial models that are out there, and it's not sustainable given the volume of patients who are trying to access the healthcare sector.

3. **What stands out as an exemplary model of the use of telehealth in your mind?**

   Here at Specialists on Call, a private telehealth services company, we provide telehealth services to acute care hospitals. As of this date we're at over 300 hospitals across the country. We provide services in emergency neurology, emergency psychiatry, and ICU or critical care. We, as a company, have done over 130,000 consultations. Our physician group, which is roughly 100 physicians who are on the current panel, supports these 300 hospitals that would not have access to care either part of the time or at all—hospitals that would not have access to the specialty care. What we've done to date is actually over 100,000 emergency neurology consults, and we have delivered TPA, which is the clot buster in stroke care, more than any other group as a unit, in the country, if not the world. Some of the biggest academic medical centers don't get the access to the number of patients that we do, and therefore don't have the ability to give that type of care. So, if you look at the size and scope of the impact of health care, . . . 100,000 consults over a six-year period is pretty massive for us. So that's something: We've been able to scale up and to deliver care to a sector that doesn't have access to it.

   Are you talking about rural, underserved hospitals that you're reaching?

   Interestingly enough, no: What we're really talking about is that group that falls right in between. It's the community hospital, 5,200 beds; the community only has one neurologist, maybe two, and he or she has no incentive, has no motivation, or is just too burned out to be taking calls whenever a patient comes into the emergency department with a neurologic situation.

So you are able to do supplementary care with specialists all over. You are able to provide exactly whatever each hospital needs in terms of supplemental care.

Correct. And they may need it 24/7 or they might just need it on weekends. They might have one physician in a community who is just fine, but that physician just can't be the only one 24/7, 365 days of the year. We assume that these are small, rural, underserved areas, but not necessarily. These are ones that just might be on the outskirts—that might be a spoke off of a hub. They just can't attract that level of expertise because the volumes don't justify it, but they still need to serve their community.

4. **What do future administrators need to know about reducing total cost of ownership (TCO) and improving their return on investment (ROI) in relationship to telehealth options?**

We talk about TCO and ROI a lot in this space. The biggest challenge for administrators today is that, in my opinion, they don't have really good data on what their real costs are. So when [they] start to implement a new service or a technology or a new solution, I don't think they have great data to demonstrate what has or hasn't changed in that ROI. So getting data from day 1 is an important [issue,] and a challenge I think for many. The second thing that I think is very hard is that the ROI is very different. It's not your traditional MBA ROI. From where I sit as a techy guy—the finance folks can battle me all they want—it's a different kind of ROI.

When I look at how telemedicine impacts care, I think about the fact that we were able to deliver something 1 day, 10 days, or maybe 30 days earlier than the traditional staffing way would have been done, and therefore we've probably reduced those costs for a patient by providing appropriate care sooner, faster, quicker—and we've therefore reduced the long-term care costs of the care. That is a very, very hard financial model to follow through because [it includes] so many variables. But I think intuitively we can all understand that by getting something checked out—let's stay with dermatology for a second—by getting that mole checked out a month, six months, a year, or two years sooner because of access to specialty care via telemedicine that you may not have had before, [it] can have a true demonstrated impact on the care of that patient. It could have turned into something much more dangerous.

5. **Talk about sustainability, standards, and relationships in regard to technology in health system management.**

Eventually telehealth needs to be considered not something unique or different, but just part of the care continuum. I think that will be an important hurdle as it gets embraced in the system of care a little bit, making telehealth a part of care. It should be delivered and it should be experienced as a standard of care. It is a different experience and you can't do everything via telemedicine that you can do in person, but it should still be included in the same care continuum. You can do many things as if you were [there] in person, but we know there are definitely some differences. It needs to be considered [a routine part of] the system of care, because, again, care doesn't have to happen within the four walls of the traditional hospital or outpatient center or doctor's office. Care should start happening with the patient at home, and then [we should] start to extend those walls elsewhere in a virtual way. I think that only becomes a better model for care as we start to think about the long-term impact of how we're managing the health of the population. Obviously that's a conversation that starts to lead into accountable care organizations and population health management, et cetera.

In thinking about technology, one of the aspects I have been interested in is the relationship building that is possible. Can you talk about the ways in which email and social media, and other creative outlets, can work with health care? What about the ways in which providers and patients might interact with these technologies?

As a visionary realist, something I like to call myself, I'm all about it. I support it; I think it's going to be a piece of health care. I think social technology is a part of how we're going to be more comfortable communicating with one another. That being said, the financial models of health care don't necessarily support this, as they currently exist today. Your doctor doesn't get paid to answer that email. I mean maybe in some cases but probably not, unless you pay a fee, and there are definitely models out there where you can email your doctor for $25. There aren't any financial models or motivating factors for physicians to engage in that kind of behavior.

Social media—social networks like Facebook, and so forth—is a fascinating [case]. The amount of information that is being shared out in that space, that individual patients put out there, is unbelievable: individuals who are writing incredible blogs about their experiences going through cancer care. Individuals who are sharing their experiences with particular hospitals or the care of their loved ones and receiving that support are incredible. But at the same time, the HIPPA police are screaming and yelling about information being on the Web. So we haven't quite figured out the balance between the two.

I believe there is a strong, strong opportunity around social networking and what it can do to improve the health of a population. I think websites like PatientsLikeMe do a fantastic job of bringing individual patients together who are sharing an experience, but not sharing an experience as just a number, or just as an individual, but really bringing it together as a community. A 25-year-old woman going through breast cancer is a much, much different story than a 65-year-old woman going through breast cancer. So we can't just send the individual patient out there and [have her] say, "I'm a breast cancer patient." Places like PatientsLikeMe as a social network, and not just an information network, really help us focus this down into these groups.

Strong impact—I don't think physicians quite understand it yet, or understand the capabilities quite yet. But it's coming.

6. **What are the primary barriers to telehealth implementation in health system environments? What are barriers to other types of technology?**

The typical barriers that you are going to find in telehealth include the cost of technology, although it's dropping tremendously, and the lack of reimbursement for care… [R]oughly 20 states, give or take a few, actually have laws on the books now—they're called telemedicine parity laws—so if you're providing a service that is normally a covered service but you happen to deliver that service via telemedicine, third-party payers, excluding Medicare and Medicaid, can actually reimburse you for delivering the services.

It's a big step in the right direction. No one is going to break even based off of just reimbursements from third-party payers. We know that. But again it's a piece of the model; it's an overall piece of the care.

Other barriers are some of the traditional barriers that are still out there. We have licensing barriers. If you're a physician, you must be licensed in the state where the patient is sitting. So if you're sitting in Maryland and you're seeing a patient in Virginia, you have to have that Virginia license. This is definitely one of the challenges of telemedicine, because it creates a much smaller geographic area. And there is definitely an investment and a cost to that. So we have the licensing; then we have credentialing. If you're delivering services to hospitals, then you must be credentialed at each of the hospitals, and hospitals may accept a credentialing by proxy, or they might not. So that's another barrier and challenge that is out there.

So many things are very archaic in health care. Some of these things have a place. There's definitely a place for credentialing and licensing, because the associations do want to try to monitor and evaluate the quality of care that is being delivered in their communities. I get that. But given the technology and where we are at today, we need to figure out ways of extending that a little bit easier.

And then the model of care, right? The availability. All of sudden it's 3 o'clock in the morning and I've sent an email. We have this expectation of, "Why didn't you email me back?" Well, it's 3 o'clock in the morning! The convenience of the technology is creating this expectation of convenience of care, and yet on the other end we're still individuals, humans who need to have some balance of life.

So there have to be boundaries and realistic expectations?

There need to be some boundaries and realistic expectations. The technologies are becoming more agnostic. The technologies are talking to each other a lot [more easily]. If you can imagine, way, way back in the day, you got a fax machine, but at the time, you know, the Panasonic fax machine could only fax a Panasonic fax machine. Then the standards were there. We're finding this now in the video space, and we're finding this now in the Web space a lot more. So we're seeing more of the standards that are making technology a lot easier in this [area].

Other barriers exist with hospitals. Their IT departments are facing a ton of challenges these days and are trying to keep up. They're challenged with EMR [electronic medical records], they're challenged with maintaining strong networks, they're challenged with Wi-Fi, they're challenged with keeping up with new technologies. You know, the iPad didn't exist five years ago, and all of a sudden it's the go-to technology for a lot of doctors. How do you have a strategy for your hospital on a technology that didn't exist five years ago? It's just moving so fast.

7. **What is the role of the entrepreneur in this new landscape of health care?**

[H]ospitals have these centers of innovation in health care—and they're all over; they all have them. I think they are great places to nurture ideas, but I think the true innovation does come out of the entrepreneurial private sector. Because they can look at things without the politics, without some of the barriers and limitations, and they can innovate that way. And we've seen this in the mobile space; it's been the biggest one—where there has really been a huge, huge opportunity there.

So are you talking about apps on the mobile phone?

Yes. Healthcare apps, for example, is one of [those opportunities]. Not the wellness apps per se, but the ones that are truly clinically focused. There is a difference there: There's a place for the wellness and the fitness apps, and then there's definitely a place for the medical ones. It's a different conversation for both.

8. **What are your thoughts on future telehealth possibilities?**

Just as we could never have imagined the iPad five years ago, or even the iPhone six or seven years ago, it's very hard to imagine what the future is going to look like. The possibilities [are] endless. I do see, though, in the transition of health care, . . . us pushing outward from the hospital more and more. I see hospitals as centers of excellence of a much higher, higher level of care. I think more and more is going to be happening in the home or alternative sites. I think the retail centers, the retail clinics, are fascinating [possibilities] but they're not doing enough to really shake the paradigm. I think we're looking for them to be much more impactful than they are, but they're very limited. I think telehealth could play a role in something like that. It could really make those locations much more engaging and much more meaningful to the healthcare sector.

9. **Paint us a picture of a health specialty in the future that may look very different from now because of technology.**

I think in the future [health care] will be pushed outward to the home. I can imagine—we already see this now with some patients—they're sent home with a box, some technology, a scale, a blood pressure cuff, and they're asked to get on that scale every day, to take their blood pressure every day, and that data is transmitted to a center. The center is monitored by a nurse, and that nurse can then call and say, "Hey, what's going on? Your weight's going up, your blood pressure is higher, I can tell you're not taking your meds." And you find that out: "Yeah, I skipped two days." So we're already doing that today.

I see us in the future being much more interactive from our home. I think that the technologies that are there—with the Xbox Kinect, there are some very smart people who are doing some stuff with physical medicine and rehab in front of your Xbox, where they can actually demonstrate an exercise. You do that exercise in front of your Xbox, which is then monitoring that and recording that with the idea of sending it to your physical therapist from there. They can say, "Yes, you're doing the exercise correctly. Keep it up. We can bring you to the next level much sooner."—as opposed to [the message] now, which is, "I'll see you next week." In the old model, . . . we leave with their exercises on a nice, pretty paper, and we've got our bands to use with our exercises, and we either (a) don't do our exercises or (b) do our exercises wrong for a whole week; then when we go back a week from now, we have now been doing our exercises wrong. They were ineffective and we're back to square one. But if we can engage from our home with these technologies, it improves that process that much faster. And I think that is one of the big opportunities out there that I believe could really shake things up.

10. **How do you see the role of future technologies in terms of time saving, waste reduction, and efficiency?**

If we're looking at "technology" as a general term, I think one of the things is data. We all know that data is changing in a lot of these spaces. There's a lot of talk about Big Data and what it means. We don't really have as much data sharing going on as many of us would like to see. I don't want to suggest that Big Brother is the way to go, but for those of us who need to engage in the health care of our life, we need to be able to be more collaborative in sharing data. Whether that's from our home, whether that's for a remote physician with a community hospital for transfers, whatever that might be, I think data is going to be really important to this aspect of connection.

Like a mobile medical file?

Whether it's mobile or whether it's in the cloud. And that's actually a very interesting point: There's a lot of debate over who owns your medical record. Is it the doctor's office, is it the ownership of the hospital, or is it the patient? We have this [attitude], "Yeah, we took your X ray. You paid me for your X ray, but if you want a copy, you've got to pay me." How does that make sense? So these are the kinds of models that need to be looked at. They're not easy ones to address. I think with telehealth, we've got a great opportunity in where things are going.

I have another futuristic view of things: I think hospitals that are smaller and more community focused will be staffed with very, very strong generalists; a very, very strong nursing staff; [and] a very strong physician assistants team. And I think virtually the specialists will come in as necessary.

Will that give specialists more choices about where they live?

If we can get over some of the licensing issues and challenges, yes. I think that's one opportunity. I think another opportunity [will emerge] around just the quality of life for that individual as well.

11. **Can you talk about technology on the horizon that may be of interest to future health system administrators?**

Obviously, video will play a big role. Video is playing a big role today—there's no doubt about that. I think going forward [a key factor] will be having that ability of your network to be strong enough to engage with alternative sites. That's one aspect of it. I think the ability for hospitals to bring in or connect to lots of data [is also important]. I think there is a great opportunity to gather data from multiple sources of information.... I know it sounds kind of Big Brother in nature, but I'm going to look at the positive of it and not the negative of it: [What] if your primary physician knew that you went to the local pharmacy and purchased a couple of over-the-counter medications, then was alerted that you're also on another medication that there could be a conflict with, and a bell went off, a red button went off someplace in that primary care physician's office that is accountable for your care, your health. [Your physician] could then say, "Whoa, whoa, whoa. Don't take that, because you're on this other medication and there's going to be some negative impact." I think it could be very, very powerful. So where does this data move? I think it's a very interesting question.

I think another big thing is just the sharing of information. Sharing of expertise, I should say—not just the data, but the expertise, the skill set. I think eventually telesurgery will be cost-effective and available. We'll get better with our bandwidth. We'll reduce the latency.

12. **Is there anything else you'd like to add for the graduate students reading this text?**

You can't ignore the role that technology will be playing in your hospital. It's a huge investment. It's an investment in your patient care, it's an investment in your operations, and it's an investment in your department. Whether we're talking about the data elements of that, or we're talking about the opportunities for physicians and patients and nurses to engage differently, technology needs to be a part of the plan. There is a possibility that someday you might be managing a completely virtual organization. Again, my company, Specialists on Call, [has] over 100 doctors. They're all over the country.

We're probably the nation's largest multispecialty practice, and we are growing tremendously. We will probably be over 200 physicians within a year and they're all over the country. They might be managing a practice from the comfort of their home!

TAKE-AWAY NOTES

1. Telehealth is the utilization of technology to connect distant pieces of the healthcare sector via technology.
2. Telemedicine is the clinical focus within the broader telehealth umbrella.
3. Telehealth can anchor a system of care around the patient.
4. Telemedicine services, in certain situations, can reach more patients and offer more services to sectors that may not have previously had access to that care.
5. The return on investment with telemedicine can be hard to track with traditional numbers. Intuitively, it can be stated that long-term costs for some patients' care will be reduced because of better, earlier access to specialty care.
6. Telehealth has an important place on the traditional care continuum.
7. Social media can play an important role in population health, especially through sites focused on specific health conditions. Financial models do not yet support better electronic communication between care providers and patients.
8. Barriers to telehealth implementation include the costs of technology, the lack of reimbursement for telehealth care, licensing restrictions, credentialing, and shifting models of care.
9. True innovation is easier to achieve in the entrepreneurial private sector, where there are fewer barriers and limitations than in the traditional healthcare sector.
10. In the future, healthcare services will increasingly be pushed into patients' homes. Technology in the home can keep patients engaged and connected to providers.
11. Collaborative sharing of data, expertise, and skill sets is an important aspect of future healthcare systems.

Healthy Communities and Health System Integration

An Interview with Rich Umbdenstock, MS, FACHE, President and Chief Executive Officer, American Hospital Association

When the American Hospital Association (AHA) recognizes a health system—urban or rural—Rich Umbdenstock travels to present the award in person. Known for his lionheartedness and visionary problem-solving skills, Umbdenstock is not the typical Washington Beltway executive. As president and CEO of the AHA, Umbdenstock encouraged association members to work with the White House during the healthcare reform effort that led to the Patient Protection and Affordable Care Act (ACA). Today, Umbdenstock recognizes that the current bill is far from perfect, but he is proud of the AHA's role in the legislation. During reform, he led his members to view the discussions as a chance to build on the bill's strengths, rather than fight inevitable change.

"The public wants a different healthcare system. We can't fight that. We have to say, 'Great. Then that's how we want to deliver,'" Umbdenstock said in a 2014 interview with *Hospitals and Health Networks*. With regard to reform, he states that the AHA's job is to read the early signals for reform, so that the organization can guide members through change and create a collaborative environment in which members can learn from one another. Many would say that he has been successful.

Umbdenstock received his master of science degree in health services administration from the State University of New York at Stony Brook, and his bachelor of arts degree in politics from Fairfield University. His career has included hospital administration; health system governance, management, and integration; association governance and management; HMO governance; and healthcare governance consulting. He has received numerous awards and accolades. His most recent award was the B'nai B'rith National Healthcare Award in 2014. In the past, he has received an honorary doctor of laws degree from Gonzaga University; the Holy Names Award from the Holy Names of Jesus and Mary (co-recipient with Barbara J. Umbdenstock), Spokane, Washington; Diplomate (Certified Healthcare Executive) from the American College of Healthcare Executives; the St. Ignatius Loyola Medal; member, American Hospital Association; and fellow, American College of Healthcare Executives.

As president and CEO of one of the most important organizations in health care since 2007, Umbdenstock defies the typical executive stereotype. His colleagues use words such as "gentle," "inclusive," and "bold" to describe him. They remark on his personal style as one "that puts people at ease." One colleague notes that Umbdenstock's humility is his greatest gift; with such humility comes the knowledge that he cannot make dramatic changes happen singlehandedly. His bold vision for transforming the hospital into a center of health, one that is patient centered and offers quality care, has brought leaders from around the country to the table.

His peer and colleague Sister Carol Keehan (see her own Insight from the Experts interview) says of Umbdenstock, "What makes Rich an exceptional leader is the fact that he is inclusive, and he has a great intelligence and competence. And he picks those causes where you most need a CEO to lead, whether the issue is healthcare enrollment or the issue is diversity in health care."

Umbdenstock is referred to as a "problem solver, not a position taker"—a beneficial leadership style for an executive to possess during the tumultuous years of healthcare reform and the rollout of the United States, first comprehensive healthcare bill, the ACA. Umbdenstock spoke from his Washington, D.C., office by phone for this interview. Here is what he had to say about health system integration, the hospitals of the future, and the role of quality care.

1. **You are in the unique position of having a sense of what is happening across the nation in terms of health system integration. Do you have examples that come immediately to mind—a system or region that is a leader in this regard?**

   Health system integration began long before the Affordable Care Act, but the Affordable Care Act takes it a step further by encouraging things like accountable care organizations. Sixty percent of AHA member hospitals are in multihospital systems—we define that as two or more hospitals—and that trend continues. Since the early part of the last decade, we've also seen a marked increase in physicians employed by hospitals; today, approximately 40% of the nation's physicians are employed by, or work exclusively in, a hospital. And multi-institutional systems are spreading out across the continuum of care; in some cases this is happening in individual hospitals, and in others, in systems that are spreading up and down the continuum of care, from prehospitalization or primary care to posthospitalization or post-acute care.

A local example is the Carilion Clinic in Roanoke, which is building upon a clinic model not unlike that used by the Cleveland and Mayo Clinics. They are continuing to build out a large group of physicians, putting the hospital and physician under one umbrella—not unlike what Geisinger also has done. Geisinger has traditionally been an integrated system in the Danville, Pennsylvania, area, but now they've integrated with more hospitals and more physician groups across their market in the greater Pennsylvania area. There are also larger groups, some of the multistate entities. Dignity Health bought U.S. HealthWorks, a series of primary care and urgent care and occupational medicine clinics.

So you see a variety of approaches. It's all still very particular to the organization—the point from which it's starting and the market or markets it's in. Some groups are doing different things in different markets. I talked to one CEO recently who explained that she can't do in the northern part of her state what she is doing in the southern part because of differences in market presence. So while integration is happening across the spectrum, its execution is as individual as the hospitals embracing it.

What would be the key components of a system that you think is really a system leader? What would be things you could list on one hand that you see happening in some of these systems that are doing a really good job?

Let me answer that question a little bit differently, if that's fair.

Sure.

What do I consider to be an integrated system?

To be an integrated system, you first must have the components of the continuum of care under your roof or within your reach through contractual relationships so that you can move the patient to the right place for care at the right time.

[Second], you must have an integrated information system so that I register once and I have one medical record.

[Third], you have to be able to integrate clinical and administrative systems such that I get one bill and set of instructions at discharge.

One admission, one record, and one bill is a *very* high order of integration. But until you achieve that, as a customer I'd say that you're integra*ting*, but I wouldn't say you're integra*ted*.

2. **The AHA has been a supporter of federal healthcare reform. Now that the ACA has passed, what do you see as still necessary on the government side of reform?**

There are a variety of things.

[Number one], even in the best case, the ACA could insure 30 million more Americans, and we know now the real number will be lower. Even with 30 million more insured, we were left with an additional 25 million without insurance. What are we going to do about them?

Number two, we need more focus on the quality improvement side of things. What are the right measures? How do we focus public and private payers and other entities on a consistent set of improvement measures that will help us [solve] some of the problems that we have among our population and across providers? Which quality improvements will make the biggest difference?

Number three, we have to move, on the payment side, from the realm of experimentation and demonstration to a new payment system. Now, if we had known what that was, I think we all would have advocated for it as part of the ACA. But we didn't know then, and we still don't. Whether we move toward accountable care, bundled payments, pay-for-performance, or some combination of those kinds of changes, we have to move away from today's fee-for-service orientation toward a system of accountability for both health and cost.

What do you see as the number one outstanding reform issue on the part of health systems?

My sense is that the biggest outstanding issue is payment reform, because that will drive delivery system reform. It will also send a clearer signal as to where hospitals should be headed. There continues to be too much uncertainty; regulatory and payment system changes and budget cuts keep coming, one by one, leaving hospitals unable to plan in a rational way. Again, the bets are pretty safe that we'll be more integrated, we'll be more accountable for outcomes, we'll be more at risk financially. But providing some degree of certainty, a known method and rate of payment, and letting the field, within reason, sort out exactly what it should be and how it should do it—these things would be wonderful for patients and for providers.

3. **What do you see as the role of hospitals in the future?**

I think the hospital will continue to be a central part, and in many communities *the* central part, of the healthcare system. Clearly, when people drive by the "H" [road sign] on a highway and need immediate assistance, they know what's there. What they may not be thinking about—and what we as hospitals have to get better at—is to be seen as a health resource, not just a treatment or response resource. And that's where you have to build the model to support that. Right now, that's not how they get paid. So, I see the hospital of the future being a lot more of a health support system. Sometimes the hospital will provide the treatment; other times—say, in the chronic care realm—it will be a treatment partner. But I see a lot less dependence in the business model of acute care and a lot more of a need to build out the business model on the wellness, prevention, and disease management side.

4. **In terms of accountability, what have hospitals and health systems done well in the past? Poorly? How do you see this improving in the future?**

I think in the last 12 or so years, hospitals have been real leaders nationally in accountability for quality, for the measurement and reporting of outcomes of care. We've been strong supporters of what was called the Hospital Quality Alliance. Since the National Quality Forum (NQF) came into being, we've been strong supporters of NQF. I'm on the board of NQF and a board officer there. The NQF runs two programs, the National Priorities Partnership and Measure Applications Partnership, that have taken away the need for the Hospital Quality Alliance, and we took that offline a year or two ago.

We've always been strong supporters. We're corporate members of The Joint Commission, and The Joint Commission has been moving in the direction of accountability with unannounced surveys, public reporting, public access, public ability to comment during the survey process, et cetera. So I think in that regard we've been strong leaders. Now, it's important to us to see it done *right*. We kind of pull our hair out at how many different entities try to rate hospitals and how many different systems they use, so in that sense we're pushing back, but not because we don't agree with the fundamental need or principle.

5. **What do you see as the most important elements of internal reform in health systems?**

The ability to do less with less. Here's what I mean. A lot of people say, "We're going to get paid less money, so we have to do more with less." But once you get to a fixed payment, you actually want to do the smallest thing that has the greatest impact. I always use the public health example of the polio vaccine. When I was a young kid, people were still being put in iron lungs. Within a decade or so, we had a sugar cube, the vaccine. That's really doing the least amount and getting the greatest payoff for it. That's why we have to move from a volume orientation to an accountable care system, one that really rewards doing the right thing at the right time—the least intensive and invasive thing that gets you the best outcome of care. And that gets you to the appropriateness question, gets you to readmissions and reutilization questions, and I think there are some really great examples of that.

One prominent example is the issue of no more voluntary inductions or early elective deliveries ([such as at] Woman's Hospital). That's a very simple but profound and challenging step, based on evidence, shown to use NICUs a lot less and shown to eliminate a lot of complications in the postnatal period. And frankly, I think, over time data will show that as kids develop in their first decade, they will be healthier kids with fewer complications. That's the perfect example of doing less and getting a much better outcome.

6. **In the pursuit of lowering healthcare costs, a focus has been on delivering only "appropriate services." Who determines what is appropriate? How is this measured?**

That's a hard question because nobody is the healthcare tsar or dictator, probably for good reasons. But to give you a bit of an elliptical answer, I think the data will tell us, the data will rule . . . we will see in a comparative effectiveness kind of way what works and what doesn't work. My chair-elect, Dr. Jonathan Perlin from HCA, who used to run the Veterans Administration system, just did a huge study that examined three totally acceptable, believed to be comparable, methods of treating people who present with MRSA [methicillin-resistant *Staphylococcus aureus* infection]. And what they found was that by giving the patient population one of the three treatments considered best practices, one was superior—it had a better outcome and cost less. I think the data and research will tell us. And, of course, it has to be done with the best methodologies and appropriate safeguards on both the patient side and the conflict-of-interest side. I think we need that kind of data and to do these studies much more rapidly than we've done them before. That will allow us to compare good things to good things, to find out if something works or not.

7. **What is the best way to measure clinical excellence? Tell us about the synergistic relationship between quality and good business.**

First, you have to have good measures, and that's where we've been with our support behind the National Quality Forum. For instance, specialty societies or payers or others keep coming up with proposed measures, but those measures have to be vetted by some neutral party, and that's the role of the National Quality Forum.

Number two, you have to show that the measures lead to improvement. Not everything that is measured necessarily gets better, or the way in which it's measured may not help the field understand how to improve. So we really need to look at these measures. The Joint Commission calls them accountability measures. There are measures and then there are measures that really lead us to better results in both the clinical and the financial realms—they call those accountability measures. We [AHA] thoroughly support that kind of further refinement. We also want to be sure that the purpose of measurement is not only to inform patients about where they can get the best care, but also to enable providers to improve. They won't be willing to spend the time and effort to pull the data and report the data and then live by the measures if they can't see how it improves things. It has to work, I guess you'd say out in the market, out in the public, and out in the clinical world.

For the second part of the question, only through measurement and further study have we absolutely made the case that better quality leads to lower cost. It leads to more efficient utilization in the current care experience, and it leads to less reutilization or repeat treatments down the line. And so that's really the business case for quality: that it lowers cost. Again, in a fee-for-service world, that hurts financially. If I get everything absolutely perfect, it probably greatly reduces my revenue opportunity, but that's *absolutely* the right thing to do. The problem is that at the moment, hospitals have made commitments based on one method of care and payment.

Now we are in a transition to another method of care and payment, but challenged to manage our way through or beyond current commitments. That's the trick—not getting to the right place, but surviving the transition.

8. **You have spoken in the past about community health partnerships—partnerships between community organizations and health systems. What would be an example of an ideal community model? If you could make this happen tomorrow, what would it look like?**

I don't know if there's an ideal community model, but you might want to reference the AHA website. We have something called the Carolyn Boone Lewis Living the Vision Award. Our vision at the AHA for the last 20 years has been a society of healthy communities where all individuals meet their highest potential for health. I was recently up in New Hampshire giving an award to Cheshire Medical Center and Dartmouth—Hitchcock Keene, which have been working for about 10 years on a vision to become the healthiest community by 2020. And they have hundreds of connections out in the broader community to really focus, again, upstream of the hospital and to work with community groups from the United Way and others.

Last May, I was in Syracuse, New York, presenting the same award to St. Joseph's Hospital and Health Center, where they have literally helped to rebuild the neighborhood and community around them, including helping employees move into the neighborhood by providing them assistance to be able to afford a home in the area—so they are truly living and working on health in the place where they live.

Before that, one more, I was up in Alaska, three years ago. We awarded the Carolyn Boone Lewis Living the Vision award to the [Alaska] Native Tribal Health Consortium for their work improving the health of Alaska Natives and American Indians through actions that go beyond traditional hospital care. ANTHC serves diverse tribal communities, 140,000 Alaska Natives, across the state. The consortium focuses on projects that improve overall health, such as wellness, community-based provision of care, and public health status and improvement to achieve their vision of Alaska Natives being the healthiest people in the world. They touch every part of an individual's health—from ensuring homes have clean water and sanitation to improving employee health to helping seniors receive appropriate care. They work on keeping people out of hospitals by preventing disease and injury. Part of this work is done in collaboration with community health aides and practitioners in rural communities and villages.

9. **What would you like to say to the next generation of health administrators?**

   I say that there has never been a better time to be in health care. We are now embarked on a path where we are truly working on the right things, and we're closer to getting it right than we ever have been. The challenge will be to manage the relationship with patients so they see the health system as a trusted partner and to refine the payment system to the point where providers partner with patients—so that it's more of a win-win and not a matter of "The more I do for you, the more I make and the more costs you have." I don't think anybody's figured that out yet. But we know it will involve truly extending care out into the community and partnering within the community so we can keep people well and productive outside of the system. The next step is building a business case for that, and creating partnerships and engaging patients so that they are also accountable.

10. **What else is on your mind today?**

   Right now, scope of practice is on my mind. For instance, how will the capacity issue be coordinated? The shortage of physicians means less MDs, and now that insurance is going to more people, there will be more demand.

   How do we increase capacity? Perhaps it will mean less reliance on MDs and more reliance on nurse practitioners and physician assistants. And how do we emphasize team-based care so there is a greater use of each member of the team?

   I see a future where we reserve the cases with the greatest ambiguity for the physicians, and what can be delegated will be delegated to other practitioners.

TAKE-AWAY NOTES

1. Integration of health systems is happening across the spectrum and the execution of integration is unique to the community and market preferences.
2. An integrated system has a continuum of care (in-house or contractual), an integrated information system with one registration and one record, and integrated clinical and administrative systems—one admission, one record, one bill.
3. Future healthcare reform requires a consistent set of improvement measures, coverage for the remaining uninsured, and a payment system that reflects accountability for both health and cost.

4. Hospitals of the future will be health support systems, a community resource. The business model is moving away from acute care and toward a larger model that includes wellness, prevention, and disease management.

5. In an accountability care organization, the focus is on doing less, but achieving better outcomes. Systems are shifting away from a volume-based model to an accountable care model.

6. The use of Big Data for comparative studies will result in more effective and appropriate care.

7. The best ways to measure clinical excellence include good measures vetted by neutral third parties and evidence that measures lead to improvement.

8. Quality lowers cost. This will be especially true with revised payment models that reward accountability and quality care.

9. Partnerships between community organizations and health systems help to create a society of healthy communities where all individuals meet their highest potential for health.

10. The challenge for administrators of the future will be to manage the system's relationship with patients so that they see the health system as a trusted partner.

Glossary

Access: The availability of healthcare services as well as the provision or delivery of actual healthcare services, the provision or delivery of the appropriate healthcare services, and some mechanism (i.e., health insurance) that facilitates access.

Accountable care organization (ACO): A group of physicians, and possibly other healthcare providers such as hospitals, who come together voluntarily to accept collective accountability for the quality and cost of care delivered to their patients.

Affordable Care Act (ACA): Federal legislation passed in 2010 that guarantees access to healthcare services for more Americans and creates incentives for medical practitioners to focus on better coordination and higher quality services. Refers to two separate pieces of legislation – The Patient Protection and Affordable Care Act (P.L 111-148) and the Health Care and Education Reconciliation Act of 2010 (P.L 11-152). Together, these laws are commonly called the Affordable Care Act (ACA).

Alternative medicine: Therapies used as replacements for conventional medicine.

Alternative transportation: Use of public or self-powered models of transportation instead of driving; additionally, the implementation of sustainable technologies in standard transportation.

Antitrust: Laws that prohibit business practices designed to restrain trade.

Appropriation authority: A legislative committee that has the authority to propose program and agency funding.

Arete: Virtue; class.

Authorization jurisdiction: A legislative committee that has the authority to establish programs and agencies.

Beneficence: Acting for the benefit of patients, with both charity and kindness.

Breach: Any unauthorized acquisition, use, or disclosure of protected health information that compromises the patient's privacy and security.

Budget: An agreement between two management levels regarding use of resources for a defined time period.

Bundled payment: A payment system in which healthcare providers receive a fixed sum for treating a patient's condition, regardless of what it costs the provider.

Business associate: A company that furnishes services to healthcare providers and has only incidental access to patient protected health information, such as telephone companies or post offices.

Business intelligence and analytics: A collection of methods to extract and analyze data for better decision making.

Care coordination: Cooperation among physicians and other medical professionals to ensure patients get the care that they require.

Centralized configuration: An information systems configuration in which most if not all, of the IS personnel work in a central headquarters or regional-based support center, rather than at each of the facilities.

Chief data officer: Also known as the chief health information officer; an emerging data-centered role in health care.

Chief information officer (CIO): The administrator responsible for information systems technology, services, and personnel in a health system.

Chief medical informatics officer (CMIO): A medically trained individual who is responsible for the physician needs of clinical systems.

Chief nursing informatics officer (CNIO): A nurse who is responsible for the nursing needs of clinical systems.

Chief security officer (CSO): The administrator responsible for the development and enforcement of policies and technologies for information security as well as business continuity and disaster recovery planning.

Chief technology officer (CTO): The administrator responsible for enterprise-level strategy and issues related to information systems technology.

Choice architecture: A framework created by decision makers that dictates the form of a default, the extent to which the default reflects what individuals would have chosen without the default, the degree of transparency of the default, and the ease with which individuals can opt out of the default.

Collaboration: In health care, a team-based effort in which team members have complementary roles and cooperatively work together, sharing responsibility for problem solving and decision making, to formulate and execute plans for patient care.

Commitment devices: Voluntary programs in which people in a rational state of mind use System 2 thinking to prepare for future situations in which they know that they will be less likely to behave rationally and fail to achieve an important goal.

Community benefit: Benefits provided by a nonprofit organization in exchange for favorable tax treatment. It may take the form of providing more uncompensated care (vis-à-vis for-profit firms), setting lower prices, or offering services that, from a financial perspective, might not be viable for for-profit firms.

Community needs assessments: Under the ACA, assessments of community health and unmet needs that are required to be initially completed as a benchmark and then conducted again in three years to document progress.

Complementary and alternative medicine (CAM): "A group of diverse medical and health care systems, practices, and products that are not generally considered part of conventional medicine" (NCCAM, 2012).

Complementary medicine: Therapies used as adjuncts to conventional medicine.

Compulsory service programs: Programs for physicians that require mandatory service with compensation, mandatory service with no compensation, or voluntary service with compensation; they are often used to provide healthcare services in remote and rural areas.

Continuum of care: The full range of healthcare services options.

Coordination: Use of practical reason to successfully balance obligations to various constituents, and to determine and take morally correct action in complex scenarios.

Coverage gaps: Areas that do not have high-speed Internet access and cell-phone service.

Critical access hospitals: Hospitals with fewer than 25 beds.

Culture of sustainability: A corporate or organizational culture that embraces sustainability as one of its core tenets, and incorporates sustainability into everyday operations from the top down.

Decentralized configuration: An information systems configuration in which at least some of the IS personnel work at each of the facilities, rather than in a central headquarters or regional-based support center.

Decision making: The selection of a course of action from a defined list of possible or feasible actions.

Duration: Either how long the disease lasts until recovery or time until death.

Economies of scale: The relationship in which costs decline as the scale (of services or production) increases.

Effectiveness: In regard to operations, the attainment of objectives through production of outputs.

Efficiency: The ratio of outputs to inputs.

Electronic health record (EHR): A record that stores all of a patient's medical information. Medical providers use the health record to document the health state of the patient as well as the care they provide.

Employee engagement: The degree of employee involvement and investment in the program, system, or action being promoted.

Employer mandate: Within the Affordable Care Act, the requirement that employers with 50 or more employees provide affordable health insurance coverage.

Endowment effect: The concept that people tend to value something—a thing, a product, an idea—more highly once they have it.

Energy management: Devising and implementing processes or systems to maximize energy efficiency and reduce energy waste.

Enterprise resource planning (ERP) system: A system that combines human capital and supply chain management with other available data to help organizations streamline equipment, supplies, personnel, and end-to-end fiscal control.

Environmentally preferable purchasing (EPP): The procurement of products and services that, throughout the entirety of the product or service life cycle, do not cause harm to the environment, patient, employees, or community, or cause less harm than alternatives.

Environmentally preferable purchasing (EPP) profile: The degree to which suppliers or other companies adhere to environmentally preferable purchasing in their operations.

Eudaimonia: Happiness; well-being.

Framing: The concept that people view alternatives in different ways depending on whether the alternatives are presented as gains or losses.

Functional medicine: A personalized approach to health care that uses basic and epidemiological science to investigate and evaluate a patient's condition; it relies on risk factor analysis and tests that evaluate the physiological ability of the body to perform basic bodily functions, with the goal of identifying factors that may be involved in mediating a patient's disease.

Going green: Taking steps to implement environmentally responsible processes and facilities.

Green construction: Designing, building, and retrofitting sustainable and environmentally friendly facilities.

Green Team: A team of leaders from across divisions who are responsible for implementing the executive vision of sustainability program(s).

Health: "A state of complete physical, mental and social well-being and not merely the absence of disease or infirmity" (World Health Organization, 1948).

Health care as a commodity: The libertarian and free market advocate view that health care is a commodity to be exchanged on open markets without governmental interference.

Health care as a human right: The liberal egalitarian notion that health care is a human right, and barriers to access to health care must be removed to ensure that all people have access to health care.

Healthcare information technology: Information systems and technologies that support the delivery of healthcare services; these information systems are tightly integrated with the business and clinical functions of the health system and are managed and supported by skilled professionals within the IS function of the organization.

Healthcare teams: Groups of healthcare providers who coordinate their efforts to ensure patient-centered care.

Health expectancy: A modified version of life expectancy considering various health states.

Health Information Technology for Economic and Clinical Health (HITECH) Act of 2009: A federal law that contains major financial incentives for health systems and other providers that incorporate electronic health records. It also addresses use and disclosure of protected health information by health systems and their business associates.

Health Insurance Portability and Accountability Act of 1996 (HIPAA): A federal law that protects patients' privacy and the security of their health information.

Health maintenance organization (HMO): A group that organizes the financing and delivery of a range of healthcare benefits for members enrolled in a health plan.

Health policy: Public policy that is related to influencing health and the diverse array of healthcare providers and functions.

Health policy process: The means through which policies are initiated, developed or formulated, negotiated, communicated, implemented and evaluated. It involves three interconnected phases: policy formulation, policy implementation, and policy modification.

Hippocratic Oath: The first and earliest code of quality in medicine.

Human capital: People, who are perceived as assets, rather than commodities or costs.

Hyperbolic discounting: The concept according to which people have a higher discount rate and prefer the present much more than the short-term future, but have a lower discount rate and are relatively indifferent between years in the long-term future.

Incidence: The rate of new cases of a disease; the number of new cases of a disease divided by the number of individuals at risk for the disease over a period of time.

Independent practice association (IPA): An organized group of independent providers who contract with one or more health plans for the purpose of providing healthcare services to a defined population.

Individual mandate: Within the Affordable Care Act, the requirement for most U.S. citizens to maintain insurance, or pay a tax penalty.

Infant mortality: The number of deaths of infants (younger than one year of age) divided by the number of live births during the same period.

Information system: A broad term describing both the technology (e.g., hardware and software) and the way that individuals use a system to perform their roles within the organization.

Integrated delivery system (IDS): A group of healthcare organizations that collectively provide an array of health-related services in a coordinated fashion to those using the system.

Integration: In health care, a system in which "care providers have established relationships and mechanisms for communicating and working together to coordinate patient care across health conditions, services, and care settings over time" (Institute of Medicine, 2001).

Integrative medicine: "The practice of medicine that reaffirms the importance of the relationship between practitioner and patient, focuses on the whole person, is informed by evidence, and makes use of all appropriate therapeutic approaches, healthcare professionals, and disciplines to achieve optimal health and healing" (Consortium of Academic Health Centers for Integrative Medicine, 2009).

Interest groups: Groups who use their economic resources and engage in a variety of strategies to successfully to promote or defeat policies they perceive as harmful to their interests.

Investor-owned firm: A firm owned by risk-based equity investors who expect the managers of the corporation to maximize shareholder wealth.

Justice: A broad notion encompassing fairness, reciprocity, equality, desert, and need.

Key health policy actors: A variety of individuals and entities such as public and private institutions and groups such as healthcare providers, healthcare practitioners, healthcare purchasers, and health insurers as well as consumers who influence public health policy.

Leadership in Energy and Environmental Design (LEED): An international certification program for green buildings, created by the United States Green Building Council.

Lean: A process improvement methodology that focuses on appropriately managing waste and variations. In health care, this concept is applied to improve customer satisfaction and to empower those involved in healthcare processes.

Life-cycle analysis: Assessment of the impact that products have at every step along the supply chain.

Life expectancy: The average number of years of survival from some point in life.

Limited liability company: Also called a limited liability partnership; a business entity that combines the tax flow-through treatment characteristics of a partnership with the liability protection of a corporation.

Limited partnership: An unincorporated business with two or more owners in which at least one general partner has unlimited liability for the partnership's debts and obligations.

Loss aversion: The contention of behavioral economics that people act to avoid losses.

Market: A place where there is an exchange of goods and services.

Mobile health applications (mHealth): Applications that connect clinical information systems to consumers in their homes and other nonclinical environments.

Morbidity: The occurrence of deviation from optimal health and well-being.

Mortality rate: The number of deaths during a period of time divided by the average population over that same period of time.

Multispecialty group practice (MSGP): A group that employs primary and specialty care physicians who share common governance, infrastructure, and finances; refer patients for services offered within the group; and are typically affiliated with a particular hospital or hospitals.

Nonmaleficence: The duty to refrain from performing certain acts; the obligation not to inflict harm on others.

Palliative care: Care that is focused on ameliorating symptoms, rather than effecting a cure; care directed toward "achieving the best-possible quality of life for patients and their family caregivers, based on patient and family needs and goals and independent of prognosis" (Meier, 2011).

Partnership: An unincorporated business with two or more owners.

Patient-centered care: The establishment of collaboration and ongoing relationships to achieve and understand all medical needs, whether those needs are primary, secondary, acute, chronic, or preventive care, while actively engaging and educating the patient throughout the duration of his or her care.

Patient-Centered Medical Home (PCMH): The National Committee for Quality Assurance (NCQA, 2014) defines a PCMH as a model of care delivery where the emphasis is on care coordination and communication among the patient, primary care providers, and specialists.

Patient portal: An "online app" available to patients of an integrated delivery system.

Period prevalence: The number of cases that exist over a period of time divided by the population over that period of time.

Personal health record (PHR): A consumer-controlled record of an individual's medical information that is independent of the provider organization.

Phronesis: Practical wisdom.

Physician–hospital organization (PHO): A partnership between a hospital and all or some of its affiliated physicians for the purpose of contracting with one or more health plans to provide health care services to a defined population.

Physician and nurse informaticist: A provider who may have received training in clinical information systems and functions as a superuser and champion of clinical systems.

Point prevalence: The number of cases of a disease state that exist at a point in time; it is calculated by dividing the number of existing cases by the population at that point in time.

Population: The entirety of individuals who possess a particular grouping characteristic.

Population health: "The health outcomes of a group of individuals, including the distribution of such outcomes within the group" (Kindig & Stoddart, 2003). A wide array of influences on individual health must be integrated to maximize the overall health of a group of individuals.

Power of the default (opt-in versus opt-out): The concept that the initial, or default, position has a powerful effect on behavior.

Practitioner bias: Practitioners' tendency to discount the community's self-knowledge and to assert that their own goals and interventions are appropriate.

Preventive care: Care that is focused on preventing disease, rather than treating disease after it develops.

Privately held company: A for-profit firm whose company stock is held by relatively few investors and is not available to the general public.

Product or service life cycle: The process of product or service creation and use, from the initial material to the final waste product.

Professional corporation: Also called a professional association; a corporate form that is created by professionals who want the advantages of incorporation, but that does not shield them from professional liability.

Program design errors: Design of healthcare interventions that fail to recognize where a community exists relative to the community members' readiness for change.

Prospective payment: A payment system under which hospitals and other inpatient providers are paid a prospectively determined fee; it is based on a fee schedule that uses diagnostic-related groups (DRGs) and the fee is paid on a per-discharge basis, which depends on the admitting diagnosis.

Protected health information (PHI): Information about health care status, treatments or conditions, and payments that can be linked to a specific individual.

Public benefit organization: A nonprofit company in which the assets (and accumulated earnings) of the organization belong to the public or to the charitable beneficiaries the trust was organized to serve.

Public health: "The science and art of preventing disease, prolonging life and promoting health and efficiency through organized community effort" (Winslow, 1920).

Publicly traded company: A for-profit firm whose company stock is bought and sold on the open market.

Public policy: An authoritative decision made in the legislative, executive, or judicial branch of government, intended to direct or influence the actions, behaviors, or decisions of others.

Quality: According to the Institute of Medicine, "the degree to which health services for individuals and populations increase the likelihood of desired health outcomes and are consistent with current professional knowledge."

Respect for persons: A key component of human dignity; an integral principle of ethics that may require considerations of autonomy, honesty, confidentiality, and fidelity.

Retention strategy: Measures to reduce workforce turnover.

Shared Savings Program (SSP): A Medicare-sponsored program for accountable care organizations (ACOs), which authorizes an ACO to share in a portion of any savings it achieves by meeting particular quality performance standards.

Six Sigma: A process improvement methodology that focuses on three steps—define the problem, obtain process performance measurements, and analyze the process and determine the cause(s) of the identified issue. These steps assist in determining whether the process in place should be redesigned or whether it can be further improved.

Social norms: Accepted and expected behaviors in a society (i.e., "This is what we do here").

Sole proprietorship: An unincorporated business owned by a single individual.

Startup costs: Costs associated with purchasing the equipment required to support a healthcare service.

Stewardship: The careful and responsible management of resources to maximize the well-being of the population (including population health). In regard to health systems, the functions associated with the stewardship role of health executives are concerned with managing resources and system performance to reconcile market inefficiencies and potential public-sector (policy) failures.

Strategic planning: A structured process that guides an organization toward the achievement of its long-term goals.

Sustainability: A method of operating that promotes the most efficient use of resources while minimizing the negative environmental effects of operations.

Sustainable care: Patient-centered care with the objective of promoting not only the patient's well-being, but also the well-being of the setting where care takes place, both in the facility and in the wider community.

Sustainable foods: Healthy, fresh local food grown and harvested in a sustainable manner, with verified sourcing.

System 1 thinking: Thinking that is fast, effortless, and automatic, and often is used when the decision maker is skilled and experienced in the task at hand.

System 2 thinking: Thinking that is relatively slow, effortful, controlled, and deductive.

Talent management: An approach to employee staffing that perceives people as assets whose current value can be measured and whose future value can be enhanced through investment.

Teamwork: The outcome of group members' willingness to collaborate toward a shared goal, have strong communication skills within the team, and devote sufficient organizational resources to sustain the team's work.

Telehealth services: The use of technology and information to support long-distance clinical health care, education, and public health activities.

Triple bottom line: A business goal that involves fiscally, socially, and environmentally responsible operations.

Uneven distribution: Workforce imbalances caused by individuals choosing to work in some areas, but not others—for example, in larger towns or familiar areas rather than in remote rural areas.

Value:

Value chain: A strategic thinking map that demonstrates how an organization can initiate and grow a partnership with both its employees and its customers. The value chain uses a systems approach and includes two subsystems—service delivery activities and support activities

Voluntary health and welfare organization: A non–business-oriented healthcare organization that performs voluntary services in its community; it is tax exempt and relies primarily on public donations for its funds.

Waste management: Devising and implementing processes and systems that improve efficiency of resource use to reduce the amount of waste generated by a healthcare facility and appropriately dispose of waste generated.

Water management: Devising and implementing processes or systems to maximize the efficient use of water, including utilizing alternative water sources.

Window of opportunity: The necessary conditions (confluence of problems and consideration of possible solutions, and political circumstances) that create the motivation and political will to stimulate the drafting or formation of legislation (new laws or amendments).

Workforce turnover: The rate at which employees leave their current job.

Years of potential life lost (YPLL): An accepted measure of premature deaths.

Index

Note: Page numbers followed by *e*, *f* or *t* indicate materials in exhibit, figures or tables respectively.